WITH THE COMPLIMENTS
OF THE AUTHOR

W9-AOD-848

HARPER & ROW, PUBLISHERS
INCORPORATED

THE GREAT MERCHANTS

THE

BOOKS BY TOM MAHONEY

The Great Merchants (*with Leonard Sloane*)

The Story of George Romney

I'm a Lucky One (*with Barry Sadler*)

The Longest Auto Race (*with George Schuster*)

The Merchants of Life

The Story of Jewelry (*with Marcus Baerwald*)

GREAT MERCHANTS

AMERICA'S FOREMOST RETAIL INSTITUTIONS AND THE PEOPLE WHO MADE THEM GREAT

by Tom Mahoney and Leonard Sloane

NEW AND ENLARGED EDITION

1817 HARPER & ROW, PUBLISHERS
NEW YORK, EVANSTON, AND LONDON

For Caroline and Annette

THE GREAT MERCHANTS—*New and Enlarged Edition. Copyright © 1966 by John Thomas Mahoney and Leonard Sloane. Copyright © 1949, 1955 by John Thomas Mahoney. Copyright 1947, 1950, 1951 by The Reader's Digest Association, Inc. Printed in the United States of America. All rights reserved. No part of this book may be used or reproduced in any manner whatsoever without written permission except in the case of brief quotations embodied in critical articles and reviews. For information address Harper & Row, Publishers, Incorporated, 49 East 33rd Street, New York, N.Y. 10016.*

LIBRARY OF CONGRESS CATALOG CARD NUMBER: 67–11328

B-R

CONTENTS

Preface : *vii*

I. PEDDLERS TO PALACES : 1
The Evolution of American Retailing

II. THE HUDSON'S BAY COMPANY : 19
Rebirth of the Oldest Retailer

III. BROOKS BROTHERS : 36
America's Oldest Men's Apparel Store

IV. TIFFANY'S : 51
The Most Famous Jewelry Store in the World

V. THE SINGER COMPANY : 66
World-Wide Pioneer of Installment Selling

VI. FILENE'S : 78
The World's Largest Specialty Store

VII. F. & R. LAZARUS & COMPANY : 100
Ohio's Famous Department-Store Dynasty

VIII. MARSHALL FIELD & COMPANY : 116
Elegance for the Middle West

IX. BRENTANO'S : 133
"Booksellers to the World"

X. MACY'S : 149
The Strauses and the Biggest Store

XI. THE FOOD GIANTS : 170
Supermarkets, the A & P and Its Rivals

XII. RICH'S : 187
"The Store That Married a City"

XIII. F. W. WOOLWORTH CO. : 198
"World's Greatest Variety Chain"

XIV. THE J. L. HUDSON COMPANY : 206
Detroit's Colossal Store

XV. SEARS, ROEBUCK AND CO. : 221
The World's Biggest Retailer

XVI. LANE BRYANT : 244
Maternity and Special-Size Fashion Pioneer

XVII. J. C. PENNEY COMPANY : 259
Merchandise Chain in a Modern World

XVIII. BULLOCK'S AND I. MAGNIN : 273
Glamour Pioneer of the West

XIX. NEIMAN-MARCUS : 286
The Pride of Texas

XX. L. L. BEAN, INC. : 299
Sporting Goods by Mail from Maine

XXI. OHRBACH'S, INC. : 310
"A Business in Millions, a Profit in Pennies"

XXII. WEBB'S CITY : 324
"The World's Most Unusual Drugstore"

XXIII. THE DISCOUNTERS ARRIVE : 336
Korvette and the Mass Merchandisers

Notes : 351

Index : 363

PREFACE

THIS BOOK PRESENTS in one volume accounts of more than a score of remarkable American retail institutions and the merchants who built them from small beginnings. They are leaders in their fields and represent the wide range of retailing in the second half of the twentieth century.

It is an enlargement of a work first published in 1955, since reprinted many times, and also translated into Spanish, Japanese, Korean and other languages. Some chapters are entirely new. All others have been rewritten and updated to include the many changes and developments of the past decade.

As collaborator on this new edition, the original author is happy to have Leonard Sloane of the *New York Times* and formerly of the *Wall Street Journal*. He is one of the foremost reporters of business and is respected throughout retailing. His help has been invaluable.

Included in the chronological order of their start are the world's largest department stores, the largest specialty shop, the largest mail-order house, the largest variety chain, the largest apparel chain, the largest drugstore and more than a dozen others that dominate their sections or their special fields. The smallest of them is a three-million-dollar business. Five have sales of more than a billion dollars a year, two more than five billion, and one more than six billion.

All have definite personalities and distinctions other than size. Though widely diverse in their operations, all have many qualities in common which will interest any student of retailing or of business in general. Several have pioneered important innovations and their founders are in the Retailing Hall of Fame at the Chicago Merchandise Mart. All are persistent and, in most cases, large advertisers.

All have made important contributions to the communities in which they operate and, in some cases, to the nation as well. All have adapted themselves to change and have survived the deaths of founders, wars, business depressions, population shifts, and the rivalry of numerous competitors.

Small parts of the Singer, Filene's and Lane Bryant chapters appeared in *The Reader's Digest,* and the material is included here with the permission of that publication. Part of the Rich's chapter was published in *The Saturday Evening Post* and is similarly acknowledged. Ralph McGill, Atlanta editor, and Mort Weisinger, New York writer, helped on the original accounts of Rich's and Tiffany's. Grace Mahoney, Helen McGinnis and Esther Vail helped on the manuscript.

In addition to the sources listed after the text, the authors are indebted for information, among others, to the following:

Douglas Alexander, Agnes Rogers Allen, Ernest L. Arms, Edith Asbury, Stanley Baar, Marcus Baerwald, Letitia Baldridge, Harold Barnett, Roger Barton, L. L. Bean, Irene Bender, Mrs. Eleanore H. Bruce, Lester A. Burcham, Philip A. Chester, Emery Cleaves, Hilliard J. Coan, Hazel Conway, Phillip Corrin, Elisa Daggs, Pendleton Dudley, Alice Encke, Margo Fischer, Lillian Friedman, Mrs. Beverley Ganschow, Mel Garber, William Gekle, Leon A. Gorman, Paul Gould, John Graham, Nixon Griffis, Carl D. Guldager.

Also Nathaniel E. Hager, Sam Harrington, Walter Hauser, Harold D. Hodgkinson, Mary Holbrook, Stacy Holmes, Charlotte Horn, O. K. Houston, Walter Hoving, William Howard, A. R. Huband, Joseph L. Hudson, Jr., Carol D. Kepple, Len Kessler, Donald Kircher, Robert C. Kirkwood, Mark Klauser, Jerome Klein, Chess Lagomarsino, Fred Lazarus, Jr., Godfrey M. Lebhar, Maude Lennox, Milton Lightner, Harold Littledale, Patricia Lochridge, John McDonald, Raphael Malsin, Stanley Marcus, Mrs. Sara W. Marshall, Paul Mazur, William Miller, James Freeman, Jess Wolf.

Also Nathan Ohrbach, Alfred G. Paulson, Raymond J. Peterson, John W. Ray, Richard Rich, Max Rosey, Carl Ruff, Leonard Schwartz, Fred D. Scott, R. E. Sheen, Jaclyn Silvern, Jack Straus, A. M. Sullivan, Albert Sussman, Irvin Taubkin, T. C. Thomsen, Bogart Thompson, Mrs. Lottie Thompson, Kendall L. Tolle, David Verlen, George Vidal, Electus B. Ward, E. B. Weiss, Robert J. Witt, John C. Wood, Robert W. Wood, Del Yannatta, Mari C. Yerian.

TOM MAHONEY

New York City

1

PEDDLERS TO PALACES

The Evolution of American Retailing

RETAILING IS THE BIGGEST FIELD of business and in many ways the most important. Discoveries in the research laboratory and the production miracles of factory and farm are meaningless until retailers place them in the hands of consumers. Nearly half of all American enterprises are retail businesses. In 1965, they had sales of $283,900,000,000—54.5 percent more than a decade earlier.

It is a field of infinite variety that has been growing in importance ever since primitive men began to trade products of the field, the hunt or their own handiwork for others that they did not have but needed or desired. As civilization developed, it became easier to do this through merchants, who often traveled from country to country, than by face-to-face exchange. From the shops of early craftsmen, who sold their own wares, and from the stalls of itinerant merchants at medieval fairs, modern stores and modern retailing have evolved.[1*]

Developments have come so fast in the middle of the twentieth century that many talk of "the revolution in retailing." This is more alliterative than accurate. By definition, a revolution is a complete overthrow, or a complete change in a system. This has not happened and is not likely to happen in retailing. The new is more profitable

* Superior figures refer to the section of Notes beginning on p. 351.

than the old but the two continue to exist next door to each other in many communities. Indeed, one of the strongest trends as of 1966, that of retailers' insuring quality in products by planning and, in many cases, manufacturing them, is a return to a virtue of the oldest retailers.

But shifts in population, the advent of the telephone, the automobile, and more recently the computer and electronic data processing have greatly affected the pattern of retailing. In 1964, retailers with sales of more than $50 million a year each for the first time drew more of their volume from suburban and outlying stores than from downtown operations.[2] In the previous decade and a half, shopping centers increased their sales volume from little or nothing to $50 billion a year—about one of every four dollars spent in retail trade, excluding automobiles.[3] Several famous stores, including some that had endured for a century, have closed. Others have thrived.

America leads the world in retailing but every nation can boast at least a few notable stores. In some places, the oldest and newest forms of retailing exist side by side. In Baghdad, there is a Sindbad supermarket and the modern Orosi-Back department store selling goods from everywhere at fixed prices while native traders a few yards away haggle with their customers exactly as in the days of Caliph Harun al-Rashid of the *Arabian Nights*.

Moscow took pride in Muir & Mirrieless, a fine department store run by Scotsmen until the Revolution, and now boasts GUM (State Department Store), an enormous government-owned gray baroque establishment facing the Kremlin on Red Square. Its goods are serviceable and it offers fashion shows five afternoons a week with new styles in overalls for factory girls among the garments modeled. It has 7,000 employees and attracts as many as 300,000 Russians a day.[4]

France has contributed the great Bon Marché, founded in Paris in 1852 by Aristide Boucicaut and in some respects the first department store; La Ville de Paris, the original Maison Blanche, and more recently the Galeries Lafayette, whose stores are visited regularly by retailers from all over the world in search of ideas. Its big Paris department store and its five branches do an annual business of

$60,000,000 and its chain of 153 smaller stores around $150,000,000 in addition. A distinction of the Paris store is a day nursery for the care of children of employees. In the food field, meals from Maxim's are sold in many countries and, thanks to transatlantic jet planes, bread baked in Paris is marketed the same day in New York.

Harrods, Ltd., of London, founded in 1849 by a grocer named Henry Charles Harrod and managed for many years by the late Sir Richard Burbidge, is the greatest store in the British Isles. Harrods business is largely food and clothing but it also arranges funerals, sells real estate, insurance and theater tickets, hires out servants and provides entertainment. Three generations of Burbidges headed Harrods until 1960, when Sir Hugh Fraser, a drapery millionaire, bought control.

The Mitsukoshi store in Tokyo, the largest department store east of Suez, is even more remarkable. It dates from 1673 and was the foundation of the fortune of the famous Mitsui merchant family. It introduced cash down, *Gen-Gin,* and fixed price, *Kakene-Nashi,* in Japan when few but Quakers practiced the latter in the Western world. From a dry-goods store selling silks and brocades, it became a full-line department store.

In addition to supplying complete wedding outfits, it has since 1944 also been furnishing brides and grooms. There is a government marriage bureau on the first floor. Men and women seeking mates leave their photographs, vital statistics and a list of qualifications they seek in a spouse. Marriage ceremonies are performed in a chapel in the basement. Mitsukoshi offers couples a bargain in services for 700 yen, about $14. This borrows trousseau for the bride, maid service to dress her, rent of an adjoining banquet hall, and tea and cakes for guests. Many Japanese literally owe everything to Mitsukoshi.

But nowhere has retailing become so important as in the United States. On its success in distributing the fruits of mass production, the prosperity of our entire economy very largely depends. Retailing is literally the biggest business in the country. It is a hard, competitive field, with one out of three new ventures failing within the first year, but in no other country have so many stores become vast enterprises.

Why have American retailing institutions grown so hugely? One obvious reason is that never before have there been such quantities of goods and so many customers able to afford them. American stores also have led the world in advertising, the use of electric lights, plate glass, packaging, air conditioning, self service, refrigeration, credit, parking lots and other devices for painlessly bringing together buyers and sellers, and causing yesterday's luxuries to become regarded as today's necessities. Nowhere else have competing retailers of every kind gone to such lengths to guarantee satisfaction to every customer. When an American consults his doctor or his lawyer, he must pay regardless of whether he likes the outcome of his case but, in virtually any store, he is assured of happiness or his money back.

Also important is the wide freedom that the retailer enjoys as to what and how he sells in the United States and the consumer's equally glorious freedom as to how and where he will spend his money. In medieval Europe, a man risked his soul as well as his capital when he attempted to sell at a profit goods that he had not made: "The man who buys it in order that he may gain by selling it again unchanged and as he bought it, that man is of the buyers and sellers who are cast forth from God's temple," warned St. Thomas Aquinas. American retailing has never had any such restrictions.

By custom and sometimes by law, for tobacco is often a state monopoly, cigarettes are purchased in Europe from the tobacconist. In the United States, you can buy cigarettes from the American equivalent of the tobacconist. You can also buy them at the drugstore, delicatessen, restaurant, gasoline filling station, and perhaps from a vending machine where you work. Sears, Roebuck and Co. will sell you a machine for making your own cigarettes. A person must be a registered pharmacist to sell prescription drugs, but almost anything else can be retailed by anybody who can obtain it.

A consumer may live in a community with but one store but even this does not necessarily mean that he is a captive customer of that store. If he has an automobile, as more and more Americans have, he can get into it and shop a hundred miles away if he likes. Or he may shop by telephone or by mail and what he wants will come to him even though his post office may be in the local store which he is not patronizing.

New forms and variations of retailing are emerging constantly despite the obstacles and harassments thrown in their way by adherents of older forms. The new usually proves neither as problem-solving as its adherents predict nor as destructive as its foes fear. The same fears that are now being voiced about discount houses, vending machines and shopping centers in the past have been shouted about department stores, mail-order houses, trading stamps and chain stores.

The first retail selling in most of America was done by peddlers. At the outset they walked. Those of more stature rode horseback and the even more prosperous rode in wagons or carriages. The father of John D. Rockefeller was a carriage peddler of patent medicines. If the peddler did not plan to return to the community, there was no limit to his chicanery, but many of them were responsible men who sold New England wares of good quality repeatedly to the same customers. The espionage of a peddler named Enoch Crosby in behalf of General Washington during the Revolution was the basis of *The Spy,* James Fenimore Cooper's first successful novel.

A peddler's life was strenuous, lonely, and hazardous. When the opportunity developed or "when they found the right place or the right girl," many were happy to settle down as storekeepers. Many dry-goods stores (so called to distinguish them from those which sold liquor or "wet" goods) were started in this way. As soon as he was established as a storekeeper, a peddler began to take a dim view of his former vocation and, as often as not, would contrive to have laws passed requiring exorbitant license fees from peddlers or even banning them entirely.

The many antipeddler efforts culminated in a Green River, Wyoming, ordinance making it a misdemeanor for a salesman to call at a home without having been previously "invited" to do so by the occupant. This was upheld by the United States Supreme Court in 1951. But, despite all the obstacles, house-to-house selling endures and more than three thousand companies were engaged in it in 1966. Three of them, the Fuller Brush Company, Avon Cosmetics and Stanley Home Products, have sales of more than $62,000,000 a year each.

As money was scarce in rural America early in the nineteenth century, the country general store of nostalgic memory did a lot of its business by barter. Phineas T. Barnum, the great circus man, in his youth learned about human nature while clerking in such a store at Bethel, Connecticut.

> Like many greenhorns before me [he wrote later in his autobiography], this was the height of my ambition. Ours was a cash, credit and barter store; and I drove many a sharp trade with old women who paid for their purchases in butter, eggs, beeswax, feathers, and rags, and with men who exchanged for our commodities, hats, axe-helves, oats, corn, buckwheat, hickory-nuts, and other commodities. It was something of a drawback upon my dignity that I was compelled to sweep the store, take down the window-shutters, and make the fire; nevertheless the thought of being a "merchant" fully compensated me for all such menial duties.
>
> There is something to be learned even in a country store. We are apt to believe that sharp trades, especially dishonest tricks and unprincipled deceptions, are confined entirely to the city, and that the unsophisticated men and women of the country do everything on the square. I believe this to be measurably true, but know that there are many exceptions to this rule. Many is the time I cut open bundles of rags, brought to the store by country women in exchange for goods, and declared to be all linen and cotton, that contained quantities of worthless trash in the interior, and sometimes stones, gravel, ashes, etc. . . .[5]

Craftsmen of various kinds, also importers, tailors and apothecaries, as well as peddlers, were among America's earliest merchants. The oldest business in the United States seems to be the Perot Malting Co., founded in Philadephia in 1687 and now in Buffalo, New York. What is now A. F. Brombacher & Company, the New York hardware firm, was founded as a cutlery and mechanics' tool business in 1760. Caswell-Massey, America's oldest chemists and perfumers, was begun in Newport, Rhode Island, in 1780 and later moved to New York. Captain Kidd, the pirate, bought perfume there. One of its employees became Sir Henry Wellcome, a founder of Burroughs & Wellcome, the British pharmaceutical firm. Schieffelin & Co., the New York drug house, dates from 1794.

R. C. Williams & Co., Inc., the wholesale grocers identified with the Royal Scarlet brand, began with a fleet of packet ships in 1811. J. H. Thorp & Co., Inc., the New York fabric house, started in 1819.

The Gunther Jaeckel, Inc., fur business, began in 1820. John Jacob Astor was once associated with it. Hager & Bro., Inc., was founded by Christopher Hager as a general store at Lancaster, Pennsylvania, in 1821. It is now a department store run by the fourth and fifth generations of the Hager family. William Mills & Son, Inc., New York dealers in fine fishing tackle, and Browning, King & Company, clothiers (whose name was later changed to Browning Fifth Avenue), date from 1822. Jacob Reed's Sons, Philadelphia clothiers famous for their uniforms, began in 1825.

Arnold Constable, the oldest New York specialty shop, was founded as a dry-goods store in that year by Aaron Arnold, an immigrant from the Isle of Wight. A century later it was joined with Stewart & Co., and Isaac Liberman, head of the latter, became president. Only a few months junior is Lord & Taylor, founded in 1826 by Samuel Lord and George Washington Taylor. It led fashion stores to Fifth Avenue and had the talent of retailers as famous as Walter Hoving and the late Dorothy Shaver. An Associated Dry Goods property, headed by Melvin Dawley, it and its suburban branches have sales of more than $110,000,000 a year. Another man from the Isle of Wight, George Arnold Hearn, founded Hearn's, the New York—and later, Bronx—department store, in 1827. The S. S. Pierce Co., Boston's fancy grocers, began in 1831. McKesson & Robbins, the wholesale drug firm, dates from 1833.

Gimbel Brothers, Inc., was founded in 1842 in the then frontier town of Vincennes, Indiana, by Adam Gimbel, an immigrant peddler from Bavaria. He inaugurated the one-price policy in the area and advertised: "Fairness and Equality of All Patrons, whether they be Residents of the City, Plainsmen, Traders or Indians." First of the modern Gimbel stores opened in Milwaukee in 1887. A Philadelphia store, since grown to many acres of space, was opened in 1894. New York was invaded in 1909. The Saks Company was absorbed in 1923, Saks Fifth Avenue was opened the next year and the Kaufmann and Baer Company of Pittsburgh purchased in 1925. Under dynamic Bernard F. Gimbel, one of the founder's grandsons, who became president in 1927 and board chairman in 1953, the firm developed unusually forceful advertising and promotion. Expansions carried it into Chicago, Detroit, Beverly Hills, Miami Beach, San Francisco and elsewhere. Bruce Alva Gimbel of the fourth generation succeeded his father as president. Gimbels had sales of $566,336,000 in the year ending April 30, 1966.

Thalhimer Brothers, Inc., began in Richmond, Virginia, and D. H. Holmes in New Orleans in 1842. The former had sales of $49,981,-264 in 1965. It boasts the first aluminum-clad building and provides showers for women shoppers. The latter was the first big store in the South to hire women and one of the first to provide free delivery service for customers. Free delivery but by wheelbarrow was the boast also of the store founded by Gerson Fox in 1847 at Hartford, Connecticut. It grew into Connecticut's biggest department store, owned and operated for years by his granddaughter, Beatrice Fox Auerbach, with sales of more than $60,000,000. She sold it to the May Company in 1965 for 720,000 shares of stock, then worth more than $40,000,000.[6]

W. & J. Sloane, the famous home-furnishings firm, started in New York in 1843. Mark Cross began as a harness store in Boston in 1845 and later moved to New York. Cartier, Inc., the jewelry firm, was founded in Paris in 1847. The Joseph Horne Co. of Pittsburgh began in 1849. Under young Richard R. Pivirotto, a former Princeton football star who became president in 1961, it had sales of $88,885,946 in 1964.[7] Famous Barr of St. Louis also began in 1849 and what became Scruggs-Vandervoort-Barney, Inc., started there in 1850.

At this time a French silk-stocking manufacturer, dissatisfied with the turn of politics in his country and hearing of gold in California, sold his business and sailed for San Francisco with a shipload of merchandise. He was Felix Verdier, who arrived in May, 1850, and set up a waterfront store which he called The City of Paris, after his ship and also the big French store of that name, giving it the motto of the French capital, *"Fluctuat nec mergitur*—It floats, and never sinks." The gold-mad Californians bought his merchandise almost as fast as he could unload it. The establishment grew into a great and distinctive store guided for generations by the Verdier family.

Eben Jordan, a ribbon clerk from Maine, started Jordan Marsh in

Boston in 1851. It is now the biggest of the 108 units of the Allied Stores Corporation, second-largest department-store chain. Under Theodore Schlesinger, this chain had record sales of $955,490,000 in 1965. Carson Pirie Scott & Co., the great Chicago store, was founded by Scotch-Irish immigrants at LaSalle, Illinois, in 1854. John T. Pirie, a grandson of one of the founders, was chairman and the store had record sales of $186,855,000 for the year ending January 29, 1966. Mandel Bros., Inc., was started in Chicago in 1855.

Younker's, the biggest store in Iowa, was founded by three Polish immigrants, Lipman, Samuel and Marcus Younker, at Keokuk in 1856 and later moved to Des Moines. Headed now by Morey Sostrin, it has nineteen branches and sales of around $70,000,000 a year.[8] Meier & Frank of Portland, Oregon's largest department store, traces its history to 1857. Julius L. Meier, of the firm, served as Governor of Oregon and organized its state police. Jack L. Meier was president in 1965 and the firm had record sales of $73,313,000. Goldwaters, Inc., was founded at Phoenix in 1860. The Higbee Co. began the same year in Cleveland and now has annual sales of more than $77,000,000. The Daniels & Fisher Stores Co., started in Denver in 1864.

Many of the stores established originally by peddlers, as their communities gained in population, grew into great specialty shops and, in some cases, famous department stores with buildings like palaces. The distinction between specialty shop and department store should be understood. A specialty shop is a store which, regardless of size, limits its merchandise to certain specialties and appeals to its customers on the basis of fashion or price rather than completeness of stocks. The limitation may simply be the broad classification of merchandise termed "soft goods." It may be as limited as clothing and accessories for brides, expectant mothers, or even tall girls.

A department store is a large store, organized by departments, selling under one management a wide variety of merchandise, including at least ready-to-wear, dry goods and home furnishings. The U.S. Census Bureau considers only stores of this type with sales of $100,000 or more as department stores.

It is difficult to determine at what date many stores met these qualifications, and the "first" department store is a matter of controversy. Macy's, Wanamaker's and Stewart's all have their partisans. Joseph Kane, the author of *Famous First Facts,* thinks the distinction belongs to Zion's Co-operative Mercantile Institution founded in Salt Lake City in 1868 by Brigham Young, the Mormon leader. This had sales of $22,342,159 and earned $685,101 in 1965. The Mormon Church has a third interest in the store.[9]

In any case, America's leading merchant in the middle of the nineteenth century was Alexander Turney Stewart, a self-made millionaire. Born at Lisburn, near Belfast, Ireland, and educated at Trinity College, Dublin, he emigrated at twenty to New York. Two years later in 1823 he opened the biggest store in the world at Broadway and Tenth Street. He was a single-price pioneer, hired handsome clerks to charm his women customers and sold quality merchandise, much of it from Europe. "I got it at Stewart's" was a phrase denoting value and satisfaction. Mrs. Abraham Lincoln redecorated the White House with goods from his store.

Stewart sent shiploads of food to famine-stricken Ireland and generously aided sufferers in the Franco-Prussian as well as the American Civil War. He was appointed Secretary of the Treasury by President Grant but was kept from office by a law forbidding importers to hold the post. He died in 1876. In one of the most bizarre crimes of the century, his body was stolen and recovered to be buried in the Episcopal Cathedral which he gave to Garden City, Long Island, a community which he founded as a model city.

A Philadelphia merchant named John Wanamaker replaced Stewart in the American scene and in 1896 acquired his New York store. The son of a bricklayer, he became a partner in 1861 of a brother-in-law in the Oak Hall Clothing Bazaar, a Philadelphia men's clothing store. On the latter's death, Wanamaker expanded the business into a department store. He was the first merchant to buy a full-page newspaper advertisement and personally wrote much of his copy which appeared in national magazines as well as the Philadelphia and New York newspapers.

As early as the Civil War, he had his famous "money back" guarantee in print. He advertised in 1865,

Any article that does not fit well, is not the proper color or quality, does not please the folks at home, or for any reason is not perfectly satisfactory, should be brought back at once, and if it is returned as purchased within ten days, we will refund the money. It is our intention always to give value for value in every sale we make, and those who are not pleased with what they buy do us a positive favor to return the goods and get the money back.[10]

In 1878, he moved his store into a vast unused Philadelphia freight depot, made it the first store completely lighted by incandescent lamps, and advertised that his ground floor of nearly three acres was "the largest space in the world devoted to retail selling on a single floor." The Wanamaker stores sold nearly everything. Their book departments were among the largest. For a time they sold airplanes and Ford automobiles.

Wanamaker, termed "Pious John" by rivals, had other interests, especially Sunday schools, the Young Men's Christian Association and the Republican party. President Harrison appointed him Postmaster General and possibly the high point of his life was in 1911 when President William Howard Taft dedicated a new Wanamaker store building in Philadelphia. Though he turned many affairs over to his son, Rodman, John Wanamaker was an alert merchant as long as he lived.

In 1920, when nearly eighty-two years old, he foresaw a postwar downturn in business. Though prices were at a peak, he ordered storewide 20 percent discount sales. On Saturday, May 8, more than $1,000,000 worth of merchandise was sold, a world record it is believed up until that time. In addition to his advertising contributions, John Wanamaker was a pioneer in employee training and public relations. One of the last lines that he wrote before his death in 1922 was this: "You have got to run a store that people will feel at home in!"

The Wanamaker stores had some adverse years during the depression. They again became profitable under John E. Raasch, a notable management consultant, who was made executive vice president in 1935, president in 1947 and chairman in 1952. Employee relations were excellent with Local 9 of the Retail Clerks International Association, AFL-CIO, which at times spent union funds to advertise

Wanamaker's. The firm adapted to changing conditions by opening branches in both the Philadelphia and New York areas but in Manhattan clung too long to its lower Broadway location and closed the week before Christmas in 1954 as uptown department stores enjoyed a record holiday business.

Mail-order or catalog selling and chain stores became important in the latter half of the nineteenth century. A lowering of postage rates and expansion of postal service made possible the former. It was government policy to aid the farmer and end his isolation.

While Benjamin Franklin has been called the "father of the mail-order catalog" on the basis of a 1744 one listing six hundred books,[11] young Montgomery Ward, previously a $23-a-week salesman at Marshall Field's, was the first to make a big thing of the idea. In 1862, he and a friend, George R. Thorne, started business in Chicago with $2,400 capital. They began in one room with a catalog of one page. "Our business," Ward recalled later, "was looked upon with suspicion by those whom we wished as customers. It was ridiculed by retail merchants, doubted by manufacturers and predicted a short life by all." The results were the opposite. In 1965, Montgomery Ward, then headed by Robert Elton "Tom" Brooker, had sales of nearly $1,800,000,000 from 500 retail stores, 864 catalog stores, 380 franchised catalog sales agencies and nine mail-order centers. Sears, Roebuck and Co. has done a great deal better.*

The idea of one merchant or one company owning and operating many stores is an old one. The Fuggers of Augsburg had branches in a score of European cities as early as the fifteenth century. It remained for George Huntington Hartford with his Great Atlantic & Pacific Tea Company and Frank W. Woolworth to develop the low-cost merchandising possibilities of chain operation to create chain-store empires.†

Notable successes in the variety and drug chain fields have been attained by J. G. McCrory, S. S. Kresge, S. H. Kress, W. T. Grant, G. C. Murphy, J. J. Newberry, H. L. Green, L. K. Liggett, Charles R. Walgreen, Cunningham Drug Stores and numerous others. There are

* See Chapter XV.
† See Chapters XI and XIII.

also highly successful clothing chains like Robert Hall, Bond's, Hughes & Hatcher and the Lerner Stores Corporation. Joseph J. Lerner, founder of the last, left an estate of more than $3,500,000 when he died in 1953.

But to go back to post–Civil War retailing, L. Hart & Son Co., Inc., began in San Diego in 1866. Stern Bros., now an important Allied unit, was founded in New York in 1867. Strawbridge & Clothier was started by Philadelphia Quakers in 1868. It had record sales of $105,756,846 in 1965 with G. Stockton Strawbridge as president. Luckey, Platt and Company, biggest store of the Hudson River valley, began in 1869 in Poughkeepsie, New York, and is now headed by William M. Smith, president and general manager. The Herpolsheimer Co. began in Grand Rapids, Michigan, in 1870.

A "Trade Palace" started in 1872 by a former wagon peddler grew into the great L. S. Ayers store in Indianapolis. With its branches, it had sales of $92,300,000 in 1965. The Joske Brothers Co. of San Antonio, Texas, was formed in 1872. Forbes and Wallace, Inc., of Springfield, Massachusetts, dates from the next year, as does Rogers Peet Co., New York and Boston men's clothiers. The Hecht Co., with big stores now in Washington, D.C., and a dozen other cities, also began in 1874. The Fair of Chicago started in 1875. Hochschild, Kohn & Co. of Baltimore began in 1876. Two famous jewelry stores, Lambert Brothers of New York and Linz Brothers of Dallas, started in 1877. Best & Co. was founded in New York in 1879. It now has annual sales of more than $52,000,000.

David May in Leadville, Colorado, that same year abandoned mining to open a clothing store. He moved it to Denver in 1888. The enterprise, now headed by his grandson, Morton D. May, has grown into the May Department Stores Co. with seventy-two great stores, many of them with branches, located from Hartford to Los Angeles. Besides stores under the May name, the company owns the Famous Barr Co. of St. Louis; Kaufmann's, the big Pittsburgh store; the M. O'Neil Co. of Akron, Ohio; the Hecht Co.; and others. It is the third-largest department-store chain and in 1965 earned a record $45,860,000 on record sales of $869,169,000.

Miller & Rhoads of Richmond began as a partnership in 1885.

Peck & Peck began as a hosiery firm in 1887. The Bon Marché of Seattle started in 1890. The Halle Bros. Co. began in Cleveland in 1891. It had sales of $62,290,952 in 1965. Stix, Baer & Fuller started in St. Louis and Abercrombie & Fitch Co. in New York in 1892. The latter does a business of more than $19,000,000 a year in sporting goods, including pith helmets, scuba suits and rifles for big-game hunting. President Lyndon B. Johnson buys fishing tackle there.[12] Earle K. Angstadt, formerly of Young & Rubicam, became president of the store at thirty-eight in 1964. Bonwit Teller, and Henri Bendel, famous New York fashion stores, were born in 1895 and 1896. Two remarkable women, Mildred Custin and Geraldine Stutz, have been placed in charge of these stores by W. Maxey Jarman, chairman of Genesco, Inc., which owns them. New York's Bergdorf Goodman store was born in 1901 when Herman Bergdorf, an Alsatian tailor, sold first half and then all of his Fifth Avenue business to Edwin Goodman, a designer and tailor from Rochester, New York. This fabulous store once employed Grand Duchess Marie of Russia as a saleslady. In 1902, Franklin Simon opened his Fifth Avenue specialty shop, the Dayton Co. began in Minneapolis, Titche-Goettinger Co. got under way in Dallas and A. Schwartz came out of Mexico to start the Popular Dry Goods Co., the big store of El Paso, Texas. Marvin and Obadiah Leonard, two energetic Texas farm boys, started a high-volume low-price food and general-merchandise business in Fort Worth at the end of World War I. It grew to be the city's biggest advertiser. Leonard's clerks some days cash more checks than local banks. In 1925, Bert Gamble and Phil Skogmo opened at St. Cloud, Minnesota, the first of many Gamble Skogmo, Inc., one-stop shopping centers. It acquired Aldens, Inc. in 1964 and the next year had sales of $608,243,214.

The depression thirties proved an opportunity for many merchants. Max Hess took over Hess Brothers, the Allentown, Pennsylvania, store founded by his father and uncle back in 1897. When he took charge in 1932, its sales were around a million dollars. By a series of dramatic innovations, the best known of which is a "Fashion Caravan" of trucks providing traveling fashion shows, he has increased sales to more than $37,000,000 a year. The caravan has been the subject of a motion picture. The store has a children's barbershop, which gives the customer a diploma and a lock of his hair on the occasion of his first haircut.

Gertz of Jamaica, Long Island, expanded from a stationery and phonograph shop to a full department store in the depression. It built a new building and added parking lots, clubs for kids and a Consumer Advisory Board of forty women's club leaders. Sales increased from less than a million to more than $60,000,000 a year, and the store boasts one of the highest sales per square foot of any department store. It was purchased by Allied Stores Corporation in 1941. It has branches at Flushing, Hicksville and elsewhere.

The late Fred Harvey, a former basement merchandise manager at Marshall Field's, found an opportunity at the same time in Nashville, Tennessee. In 1943, he took over a moribund department store there with sales of $560,000. He remodeled, introduced night openings and advertised with blimps. In a decade, he raised sales to $11,000,000 and made Harvey's Nashville's leading store.

Discount houses* and shopping centers flowered after World War II but had their beginnings earlier. Nijni Novgorod took a step toward the shopping center in the fifteenth century when traders at the ancient fair there began to have "permanent buildings and bazaars, often of stone." When automobiles spurred growth of the suburbs and at the same time began to clog downtown streets, stores in several cities began to establish outlying branches with parking areas. One of the earliest was the Country Club Plaza of Kansas City, Missouri, developed by the J. C. Nichols real-estate interests in the twenties.

What is a shopping center? Any wide place in the road with a strip of stores and some parking can call itself a shopping center. But those of importance are groups of retail establishments, planned, developed and managed as units, with off-street parking and all readily accessible by auto or public transportation to at least thirty thousand people. There were fewer than one hundred such centers in 1950.

Three of the oldest are noteworthy because all big centers follow to some degree one of their designs. Northgate, in Seattle, Washington, built at a cost of $12,000,000 by Allied Stores, was opened in 1950.

* See Chapter XXIII.

The Bon Marché, Butler Bros. and other stores pull shoppers back and forth across a pedestrian mall. It has an underground service concourse. The eighty-odd stores are grouped by merchandise and emphasize competition. This design proved so successful that the architect, John Graham, has since designed seventy more mall-type centers, such as Ala Moana in Honolulu; Gulfgate in Houston, Texas; the Halifax Shopping Center in Nova Scotia; Bergen Mall in Paramus, New Jersey; Tacoma Mall in Tacoma, Washington. Newer ones are air-conditioned.

Shoppers' World in Framingham, Massachusetts, first big center in the East, was opened in 1951 and has had a less happy history. A domed Jordan Marsh store dominated a U-shaped building containing some forty stores doubledecked around a wide mall or court. There was no separation of service and customer traffic and many customers did not walk past Jordan Marsh to the other stores. The center went bankrupt in 1954 and was taken over by an insurance company. It has been operated since 1957 by Alstores Realty Corporation, an Allied subsidiary. With more parking space, a large theater, an increased population in the area, it is now prospering.[13]

Northland, the third basic type, was completed at a cost of $25,000,000 in 1954 by the J. L. Hudson Company twelve miles northwest of downtown Detroit, Michigan.* Truck delivery is underground. To reach the Hudson store in the center from the seventy-five-hundred-car parking areas, a shopper must pass a great many of the development's eighty smaller shops. Designed by Vienna-born Victor Gruen, Northland has parlayed beauty and efficiency into success.

In the decade and a half after 1950, shopping centers in the U.S. increased from fewer than one hundred to more than ten thousand, according to the International Council of Shopping Centers. Their effect on downtown shopping has been serious. But downtown is fighting back successfully in many cities.

Shopping developments with nearly all the advantages of a suburban center can be constructed downtown. The great Lloyd Center, only a mile from the heart of Portland, Oregon, is an example of this. This city-within-a city is America's largest central, downtown shop-

* See Chapter XIV.

ping center. A big Meier & Frank branch is at the center. J. J. Newberry, F. W. Woolworth and Best's Apparel stores are at the ends of pedestrian malls. Stores with complementary merchandise are grouped. Sidewalks and second-floor balconies are covered. Pedestrian malls are fifty feet wide and landscaped with flowers and fountains. Lloyd Center has 1,200,000 square feet of floor space, more than one hundred stores, a medical arts building, an outdoor skating rink, a Sheraton Hotel, and parking for nine thousand automobiles.

Rochester, New York, has revitalized downtown with a $30,000,000 Midtown Plaza designed by Gruen. A two-level, air-conditioned mall that makes shopping pleasant even when icy winds sweep off Lake Ontario connects the big B. Forman and McCurdy stores and forty shops. The complex includes a nineteen-story office building with a hotel on the top four floors, a post office, a bus station, and an $8,500,000 underground garage where closed-circuit television cameras watch cars. The city built the garage, is paying off bonds with parking charges, closed a street bisecting the site and with state aid built limited-access highways leading to it. This came only after the merchants gambled $5,000,000 in quietly buying the land required.

Shopping centers accounted for $78.7 billion in annual trade in the United States and Canada as of the end of 1966, according to *Chain Store Age*. This was 36.84 percent of total retail trade excluding automobiles, gas stations, building materials, hay, grain, fuel and ice. The percentage was as high as 43.4 for the Texas-Oklahoma and Arkansas-Louisiana areas.

The shopping-center idea has spread to many lands. Japan has underground shopping centers in Tokyo, Nampa and Osaka, the last a development of 4.4 acres two levels below the streets and opened in 1963 at a cost of $88,000,000. The Osaka municipal government owns 51 percent of the shares. It contains 80 general stores, 55 restaurants and coffee shops, 47 food stores, a barbershop, travel agency and other service establishments. It adjoins a railroad station and two electric lines. Some 700,000 people shop there daily.[14]

There are shopping centers in England, West Germany, the Netherlands, Australia, Mexico, Argentina, France and Sweden. Topping them all for imagination and flair is the Helicoid, a terraced pyramid of 300 stores being built on huge Tarpeya Rock in Caracas, Venezuela. It is a $40,000,000 project. Access is by a road which spirals for a mile and a quarter to the summit, which features a gigantic aluminum dome covering a 2,000-seat auditorium. From this point a shopper can view Caracas from an observation deck 492 feet above sea level, a height equivalent to that of a 45-story building.

II

THE HUDSON'S BAY COMPANY

Rebirth of the Oldest Retailer

THE HUDSON'S BAY COMPANY is the world's oldest retailer. Founded in 1670 to develop the fur trade of then largely unexplored Canada, it is North America's oldest company.[1] It is older than the Bank of England. For years it issued its own money and maintained forts. Over its ships, stores and trading posts it still flies its own flag, a British merchant ship ensign initialed "HBC."

For fiscal 1966, sales of $370,611,000 and profits of $12,309,000, both the greatest in the company's long history, were announced in London by Viscount Amory in his first annual report as the company's thirty-second governor. Some of the income came from oil and gas royalties on the vast land "The Bay" once owned. Some came from its traditional fur trade, now mostly ranch-bred pelts. Some came from its wholesale trade in tobacco, whiskey and other products. But 70 percent came from The Bay's retail stores, which now stretch from Newfoundland to the Pacific Coast with some even offering a new "U-Paddle Canoe Rental Service," where for $25 a week you can rent a canoe at one of the company's northern stores and leave it at another.

Hudson's Bay has been called "the most rambunctiously modern old-fashioned company in the world." Airplanes and radio telephones have replaced canoes and dog teams in supplying and communicating with the company's Arctic posts. It is the most outstanding example of a commercial enterprise successfully adapting its operations to tremendous economic, social and political changes. It might easily have vanished into the mists of history along with the East India Company, the Muscovy Company and the other great companies chartered by the British Crown in the century of the first Queen Elizabeth. Instead, the venerable company, largely owing to shrewd and courageous British leaders, many of them Scottish, developed a vitality that enabled it to survive Arctic cold, wars, disasters, and rivalries of all kinds, to become one of modern Canada's most interesting and important enterprises.[2]

One of the architects of the modern company is James Richard Murray, who became managing director in 1959 and the next year moved The Bay into eastern Canada through a merger with the ten-store Henry Morgan & Co. Ronald E. Sheen and Hugh W. Sutherland are deputy managing directors. Important builders of The Bay of today also have been Philip Alfred Chester, general manager or managing director from 1930 to 1959; the late Sir Patrick Ashley Cooper, governor from 1931 to 1951, and William Johnston Keswick, governor from 1951 to 1965.

While The Bay continues to operate under its old charter and to hold its annual meetings in the United Kingdom, where four-fifths of its thirty thousand "proprietors" live, it has become increasingly a Canadian enterprise. Members of the Canadian Committee, of which D. E. Kilgour is now chairman, were named to the board in 1957. From two out of nine in 1954, they have increased to ten out of seventeen at present. Company shares were listed on the Montreal Stock Exchange in 1961 and on the Toronto Exchange in 1963. Canadians now own 15 percent of them. Six-months operating figures began to be announced in 1966.

The company owns a 21.9 percent interest in Hudson's Bay Oil and Gas Company Limited, a company organized in 1926 with the Continental Oil Company of Delaware to develop the oil and gas in western Canada. This contributed $1,827,000 in royalties to The Bay in 1966. The oil company has oil and gas rights to more than

12,000,000 acres, of which 4,500,000 are mineral rights of The Bay. In 1951–52 speculators attempted to buy control with a view toward exploiting the oil and possibly liquidating other activities. But the management was alert to the threat and the proprietors cold shouldered the idea. The agreement with the Continental Oil Company was extended to 1999.

The big and little Hudson's Bay retail stores have been enlarged and expanded to keep pace with Canada's quickening economy. While it still trails Eaton's and Simpson's in this field, retail sales of The Bay have increased at a greater rate than for Canadian retailers generally. Let a new uranium mine open or a new hydroelectric development start and the company is likely to have a new store adjoining. While the bulk of retail expansion in recent years has been in Montreal, Toronto, Vancouver and Regina, The Bay opened a store in 1964 at Pinawa, Manitoba, site of the Canadian Government Nuclear Research Station.

Retail sales increased from $126,000,000 for the year ending January 31, 1956, to $307,626,000 for the year ending the same date in 1966. Retail business now accounts for 70 percent of the company's net profits.

It is possible to buy a marriage license in the great Hudson's Bay department store in Winnipeg. The company also has big department stores in Vancouver, Calgary, Edmonton, Victoria and Saskatoon, and thanks to the Morgan merger in Montreal, Toronto and Ottawa. All carry a complete line of ready-to-wear apparel for men, women and children; house furnishings and floor coverings, appliances, smallwares, sporting goods, china, furs, diamonds, drugs and other types of merchandise.

The company also operates ninety-five "junior" department stores in small cities or towns, usually built around primary industries, and scattered from British Columbia to Quebec. In addition, the company sells merchandise at its 135 fur-trading posts, now known as Northern Stores, nineteen of which are north of the Arctic Circle. Transportation expense in some places is many times the initial cost of the goods. It is the company policy, however, to maintain low prices on the necessities of life.

A wholesale department, which accounts for 10 to 15 percent of the profits, had sales of $56,121,000 in 1966. This division supplies its "Best Procurable" Scotch whiskey and other products bearing company brands not only to its outlets but to many others, some outside of Canada. The wonderful woolen Hudson's Bay "Point" blankets, which have warmed Antarctic explorers and the climbers of Mt. Everest, indicate how conditions have changed for the company. A four-point blanket once meant that it could be exchanged for four first-grade beaver skins. It now means that it fits a double bed. The company gives every woman employee who has worked five years a four-point blanket as a wedding present when she marries. The wholesale department has nineteen branches and is the largest distributor of tobacco in Canada.

Though a smaller proportion of company business than in the past, the Hudson's Bay fur business of around $116,000,000 a year is much larger than when this was the company's only activity. Only the fur operations of Soviet Russia are larger. The company's traders buy furs in Iran and Tibet. Prior to World War II, it sold only its own furs through auctions in London. It now sells also in Montreal and New York and handles furs of others as well as its own, including all of the karakul skins from South Africa.

The story of the fabulous company began with two Indianized Frenchmen, Pierre Esprit Radisson and his brother-in-law, Médart Chouart, Sieur des Groseilliers, of Three Rivers, Quebec. "A more daring pair of international promoters cannot be found in the history of commerce," wrote one historian of them. "Glib, plausible, ambitious, supported by unquestionable physical courage, they were completely equipped fortune hunters."

Less than fifty years after Henry Hudson sailed into the bay while seeking the Northwest Passage, Groseilliers and Radisson made their way there overland from the French settlements and returned in 1660 to Quebec with Indians carrying beaver skins worth $300,000. Of this, the colonial authorities took in taxes and fines for illicit trading all except $20,000. Unable to obtain redress in France, Groseilliers and Radisson turned to England.

They met rebuffs. London was ravaged by the bubonic plague and in 1666 was destroyed by the great fire. There was war with Holland. At last in 1668, they talked Prince Rupert, a cousin of King Charles II, and others into outfitting two ships for Hudson's Bay. One was damaged in a storm and turned back.

The other, the *Nonsuch,* a fifty-ton ketch in which Groseilliers sailed, won through to Hudson's Bay and after 118 days anchored in what was christened Rupert's River. The Hudson's Bay Company still has a fur-trading post at the spot. After a winter of trade with the Indians, the *Nonsuch* returned to England with a fortune in beaver skins, then highly valued for men's hats. Thus encouraged, the adventurers and Prince Rupert, their first governor, on May 2, 1670, obtained from King Charles their celebrated charter, with privileges greater than any ever granted before or since.

This assured "The Governor and Company of Adventurers of England trading into Hudson's Bay . . . the sole trade and commerce" and absolute control of all lands they should discover through Hudson Strait. It was later interpreted to mean the watershed of Hudson's Bay. This was 1,486,000 square miles of territory, nearly a sixth of North America. The Company was given "the fishing of all sorts of fish . . . and all Mines Royal, as well discovered as not discovered, of gold, silver, gems and precious stones. . . ."

Obligations of the company included a promise to seek the Northwest Passage. Two of its ships eventually made this voyage and its *Fort James* sailed almost entirely around North America. King Charles also required the company "To yield and pay" two elks and two black beavers "whensoever and as often as we our heirs and successors shall happen to enter into . . . the regions hereby granted." This curious tribute, compromised to elk heads and beaver skins, has been paid twice to reigning monarchs, King George VI in 1939 and Queen Elizabeth II in 1959.

The company adopted as a coat-of-arms a design of elks and beaver with the motto "Pro Pelle Cutem," meaning "a man risks his own skin for the skin of an animal." This represented accurately its activity for almost two centuries. Ships took out guns, knives, hatchets, glass beads, brass kettles, blankets and other items and brought back furs. Hudson's Bay men early established a reputation for integrity and fair dealing in their trading with the Indians. The company's affairs prospered. In 1684, the company paid its first dividend, 50 percent on the original capital of 10,500 pounds.

Prince Rupert died and was succeeded as governor by James, Duke of York, an early shareholder. When he became King James II in 1685, he yielded the position to Lord Churchill, the future Duke of Marlborough, an ancestor of Winston Churchill. Dividends were paid to British rulers until 1813.

The early struggles of the Hudson's Bay Company with the French and other rival traders in North America have supplied material for many novels and motion pictures. A young Scot, R. M. Ballantyne, a nephew of Sir Walter Scott's publisher, was one who found romance in the fur trade. He joined the company as a clerk in 1841. After six years at York Factory, Norway House and other posts, he quit and wrote eighty books, most of them novels for boys, based on his adventures. Some are still in print and many a later Hudson's Bay man has confessed that he joined the company after reading Ballantyne's *The Young Fur Traders* or *Hudson's Bay*. The Hudson's Bay Record Society has published twenty-five scholarly volumes of papers covering events before 1870 and half the company's magazine, *The Beaver*, is devoted to history.

French attacks reduced the enterprise to a single trading post toward the end of the seventeenth century. In 1697, the company's ships and the French fought the greatest naval action in Arctic history, with the latter victorious. The Treaty of Ryswick that year confirmed the French in their conquests. The Duke of Marlborough, the company's former governor, however, led the British to victory in the War of the Spanish Succession that followed. In 1713, the Treaty of Utrecht gave all of Hudson's Bay back to the British. From 1690 to 1718, the company paid no dividends. Wolfe's capture of Quebec in 1759 and the surrender of Montreal the next year ended French authority in Canada, but in 1782, during the American revolution, La Pérouse, the French admiral, led a final raid into the bay, capturing and burning the company's forts.

As trading moved inland, Hudson's Bay men came into conflict with other fur traders as shrewd and as tough as themselves, who ignored the Royal Charter. These were Scottish-Canadians from Montreal who moved west and in 1784 formed the North West Company. Alexander Mackenzie, who explored the great river which bears his name, was employed by the North West Company. By 1818, this was powerful enough to buy the Pacific Fur Company of John Jacob Astor, which had sent traders from the United States into what is now Oregon.

Meanwhile, rivalry of the traders from Hudson's Bay and Montreal reached a bloody peak in 1816. In that year, Northwesters encouraged half breeds to massacre settlers established in the Winnipeg area by Lord Selkirk, a Hudson's Bay Company stockholder. Twenty men, including the local governor, were killed. Merger of the companies in 1821 ended this struggle.

From this struggle, Sir George Simpson, one of the most forceful figures in the company's history, rose to head its operations in Canada. Being better managed and free of debt, the Hudson's Bay Company was dominant in the merger, but adopted were a number of North West activities, notably the sharing of 40 percent of the profits among the chief factors and chief traders. The merged company began to use the St. Lawrence River as well as the bay of its name for its shipping.

An illegitimate son, Simpson was born in Ross-shire, Scotland, in 1787. At thirty-three, he was a clerk in a London office when he was noticed and sent to Canada by Andrew Colvile, a member of the Hudson's Bay Company's governing London committee. Though bland in manner and short in stature, Simpson proved a man of iron will and advanced rapidly. Some contemporaries called Simpson the "Little Emperor" and one historian described him as "a composite of fur trader, merchant prince, Machiavelli and statesman." With the companies merged, he eliminated duplicating operations and found new sources of revenue.

One of these was the shipment of ice from Alaska, then in Russian hands, to what is now San Francisco. This added "the first ice man of the Pacific" to his distinctions. Under Simpson, the company added posts in San Francisco; Honolulu; Okhotsk, Siberia; and Fort Yukon,

Alaska. Hudson's Bay furs were sold profitably to the Russian American Fur Company and two thousand skins a year were paid for rent of Alaskan territory. When British and Russians fought in the Crimea, and the Light Brigade charged at Balaklava, the companies by one of the most curious agreements of history preserved neutrality in North America.

Simpson's firm rule was abhorrent to some of his subordinates, notably Dr. John McLoughlin, the "father of Oregon," who resigned, but the company prospered. Dividends were paid every year and additional stock was issued in 1825, 1850, 1852 and 1854 to bring the capital to 500,000 pounds. Simpson made incredible journeys and in 1841 crossed Siberia in a trip entirely around the world, to be knighted by Queen Victoria in recognition of the Hudson's Bay Company's exploration in the Arctic. Sir George entertained the Prince of Wales lavishly on his Canadian tour in 1860 and died of apoplexy a few days later. He was mourned not only by Lady Simpson's four children but by at least seven others from extramarital unions of his lusty early years.

By this time it was obvious that the Canadian West would be opened to settlers and that the Hudson's Bay Company would have to surrender some of its unique privileges. Its charter had been assailed at intervals through the years and had been the subject of a Parliamentary inquiry in 1857. Sensing the chance for a bold financial coup, Sir Edward Watkin, a railroad builder, and others in 1863 bought control of the company, paying stockholders 300 pounds for shares previously valued at less than 200 pounds. As soon as control was gained, Watkin and his friends named a new London committee and increased the stock to 2,000,000 pounds, most of which was sold to the public.

In 1867, the Dominion of Canada was proclaimed by authority of the British North America Act, a clause of which provided for admission of the company's territory into the new confederation. The details were worked out in a Deed of Surrender. Under this, the Hudson's Bay Company gave up its governmental powers and most of its vast lands. In exchange, the Canadian government paid the Hudson's Bay Company 300,000 pounds. The company retained 5 to

3,000 acres around each of its 120 posts and, in addition, was allowed to claim one-twentieth of the fertile plain area, a matter of seven million acres, for sale to settlers.

This led to a new crisis. Some of the Indians who had depended on the paternalistic company for food, shelter and government feared the coming of hordes of settlers and Dominion authority. Under Louis Riel, a persuasive half breed, the métis rose in rebellion and for a time held Fort Garry, the forerunner of modern Winnipeg. As troops approached, Riel, a tragic figure, fled to the United States but later returned, led a new uprising, was captured and hanged.

From this turmoil Donald A. Smith, later Baron Strathcona and Mount Royal, emerged as a powerful Hudson's Bay figure. He was born in the Scotch village of Forres, grim scene of Shakespeare's *Macbeth*, and joined the company as a boy apprentice. A man of thirty years' company experience, he dashed six hundred miles by sleigh to prevent serious bloodshed in the rebellion. He also induced the new management of the company to distribute 107,000 pounds from its Oregon indemnity to the traders hitherto entitled to share in the company profits.

Lord Strathcona speculated successfully in the building of the Canadian Pacific Railroad and many other ventures and became such a large stockholder in the Hudson's Bay Company that he was made deputy governor and, in 1889, governor of the company, becoming the first man from Canada ever to rise to the top post. He was then sixty-nine years old and divided his energies among many projects. He believed the fur trade doomed and was interested only in sale of the company's seven million acres of land. Oil was undreamed of but coal was a possibility and mineral rights were reserved as the acreage was sold to settlers.

As the population grew and gold seekers rushed to the Klondike, the western trading posts became stores, but aged Lord Strathcona was more interested in other matters, including a regiment of Canadian cavalry which he sent to the Boer War. He let Timothy Eaton and James Simpson launch and spread their great retail enterprises in the Canadian cities without challenge. He was still governor of the Hudson's Bay Company when he died at ninety-three on January 21,

1914, leaving an estate of $25,000,000 to numerous beneficiaries, including some Eskimo friends of his youth.

His successors took charge vigorously. With the outbreak of World War I, the Hudson's Bay Company became purchasing agent for the French government on a 2½ percent commission basis and also undertook to deliver supplies to Russia via the Arctic port of Archangel. A subsidiary shipping company was formed and it amassed a fleet of 275 vessels. Of these, 110 were lost, principally to submarines.

Five of the company's vessels were frozen in the ice in the winter of 1915-16. An explosion at Bakaritsa gravely damaged five other vessels. In 1917, the icebreaker *Iceland* blew up at Economia, wrecking a steamer alongside, damaging three more and setting munitions on shore afire to start a blaze which lasted for days in weather eighteen degrees below zero. To replace cranes destroyed at the time, the company located a floating one, capable of lifting 125 tons, at the Spanish port of Cadiz and one even larger in Holland and towed them safely to the Arctic port.

Despite mishaps such as these, the company procured and delivered safely some eighteen million tons of cargo. In addition to munitions, this included breadstuffs secured from Algeria, Australia, the Argentine and Canada; sugar from Cuba, Java and Martinique; timber and wood pulp from Canada; coal from England, Canada and the United States; groundnuts, palm kernels and other produce from West Africa and Morocco. During 1918, the company delivered one thousand tons of freight daily in French ports.

One of the most exciting war episodes involved the tug *Vigilant*. Caught in a heavy gale 480 miles out of Queenstown, the eighty-six-ton vessel seemed doomed. Her captain and most of the crew abandoned her and were picked up by a passing steamer. The second mate, a fireman and a greaser, however, refused to quit the ship and brought her safely to Ireland. The company gave them 5,000 pounds as a reward for their heroic work.

The S. S. *Nascopie*, an icebreaker named for a tribe of Indians in Labrador and in time of peace the summer supply ship for the company's Arctic posts, made many wartime voyages to Murmansk and Archangel. In June, 1917, shortly after sailing from Archangel for Montreal, she was attacked by a large enemy submarine. The *Nascopie* shot back. Her fourth shell was a direct hit. The submarine exploded and disappeared. The captain and crew received the thanks of the Admiralty. With peace the *Nascopie* returned to her supply-ship duties and was the best-known ship of the Arctic until her thirty-five years of service ended in July, 1947, when she sank after striking a reef at the entrance to Dorset Harbour.

In 1920, Sir Robert Kindersley, the twenty-eighth governor of the company, visited Canada for celebration with some pageantry of the 250th anniversary of the old company. With the war profits, the company built a new London headquarters, Beaver House, on Great Trinity Lane. This contained the finest facilities for the storage and sale of pelts from all over the world. It also provided a magnificent board room, on the walls of which were hung portraits of Prince Rupert, King James II and other great figures of its long history.

Under the leadership of Charles Vincent Sale, deputy governor from 1916 to 1925 and governor from then until 1931, the company belatedly spent lavishly on new store buildings in Canada. Before amassing a fortune as a trader in Japan, Sale had married a Canadian girl and was interested in the Dominion. He created the company's Canadian Committee for on-the-spot direction. He was the first to interest the company in fur farming and also the first to throw open the company's archives to historians.

There had been some store building earlier. In Edmonton, for example, a store building completed in 1905 had been one of the first in the area to have elevators. These and also mirrors were a source of wonder to the Indians. On seeing his reflection for the first time, a chief once said: "Now I can see into the Spirit World."

Employing some of the experts who had built Harrod's great store in London, the Hudson's Bay Company in the twenties erected new and magnificent store buildings in Winnipeg, Vancouver and several other cities. These were no sooner completed than the depression struck. The company began to lose money in all departments and was soon in arrears on dividends on preferred stock which had been issued in 1912 and later. Even in the land department, sales failed to cover salaries and taxes. The London Committee resigned and a committee of stockholders chose a new governor in 1931.

Major and later Sir Patrick Ashley Cooper, who had been born in Aberdeen, Scotland, in 1887 and had studied law there and in Cambridge, was their choice. He had also seen Army service in World War I. He at once made a tour of the company's Canadian properties and, something that no previous governor had done, began to make annual visits to Canada.

"On arriving in Canada on my first visit," he reported later, "I was dismayed at what I found—a very extravagant administration and, worse still, a disheartened staff." Fur prices in 1931 were only 17 percent of what they had been ten years earlier. Major Cooper found such heavy losses in the wholesale department that closing it down was considered. He found the magnificent retail store buildings "filled with merchandise instead of customers, with staff despondent and with little faith in the future. This unhappy situation was partly the result of the economic conditions then prevailing in Canada but also due to too rapid expansion, bringing with it over-costly administration and lack of coordination. The absence of a strong guiding hand was only too obvious."

In Philip Alfred Chester, a six-foot astute former accountant, Major Cooper found the executive to lead the company's rehabilitation. Born in Long Eaton, Derbyshire, March 14, 1896, Chester had run away from home to serve with the King's Rifle Corps in World War I. He then earned his articles as an accountant and joined this department of the Hudson's Bay Company in London in 1923. He was transferred to Winnipeg the next year and became chief accountant in 1925. He was promoted to general manager in 1930.

At the 1932 annual meeting, Major Cooper read a letter from a Canadian farmer setting forth the plight of many of the company's customers. "I got your letter about what I owe," wrote the man. "Now be pachant. I ain't forgot you. Please wait. When I have the money I will pay you. If this was the Judgement Day and you was no more prepared to meet your maker than I am to meet your account you sure would go to hell. Trusting you will do this."

Major Cooper was convinced that much of the company's trouble stemmed from the remote control which the London committee had attempted to exercise over its operations. He turned to the Canadian Committee, which had been given real power only in 1930, and it began to function as a frequently meeting board of directors. Drastic economies were instituted to meet the depression. Many positions were abolished. New executives took charge in all departments. The organization was strengthened by new attention to the selection, training and welfare of the company's employees.

No employer looks after his workers with greater care than the Hudson's Bay Company expends on its fur-trade post managers and their families. All the resources of science are employed to mitigate the hardships of the Arctic. Each manager and his family have a completely furnished rent-free six-room home especially designed for the climate. The company looks after the household needs, supplying and replacing some twenty-seven hundred different items as required.

There are books for adults and children, toys and textbooks for the latter. There are free government-approved correspondence courses for children up to ten years old. The company will pay the fare of those between ten and seventeen to the nearest urban school and $350 a year toward the tuition.

For a flat fee of $50 a month for adults and $4 to $15 for children, depending on age, the family can order almost anything it wants in the way of food from the company's nearest supply depot. The company supplies its employees with a wealth of booklets with titles like *Your Food and Health in the North, How to Grow Gardens at HBC Posts* and *Prenatal Care*. The last explains how to use dried milk instead of fresh, and the importance of vitamins. Each post has a company-supplied medicine chest, full of sulfa drugs, vitamins, and first-aid supplies, but the seriously ill and women expecting babies are taken to city hospitals, often by airplane.

"A striking feature of life in the far north," noted the company's 285th Annual Report in 1954, "is the very close cooperation, both official and personal, which exists between representatives of the Federal and Provincial Governments, the Royal Canadian Mounted Police, the Missions, and the Company's personnel." Each fur-trade post usually consists of a store, warehouse, and the residence of the manager, all immaculate white buildings with red roofs. Electric power for these, and sometimes for neighboring missions and police stations, is generated by a company-developed gasoline-powered unit. There are stoves which operate on electricity as well as on wood or coal.

Many of the posts have radio-telephone facilities. During World War II these became weather-observing posts and in many cases sent out hourly observations for the guidance of airplane pilots. The company's three airplanes and dozen or so ships travel more than a quarter of a million miles a year, taking supplies and personnel to these posts and bringing out furs.

But the company's greatest rejuvenation has come in its retail-stores department. One of the new executives employed in the 1931 search for fresh talent was Frank F. Martin, a six-foot New Englander who for some years had done an outstanding job as controller of The Wm. Taylor Son & Co. department store in Cleveland, Ohio. As a boy in Lynn, Massachusetts, Martin had worked briefly for the famous Lydia Pinkham patent-medicine company and also in General Electric's personnel department. During World War I, he served with the Quartermaster Department in Washington. He joined the Hudson's Bay Company as controller of its Vancouver store. He later became assistant general manager and in 1935 was promoted to general manager of the department.

Merchandise lines were expanded and improved. The company became the exclusive Canadian outlet for products developed by the Associated Merchandising Corporation buying organization. Advertising was increased. The big stores gave more attention to lower-priced merchandise and basement operations. Food departments, which account for half the business of some of the small stores, were enlarged. This is usually self-service and the company pioneered the self-service sale of meats in Western Canada. The average sales ticket in Canadian department stores is only about half that in United States stores but with food stocked the customers come in oftener.

Almost anything is obtainable in the great Winnipeg store. It once sold in one day six thousand dozen cut daffodils flown in by airplane. It regularly does a big business in diamond rings, television sets, pianos, fine chinaware, boats, canoes, hardware, food and drugs. It has one of the largest book departments in Canada. This also sells magazines and daily newspapers. There are parking facilities for customers, and an arrangement for delivering their parcels to their cars. Shopping mothers can leave their children in a store playroom or wheel them about in red strollers supplied by the store. There is no adjustment bureau. Clerks are empowered to accept returns and make refunds.

Executive salaries were increased. Prior to 1931, no Hudson's Bay buyer earned as much as $15,000 a year. Systematic training and profit-sharing programs were introduced.

In addition to the usual employee benefits of discounts and vacations, the company pays its employees interest on their savings, 5 percent up to $10,000 and 4 percent over $10,000. At sixty-five, those employed for twenty years are eligible for pensions. Cash awards and extra holidays with pay are given veterans. An employee with fifteen years' service can be discharged only with the approval of the Canadian Committee.

All of this plus Canada's improved economy made the retail-stores department profitable. In 1936, the company resumed payments of dividends on its preferred stock and retired all of this stock by 1945. Dividends were resumed on the common stock in 1938 and since then have been paid continuously.

Managing Director Murray, a native of Winnipeg and a graduate of McGill University, was a lieutenant in the Canadian Navy during World War II and then a Canadian foreign service officer for five years, four with the Canadian Embassy in Washington, before joining The Bay in 1951. After training in the fur-sales department in Montreal, he joined the fur-sales office in New York, became head of this operation in 1953, and returned to Winnipeg in 1955 as general manager for Canada. Most executives have spent all of their business careers with the company. Deputy Managing Director Sutherland, a chartered accountant, has been with the company since graduation from the University of Manitoba and Deputy Managing Director Sheen since graduation from the University of Toronto.

Canadian universities are scouted for talent each year and, as in years past, adventurous young men are enlisted by advertising in British newspapers, especially in the Northern Islands of Scotland. The Northern Stores Department seeks physically fit single men, between seventeen and twenty-three, with a high-school education, pays their travel expenses and $200 to $250 a month during training. During the period of training, a young man must remain single "since living accommodation is not generally provided for married assistants." Many become store managers in three to five years, earning $300 to $600 a month and upward. An initial two-year employment contract is required. Only those volunteering for Arctic posts are sent to them.

Following the 1960 merger with 115-year-old Henry Morgan & Co., Ltd. (effected by the exchange of a share of Hudson's Bay stock and $14 for each of the 428,000 common shares of the Morgan firm), retail activities of The Bay were reorganized into four geographical regions: Central, General Manager Sheen; Western, General Manager N. H. Abramson; Northern Stores Department, Chief Executive Officer Sutherland; and Morgan's Montreal and Ottawa, President E. W. H. Brown. To finance the acquisition, The Bay issued $10,000,000 in twenty-year debentures. Besides the large department store in downtown Montreal, The Bay acquired several shopping centers and other small units in that city as well as in Toronto, Hamilton and Ottawa. The Montreal department store has a number of restaurants, including one selling only soup and pie. These as well as older units have been expanded and modernized. The big Montreal store benefits from the city's new subway.

In 1965, the company adopted "The Bay" as its name for all retail activities except the Morgan store in Montreal, and had Lippincott & Marguiles, Inc., the industrial designers, create new letterheads, wrappings and boxes, using the short name in English or French. It also chose ochre and white as colors for the retail stores.

Sir Patrick Ashley Cooper, who had been a director of the Bank of England and many other institutions, retired as governer of The Bay in 1952 and died at sea in 1961 while returning to England from South Africa. His successor was William Johnston Keswick, previously managing director of Jardine, Matheson, Ltd., Far Eastern

Trading Company. He had flown out of Singapore on the last airplane before occupation by the Japanese. He had helped Field Marshal Montgomery plan the Normandy invasion.

In his report to the 296th Annual General Court of the company as he retired as governor in 1965, Keswick reported that by reinvesting 61 percent of the profits, The Bay's business had increased by a greater percent than the Canadian gross national product in the previous twelve years ($24 billion in 1952 and $47 billion in 1964, an increase of 96 percent). In the same period, The Bay's retail sales increased 180 percent; fur sales 112 percent, and total profits 320 percent; income from oil royalties from nothing to $1,400,000; and the value of The Bay's equity in Hudson's Bay Oil and Gas Company, Ltd., from $2,500,000 to $75,000,000.

Lord Amory was previously British High Commissioner to Canada. Born Derick Heathcoat Amory on December 26, 1899, and educated at Eton and Oxford, he has won distinction in business, politics and military service. He is a director of his family's firm of John Heathcoat & Co., textile manufacturers, and Imperial Chemical Industries. He has been a Member of Parliament and has held several British Cabinet posts, including Minister of Agriculture, Fisheries and Food, and Chancellor of the Exchequer. He was an officer in the Territorial Army for twenty years, broke a leg in a parachute jump and was captured by the Germans at the siege of Arnhem during World War II. After nearly three centuries The Bay is still directed by adventurers.

III

BROOKS BROTHERS

America's Oldest Men's Apparel Store

WHAT DO THESE ILLUSTRIOUS PEOPLE have in common: Abraham Lincoln, Theodore Roosevelt, Franklin D. Roosevelt, John Foster Dulles, Charles Lindbergh, Gene Tunney, the Duchess of Windsor and Marlene Dietrich? The answer, surprising as it may seem, is that all have been customers of Brooks Brothers, the New York firm whose unparalleled existence since 1818 gives it the distinction of being America's oldest men's clothing store.

Theodore Roosevelt, Ulysses S. Grant and Woodrow Wilson were all clad in Brooks Brothers suits when they took their oaths of office as Presidents of the United States. At the Yalta Conference President Franklin D. Roosevelt wore a Navy cape made by Brooks and it is immortalized in a statue of him in London's Grosvenor Square. President Lincoln was wearing a Prince Albert coat, a waistcoat and trousers from Brooks Brothers when he was assassinated.

Other famous Brooks customers included Herbert Hoover, Charles Evans Hughes, Adlai Stevenson and John Foster Dulles. In fact, this predilection of the diplomatic set for the store led Charles Lindbergh to it. When the famed airman landed in Paris without luggage after his historic flight alone across the Atlantic Ocean, Ambassador

Myron T. Herrick loaned him a Brooks Brothers suit. Lindbergh liked it and became a staunch customer.

To wear clothing made by Brooks Brothers is the virtual equivalent of membership in an exclusive club. Identification as a Brooks Brothers customer is usually inescapable. A novelist has only to write that one of his characters is wearing a shirt, suit or coat made by Brooks Brothers and the reader knows instantly what type of person is being described.

Such a person is an executive or would-be executive, well born and well schooled and invariably well behaved. In his appearance, he follows the advice of Lord Chesterfield to "take great care to be dressed like the reasonable people of our own age, in the place where you are; whose dress is never spoken of one way or another." Such a man always wears the right clothes to the right place at the right time.

The quiet conservatism that characterizes clothing made by Brooks Brothers is one of the factors that has made the concern such an American institution. In a nation dedicated to speed, change and flamboyance, Brooks Brothers has endured under the founder's original policies of good taste, fine-quality merchandise and expert workmanship in everything made and sold. There is no high-pressure salesmanship. Its advertising features understatement rather than strident superlatives and comparisons.

Some old-line customers feared this might come to an end when Brooks Brothers was purchased in 1946 by Julius Garfinckel & Co., the Washington specialty store. The new management, however, attempted few changes. For, when it removed the button behind the collar of a button-down shirt because men no longer buttoned down collars in back and eliminated shirttails that reach all the way to the knee, certain customers complained. The long shirttail was at once restored and those who want it can have a button sewed behind their collar and a buttonhole added.

The store's dignity and graciousness were maintained. The new owners merely introduced more efficiency in the production of Brooks's fine merchandise and brought it to the attention of more people. Six-foot John C. Wood, who had just taken off a lieutenant colonel's uniform, was installed as president. A native of Newark, New Jersey, and a 1922 graduate of Dartmouth, he had been prior to Army service a vice president for ten years at B. Altman & Co., a store also known for its taste.

Wood opened new Brooks stores in Chicago and Pittsburgh and greatly increased Brooks's advertising program. Under his leadership, sales increased to $30,000,000 in 1965, more than quadruple the volume in the best year of the old regime. The average Brooks sales ticket jumped to $35, much higher than the average for the big department stores.

Suits for sale are still piled neatly on table tops, as was customary in the early days. "It's the most inefficient way in the world to handle suits," says President Wood. "But we continue to do it because we've learned that you don't change the brand of oats on a winning horse."

Brooks Brothers has never been averse to changes of the right sort in clothing and has pioneered dozens of innovations that rival clothiers have adopted. These include the button-down shirt (still called by Brooks the polo model), the foulard tie, the four-button suit, the rounded collar, the Shetland sweater and the polo coat. Its famous No. 1 sack suit, three-buttoned and single-breasted with natural shoulders and straight hang, has been for about five decades the "uniform" that stamps a man as being "correctly dressed."

Brooks was also the first in modern times to sponsor linen crash, shantung silk, seersucker, cotton cord and other cooler summer suits for men, jackets with odd trousers, and many styles in boys' clothing. It has introduced such items as the Norfolk jacket, the Tattersall vest and the "deerstalker" cap, and was in great measure responsible for the once overwhelming vogue of the box-cloth spat. More recently it launched new man-made materials and was the first in the world to offer shirts made of Dacron and cotton oxford, called Brooksweave, and Dacron and cotton broadcloth, copyrighted as Brookscloth.

Possibly the most important feature of the Brooks tradition is the personal service given to regular customers. Brooks salesmen refer to these people as "see-you" customers. Because of a policy of "open book" selling—whereby one clerk may serve all the needs of a customer regardless of where the merchandise is selected—strong relationships are established. These customers are frequently reluctant to be served by any other than their favorite salesman, who remembers their apparel preferences and tastes, and wait until his return if he is ill or on vacation. "Mr. So-and-So wants to see you," goes the word. Some customers never bother to learn their own measurements but rely wholly on the little black book of their favorite salesman.

So unswerving in their loyalty to the store are these "see-you" customers that salesmen have been known to serve four or five generations from one family. One salesman, the late Frederick Webb, served five generations of Morgans, calling them by their first names. It is doubtful if any store in the world can equal such continuous patronage as that given Brooks Brothers by the late John R. Voorhis, one-time Grand Sachem of Tammany Hall and a man noted for his immaculate dress. When he was 10, his mother bought him his first long pants at Brooks Brothers and, until his death at 102, he never bought a suit elsewhere.

Other long-term customers include notables in every walk of life—Presidents, bankers, diplomats, prize fighters, military officers, Hollywood stars and European royalty. Eighteen hundred elite European customers order by mail when necessary and embassies abroad keep extra Brooks Brothers suits on hand in case of emergencies.

John Stahl, the former California postal clerk known as "Old Iron Legs" because he walked thirteen thousand miles *after* retiring, once landed in Madrid with his clothes shabby and unpressed. He appealed to the American Embassy there for a change of clothes and was loaned a custom-made Brooks suit that had the name Nicholas Duke Biddle sewed in it. Stahl wore the suit for an audience with Pope Pius XII.

That consideration of customer whims pays off is evidenced by the fact that today the firm has, in addition to two New York stores, branches in Chicago, Boston, Pittsburgh, San Francisco and Los Angeles. Its mail-order business services customers from coast to coast. Customers in thirty-three other large cities are also served seven or eight times a year by Brooks "travelers," who, with some six hundred swatches of materials and a variety of samples, set up shop for short periods in the leading hotels.

The company has its own clothing factory in Long Island City, New York, and its own shirt factory in Paterson, New Jersey, that supply almost 45 percent of all merchandise sold in its stores. Brooks Brothers is thus its own largest supplier.

Brooks Brothers' history parallels the growth of both New York and the nation. The founder of the business, Henry Sands Brooks, son of a Connecticut physician, opened his shop on the northwest corner of Catherine and Cherry streets on April 7, 1817, a month after James Monroe was inaugurated President. New York, with less than 125,000 inhabitants, was then a seafaring city. Four months after the clothing shop was opened, the *Savannah*, the first American ocean-going steamship, was launched a few blocks away.

Henry Sands Brooks, who was forty-six years old when he opened his shop, was noted for his fine taste in clothes. Prior to that time, he had been a successful provisioner. He was a dapper gentleman who made frequent trips on sailing ships to England, from which he returned with new items for his wardrobe. Each time he sailed some friend invariably said, "Henry, bring me back a waistcoat like yours." Or "Henry, have your London tailor make me a coat like yours."

Just when the idea struck him to pioneer in ready-made clothing nobody knows, but Brooks was among the first in the world, if not *the* first, to offer such clothing. His sea captain friends often couldn't wait for something to be made. He also tailored clothes "to measure" as did clothiers everywhere, but his shop, offering the dual service, was unique in those days.

The site selected for the shop was in the center of New York's busiest mercantile district and within a block or two of the most fashionable residences. Brooks bought the ground and a frame building for a little over $17,000, and his first entry on opening day is significant.

It wasn't for a sale but rather for a loan of $25 to a friend. Then and there was established the Brooks dictum to make friends of all customers. He also treated seafaring customers to a drink of Medford rum and often wrapped packages in black silk kerchiefs for which he did not charge.

Henry Sands Brooks guided the first store for fifteen years until his death in 1833. By then he had initiated his two older sons, Henry and Daniel H., into the business, firmly implanting in them this principle: "To make and deal *only* in merchandise of the best quality, to sell it at a fair profit *only* and to deal *only* with people who seek and are capable of appreciating such merchandise." In 1850, the company name was changed from H. & D. H. Brooks & Co., to Brooks Brothers.

By this time, the familiar Golden Fleece trademark of the firm was in use. A sheep suspended in a ribbon, the Golden Fleece had long been a symbol of British woolen merchants. Dating from the fifteenth century, it had been the emblem of the Knights of the Golden Fleece, founded by Philip the Good, Duke of Burgundy. Worn suspended over each knight's heart, it symbolized the Lamb of God.

As New York City grew and moved northward, the firm followed. While the original store was occupied until 1874, a second and larger store was opened in 1858 in new quarters at Broadway and Grand Street. Henry Brooks, the eldest son of the founder, was dead by then and control passed to the four younger brothers, Daniel H., already initiated, and John, Elisha and Edward S. Brooks.

The elaborateness of the new premises is indicated by an entry in Mrs. George Shepard's diary of 1861, now in the Burton Historical Collection of the Detroit Public Library. Mrs. Shepard, a cousin of Ralph Waldo Emerson, was spending the winter with her husband at the Astor House in New York. On December 9, 1861, she wrote:

> Fair warm like the spring of the year. . . . Smith came with his carriage we drove to Brooks Brothers Clothing House corner of Broadway & Grand Street where Mr. Shepard changes his Scotch wool Drawers for 2 pair English Merinos we went upstairs and looked over this large establishment where all kinds of Garments for Men were cutting out & making . . . they employ 400 persons cutting and sewing. . . . Columns & pillars bronze colour, with large looking glasses: were well worth seeing.

Mrs. Shepard did not mention the unique pagoda in the store, a structure fifteen feet in diameter by thirty feet in height, which was occupied by the desks of the "measurers" for all clothing made to order. Another feature of the store was an enormous four-dialed globe clock, illuminated from the inside by gaslight.

A store advertisement of the time stated that

> Our Custom Department will at all times be found complete in stock and variety of piece goods, imported expressly for our trade, consisting of French, English and German Cloths, Cassimere, Doeskins, rich Velvet, Silk, Satin and every new style of cloths, etc. of the finest quality, which will be made to order in the best manner and most fashionable mode.

During the Civil War, many of the Union Army notables patronized this five-story establishment, then probably the largest of its kind in the world. Generals Grant, Sheridan, Sherman and Hooker, and thousands of the men they led, were outfitted in uniforms made by Brooks Brothers. The contract for these came from Governor E. D. Morgan of New York.

Most illustrious of all Civil War customers was President Abraham Lincoln. He bought the overcoat for his Second Inaugural —its lining was embroidered with an eagle holding in its beak a pennant inscribed, "One Country, One Destiny"—and many other articles at the Grand Street store. One of Brooks Brothers' present-day customers is Raymond Massey, the actor whose portrayal of Lincoln has been so masterful as to make him seem a reincarnation of the President. One of the store clerks tells of the eerie feeling he had on a Lincoln's Birthday when the first customer was Raymond Massey.

Times were perilous while the Civil War raged and the Cherry Street store was sacked from top to bottom by a rowdy mob during the draft riots of 1863. *Valentine's Manual*, a publication of the time, in its account of the sacking has probably given one of the best descriptions ever made of the character of the Brooks brothers and their associates. The reporter states: "We can find no reason for the looting, for the Messrs. Brooks are fair, upright gentlemen, of mild manners and such simplicity of deportment as to allay and conciliate rather than excite ill feeling in any with whom they come into intercourse."

In 1868, store spokesmen mentioned "having the most fastidious among our regular customers," and said that "the one-price system is always observed." The firm valued its property at $750,000 and stated that "half of the sales of this house are for cash, yet the firm carries from 3,000 to 4,000 accounts which are extended to approved credit."

In 1869, Brooks Brothers became a neighbor of the Singer Company on Union Square and began to use Singer sewing machines. Garments, however, continued to be finished by hand, as they still are today.

The day of the famous blizzard of 1888, March 12, Brooks Brothers had only one customer. What did he buy? Nothing but a pair of white flannel trousers.

During migrations farther north, two of Henry Sands Brooks's grandsons entered into a partnership with six of the oldest employees. In 1889, two more grandsons came into the business. The four grandsons and six veteran employees incorporated the business in 1903.

The presidency went to one of the old employees, Francis Guerin Lloyd, who had been senior partner. Frederick Brooks, one of the grandsons of Henry Sands Brooks, became first vice president and Eugene Mapes, an employee since 1880, became secretary. Lloyd had been with the firm for forty-one years when he became president. He stayed at the helm until his death in 1920, making in all fifty-eight years of service to the store.

There were many reasons why the group selected Lloyd for president, but certainly one was his appearance. A man addicted to bow ties and a goatee, he was as impeccable in dress as any member of the Brooks clan. He had an exceptionally fine color sense and many of the East Indian and British design blocks still used for printing Brooks's exclusive ties were selected by Lloyd in England.

During his regime, a branch was opened in fashionable Newport, Rhode Island, at 220 Bellevue Avenue. It was more of a club than a store and some of society's most colorful notables dropped in daily.

Charley Sands stopped in every morning to buy just one polo shirt and Joe Harrison would flip coins with friends for $50 polo coats.

In 1915, Lloyd supervised the move of the firm's executive offices and main store to its present ten-story walnut-paneled building at 346 Madison Avenue. Although the building was modern in every respect, Lloyd persisted in a few antiquated business methods. Since he was able to add up columns of four-digit figures faster than the first adding machines, he saw no reason why everyone else couldn't do the same and the store had none of these machines until after his death.

Lloyd, who had a fine Spencerian style, continued to write the company's direct-mail advertising by hand just as he had in the early years. This was mailed as a personal letter to customers and called their attention to new imports, new styles or new patterns.

Under Lloyd's guidance, the store weathered World War I, outfitting General John J. Pershing and many other officers, some of them the store's own employees.

When the war made it increasingly difficult to import woolens, Frederick Brooks, then chairman of the board, exhibited the same paternalistic attitude toward regular customers that has always characterized the store. Outsiders who had never been in the place before started flocking to Brooks Brothers, particularly on Saturdays, to buy up as many woolen items as their budgets permitted. One Saturday morning in May, 1917, Brooks came down to the main floor and, for the first time, saw them.

"Who are all these people?" he wanted to know.

When told who they were and why they were there, he said firmly: "Close the store on Saturdays. We must save this merchandise for our regular customers."

And every Saturday thereafter during the summer of 1917 the store remained closed, the first time in its history for it to have Saturday closings in any month other than August.

After Lloyd died, Mapes, who had then been with the store for forty-three years, became president. He had started to work for Brooks Brothers at the age of fifteen and progressed to the top through the uniform and livery department. The store's collection of livery buttons, incidentally, dates back to about 1870 and is a museum record of the Goulds, Vanderbilts, Morgans, Rockefellers and other families prominent in American society.

Mapes held the post of president until 1935. During this time the firm continued to expand, opening branch stores in Boston and in Palm Beach. The latter had a distinguished but short-lived history.

The firm had started wooing college and prep-school trade back around 1900. By the 1920's, to look "Brooksy" was practically a requirement for entering any of the Eastern or Ivy League schools.

F. Scott Fitzgerald, who chronicled American life in this era, alluded to Brooks Brothers so often in his novels that quotations from *This Side of Paradise* helped the firm obtain an injunction against a California company using the Brooks name. Characters also wore Brooks Brothers clothing in novels by Ernest Hemingway, Somerset Maugham, and John P. Marquand. Mary McCarthy called a short story about a romance aboard a transcontinental train "The Man in the Brooks Brothers Shirt."

Mapes increased the store's display advertising and Donald G. Vaughan, advertising manager, wrote most of the copy. It helped increase the sales volume to over $6,500,000 in 1929, a record figure at that time. Vaughan, a slight, bookish man who retired in 1948 and died in 1959, described the Brooks Brothers advertising policy of those days as "no policy at all," adding that the store's real advertising was "done by loving friends."

One of these friends was another literary man, Frederick Lewis Allen, who was editor of *Harper's Magazine*, a Brooks customer and a Vaughan friend for thirty years. Vaughan translated and adapted Honoré de Balzac's *Art of Tying the Cravat* for the firm in 1921 and the booklet proved as useful to customers as an earlier compilation called *On Going Away*, a handbook for travelers.

Age forced Mapes to resign in 1935 and the presidency was then taken over by Winthrop Holley Brooks, a great-grandson of the founder and a son of Frederick Brooks. Winthrop Brooks had entered the store four years after graduating from Yale in 1915. Although professing to dislike the clothing business—he had been living on a Wyoming ranch his father gave him—he headed the store for eleven years.

Douglas Fairbanks and other motion-picture stars had been hounding the store management for years to open a branch in or near Hollywood. In 1939, Winthrop Brooks reluctantly consented to opening shops in San Francisco and Los Angeles. There the stars could at least examine samples of clothing and buy furnishings. It was not at all unusual in those days to see the sartorially correct movie stars shopping leisurely there—among them Fred Astaire, Burt Lancaster, Robert Montgomery, Tyrone Power, Chester Morris, Cary Grant and Clark Gable—and the Brooks Brothers clerks were instructed to pay no more attention to them than to less-celebrated individuals.

Occasionally a customer recognized one of the movie greats with unmistakable delight. One Christmas, for example, an elderly little woman was buying a cashmere muffler as a present for her husband when she recognized a tall, lanky figure beside her.

"Why, you're Gary Cooper, aren't you?" she said. With characteristic aplomb, Cooper raised his hat, bowed and said, "Howdy, ma'am" and went on with his shopping.

No one could much blame Winthrop Brooks if he found the clothing business a pretty big task when he took over. He had the responsibility of directing the store through World War II and of seeing many of its employees march off to fight, including his own son, Frederick. It was an honor to outfit Generals Wainwright and Doolittle and other illustrious military figures, but the employees experienced real grief when customers like Theodore Roosevelt, Jr., failed to return. Roosevelts from both Oyster Bay and Hyde Park have always been among the favorite Brooks Brothers customers.

Because Brooks Brothers depends so heavily on materials from abroad, especially Great Britain, for its merchandise, World War II was a special hardship. Its volume was down to about $4,750,000 and the 1946 sale to Garfinckel followed.

This did not end the Brooks blood in the business. Winthrop Brooks, who died in 1963, had continued as chairman until 1951. His nephew, Ashbel T. Wall, a fifth-generation representative of the Brooks family, became a vice president under the new management.

While no change was made in the original Brooks policy of quality merchandise for quality customers—President Wood describes Brooks Brothers as "not a business but a world standard for men's good taste"—there have been some changes made under the Garfinckel ownership. Advertising remains distinctive and underwritten, but the linage in the leading newspapers has been upped considerably. More clothing in a greater variety of styles is being stocked and customers can get what they want when they want it. Special-order clothing, made in the ready-to-wear factories but to specific measurements, is widely available too.

"Now you can order anything," says President Wood, "even an African bush coat, if you have it custom made. You can get it *when* you need it, it will be the *best* of its kind, and it will be correct for the *locale* where it is to be worn."

Wood quickly established a "346" department—named after the store's address—aimed at the younger man who wants the Brooks look and label but cannot afford the prices of its regular merchandise. The "346" merchandise is made by outside contractors to Brooks Brothers designs and specifications, while its other clothing is made in the company's own workrooms.

More emphasis is also being placed on the rapidly growing boys department. A young man of four can be completely outfitted by the store, the idea being that potentially long-time customers ought to be caught early in the Brooks Brothers habit.

Not that all small fry want to be little gentlemen. Abe Burrows, the theater writer and director, once took his young son into the New York store for an outfit. Master Burrows shied away from a suit with coat and trousers that matched until reassured by a diplomatic salesman that such an outfit was really being worn. It was then suggested that some new shirts be purchased to go with the suit.

"I want the kind with writin'," announced young Burrows.

"You mean shirts with your monogram?" asked the clerk.

"I mean with writin'—like the Dodgers and Giants," was the answer.

President Wood sometimes growls about women invading a store run for men. Nonetheless, it's quite a tribute when some of the nation's best-dressed and most glamorous women adopt a man's store for their very own. The Duchess of Windsor, Marlene Dietrich, Elizabeth Taylor, Katharine Hepburn and Audrey Hepburn are among the women who have insisted upon wearing Brooks dressing gowns, slacks, pajamas, sweaters and shirts. In fact, it was the pink shirt Brooks Brothers first made at the turn of the century to stir up color consciousness in men that caused the first big invasion of the store by women, when they finally "discovered" it in 1949 and 1950. Women bought thousands of these shirts at $8 each.

The little-boy look, popular with women since 1953, has caused Brooks Brothers to "allow" women to buy Bermuda shorts and English raincoats originally designed for boys. But Brooks Brothers has no intention of sacrificing its men's business or changing the character of its merchandise to cater to women.

"If colors or styles change, and if, for example, women's sweaters become longer or shorter, we will be out of the women's business," says Vice President Wall. "Women's styles just aren't our dish of tea. We believe in the maxim 'Shoemaker, stick to your last.' "

The Brooks management takes pride in the store's old-time employees. Twenty-five years of service makes an employee eligible for membership in the Quarter Century Club, an organization that meets once each year in September. The club has over 150 members, well over 10 percent of all employees. Many of these have worked for the firm much longer than twenty-five years. The record for continuous service, however, is held by the late Horatio Kiernan, who served the firm sixty-seven years.

Many of the Brooks employees speak foreign languages. When the United Nations sent a letter to the store in 1954 asking how many languages were spoken, in case some of the foreign delegates wanted to shop there, the personnel department counted up and returned a letter enumerating twenty-five languages.

Anecdotes about Brooks Brothers are legion. One of these concerns the wife of an elderly Boston Brooks customer who announced that he intended to do away with himself. "I'm seventy-two years old," he complained. "And I'm no use to you or anybody else. I'm going out and drown myself." He took a coat from a clothes rack and started for the door.

His wife, weary of the oft-repeated threat, looked up briefly from her knitting. "No need to wear your new Brooks coat," she told him calmly. "Not if you're going to drown yourself. Leave it for John. He's being proposed for membership in the Somerset Club this week."

Brooks Brothers has become such an institution in New York City that when its lower Manhattan store was robbed of 1,250 suits and sport jackets in 1964, newspapers covered the story with both seriousness about the $200,000 loss and humor about the style-conscious thieves in their three-button suits. Said one clerk at the time: "We could have saved 20 percent if they had stolen it during our sale two weeks ago."[1]

What does Mr. Wood believe to be the major reason for the Brooks Brothers growth? "We have a definite goal and we never deviate," he says. "When we think we're right, we go at it in depth. We try to run this thing with courage."

The Brooks Brothers president is a walking advertisement for his store. He wears conservative, natural-shoulder, three-button suits, striped button-down shirts and narrow solid-color ties. He owns thirty ties—all of them, incidentally, navy blue.

Mr. Wood feels that Brooks's success is based on the principle that "nobody can kid the public for a long time. We have been able to maintain our standards of quality and the public knows it."

To make sure that these standards are always maintained, Mr. Wood personally reads all letters of complaint that are mailed to the store. Any unsatisfactory patterns that crop up are immediately investigated in order to purge the offending department of whatever problems may exist.[2]

Early in 1966, the quiet selling floors and offices of Brooks Brothers reverberated when a bid for control of its parent company was made by Genesco, Inc., one of the nation's largest manufacturers and retailers of apparel and footwear. After making two acquisition offers to the management of Garfinckel since 1961, Genesco took its case directly to the stockholders with a tender offer to buy more than 50 percent of the common stock for cash.

When the tender offer expired in April, 1966, Genesco had obtained only about 10 percent of the Garfinckel shares. As a result, it appeared then that there would be no radical changes in the modus operandi and merchandising practices of Brooks Brothers.

Brooks thus intends to continue to stress its century-old traditions of taste, quality and workmanship. There's no doubt, moreover, that its customers like it that way.

IV

TIFFANY'S

The Most Famous Jewelry Store in the World

A SPIRITED STRUGGLE developed in 1955 for control of Tiffany & Company, the New York jewelry firm founded in 1837 and owned by the Tiffany and Moore families. Sales and earnings were low. The latter failed to cover a modest $1 annual dividend on the company's 132,451 shares in 1953 and barely did so in 1954. There was an air of somnolent splendor about the store. Promotion in the usual sense was nonexistent. But the company had a surplus of $4,544,395, its stock was selling at less than half of book value, and it was the most famous jewelry store in the world.

Several entrepreneurs began to buy Tiffany stock and in a few months it soared from $19 to more than $70 a share on the over-the-counter market. Irving Maidman, a New York builder and real-estate man, amassed 33,000 shares and the Bulova Watch Company 12,000 shares, but Walter Hoving, president of the Hoving Corporation, which then owned the adjoining Bonwit Teller fashion-apparel store on Fifth Avenue, captured the prize.

By frantic efforts, including an airplane trip to New Hampshire to talk to a ninety-two-year-old woman stockholder, Hoving induced the family owners, who were anxious to maintain the store's high standards, to sell their 40 percent to his company.[1] They sold him 68,000 shares for $3,825,000, an average of $56.25 a share. He became board chairman, a post vacant since 1946.

Vice President William T. Lusk, a great-grandson of the founder and a member of the firm since graduation from Yale in 1924, on October 20, 1955, became the fifth president of Tiffany's, succeeding President Louis de Bebian Moore, a great-grandson of the original Moore, who retired at sixty-five. Chairman Hoving became chief executive officer.[2] In the next decade he had Tiffany in the news more than in all its previous history.

He began with a store-wide sale, the first in a century. Markdowns of as much as 50 percent cleared white elephants from the stock. He threw out a line of American china stocked for years because he felt the designs were dull. He eliminated leather, silver plate and antique silver items. He added cultured pearls, which the old regime at Tiffany's had refused to stock.

Hoving purchased the business of French-born Jean Schlumberger, previously proprietor of a small shop on East Sixty-third Street, and he began to design Tiffany's fine jewelry. Hoving put Van Day Truex, formerly president of the Parsons School of Design, in charge of china and silver design development. Hoving brought Gene Moore from Bonwit Teller to do Tiffany's windows. During one of New York's water shortages, Moore substituted gin for water in a fountain display and the news went around the world.

Hoving added a publicity director to the staff and instead of avoiding publicity the store began aggressively to seek it. Letitia Baldridge, a tall daughter of a Yale football star and a graduate of Vassar, was the first to hold the post. She helped Tiffany stage a great benefit ball at Newport, Rhode Island,[3] and held the post until she became social secretary to a Tiffany customer, Mrs. John F. Kennedy, in the White House.

Tiffany's opened one Sunday in 1960 to allow the filming of Audrey Hepburn in a scene for the movie version of Truman Capote's *Breakfast at Tiffany's*. The sequence was short but favorable. Miss Hepburn, as the heroine Holly Golightly, explained that her remedy for worry is "to get into a taxi and go to Tiffany's. It calms me down right away, the quietness and the proud look of it;

nothing very bad could happen to you there. . . ." The store adopted "breakfast at Tiffany's" as a promotion ploy. There have since been breakfasts, usually just coffee and rolls, for wives of businessmen attending conventions of the National Association of Manufacturers and many others.

With the backing of some of his associates, Hoving in 1961 bought control of Tiffany's from W. Maxey Jarman's General Shoe Company (later called Genesco, Inc.), which in 1956 had increased its holdings of Hoving Corporation stock to 65 percent.[4] Additional stock was authorized and some of it distributed in dividends.

Hoving opened a Tiffany branch in San Francisco in 1963, at 223 Post Street, opposite Gump's and Shreve's. The branch soon increased the number of Tiffany's San Francisco charge accounts from four hundred to more than eight thousand. Branches followed at Houston, the same year, in Beverly Hills in 1964 and Chicago in 1966. Promotion was stepped up further. Advertising in *Vogue, Harper's Bazaar* and *Town & Country* was increased and Hoving bought a page in the November 16, 1962, *Life* to report Tiffany progress and explain his ideas on the Tiffany point of view. He personally dashed off a book, *Tiffany's Table Manners for Teen-Agers,* published by Ives Washburn, and launched it with a press breakfast. In 1963 he began to give awards for outstanding industrial design and to business executives who encourage it, the first going to Frederick R. Kappel of A.T. & T. Thomas J. Watson, Jr., of I.B.M. received one in 1966 for, in his words, "trying to make machines glisten like jewels." The Ford "Mustang" earned one.

It all added up to success for Tiffany's. In his first decade in charge, Hoving increased the company's sales volume 170 percent (the New York store alone gained 140 percent), and the company's profits increased over 900 percent.[5] For the fiscal year ending January 31, 1966, there were earnings of $1,500,989 on sales of $19,437-032 and these were still soaring.

Tiffany's is not the oldest jewelry store in America. Bixler's of Easton, Pennsylvania, dates from 1785. Shreve, Crump & Low of Boston began in 1800. Galt & Bro. of Washington, D.C., whose widowed owner married President Woodrow Wilson, dates from

1802. Black, Starr & Frost of New York and White Plains has a history extending back to 1810. C. D. Peacock started in Chicago, the year Tiffany's opened in New York.

To appreciate Tiffany's and these firms, it is necessary only to review the difficulties of the jewelry business. Jewelry is a romantic luxury, not a necessity. Many persons live and die without buying or wearing a diamond, a ring or a brooch. There are even religious denominations which regard such display as sinful. Jewelry sales are the first to drop when general business declines and are among the first to be taxed when governments need extra revenues. The levy has been as high as 100 percent in England.

There are also merchandising problems. Selling fine jewelry demands not only probity but expertness, technical knowledge and taste. It is difficult to find individuals with all these qualities. The jeweler selling precious stones competes not only with department stores and mail-order houses selling them but with countless outlets offering synthetic and imitation stones in costume jewelry.

While the Jewelry Industry Council has achieved some success in promoting jeweled gifts for anniversaries and birthdays, the business continues to be largely seasonal. Thirty percent of the year's volume comes in December and about 8 percent in the graduation and wedding month of June. Expenses continue all year. To operate profitably, Dun & Bradstreet figures reveal, a jeweler must have a markup of around 100 percent and can hope to turn his inventory only about 1.2 times a year, about the same as the merchant who sells tombstones instead of precious stones. If the inventory is too low, impulse sales will be lost. If it is too high, some of it may go out of style, and costs of insuring and safeguarding it will increase.

Tiffany's serenely survives such difficulties and, if a fine stone doesn't immediately find a purchaser, the store will keep it until somebody with the proper discernment comes along. It thus held for several years a fine emerald from the belt buckle of Abdul-Hamid, the last Sultan of Turkey.

"Tiffany's isn't just a place of business," the head of a neighboring store once remarked. "It's part showplace, part museum, part institution and part legend." This is no overstatement. No other store has so impressed itself on the business world, and the greatest accolade that any company can earn is to be called the "Tiffany" of its industry.

The store's reputation for integrity and fair dealing extends far beyond Fifth Avenue. Poor pensioners have been customers. There was the farm girl who turned up an unusual stone while helping her father "chop cotton" at Searcy, Arkansas. She cherished it until she grew up and, in 1946, mailed it to Tiffany's. The stone proved to be a 27.21-carat diamond, the third largest found in North America.

Man or nature somehow had moved the single stone to Searcy from a little-worked diamond mine 140 miles to the southwest. Tiffany's bought the stone. Today it is displayed in the store, not far from the celebrated Tiffany Diamond.

This is a 128.51-carat yellow gem as big as a bird's egg, the largest and finest canary-colored diamond in the world. It was purchased by Tiffany's soon after it was found as a 287-carat rough in a De Beers mine at Kimberley in 1878. It is a showpiece, not for sale. The name of the store also was given to the Tiffany Queen Pearl, an 83-grain pink freshwater pearl found only seventeen miles away at Notch Brook, New Jersey. Tiffany's paid the carpenter who found it $2,500 cash and $250 in trade. It was sold to the Empress Eugénie, then to a German industrialist and later to the King of Saxony.

Tiffany's has also enriched the vocabulary of the jewelers' world with its creation of the Tiffany catch and the Tiffany setting. The first is a device for the safe locking of a brooch. The latter is the almost universally used six-prong setting for engagement rings created years ago by the firm. It holds and protects a stone and at the same time makes it appear a little larger.

The fame of the Tiffany setting is attested by a straight-faced account in a Johannesburg, South Africa, newspaper of the attempted theft by a native of a large diamond from a mine. A sharp-eyed inspector detected the gem and reported: "The inspector noted that the accused had allowed his left large toenail to grow two-thirds of an inch and had cut from the inner surface six swaths of nail, which he bent to encase the stone in a Tiffany setting."

At the Fifth Avenue edifice, you can usually find a $250,000 diamond necklace. However, if you are not in a hurry, the sky is the limit. The store's Christmas catalog offers diamond solitaires as high as $25,000 and bracelets at $20,000 some years. But there are many items under $100 and a few as low as $5, such as silver thimbles, baby spoons and letter openers. You can purchase a champagne swizzle stick of solid gold or have your door key set with diamonds.

On the upper floors are Tiffany's famed wedding gifts, silver, china and glassware. Brides cherish even the boxes in which they are sent. In addition to American products, Tiffany's has big stocks of Swiss watches and English chinaware. At one time, it owned a watch factory in Geneva, Switzerland. The firm's metalsmiths fashion its own jewelry and set its own gems in the building. Its silversmiths create Tiffany silverware in a factory at Newark, New Jersey.

Surprising as it may sound to the uninitiated, Tiffany prices on fairly standard items, like men's gold cuff links, where the principal cost is the weight of pure metal, are sometimes less than the prices at which other stores sell comparable items. This is simply the result of manufacturer-to-user operation. The store's repair department often pleasantly surprises customers by doing jobs at less than the estimated cost and most items are initialed or inscribed gratis.

Tiffany executives would sooner commit hara-kiri than reveal the names of their customers, but the identity of many is well known. Mrs. Cornelius Vanderbilt, queen for many years of New York's Four Hundred, was one. The elder J. P. Morgan bought whole collections of Tiffany jewels. The late Payne Whitney is reputed to have spent $1,000,000 at the store in a single year. Jewels were a sizable part of his estate, the largest ever probated in America. Charles M. Schwab once strolled into the store, wrote a check for $91,000 and walked out with a sixty-carat diamond pendant for his wife.

Shirley Booth, the actress, and perhaps half a million other women have been given Tiffany wedding rings which sell for $7.75 to $450 and higher. Tom Girdler, the industrialist, had Tiffany's make for him a solid-gold miniature of an airplane that one of his firms produced. William Durant, the dynamic founder of General Motors, regularly ordered golden small-scale duplicates of his latest car models. A Texas millionaire once sauntered into the store and had made a golden model of an oil well which was the source of his fortune. A judge had Tiffany's make him a jeweled weathervane in the likeness of his favorite horse.

When friends of the late Al Smith wanted to honor his successful completion of the Empire State Building, they could think of nothing more appropriate than a fourteen-carat Tiffany model of the world's tallest skyscraper. Smith later gave it to Pope Pius XI. James W. Gerard bought many jewelry items and had Tiffany bind for presentation to President Wilson a historic letter written to him in Kaiser Wilhelm's own hand. Probably the most expensive paperweight of all time is the Tiffany all-gold replica of the S.S. *Nieuw Amsterdam* which a shipping official ordered for his desk at a price of $5,000. The late Crosby Gaige, when running a Broadway theater, had Tiffany's make permanent sterling silver tickets for dramatic critics of the New York newspapers, each engraved with the recipient's name and the location of his opening-night seats.

Scores of noted trophies have come from the Tiffany workrooms, among them the Vanderbilt Cup, the Horse Show Military Trophy and the International Polo Cup. The rifle prizes, pigeon-shooting cups, racing cups and other coveted sportsmen's prizes which have been made by Tiffany's have filled several showcases at famous expositions. The firm also has struck medals for military heroes throughout the world.

By royal appointment, Tiffany's has served kings, queens and princes. Its rare gems have sparkled through the years in the palaces of the rulers of England, the czars of Russia, the kings of Belgium, Italy, Greece, Spain, Denmark and Portugal. Tiffany's glitter has also brightened the thrones of the Khedive of Egypt, the Shah of Persia and the Emperor of Brazil. Kings and nobility are few these days but Tiffany's has on an upper floor a file of all the peerages and almanacs of blue blood. With no more than normal delay, its craftsmen can turn out articles authentically marked with any current or past coat of arms. Nor will the firm knowingly make such items for persons not entitled to display the arms.

The famous firm is named for Charles Lewis Tiffany, who was born February 15, 1812, at Killingly, Connecticut. At fifteen, he ran a general store started by his father, a small cotton manufacturer. In September of the depression year of 1837, when Charles was twenty-five, he borrowed $1,000 from his father and came to New York. He went into partnership with a schoolmate, John D. Young, who had preceded him by six months and had been working in a stationery store. They rented half of a lower floor of a dwelling on lower Broadway. A dressmaker had the other half. From the beginning they stocked unusual items: Chinese goods, Japanese papier-mâché and terra-cotta ware, umbrellas, walking sticks, cabinets, fans, fine stationery, pottery and all manner of novel bric-a-brac.[6]

Receipts for the first three days totaled only $4.98. But on Christmas Eve their sales reached $236 and on the last day of the year $675. In 1839, burglars carried away $4,000 worth of merchandise, virtually the whole stock of the fledgling establishment. But it continued to grow.

Tiffany further united the business by marrying Young's sister in 1841. This was an eventful year. Young made the first of many trips to Europe to buy French and Dresden porcelain, cutlery and clocks and Parisian jewelry. A third partner, J. L. Ellis, joined the firm and the store expanded into adjoining quarters.

But until 1848 Tiffany jewelry was of the sort that is not now allowed in the store. In that year the partners decided to go into precious gems and to manufacture as well as sell gold jewelry. This was a year of revolution in Europe. Prices of diamonds declined 50 percent in Paris, and Tiffany, Young and Ellis, as the firm was then known, bought all that they could, including a necklace once owned by Marie Antoinette. They opened a Paris branch for both buying and selling.

When gold from California began to arrive in New York the next year, Tiffany and his partners had merchandise for which the newly rich were glad to trade their wealth. In 1850, when P. T. Barnum brought Jenny Lind to America, one of the first shops she visited was Tiffany's. She ordered a costly silver tankard as a gift for the captain of the vessel which had brought her over. Barnum was so impressed with the tankard that when his two famous midgets, General Tom Thumb and Lavinia Warren, were married, he gave them a silver chariot from Tiffany's almost big enough to carry the tiny couple.

Young Tiffany had no special training for the jewelry business, but brought to it qualities valuable in any business. These included old-fashioned New England integrity, energy and courtesy, love for the genuine and scorn for the spurious, a belief that bills should be paid and debts collected promptly. This became store policy. Anybody who doesn't pay Tiffany's is likely to be sued and the store has obtained judgments against some notable heiresses, playboys and at least one diplomat's wife.

Tiffany's early introduced the sterling silver standard from England and advertised "every silver article we sell is guaranteed English sterling (925/000)." In 1851 the firm also advertised that "every article is marked in plain figures, upon which there will not be the slightest variation." The one-price system was then far from general.

Tiffany's unique advertising began at this time and has continued ever since. The partners advertised "their magnificent stock, believing it to exceed in extent, variety and richness, any other in the country." This was modest in comparison with the flamboyant claims of the day and soon their copy became so restrained that for many years all adjectives were eliminated. But when an authority on the subject chose the "One Hundred Greatest Advertisements in History," he picked one just saying: "Tiffany & Co., Pearls, Pearl Necklaces."

Completion of the Atlantic cable gave the firm an opportunity for a publicity stunt. The store bought cable fragments and fashioned them into paper weights, cane and umbrella handles. A jeweled inkstand for President Lincoln and a fabulous sword for General U. S. Grant were among the Civil War products made by Tiffany's. The hilt of the latter was encrusted with precious stones. The scabbard was of gold and richly studded with rubies, diamonds and sapphires to represent the national colors. The firm made lockets which girls wore to carry hair of a favorite soldier. Medals and flags, the latter priced as high as $500 each, also were produced. But the firm's factory soon was converted to the actual making of military supplies. This set a pattern for World War I when Tiffany's made surgical instruments and World War II when precision airplane-engine parts were made.

Tiffany & Company, the present firm, was incorporated in 1868 coincident with the merger of the partnership, from which Ellis and Young had retired, with John C. Moore's Silverware Company, which had been supplying its American-made silverware. Tiffany was the first president. Members of the Tiffany or Moore families have been officers of the company ever since and, as mentioned, William T. Lusk, a great-grandson of the founding Tiffany, is currently president. His nephew, Henry B. Platt, is a vice president and director.

Of the intervening Tiffanys, the founder's son, Louis Comfort Tiffany, was the most famous. He was a vice president of the store, but spent most of his long life in art. He developed a remarkable iridescent glass, Tiffany Favrile, used for vases and bowls sold in the store and also for stained-glass windows. A perfectionist, Louis Comfort inspected every product before it left the factory, stalking down the aisles carrying a long stick and breaking faulty pieces. He redecorated the White House for President Chester A. Arthur, putting in some glass screens, and supplied a $100,000 curtain made of small crystals for the National Theater in Mexico City. A noted oil and water-color painter himself, he established with $1,000,000 the Louis Comfort Tiffany Foundation, which gives annual cash grants to promising painters and sculptors. His glass company went bankrupt in 1932 but many of its creations are exhibited in museums and survive in the Cathedral of St. John the Divine and other churches.[7]

Tiffany's won medals at countless expositions and opened an office in London. When the French Republic sold the French crown jewels, Tiffany's was the largest purchaser, buying a third of them. The store also bought heavily at the sale of diamonds of Prince Esterhazy of Hungary. A Tiffany-made silver centerpiece, reproducing the Statue of Liberty, was presented by grateful New Yorkers to Frédéric Auguste Bartholdi, the French sculptor, on completion of this famous symbol of freedom. Mrs. Finley J. Shephard, daughter of Jay Gould, also had Tiffany's make a five-pound sterling-silver copy of the statue's torch for New York University academic processions.

After three locations on lower Broadway, the store moved in 1870 to Union Square and in 1905 to Fifth Avenue and Thirty-seventh Street. This was near the first Waldorf-Astoria Hotel, where John W. "Bet-a-Million" Gates and some other Tiffany customers resided. There the firm erected its own seven-story building modeled on the Palazzo Grimani on the Grand Canal in Venice.

A remarkable feature of this building was the fact that for thirty years it bore no sign of any kind. It was not until 1935 that a modest "Tiffany & Co." went up over the doors. Five years later, the store moved to its present site. In this move, an old whistle that had long sent Tiffany craftsmen to lunch was discarded, but taken along was the old Tiffany clock, supported by a carved wood figure of Atlas, which dates from 1853. The store's Union Square building was one of the first to boast burglar-proof vaults and the present store has a protective system of visible guards and secret alarms that probably rivals Fort Knox.

Men outside the Tiffany and Moore families, of course, contributed to the success of the store. One of these was Charles Cook, a Tiffany man for fifty-nine years. He was president from the death at ninety-four in 1902 of the first Tiffany, who left an estate of $35,000,000, to the accession of John Chandler Moore in 1907.

Of greater renown was Dr. George Frederick Kunz, dean of the world's gem experts. As a New York boy of ten, he began to collect colored stones from excavations. He sold a tourmaline to Charles Lewis Tiffany, who like other leading jewelers until then had been interested only in diamonds, emeralds, rubies, sapphires and pearls. Educated at Cooper Union, Kunz went to work at twenty-three as Tiffany's gem expert and continued there until his death fifty-three years later. In a score of books and countless lectures, he championed the beauty of gemstones. One of his chance remarks about their abrasive qualities led an admirer, Dr. Edward G. Acheson, to invent the valuable abrasive carborundum.

Dr. Kunz was the confidant of the elder J. P. Morgan and sold him collection after collection of rare gems. The greatest of these, representing twenty years of searching by Kunz, is now at the American Museum of Natural History. Kunz could sell Morgan any gem except an opal. The financier was among the superstitious who considered this gem one of ill omen.

Dr. Kunz named a newly discovered pink beryl gem morganite in honor of Tiffany's great customer and also dedicated his best-known book, *The Curious Lore of Precious Stones,* to him. In this work, the gem expert reviewed all of history's superstitions about jewels. These he did not accept, but wrote: "Nevertheless, the possession of a necklace or a ring adorned with brilliant diamonds, fair pearls, warm, glowing rubies, or celestial-hued sapphires, will today make a woman's heart beat faster and bring a blush of pleasure to her cheek."

A rare milky blue Brazilian diamond, which Dr. Kunz noticed glowing in his wife's ring when she hung a gown in a dark closet, he named tiffanyite in honor of the store founder. This gem has a phosphorescent inclusion. In addition to receiving decorations from France, Norway, Japan and other nations, Kunz was honored by one of his admirers giving the name kunzite to a lilac-colored variety of spodumene discovered in California which the expert had identified. It has since also been found in Madagascar.

Tiffany's present scientific laboratory, the most elaborate of any store, includes specially constructed X-ray and camera equipment. Every important stone is photographically "fingerprinted." There is a density balance for the separation of jadeite and nephrite, the two varieties of jade. There are five different instruments for the testing of pearls and the staff includes a scientist.

In most cases, the instruments merely confirm the judgment of Tiffany men. Only the store's senior officers buy stones. The staff includes many specialists. A dozen designers, some of them graduates of art schools, are available to sketch the possible settings for a gem or to show visually how an old piece can be modernized. There are fashions in the design of jewelry just as in the design of dresses.

Two women string pearls. Dowagers who don't want their pearls out of their sight make appointments and watch the job done in private rooms. The cost is according to the length of the strand. Some million-dollar necklaces, mostly the property of Indian Maharajas, have been in and out of Tiffany's.

One of the few people ever to out-expert Tiffany's was Louis Marks, famous dealer in rubies and star sapphires. He found a fine star sapphire underpriced at Tiffany's in London, bought it and brought it to America and sold it to Tiffany's in New York at a much higher price. Marks never tired of telling the story.

Tiffany's employees are a devoted group. Legend has it that one of them made his way through the German lines into besieged Paris in 1870 to safeguard the Tiffany branch there. More than half of the slightly more than six hundred store and factory employees belong to the firm's Twenty-five Year Club; thirty-five have been employed for more than fifty years. The late George F. Heydt, who began as secretary to the founder and rose to advertising manager, served the firm sixty-eight years before retiring.

Only rarely has Tiffany's faith in its employees been betrayed. One embezzled $10,000 long ago by payroll padding. From an inside caged-off enclosure on the repair and manufacturing floor, three pear-shaped diamonds, weighing twelve carats each and valued at $80,000, later disappeared and were never located. These stones, cut from the famed Excelsior diamond, once the largest in the world, were Tiffany's most spectacular loss.

More recently a Tiffany man was victimized by one of the oldest swindles in the confidence man's book. An attractive blonde entered the store and, with the bored nonchalance of the rich, said her fiancé had asked her to select some rings. She chose two, a solitaire and a diamond wedding band, valued at $6,300, then told the clerk she would like her mother's approval before buying. She demurely asked the clerk to deliver the rings at her Riverside Drive apartment.

When the clerk arrived, she took the kid-covered box and walked through a door, calling, "Mother, the Tiffany man is here with the rings." When she failed to reappear after fifteen minutes, the clerk became alarmed. He knocked on the door, got no answer and turned the knob. The door was another exit into the hall. Tiffany's never saw the blonde or the rings again.

Tiffany's is concerned with its dignity. The firm obtained a permanent injunction, for example, against a motion-picture company which adopted the name Tiffany, used a sparkling diamond as an emblem and referred to its productions as gems and pearls. In the course of this litigation, Tiffany's in 1932 revealed some sales figures for the first time but only to the extent of saying that it had done a gross business of more than $350,000,000 in the previous forty years and had spent $3,500,000 for advertising in the previous twenty-three years.

During the depression, the store reduced its capital and adjusted its operations to a much lower volume than during the lush twenties and earlier years. World War II closed the Paris and London branches and they were not reopened. The New York City sales tax, increased many times, and the 20 percent federal excise tax, not reduced until 1954, hardly encouraged profligate buying.

Nevertheless, Tiffany's dividends continued. The shares were split five for one in 1920 and again sixteen for one in 1949, and a few investors outside the Moore and Tiffany families became stockholders. The firm began to publish a brief balance sheet and profit statement. Earnings fell to $14,787 in 1952 and were but $24,906 in 1953 despite a reduction in operating expenses from $2,516,960 to $2,482,869. But the firm still had a surplus from previous years of $4,544,395 after paying a per share dividend of $2 in 1952 and $1 in 1953 on its 132,451 outstanding shares. For the jewelry industry as a whole, Department of Commerce figures showed larger sales in 1952 and 1953.

Back in 1916, court appraisal of the estate of Charles M. Moore, for many years manager of the Paris branch of the firm, revealed that in the seven years prior to 1914, when he died, Tiffany & Company earned a total of $7,544,319, or an average of $1,077,759 a year.

With the advent of Walter Hoving, his introduction of what he calls "esthetic excitement" in the merchandise and the opening of branches in other American cities, Tiffany's has had profits greater than these and with more branches expects to do even better. A Tiffany branch is designed to break even on sales of $400,000 and Hoving believes there are at least fifty metropolitan communities where there can be sales of $500,000 without compromising Tiffany standards.

Hoving has dedicated Tiffany's to proving wrong the prediction of Alexis de Tocqueville in his *Democracy in America* that a decline in taste is inevitable in a democracy. Most retailers study their customers and try in every possible way to give them what they want. Tiffany's doesn't. At Tiffany's, customers can have only what Tiffany's thinks they should have and more and more of them are happy to put their trust in the store.

It is a classic example of a store shifting its location—it has moved five times—to keep abreast of shopping and of a store "trading up" in its merchandise. By adherence to self-imposed standards, it has become a world-wide synonym for quality, integrity and exclusiveness. Its "trademarks, designs and patents" are listed at just $1 on the company's balance sheet but the frequency with which the world-famous name figures in song and anecdote attests its great value.

When Mrs. Stuyvesant Fish, the famous Newport hostess, coughed in the night air, her husband considerately asked: "Can I get you something for your throat, my dear?"

"Yes, you can," she replied. "That diamond necklace I saw today at Tiffany's."

Eartha Kitt has entertained Broadway audiences more recently with a song demanding that somebody trim her Christmas tree "with ornaments from Tiffany."

V

THE SINGER COMPANY

World-Wide Pioneer of Installment Selling

PENNILESS AND BESET BY LAWSUITS, a forty-year-old sewing-machine inventor named Isaac Merritt Singer turned for help in 1851 to a New York attorney named Edward Clark and they became partners. From this modest beginning grew The Singer Company, with factories in twenty-nine countries and world-wide sales affiliates which in 1965 sold mostly direct to the user $642,800,000 in home products, including $534,800,000 in sewing machines and items related to sewing, the most in the company's long history.

Thanks to the successful diversification program pursued by Donald P. Kircher, who became president and chief executive officer in 1958, Singer in 1965 also sold $138,300,000 in business-machine products and $198,700,000 in products for industry for total sales of $979,800,000 and was about to become a billion-dollar company. In 1958, sewing sales were $414,400,000 and 93 percent of the company's total. The greater 1965 sewing sales were only 54.6 percent of the volume.[1] While Singer now makes and sells home appliances of all kinds, its marketing innovations came with its original product.

In addition to making sewing machines of a mechanical excellence that is the standard of the world, the Singer organization has facilitated their sale by everywhere pioneering installment selling, a development that has affected the economy of mankind almost as much as the sewing machine itself. This innovation has helped the organization, under statesmanlike management, to sell more than 125 million Singer machines and to pay dividends since incorporation in 1863.

Singer is the foremost exponent of manufacturer-to-consumer selling and its family sewing machine is the most widely used product in the world.

Mahatma Gandhi, the late Indian leader, while in jail learned to sew on a Singer and exempted the sewing machine in his ban on Western machinery. "It," he said, "is one of the few useful things ever invented." Singer is better known and occupies bigger buildings than the United States government in parts of India. A native-language letter, for example, was delivered addressed: "Exalted Holiness of the Consul General of the United States of America by the backside of the Singer Sewing Machine Company, Calcutta."[2]

The company prints directions for using Singers in fifty-four languages. South Pacific islanders rate a Singer high among the necessities of life. First comes food, then shelter, and next the sewing machine. The only reason shelter comes ahead of the Singer is to protect it from the rain.

It might be an exaggeration to say that Japanese dress was Westernized to provide a market for Singer machines but the company had a great deal to do with the process. With the encouragement of Marquis Okuma, one of the last elder statesmen, Singer opened the first sewing school in Japan. Its graduates taught the nation.

Singers are popular throughout Europe. A shop in Norway is above the Arctic Circle. Africa had Singers before Stanley went searching for Livingstone and there is a Singer-equipped shirt factory in the heart of the Congo. In the Americas, Singer Centers marked with the big red "S" extend from Anchorage, Alaska, to Magallanes, Chile.

Singer executives smilingly describe the workings of the organization in a deceptively modest sentence. "All we do," they explain, "is make a machine, take it out and sell it, collect the money and then send it back to make another machine."

As most sewing machines are sold on the installment plan, this may require two or three years. Singer fathered installment selling and is possibly its foremost exponent. Singers are made in dollar, sterling, franc and lira nations and sold not only in those currencies but also elsewhere for pesos, pesetas, yen, krone, rupees, guilders and other moneys. In consequence Singer probably does business in more currencies than any other company.

Isaac Merritt Singer, for whom the companies are named, was a restless Yankee machinist. When thirty-nine years old, he borrowed $40 for capital and made his first sewing machine in Boston in 1850. When completed, it would not work. He was about to give up in despair when he recalled a neglected thread adjustment. He returned to the shop after midnight, made the change and the machine functioned. It was the first device with which it was possible to sew continuously. He was granted patents and began to make machines, first in Boston and then in New York.

As a relic in the Smithsonian Institution shows, the Singer was the first practical sewing machine and the first to resemble modern models. It was far from being the first sewing machine. As early as 1790, Thomas Saint, "cabinetmaker of Greenhill Rents, Parish of St. Sepulchre," obtained an English patent on a forgotten machine for chain-stitching leather.

The first sewing machine of any tangible success was made by Barthélemy Thimonnier, a French provincial tailor, and patented in 1830. Eighty of his machines, which employed a single thread to make a chain stitch, were put to work making French army uniforms only to be smashed by a mob of jealous tailors. Walter Hunt, an American Quaker genius who invented the safety pin and paper collar, made a machine in 1834 but abandoned it when his daughter told him it would throw seamstresses out of work. In 1843, Dr. Frank Goulding, a Presbyterian Clergyman of Macon, Georgia, made a machine. Neither he nor Hunt patented their machines.

Elias Howe, Jr., a Cambridge, Massachusetts, machinist with much more forethought, in 1846 won the recognition of history with a patent on a sewing machine employing an eye-pointed needle with a shuttle. When Singer and two other makers appeared with their improved machines, Howe sued them. After a few lawsuits, in one of which Rufus Choate, the greatest attorney of the day, represented

Howe, it was apparent that the new machines could not be made without the needle and shuttle idea. At the same time, it was obvious that Howe's machine, which sewed only straight seams a few inches at a time, could be sold only with the new improvements.

Soon each of four manufacturers was suing all of the others. Each maker also denounced his rivals in scathing newspaper advertisements and what the public called "the sewing machine war" was under way.

For help on the legal front, Singer turned to the New York law firm of Jordan & Clark. As Ambrose Jordan, the senior partner of the firm, was state attorney general, Singer saw Jordan's junior partner and son-in-law, Edward Clark. For a third interest in the company, he agreed to fight the legal battles. The man who had advanced the original $40 a little later fell ill and for $6,000 sold his third to Clark and Singer. They became equal partners in I. M. Singer and Company in 1851. Singer remained in charge of manufacturing. Clark took charge of finances and sales as well as legal matters.

Two more different men than Clark and Singer would be difficult to imagine. Born of poor German immigrant parents, Singer had little education and left his Oswego, New York, home when twelve years old. He grew up to be a truculent man of lusty appetites. He was without success a farmer, a machinist, an actor in a Shakespearean troupe, and an inventor of machines for excavating rock and carving wood. He employed the vertical action and horizontal work platform of the latter device in his sewing machine.

By contrast, Clark, a man of the same age, was a well-educated, quiet-spoken lawyer from upstate New York. He was a graduate of Williams College and a building there later was named for him. As his father was a pottery manufacturer, Clark grew up with some knowledge of business.

He and other lawyers ended the "sewing machine war" by organizing the Sewing Machine Combination, America's first patent pool. Manufacture was licensed at $15 a machine. Because of the greater importance of their patents, the Howe and Singer interests received $5 each and the others less. Twenty-four companies were licensed and machine making greatly increased. Though he made few machines himself, Howe received at least $1,185,000 in royalties before his death in 1867. The Combination continued until 1877, when the last of the patents involved expired.

The earliest sewing machines were heavy devices for tailors and harness makers but by 1856 all the leading companies were making lighter models for home use. A machine enabled a housewife to do in one hour what took ten to fourteen hours by hand. The great obstacle was the fact that the average family income was less than $500 a year and the price of a sewing machine was $125 or more. Edward Clark attacked this problem with a trade-in allowance for old machines, the barter of machines for advertising, discounts to schools, and, most important and enduring of all, the development of installment selling.

Installment sales kept the Singer business going when the panic of 1857 struck the next summer with the failure of many banks, railroads and insurance companies. Only $5 was needed now to place a new Singer sewing machine in a home. The remainder was paid in small monthly payments. If the purchaser failed to make payments, the machine was repossessed.

The idea became popular so rapidly that Clark was apprehensive about the results. "It appears," he wrote a Milwaukee agent, "that $955.50 worth of machines were sold, of which you received $76 in cash. This is too small a proportion . . . leave the doubtful customers to your competitors." The firm's *Gazette*, one of the first house organs in American business, published a warning against the pawning or selling of machines on which payments had not been completed.

But losses were slight. Various special printed forms were worked out for this form of sales. Sometimes stamp receipts were given for payments and these were affixed to the contract until the full amount was paid. If a customer could make a larger payment than $5, he, of course, was encouraged to do so.

Installment selling became a bulwark of Singer sales in the United States and soon was instituted in Great Britain and many overseas countries under the original term of "hire-purchase." Nearly all machine purchasers everywhere were found to be honest. All Singer records in Manila, for example, were destroyed during World War II but with peace fifty thousand persons owing money on machines voluntarily paid up their accounts. A small army of collector-agents long collected the installments but most payments are now made by mail.

Clark managed so well that Singer was happy to leave everything to his partner or others while he pursued pleasures he could not afford in his youth. After incorporation of the business as The Singer Manufacturing Company in 1863, the inventor spent nearly all of his time in Europe. He was completing a great house, called "The Wigwam," at Paignton, England, when he died there in 1875, leaving $13,000,000, mostly in Singer stock, to a numerous progeny. Clark, who then became president of the company, left an even larger estate when he died in 1882 at Cooperstown, the beautiful upstate New York community to which his family was devoted. The Civil War, meantime, demonstrated the advantages to the Singer Company of foreign trade, when the dollar was depreciated temporarily, and of integration. With establishment of its own cabinet factory in 1867, Singer became virtually a maker-to-user manufacturer and has remained so. Starting from pig iron, rough forgings or wire, Singer makes its machines in four thousand varieties and its own needles in ten thousand sizes. It makes its own electric motors. Equally important, nearly all of its machines have been sold direct to the user through the company's own salesmen and shops.

Some extraordinary salesmen introduced Singer machines to the world. It was a difficult business at first. James Bolton, an early agent in New Haven, recalled in his memoirs that as he started for his post Isaac Singer slapped him on the shoulder and said: "Jim, we'll send you all the machines you want but not one cent of money." Singer men had to be mechanics, collection agents, sewing teachers and versatile adventurers. They traveled mostly in well-marked buggies but also by dugout canoe and every other form of conveyance.

Some Singer machines moved abroad early. One took a grand prize at a world's fair in Paris in 1855. Singers were advertised the next year in Rio de Janeiro. Despite great growth in domestic business, the company by 1861 was selling more sewing machines abroad than in the United States.

First manufacture of Singers overseas began in 1867 in Glasgow,

Scotland. Fifteen years later, Clark's successor as head of the company, George Ross McKenzie, who left Scotland as a barefoot immigrant boy, returned there and built the biggest of all Singer plants at nearby Clydebank. It is so important in the community that a Singer machine is now part of the city's coat of arms. Assembly of Singers began in Montreal, Canada, in 1873, the same year that the big Elizabethport, New Jersey, plant was completed and United States manufacturing shifted there from New York.

When Singer salesmen found people lacking the coordination to operate the usual treadle machine, they were sold hand machines. When one African tribe, believing "good iron makes good noise," demanded noisy machines, a Singer man obligingly loosened up his machines until they achieved the required clatter. Agents even sold Singers to customers who thought the machine witchcraft.

As the native Japanese kimono was sewed with a few long stitches, which allowed it to be taken apart for washing and drying, the first Singers introduced there were adjusted to make such stitches. The company then taught thousands of Japanese how to make Westernized garments by machine. In later years, sewing lessons were broadcast by radio with thousands at times listening in the Tokyo and Yokohama municipal halls.

One of the most amazing Singer pioneers was George Neidlinger, first employed as a factory waterboy in New York. At twenty-two, he went to Hamburg as a European agent. Against heavy competition, including that of machines sold under imitation Singer labels, he introduced the Singer into Germany, Denmark, Sweden, Norway, the Balkans and eventually into Russia. As a step in the last, he had 250,000 tents for the Czar's army made on Singer machines.

Singer sales organizations employ where possible the citizens of the countries in which they function. "A Frenchman," a Singer executive once remarked, "knows better than anybody else how to sell a sewing machine to another Frenchman." Natives head the Singer organizations in every European country. The Australian and South African Singer organizations are 100 percent national.

Singer has had only four presidents since the retirement in 1889 of George Ross McKenzie. These have been Commodore Frederick G.

Bourne, Sir Douglas Alexander, Milton C. Lightner and Donald P. Kircher, all of them world-traveling forceful executives.

Under Commodore Bourne (the title was from the New York Yacht Club), Singer made its first electrically-powered machines, separated the family and factory business in the United States, and began to organize overseas subsidiaries. Sales of machines passed the million-a-year mark.[3]

Sir Douglas, a Canadian subject, rose from a clerical job to head the company for forty-four years. These saw erection of the Singer Building in New York and world-wide expansion. This included construction of a great Singer plant at Podolsk, near Moscow, and the opening of Singer shops across Russia to Vladivostok. In recognition of his and the company's services in World War I, he was made a baronet by King George V.

World War I saw the end of the vast Russian development. All of the Singer property, representing an investment estimated at $115,000,000 was seized by the Soviet government. After World War II Russians also stripped the machinery from a Singer plant in Wittenberge, Germany, and took it to Podolsk.

Singer suffered other serious World War II losses while winning acclaim with record production of intricate fire controls, airplane parts and other military items. Thirty-nine Singer workers were killed in the vicinity when the great Clydebank Singer plant was blitzed by high explosives and incendiary bombs. The fire burned for days. Bombs also hit two hundred Singer shops in Great Britain and many on the Continent. Some Singer workers were killed in the French factory at Bonnières which was both bombed and sabotaged. Singer men also died in the Far East while several executives suffered in Santo Tomas and other concentration camps.

Two Singer men, one Japanese and one American, helped effect the surrender of the Korean port of Inchon in 1945. The latter, George Jones, who had traveled for Singer in the Orient, served with Army Intelligence and was with the fleet that steamed in to accept the surrender. Because of his knowledge of English, one Tani, who had been a Singer agent in Seoul under the Japanese, headed the Korean party that came out in a small boat.

"Why, it's our Mr. Jones!" shouted Tani as he saw the American.

Singers are found in all sorts of places. Nearly every ship carries at least one. They are used in prison, leper colonies and mental institutions, where the satisfaction of creating something is an important factor in rehabilitation. The Wright brothers stitched the wings of the first airplane on a Singer, preserved in Dayton, Ohio. Admiral Richard Byrd took six Singers with him to the Antarctic.

Both the gowns and shoes of Queen Elizabeth of England are made on Singers and Westminster Abbey has a Singer for repair of the ceremonial robes of the British Royal Family. The Empress of Ethiopia visited the Singer shop in Addis Ababa and enrolled two of her ladies-in-wating for a sewing course.

Long before the basic sewing machine patents expired, the Singer management shifted emphasis to quality, service, advertising and trademarks. As maker of the first article sold all over the world, Singer pioneered the use of trademarks in many lands. Singer machines were marked with the name from the first and the stands of many spelled "Singer" in metal. By 1870, the company had an oval trademark. It included a large "S," crossed needles and a shuttle.

Early in the seventies, the famous red "S" with a woman at a sewing machine also began to be used. Since then it has become the world's best-known trademark. The woman has been drawn in appropriate costume as the native of many lands. Her machine is always up-to-date and every few years the woman herself is given a new hairdress and has her skirt lengthened or shortened to keep her modern.

There had been surreptitious counterfeiting of Singer trademarks earlier, but with expiration of the last basic patent in 1877 many imitators came into the open. They imitated the Singer design. They also called their machines Singers and imitated the Singer trademarks. The Singer Manufacturing Company filed suits.

Hardest-fought was one against Frank T. June, head of the June Manufacturing Company of Chicago, and George P. Bent, a Chicago and Kansas City sewing machine dealer. Stationery of the June firm described it as "manufacturers of the new and greatly improved Singer Sewing Machine." Metal stands of its machines embodied the word Singer and a monogram, "S. M. Co.," which was explained as standing for Standard Machine Co., an earlier name of the June enterprise. Bent sold the June-made machine as the "Improved Singer," "June Singer," "New York Singer" and "Philadelphia Singer," though he had offices neither in New York nor Philadelphia.

Litigation lasted nineteen years. The defendants contended that the name Singer had reverted to the public with the Singer patents as in the case of the harmonica, the macintosh coat and linoleum, all names of once patent-protected articles that had become generic. Singer attorneys put forth the trademarks, introduced the full line of Singer machines, and argued that the name meant "the source of manufacture" rather than a type.

In a decision by Justice Edward D. White, the Supreme Court ruled finally against June and Bent, saying each manufacturer should indicate who made his machine and "unmistakably" inform the public. Justice White termed June's imitation of the Singer marks "an injury to private rights and a deceit upon the public." The deceptive practices of the defendants were "perpetually enjoined."

Since then Singer has consistently succeeded in protecting its famous trademarks against efforts at imitation in many lands.

Milton Lightner became head of the Singer empire on the death of Sir Douglas in 1949 after twenty-two years as vice president and earlier service as legal counsel. He rehabilitated the war-damaged European properties and built new plants in Anderson, South Carolina; Campinas, Brazil; Karachi, Pakistan; Penrith, Australia; Taytay, the Philippines; Queretaro, Mexico; and Maltete, Turkey. He met German and Italian competition with a slant-needle, zig-zag machine. In the face of a flood of Japanese machines encouraged by the U.S. occupation authorities, he preserved part of Singer's market there by buying a half interest in the Pine factory in Japan. He replaced the single sheet of figures given by Sir Douglas to stockholders with a conventional annual report. He chose as his assistant and successor another lawyer, Donald Peter Kircher, a native of St. Paul, Minnesota, who had been a twice-wounded, eight-times-decorated tank captain in the U.S. Third Army.

Under Kircher, who became president at forty-two in 1958, executive offices were moved uptown in New York from the Singer Building, later sold for $8,000,000, to the Radio Corporation of America Building in Rockefeller Center. They were adorned with new abstract art. Into Kircher's office went James Brooks's "Sarpolo," catalogued as creating "an atmosphere of suspension and potential action." This came fast.

Kircher launched a world-wide planned internal and external diversification, which dwarfed the company's previous success and doubled sales and earnings. He met Japanese competition with low-priced machines from Singer plants in Italy and Scotland. Medium-priced machine production was concentrated in Scotland and that of higher-priced models in U.S. and West German plants.

Scores of additional items began to be sold in Singer shops. To machines and vacuum cleaners were added radio and television sets, record players, records, fabrics and many other items. Singer began to produce its own patterns and to promote them with *Singer Showcase—Sewing Fashions,* a consumer quarterly. Singer plants began to make a greater variety, such as the one at Pickens, South Carolina, for example, producing millions of dollars worth of portable power tools for Sears, Roebuck and Co. Electric guitars were made in Japan and power lawn mowers in Australia.

In outside diversification, Friden Inc., an important maker of office equipment, was purchased for stock then worth $175,000,000. In nine years, Singer also bought a research company, five textile equipment companies, four makers of laboratory instruments, a home-entertainment equipment manufacturer, a maker of home-laundry and refrigerator products and two makers of heating and air-conditioning equipment. The word "manufacturing" was dropped from the company name and its stock was listed on the New York Stock Exchange. Mandatory retirement for executives at age sixty-five was instituted.

A new type of Singer executive, concerned more with management and profit than specific sales or manufacturing, came to the front. Most continued to rise from the ranks. Vice President Charles F. Bruder, in charge of long-range planning and screening of acquisitions, was formerly in charge of U.S. sales. The father of Newton H. Hoyt, Jr., vice president and treasurer, worked for Singer and Vice President Herbert Burchill, in charge of product policy, is a third-generation Singer man. But there are now also some from the outside. Vice President Alfred di Scipio, in charge of the consumer products division, came from International Telephone & Telegraph; Vice President Elliott E. Vose, from President Kircher's old law firm; and Vice President George A. Downsbrough, technical products division, from American Standard. Outsiders also were added as directors, the first being Gilbert W. Fitzhugh, president of Metropolitan Life, and Henry R. Labouisse, executive director of the United Nations Children's Fund, and the husband of Eve Curie, the writer.

With few exceptions everything was successful. The company lost several millions in the Thurso Pulp and Paper Company in Canada and its interest in the enterprise was sold in 1964. Selling by catalogue proved unproductive in the United States but successful in Europe, and Singer paid $14,000,000 for control of Friedrich Schwab & Co. third largest mail-order house in Germany. In the "culture boom" even the abstract art in the executive offices increased in value. For the first six months of 1966, sales were $506,015,000.

VI

FILENE'S

The World's Largest Specialty Store

BOSTON HAS BEEN FAMOUS for the excellence and enterprise of its stores for generations. More than one hopeful retailer opening far from New England has paid tribute to this reputation by calling his establishment "The Boston Store." In some places the effort was successful. Milwaukee's Boston Store grew into a great institution, and in Rochester, New York, a Boston Store later prospered as the Sibley, Lindsay & Curr Co.

Biggest store volume-wise in Boston long has been that of the Jordan Marsh Company. Eben Jordan,[1] one of its founders, gave Boston an opera house. Its magnitude is epitomized by its boast "New England's Greatest Store." It is a complete department store, headed in 1966 by William P. Reed, and is the biggest unit of the Allied Stores Corporation. Other notable Boston stores, some of them more than a century old, include Chandler & Co., Gilchrist Co., R. H. Stearns Co., and the E. T. Slattery Co. In Raymond's, Inc., the city has a remarkable helter-skelter bargain spot. The Shreve, Crump & Low jewelry store and Goodspeed's bookshop are nationally known.

It is Filene's, short for the William Filene's Sons Company, however, that is the Boston store that has been oftenest in the headlines. This is the world's largest specialty store. Its main building, a city block in width, was one of the last designed by the late Daniel H. Burnham. It stands at Washington and Summer streets and the spot is brass plaqued as "the hub of the universe" of which Oliver Wendell Holmes spoke. Thanks to this location, with access to two subways, and its fame as a store with a successfully split personality, high fashion upstairs and low prices downstairs in a unique basement, its dollar sales volume per square foot, more than $1,000 a year in some departments, is one of the highest in the world.

Filene's contributions to retailing include important advances in employee selection and training, sustained showmanship and community service, and merchandising innovations which have been adopted widely. Cycle billing, which changed a frantic end-of-the-month operation to an orderly procedure, was born at Filene's. The need of the store for a simple identification device for charge customers spurred invention of the Charga-Plate and Filene's was the first to use it. Since then it has been adopted by more than 650 stores and carried by at least twenty-five million shoppers. Branch-store operation was pioneered by Filene's and, as many branches were in college towns, led the store to develop first college and then high-school student advisory fashion boards.

William Filene was born in 1830 in the Polish city of Posen, when it was within the borders of Prussia, where the name was sometimes spelled Filehne. There his father sold ribbons, then an important part of fashionable dress, profitably enough to send William and another son to Berlin to study law. The latter died there and William, discouraged, abandoned the law. It was 1848, a year of revolt in Europe which brought a bloody uprising in Posen. Instead of returning home, William renounced the religion of his Jewish fathers and emigrated first to England and then to the United States.

At eighteen, William went to work as a tailor in Boston. Three years later in 1851, he opened a tiny shop, stocking some dry goods, on Hanover Street. This lasted only a short time and 1856 found him with a small store on Essex Street in nearby Salem. There in 1856, he married Clara Ballin, an immigrant from Bavaria who proved a remarkable wife. To them were born four sons and a daughter.

Of these, only the second son, Edward Albert, born in 1860 in Salem and named for the Prince of Wales, who had just visited America, and the youngest son, Abraham Lincoln, born April 5, 1865, in Boston, figure importantly in the history of Filene's. The latter shortened his name to A. Lincoln Filene and eventually legally dropped the first name.

During the Civil War, William Filene left retailing for an unsuccessful manufacturing venture in New York, moving there in 1863 and losing all of his money in the metal trade by 1870. He then moved his family back to Lynn, Massachusetts. Despite the business troubles which culminated in the panic of 1873, he launched two small stores at Lynn, one at Salem and one at Bath, Maine.

The older boys had a year at the Handels Institut, a famous boys' school in Segnitz, Bavaria, their mother's birthplace, before collapse of the New York venture. They continued in the Lynn High School. After classes, they ran errands, washed floors and cleaned the windows of their father's Lynn stores, one of which was devoted to women's wear and the other to men's and boys' clothing.

These prospered and college was planned for Edward. But he had no sooner passed the Harvard University entrance examinations in 1879 than the father fell ill. As the eldest son Rudolph had no aptitude for or interest in the work, Edward had to abandon his college plans and at nineteen go to work full time. He cherished his Harvard entrance certificate, "No. 276," all of his life, however, and became a benefactor of the Harvard Business School. Young Lincoln soon followed his brother into the stores. It was William Filene's hope that each of his sons would take over one of the four stores, and the store at Bath, Maine, eventually was given to Bertram Filene, the brother born between Edward and Lincoln.

In 1881, the father and sons opened a store at 10 Winter Street in Boston and soon afterward sold the Lynn and Salem properties. The Boston store was only twenty-four feet square but was described as "one of the most modern of the day with its genuine white marble floor and most artistic windows." Bearded William Filene respectfully advertised that "purchasers can save a large percentage on esmeralda and embroidered sleeves from 25 cents to $3 a pair . . . dress trimmings in the latest patterns . . . lisle thread and silk gloves and mitts . . . and cotton stockings." A glove shop was added the next year also on Winter Street.

With the sons gradually relieving their ailing father of responsibilities, the business grew. The brothers came in on Sunday to clean the store. Father and sons did all of the buying and employees were few enough for all to discuss their plans every Friday evening at William Filene's home. In 1890, much larger quarters were leased in a five-story-and-basement building at 445–447 Washington Street, and the business was moved there. The space was the largest in Boston at that time devoted exclusively to women's wear and accessories.

The father, who suffered from a heart ailment, turned the management over to Edward and Lincoln in 1891 and they inherited the store at his death in 1901. The company was organized briefly as William Filene, Sons and Company and then as William Filene's Sons Company. Edward proved a wizard at merchandising, and Lincoln a genius at managing a store staff. They owned equal shares of the business, took turns using the title of general manager, and became one of the most famous brother teams in retailing.

They were among the first to recognize the value of good employee relations and systematic employee training. They went on record against absentee ownership and nepotism. As Edward remained a bachelor and Lincoln, who married in 1895, fathered only daughters, this action, of course, was no personal hardship but it helped establish a remarkable spirit among the workers.

"If we were to create contentment in front of the counter," once explained Lincoln Filene, "we had first to create contentment behind it. Many employees learn their manner of serving the public from the manner in which they are served by their managers."

Without offending its carriage trade in piece goods, the store stocked machine-made dresses and lingerie as they became available. Its sales passed the half-million-dollar mark in 1900. The exact figure was $554,425. The next year the store trebled its space by moving to the buildings numbered 453 to 463 on Washington Street. In 1902 sales exceeded a million dollars for the first time, with a volume of

$1,165,183. The next year the previous quarters were leased again and designated as a "Baby-to-Miss" annex. In 1904, the intervening structure, Oliver Ditson's music shop, was occupied and the two Filene stores became one. But more space was needed.

Burnham, the famous architect and city planner, was employed to design a great store building to include eight floors above ground and a basement, sub-basement and cellar beneath it. The greater space would enable the store to enter the men's wear field. Plans provided for underground access to the new Boston subway to permit customers to arrive in comfort regardless of the weather.

When the new building was completed, so great was the interest that 235,000 persons visited it when it opened, decorated with American Beauty roses, on September 3, 1912. Within a week, 715,000 persons went through the doors. So well planned and constructed was the building that, with only slight changes, it was still in service more than fifty years later.

To obtain the well-known Hart Schaffner & Marx line of clothing for its men's department, Filene's bought two Boston stores of the Continental Clothing House. One was resold and the other, a nearby structure, was absorbed into Filene's when the store spread over the entire block. A public-address system and air conditioning were added later, with the Filene basement becoming the first large-scale application of air conditioning in retailing.

Outlying branches began to be established immediately after World War I. Taxation rather than traffic was the initial impetus. Many places undertook to collect a year's taxes from any store that presented a fashion show or showed merchandise there. Some of the early branches at Providence, Rhode Island; Falmouth, Massachusetts; and Portland, Maine, did not survive. Those remaining at Wellesley, Belmont, Winchester and Hyannis proved very profitable small specialty-shop branches. Much larger Filene high-fashion branches have been opened at South Shore Shopping Plaza, Braintree; Natick Mall in Natick; North Shore Shopping Center, Peabody; Chestnut Hill on Route 9; and in Worcester, Massachusetts, with all except the last designed by Raymond Loewy–William Snaith, Inc. Burlington, Massachusetts, will have another.

Some of the first Filene branches were in college towns such as Northampton and South Hadley. Out of them grew the store's college board, which helps it select and test fashion apparel for college girls. At times members have been rewarded with trips to Europe and South America. As an extension of this activity, Filene's also has a high-school fashion board selected annually on a competitive basis from several hundred eager applicants. Many board members have graduated to the store staff.

As the store became a great business, sales leaped from $4,810,-899 in 1912 to $8,466,467 in 1913. With completion of the new building the Filenes pioneered a four-pyramid organization for their business modeled somewhat on the branches of the national government. Under the top authority, originally the Filene brothers, were four executives. One headed merchandising, another supervised advertising and publicity, another managed the store's services, and a fourth was the controller, in charge of accounts and money. These divisions successfully checked and balanced each other and this form of organization was adopted by many big stores as a result of its use at Filene's.[2]

"I always believed that the store would grow if it had the right people," said Lincoln Filene, "and that if it didn't have the right people, it wouldn't grow." Booklets outlining opportunities in retailing and containing an application blank for employment at Filene's were distributed to graduating high-school and college students in the area.

Promising young men and women were hired, systematically trained, their progress recorded and evaluated long before such personnel methods were general. Among those employed in the work were the late Professor Frank Parsons of Boston University, "the father of vocational guidance," Robert G. Valentine, one of the first industrial counselors, and Frank B. Gilbreth, noted motion-study specialist and exponent of scientific management. In recognition of his own contributions to vocational training, Lincoln Filene, whose formal education stopped with high school, was awarded an honorary Master of Arts degree by Dartmouth College in 1916 and elected to honorary membership in Phi Beta Kappa by the parent William and Mary College chapter in 1922.

Filene training ranges from instruction in how a waitress shall place silver in the store restaurant, to courses in the Harvard Graduate School. Job specifications are mimeographed. Workers are told how to perform their duties, how these fit into the store operations, why they are important. Workers are encouraged to make suggestions. An employee suggestion system, something which many businesses discovered only in World War II, was in effect as early as 1899 and $25,000 was once distributed in a single contest.

Humorous drawings by Francis Dahl, famous cartoonist of the Boston *Herald*, have enlivened Filene's instructions to salespeople. These are taught not that the customer is always right but that she is a guest and must be treated with consideration and tact.[3]

In line with their oft-expressed belief that it is possible to attain more by cooperation than by conflict, the Filenes encouraged formation in 1898 of a remarkable employee organization called the Filene Cooperative Association. The complaint of a cashier whose pay had been docked for a shortage was responsible for the start of a liberal system of settling employee grievance through this organization.

"If I'm short in my accounts," said the girl, "it's supposed that I've stolen the money. If I happen to be over, it's a 'clerical error,' and you pocket the money. It isn't fair."

Three arbiters decided for the girl. As a consequence an elected Board of Arbitration was made part of the Filene Cooperative Association. It was given power to settle, without interference from management, any matter regarded as an injustice to an employee, or group of employees, resulting from a store rule, a discharge or a question of wages. The rules were drawn by the great Louis D. Brandeis, attorney for Filene's who later became a Justice of the United States Supreme Court. As they gave the employees on the board greater power over management than was later possessed by any labor union, some business leaders predicted dire consequences.

These did not develop, nor did the leaders of the F.C.A. evince any ambition to assume responsibilities of the management. This was a sad disappointment for Edward Filene. He hoped the organization might be the means eventually of turning over ownership of the store, in whole or in part, to its employees. The workers proved more interested in immediate problems of hours, wages and various disputes and the management met them more than halfway.

The store was one of the first to establish a minimum wage for women and girls. In 1913, the store inaugurated Saturday closing during the summer months and was the first in Boston to do so. In 1924, winter vacations were instituted in addition to the usual summer holiday.

In its thirty years of existence, the Board of Arbitration handled nearly a thousand disputes. In 308 cases studied by Russell Sage Foundation investigators, the board ruled for employees in 55 percent of its decisions, for the management in 42 percent, while 3 percent were compromises.[4]

With passage of the Wagner Act, the Filene Cooperative Association became the Independent Union of Retail Store Employees and conventional bargaining replaced the Board of Arbitration. But relations between Filene's and its thirty-five hundred to forty-two hundred workers continued smooth. For its personnel who served in World War II, the store made up any difference between the service pay and regular earnings and sent checks to families each month. The store became the first in Boston to establish a year-round forty-hour five-day work week. Filene's and the union shared the expense of a job evaluation study. Filene workers have group insurance, their own magazine, *The Echo*, a library, a card room, restaurants and cafeterias, a twenty-five-bed clinic with two doctors and two nurses in attendance.

The Filene employees' Credit Union, which has loaned $10,000,000 for the purchase of homes, payment of doctors' bills and similar purposes, is the prototype of credit unions throughout the country. While on a trip around the world, Edward Filene in 1907 found credit unions functioning successfully in Bombay, India. As a result, an informal loan fund which the store maintained to keep its employees out of the hands of loan sharks eventually was changed into a credit union operated by employees with their own money.

So enthusiastic was Edward Filene about the economic value of credit unions that he personally employed Roy Frederick Bergengren, a lawyer who had been an outstanding finance commissioner for

Lynn, to lead a national credit-union movement. A Credit Union National Extension Bureau was formed and later reorganized as the Credit Union National Association. State and then national legislation was obtained authorizing credit unions. There are now thousands of credit unions lending millions of dollars to workers. Filene and Bergengren quarreled over the tactics to be pursued and the views of the latter prevailed, but the "shopkeeper from Boston," as Edward Filene often called himself, is entitled to a sizable share of credit for the success of the credit unions. This was acknowledged when the Credit Union National Association's headquarters building at Madison, Wisconsin, was dedicated by President Truman as "Filene House" and in 1960 when a monument on Boston Common recognized Edward Filene's role in the movement.

It was also from his restless brain that came the store's unique contribution to retailing. This is the world-famous Automatic Bargain Basement started in 1909. There was nothing remarkable about a basement store. Many firms had one, often as an outlet for the mistakes of buyers on the upper floors. But a basement in which prices were plainly marked and automatically reduced by a definite percent on a definite day, if the goods remained unsold, was unique in 1909 and after nearly sixty years still is unique.[5]

Under the Filene system, basement goods are automatically reduced 25 percent after twelve selling days, another 25 percent if still unsold at the end of eighteen selling days, a third 25 percent if remaining after twenty-four selling days. If still on hand after thirty days, items are given away to organized Boston charities.

The business world predicted failure for the scheme, but by faithfully adhering to these rules, candid institutional and item advertising, and paying cash for distress stocks, the Automatic Basement became a spectacular success. In the depression, earnings of the basement were great enough to keep the store profitable when every upstairs floor was operating at a loss. When President Roosevelt closed all banks in 1933, the entire Filene payroll was met from the basement cash sales. Items as costly as mink coats and diamond jewelry have been handled.

Buyers for the basement, which has a staff entirely separate from the rest of the store, have scoured the world for bargains. As the Germans approached Paris in 1940, buyers for Filene's basement picked up four hundred of the latest dresses by Schiaparelli, Lelong, Chanel and other famous modistes and shipped them out through Spain. A week after Paris fell, the basement announced a sale of the dresses, normally priced at several hundred dollars for $11 to $49 each. Fifteen thousand women were on hand when the doors opened. Several had come from New York, and the wife of a famous radio executive and the wife of a great manufacturer had flown together from Chicago. Within sixty seconds, every dress was off the racks. Fifteen minutes later all had been sold.

Another wartime coup was the Austin Reed of London haberdashery from the liner *Queen Mary*. Buyers laid out the inventory in the liner's swimming pool and, after intricate negotiations involving international exchange and British and American officialdom, acquired it for Filene's basement. Included were cashmere sweaters, lounging robes, pajamas and ties of the highest quality. Among the ties were 412 of an identical design, yellow, royal purple and red stripes against a dark blue background, made for the *Queen Mary*. These were marked down to $1 each and, along with everything else, sold out in two and a half hours. For years afterward, strangers wearing the ties would greet each other as fellow members of Filene's *Queen Mary* club.

As many as 150,000 bargain hunters have swarmed through the basement in an eight-and-a-half-hour day. This mark was hit during a 1947 sale of $1,400,000 worth of smoke-damaged luxury goods from Neiman-Marcus, the famous Dallas store. An imported $190 black lace brassière then went for $8.95. In 1965, this renowned store's $410,000 stock of slightly smoke-damaged fur coats was sold in a few hours. Included were a $1,500 polar bear rug and a $17,000 Russian sable. Women also stormed the basement in 1949 to buy $514,000 worth of coats and dresses from Saks Fifth Avenue. That same year the two-million-dollar surplus inventory of the famous Waltham Watch Company was sold upstairs at half price. Many men bought three and four each, and the $200 watches were the first to go.

Probably the biggest crowd of expectant mothers ever assembled in Boston showed up for the sale of two thousand baby carriages. There wasn't room for these in the basement and they were sold in a single morning from the store's Charles River warehouse. Mourning handkerchiefs from Ireland were once sold at three cents each. At the end of one Folies-Bergère season, a Paris buyer sent to Filene's a lot of hip-length silk stockings made especially for the chorus. They went fast at 59 cents a pair. The basement had the first sale of famous-brand "irregular" nylon stockings, customers lining up for four blocks to buy nearly 200,000 the first day.

Charity gets less than 1 percent of the basement merchandise but the basement has had some long-remembered mistakes. One involved two thousand woolen overcoats bought to sell at $12. The sample was all right but when the whole lot arrived the coats literally stank. They still stank at $9 and $6 but most moved at $3. Another involved a whole carload of 50-cent "hard" collars, some 1,100,000 in number, from Van Heusen. These were seconds and Filene's offered them at 25 cents each. That day neighboring stores offered first-quality Van Heusen collars at 15 cents each. In addition, the lot contained many size eighteen and thirteen collars which even the Salvation Army refused as they had no necks that big or small. Filene's finally made a bonfire of the remaining collars.

The Automatic Basement has had famous customers and noted help. John Roosevelt began his business career in the basement at $18.50 a week while his father was President of the United States. The youth's job was to keep the bins filled. He worked faithfully and modestly but for a time attracted so much attention that he had to be hidden in the stockrooms. Failing to find him, one portly lady unrolled and gave to the manager a big scroll bearing an ode starting, "Oh thou youth of sterling character."

Show-business notables regularly visit the basement. One of the principal ballerinas of Britain's Royal Ballet buys formal dresses there. Joe E. Brown has boasted in the Hollywood Brown Derby of shirts from Filene's basement. The famous Joseph Kennedy family of Boston like the place. The entire population of remote Pitcairn Island, descendants of the *Bounty* mutineers, buy their shoes in the basement by sending a sailor there once a year with pencil tracings of all the feet in the colony.

Why haven't other stores been able to establish similar operations? Attempts have been made in Boston, Philadelphia and a few other places but without success. The principal reason seems to be that there is only a limited amount of worthwhile distress merchandise and the fame of Filene's is likely to give it first call. Some rivals have been unable to bring themselves to follow through on the automatic reductions when sizable quantities of goods failed to sell, and customers were quick to detect this. None has promoted its efforts as faithfully and as forcefully as Filene's. The first motion picture made in a store, a silent called *One Flight Down*, was filmed in the basement. It has used illuminated blimps to advertise anniversary sales.

While the basement was winning its fame, Filene's upstairs also had the benefit of some of the most notable talents in retailing. One of these was Louis E. Kirstein of Rochester, New York. He was induced to leave the Stein-Bloch Company, a men's clothing manufacturer there, and join Filene's in 1911 as a vice president when the store entered the men's wear field. The store became successful in this in the face of fierce competition. He later was given charge of all upstairs merchandising and publicity as well. He made great contributions to the store for thirty-one years until his death in 1942.

A colorful and forceful figure, his aphorisms on management are still quoted. Some of the best known are:

The expense rate cannot be lowered by worrying about it.
Overnight we have all become accountants rather than merchants.
Retailing needs less figuring; more fingering.
One thing wrong with business is that business men do not attend to it.
We need more individuality and less foolish straining to be all things to all men.
No industry can rise higher than the caliber of men in it.
Advertising pays when it is believed.

Expenditures for advertising, he believed, should be increased and not curtailed when business became sluggish. He argued that it was a waste to use huge newspaper space at Christmastime, when without persuasion customers were struggling to get into the store.

A major contribution to merchandising initiated by Lincoln Filene enabled the company to exchange information hitherto regarded as confidential with important stores in other cities. After some preliminary discussion, he invited the principals of eighteen stores to lunch on September 6, 1916, at the Aldine Club in New York. Stores represented included L. S. Ayres & Company of Indianapolis, The Dayton Company of Minneapolis, The Emporium of San Francisco, B. Forman Company of Rochester, Joseph Horne Company of Pittsburgh, The J. L. Hudson Company of Detroit, F. & R. Lazarus & Company of Columbus, The Rike-Kumler Company of Dayton, and the William Taylor Son & Company of Cleveland.

Lincoln Filene suggested that an organization be formed for the scientific study of the problems of merchandising and store operation. He contended that this would enable all to operate more efficiently, cut expenses and reduce distribution costs. Two months later the Retail Research Association was organized and opened a modest office in New York with Alvin E. Dodd, previously secretary of the Society for Vocational Education, as director. When he joined the U.S. Chamber of Commerce five years later, he was succeeded by Dr. Paul H. Nystrom, Columbia University professor of marketing.

One of the first projects of the association was the working out of a uniform system of records so figures of the cooperating stores could be compared. Some of these later were telegraphed to permit the prompt detection of any new trend. Detailed studies also have been made of every store activity and members often have helped each other on special problems without going through the association office. Of the many reports supplied its members, the most important are the annual and semiannual general manager's reports. These are as large as an atlas and present a complete picture of every department.

As an outgrowth of this activity, the same stores beginning in 1918 formed a twin organization, the Associated Merchandising Corporation and recently the A.M.C. Wholesale Corporation, for the cooperative mass buying of many of the items which all sold. In 1920 a committee chairmaned by Vice President Kirstein of Filene's toured Europe and opened A.M.C. buying offices in London, Paris, Brussels, Berlin and Milan, the last later removed to Florence. Buying offices subsequently were opened in the Orient—Hong Kong, Tokyo, Bombay—as well as in Munich, Copenhagen, Barcelona and Dublin. At the same time, A.M.C. began to buy in the American markets for important foreign stores as well as for its members. Firms thus represented included Harrods Ltd., of London, John Orr and Garlicks of South Africa; Hudson's Bay Company of Canada; and the Panama Railroad Co., which operates stores in the Canal Zone.

As A.M.C. buying became a multi-million-dollar activity more famous stores joined. Bullock's of Los Angeles became a member in 1919; Strawbridge & Clothier of Philadelphia, in 1921; Abraham & Straus of Brooklyn, in 1923; Hutzler Brothers Company of Baltimore, in 1925; the H. C. Capwell Company, Oakland, California, in 1927 (which afterwards merged with The Emporium) and others later.

Lincoln Filene served as president and chairman of the executive committee of the R.R.A. from its organization until 1943 and of the A.M.C. from 1921 until that date, when he retired with a notable collection of gavels as souvenirs of his long service. A.M.C. had annual sales of around three billion dollars as of 1966 and was headed by William T. French as chairman and chief executive officer. Steven L. Osterweis, formerly head of Gimbels Pittsburgh and a graduate of the Harvard Business School, became A.M.C. president that year. It had long been the largest central buying organization outside the chain and mail-order fields.

At Filene's, top management, meanwhile, went through a grave crisis. On March 1, 1913, in a reorganization after completion of the new building, control was vested in six executives, the Filene brothers and the heads of the four pyramids in the store's organization chart. Each brother had 26 percent of the stock. Each of the other four had 12 percent. These were Vice President Kirstein, merchandising; John R. Simpson, publicity; Thomas K. Cory, the store manager; and Edward J. Frost, the comptroller. The Filenes pledged that they or their heirs by the same date in 1928 would transfer 4 percent of their holdings to the others and yield them control of the store. These six men and five other employees composed the company's board of directors.[6]

All went smoothly for a time but tension and antipathy developed between Edward A. Filene, who under the reorganization had the title of president of the company, and Vice President Kirstein. Both were intense, ambitious, driving personalities. As both were merchandising men, collision possibly was inevitable. Kirstein was a big kindly bear of a man. "Little Eddie," as some old employees termed him, was a small dapper fashion plate with a close-cropped bristling mustache. They differed more in ideas.

Kirstein was a man of family, interested in the Boy Scouts, headed the Boston Jewish charities for a time, and was a conventional and understandable executive. Sigmund Freud would have been greatly interested in Edward A. Filene. From a shy youth who suffered from eczema, he grew into an aggressive, complicated, tactless, restless, brilliant and dictatorial man.[7] In his thirties, he became engaged to a young woman but, as he explained later, the engagement came to an end one evening on a streetcar when he neglected her to conclude a business deal with a man he had been seeking who chanced to be on the car. He had little use for conventional charities. With no family interests, he flung himself intensely into all manner of causes. He was the leading spirit in the organization of the Boston Chamber of Commerce, the U.S. Chamber of Commerce and finally the International Chamber of Commerce.

He made an annual trip to Europe at first to buy merchandise but soon to visit leaders of all sorts and pursue his causes. Outbreak of World War I found him in Paris helping Ambassador Myron Herrick mark American property and care for stranded Americans. During the war, Filene was a dollar-a-year organizer of procurement. After the war, he resumed his European trips, even studying retail stores in Soviet Russia. With writers as notable as Lincoln Steffens polishing his sentences, he spoke in favor of the League of Nations, the Dawes Plan, daylight saving time, sickness insurance which evolved into the Blue Cross plan, tourist rates on steamships, and low-cost housing.

Invention also interested him. A footstool of his design came to nothing but, with Tom Watson of International Business Machines, he worked out the Filene-Finlay simultaneous translator for the proceedings of the League of Nations. With this, earphone-equipped listeners hear in their own tongues addresses as they are made. Produced by I.B.M., the equipment later was adopted for the

Nuremberg war criminal trials and sessions of the United Nations. All of these interests, of course, took Edward A. Filene away from Boston for long periods and responsibility fell increasingly on his associates.

The cleavage with Vice President Kirstein became evident in 1918 when Vice President Simpson enlisted for war service and resigned. His associates could not agree on a successor. His stock was purchased and placed in trust and his duties were assumed by Vice President Kirstein. In 1925, Vice President Cory died. With Edward A. Filene dissenting, the directors allowed Cory's stock to be purchased and divided by Vice Presidents Kirstein and Frost and the latter assumed the late executive's duties.

Events came to a head in 1928. A further reorganization of the store's financial structure that year and a compromise division between Edward A. Filene and the others of what had been Simpson's share of the business left the original 100 units of common stock divided this way: Edward A. Filene 30; Lincoln Filene 24; Frost 19.5; Kirstein 19.5 and the last three together 7. In that year, it was proposed that the store join Abraham & Straus of Brooklyn and The F. & R. Lazarus & Co. of Columbus, Ohio, with whose principals the Filene executives had worked successfully for a decade in the Associated Merchandising Corporation, in formation of a holding company to be known as Federated Department Stores, Inc. One aim was the stabilizing of earnings through a geographical distribution of risk. Edward A. Filene opposed the idea. All his associates favored it.

Weary of the quarreling and fearful of the future of the store, Lincoln Filene then voted his stock with the others and deposed his brother as head of the company, but not without conditions. No loser in a store struggle was ever treated more generously. The elder brother was to continue to have the title of president for life, occupy the president's office and draw a salary of $100,000 a year, the same as the younger brother, Frost and Kirstein (all these salaries came down in the depression). He could make suggestions to the operating committee of the store but was not to interfere in its management. He could not start a business in competition with Filene's but he was free to do anything else he liked.

For the next nine years, the man derided by some "as a cross between a pack peddler and the prophet Isaiah" did exactly this. He spoke and traveled more than ever. He offered but never awarded a $25,000 prize for an essay on world peace. He became a well-known figure of the New Deal, serving as Massachusetts administrator for the National Recovery Administration, and campaigning for President Roosevelt. The night before the 1936 national election, the President, Senator Robert Wagner, National Chairman James A. Farley and Edward A. Filene spoke over the combined National Broadcasting Company and Columbia Broadcasting System networks. The next day his candidate swept every state except Maine and Vermont. It was the happiest day of Edward A. Filene's restless, lonely and ambitious life.

Death in the form of pneumonia overtook him less than a year later on September 25, 1937, in Paris. In accordance with his wishes, his ashes were returned to Boston and cast into the Charles River Basin, which his apartment at 12 Otis Place overlooked. His will left the bulk of his $2,000,000 estate to two foundations which he had started and to which he had given larger sums earlier. These were the Twentieth Century Fund, Inc., and an organization that was renamed the Edward A. Filene Good Will Fund, Inc.

One of the obligations of the latter was to advance $1,000,000 to the Consumer Distribution Corporation, founded earlier to start cooperative department stores as part of the donor's hope of finding ways to cut distribution costs. This action by a merchant who had made a fortune in private enterprise gave critics an excuse to call him a traitor to his class. It was not until 1948 that the first cooperative department store backed by $550,000 of Filene's money was opened in Shirlington, Virginia, a suburb of Washington, D.C. Five years later its assets were sold for $260,000. A similar experiment failed, not necessarily because of the form of operation, in Providence, Rhode Island.

The Twentieth Century Fund proved more fortunate. Since 1919 when E. A. Filene founded it with $5,000,000 in securities, by grants to others and through its own operations the Fund has conducted economic research on timely subjects of public importance and disseminated the results by pamphlets, books, motion pictures, radio and, in recent years, television. Though expenditures have been more than $600,000 year, the Twentieth Century Fund has been so well managed that the endowment in 1966 had increased to more than $30,000,000.

In large part this was due to the dividends of Filene's and Federated Department Stores, Inc., of which Filene's became a unit by a share-for-share exchange of common stock in 1929. Net sales of Filene's for the year ending January 31, 1929, were $34,173,186. Sales reached $47,422,264 the next year as the depression hit the nation. "The honeymoon is over," Vice President Kirstein then told the store staff. "Now the labor pains begin."

Thanks to the remarkable basement, Filene's sales during the depression were never less than the $30,620,089 for the fiscal year ending January 31, 1934. On this figure there was a profit of 3.35 percent though only 1.90 percent had been earned on sales of $32,593,795 the previous year. Filene's sales reached $52,320,951 during World War II and a few years afterward passed $70,000,000. As of 1966, sales were well over $100,000,000 and profits greater than average specialty-store earnings.[8]

Lincoln Filene, a serene and courtly gentleman, died at ninety-two on August 27, 1957, at his summer home in Marstons Mills, Massachusetts, after outliving all of the men he and his brother had picked in 1913 as their possible successors. After his brother's departure, he became president of the firm, relinquished the title for a time to Vice President Frost, who died in 1944, and again resumed it. Vice President Kirstein died in 1942. His successor in charge of publicity, Vice President William McLeod, died in 1946. The store survived these deaths just as it had the loss of Edward A. Filene. A new generation of executives came from its training system.

Chief of these was Harold Daniel Hodgkinson, a six-foot-three executive of boundless energy. He was born May 8, 1890, in Wallingford, Connecticut, where his father, Samuel Hodgkinson, was a small silverware manufacturer, and attended Yale. There he studied engineering and earned his first money by breaking in pipes for his less robust classmates at ten cents a pipe. Work as a campus correspondent for the Associated Press shifted his interest to journalism but the AP had no job for him when he received a degree in 1912 from Yale's Sheffield Scientific School.

"Why don't you try Filene's in Boston?" suggested the New Haven correspondent of the news service. "They are expanding into a new building and I hear it's a good place for college men."

Hodgkinson obediently went to Filene's and was hired by Ernest Martin Hopkins, a personnel man who later became president of Dartmouth College. Hodgkinson first addressed envelopes and then sorted overshoes in a sub-basement. Meanwhile, he studied at the Harvard Graduate School, a bit of application that later gave him the distinction of being the first Yale man ever to become a governor of the Harvard Club of Boston. He married Laura White Cabot, descendant of two old Back Bay families.

After Navy service in World War I, he became copywriter, advertising manager, buyer and merchandiser and then, in 1931, manager of the Automatic Basement. Hodgkinson traveled widely for the basement, buying linen in Ireland, rugs in Africa and even the wardrobes of movie stars in Hollywood. In 1942, he became top executive for the whole store as vice president and general manager and two years later chairman and chief executive officer.

To next in rank rose Samuel Seegal, a statistician with a notable talent for merchandising, who modernized E. A. Filene's "model stock plan." A graduate of both the Massachusetts Institute of Technology and Harvard, he joined Filene's after work as an aide to Secretary of Commerce Herbert Hoover. Jack Goldberg took charge of the basement; John Perkins, acquired from Boston University, operations; California-born Alvah Kindall, personnel; William Lee, the branches; and Francis B. Gummere, planning and research.

The store was rebuilt and remodeled at a cost of $5,000,000. Its showmanship continued. Some World War II war bond promotions earned congratulatory advertisements from rival Jordan Marsh. Ackley Slee, an assistant store superintendent at Filene's, single-handedly sold $4,824,525 in bonds to lead individual sales in the Seventh War Loan. A liberty ship launched during the war was named the S.S. *Edward A. Filene*. The day the atom bomb was announced, the store assembled, with the aid of Harvard scientists, a window display explaining fission of the uranium atom. When President Truman announced an end to price ceilings at 10 P.M. one Saturday, many stores took pride in pledging to hold the line on prices in Monday advertisements. Filene's had one in the Sunday newspapers. A Filene's window display modeled President Eisenhower's inauguration and won an award as the best retail-store institutional window of the the year.

A series of postwar promotions, many of them planned by a notable woman executive, Harriet Wilinsky, fashion director and later sales manager, attracted wide attention. She flew to France on the first Boston-to-Paris plane and conducted a fashion show there for French war brides awaiting passage to the United States. After showing clothes suitable for various sections of America, she answered questions like, "How do I get along with an American mother-in-law?" and "Is it true that American men go out at night without their wives?" Back in Paris later, she was hostess at a party at which French friends of Bostonians heard recordings of messages from them and posed for movies which she took back to Boston. Goods from Ireland, Italy and other foreign lands were the subject of promotions, sometimes in cooperation with *Life, Vogue* or other national publications. The maiden voyage of the American Export Liner *Constitution* featured a Filene fashion show and the French line *Ile de France* made a special stop in Boston for a Filene event.

An annual promotion of New England products, called the "New England Revelation," was started with a special New Haven train carrying designers, manufacturers and editors from New York to Boston for the initial affair. A fashion show was presented en route to the tune of a specially composed musical number titled "New England—It's Grand."

A cartoon-illustrated 1947 advertisement in the *New York Times* headed, "One doesn't wear Jones Beach fashions on Cape Cod," urged vacationing New Yorkers to take empty suitcases to New England and let Filene's outfit them. This made New York merchants seethe but drew business and a favorable reaction for Filene's. "You are helping all New England," wrote a hosiery mill president. "This is a conspicuous example of regional promotion at its best," commented a recreation leader.

All innovations of Filene's have not, of course, proved successful.

Those that failed to justify expectations have been abandoned and usually without delay. In an effort to reduce and equate distribution costs among different classes of customers, the store during World War I undertook to collect a fee of fifty cents a month from customers who maintained charge accounts. It also began to collect a ten-cent fee for each parcel delivered. Both ideas were abandoned when customers complained and rival stores continued to provide the services without special charges.

In 1929, Filene's acquired R. H. White's, an important Boston store dating from 1859. It was the first store to have an electric stairway and to use pneumatic cash tubes. The purchase was made with the idea of shifting some nonfashion departments out of Filene's and operating the stores as complementary institutions. This was not realized and in 1944 White's was sold to the City Stores Company. A ten-year experiment in discount selling in a warehouse at Needham, Massachusetts, was concluded in 1966 as not consistent with Filene's merchandising.

Few civic enterprises are launched in Boston without somebody from the store having a part. "I always tell people," Lincoln Filene once remarked, "that just making money out of a city and its inhabitants isn't the only thing to do." He became the leading spirit of the New England Industrial Development Corporation, a nonprofit organization aiding small business. Among many other activities, Chairman–General Manager Hodgkinson served as chairman of the Federal Reserve Bank of Boston, vice president of the American Academy of Arts and Sciences, chairman of the Associated Merchandising Corporation, president of the American Retail Federation, trustee of Boston University, Northeastern University, Simmons College and the Boston Symphony Orchestra.

A Lincoln Filene Professorship of Retailing in the Harvard Graduate School of Business Administration was established with $300,000 given by Federated Department Stores, Inc., and the Lincoln and Therese Filene Foundation. Coincident with Lincoln Filene's eighty-fifth birthday, Professor Malcolm P. McNair was chosen as the first to fill the chair.

In 1954, Edward S. Filene was elected to the Retailing Hall of

Fame at the Chicago Merchandise Mart and Hodgkinson helped Ralph Lowell, Boston banker, secure the license and more than half the funds for the building of WGBH, Channel 2, an $800,000 educational television station, one of the first, as a memorial to the Filene brothers. The Ford Foundation joined the Twentieth Century Fund and other Filene foundations in paying for the transmitter at Blue Hill adjoining the Harvard Observatory. It is operated by the Lowell Institute Cooperative Broadcasting Council, which includes the Boston Symphony Orchestra, Boston University, Harvard University, Lowell Institute, M.I.T., Museum of Fine Arts, New England Conservatory of Music, Yale University, Northeastern University, Simmons College and Tufts College.

After fourteen years as chief executive, Hodgkinson was succeeded in 1958 by Maurice Lazarus, son of Fred Lazarus, Jr., and previously executive vice president of Foley's, Federated's Houston store. Harold Krensky, previously at Bloomingdale's, became president in 1963. Maurice Lazarus went to Federated Department Stores in 1964 as vice chairman, Hodgkinson became chairman of the executive committee, and Krensky took over as chairman and chief executive officer. Richard G. Shapiro, formerly a Lord & Taylor executive, became president in 1965.

In the retail world, a man trained at Filene's has something of the prestige of a hotel man who worked for E. M. Statler or a surgeon who interned at the Mayo Clinic. At least sixty great stores, at one time nine in New York alone, have been headed by alumni of Filene's.

Graduates of Filene's also have won fame in other fields. Ernest Martin Hopkins became president of Dartmouth College. Donald David was dean of the Graduate School of Business Administration at Harvard University and vice chairman of the Ford Foundation. Paul Mazur became a partner of Lehman Brothers. Muriel Cox became director of the Chamberlain School of Retailing. Owen Stoner became president of Prince Matchabelli, Inc. and Glenn Frank later was president of the University of Wisconsin. Robert L. Moore helped start the Sheraton Hotel chain. And Wheeler Sammons and Charles Merz became publishers of *Who's Who in America* and the *New York Times,* respectively.

VII

F. & R. LAZARUS & COMPANY

Ohio's Famous Department-Store Dynasty

A SHOPPER IS LIKE A BABY who wants milk. When he cries for milk, he doesn't want a meal ticket. He doesn't want an argument or an excuse. He wants warm milk that is right for him—and he wants it at once.

Providing this sort of service is all there is to success in retailing, says Fred Lazarus, Jr., the most famous member of the Ohio family which has built the extraordinary Lazarus and Shillito department-store businesses in Columbus and Cincinnati. From 1946 to 1966, he also was chief executive officer of Federated Department Stores, Inc., of which these big stores are model units. He continues to work nine to four as chairman of its board and also of its executive committee.

When Mr. Fred, as the 5-foot-5½-inch, cocky, bantamlike gentleman is called to distinguish him from his numerous relatives in retailing, became head of Federated, the group consisted of five stores, only one with branches, and sales totaled $200,900,942. When, at eighty-one, he yielded the executive title to his Dartmouth-educated fifty-two-year-old eldest son, Ralph, Federated for the year ending January 29, 1966, had sales of $1,330,736,617. Federated common was the department-store stock most widely held by mutual funds.[1]

As of 1966, Federated had big stores in twelve cities. Through branches of these and a division of small-city Fedway stores, located in the Southwest and West, Federated units were operating in ninety communities from Hyannis, Massachusetts, to Del Amo, California. So dominant was the chain in the department-store field by then that the Federal Trade Commission demanded a five-year moratorium on Federated mergers. The company denied the dominance but, to avoid litigation, agreed. This did not prevent expansion abroad, such as the 1964 purchase in Spain for $4,000,000 of a tenth interest in Galerias Preciadas, or the building of more branches.

All the stores reflect Mr. Fred's restless ideas. These also have found expression in the Ohio State Council of Retail Merchants, formed in 1922 at his instance to represent Ohio retailers of all kinds, and the American Retail Federation, similarly organized in 1935 to speak for many retail groups in Washington. For his ideas, he has received the gold medal of the National Retail Merchants Association, a Tobé award and other retail honors. At least one of his ideas affected everybody in the country.

This was the matter of the date of Thanksgiving, which traditionally starts the Christmas shopping season. In 1939, when the depression still lingered, the last Thursday of November, on which the holiday was then observed, fell on the very last day of the month. At a dinner in Cincinnati on June 14, Mr. Fred remarked to George V. Sheridan, executive director of the Ohio State Council of Retail Merchants, that there would be six more days of Christmas business if Thanksgiving could be advanced a week.

Next day Sheridan visited a library and found no legal bar to changing the date; in fact, it had been observed on many different dates in American history. The late William F. Wiley, then publisher of the Cincinnati *Enquirer*, endorsed the idea. Sheridan and Ed Martin, secretary of the Ohio Newspaper Association, took the proposal to Washington and through Lowell Mellett presented it to the White House, where President Roosevelt gave it a warm welcome. He promised to proclaim the earlier date and to give Lazarus and Wiley advance notice of his proclamation.

"But he forgot that part," recalls Lazarus. "The announcement came just as I was sitting down to the first company dinner of the bride of my son Ralph. She had broken her back over it but I spent the evening on the long-distance telephone talking to retailers. Wiley did the same with publishers. But it was too late. Everybody knows about the big squabble that broke out and continued for three years. We hadn't thought of the long-planned football schedules, school holidays, almanacs and calendars, railroad timetables and other things. Even my brothers who were interested in Ohio State's football team were annoyed."

Eventually everybody conceded the value of the change and Congress on December 29, 1941 legalized the fourth Thursday in November as Thanksgiving. This can fall no later than November 28, and may be as early as November 22. Manufacturers, shoppers and store workers as well as retailers benefit.[2]

Some less spectacular Lazarus ideas have been the conversion of store buyers into department managers, making them responsible for operating costs, including selling, warehousing and delivery, as well as the selection and sale of merchandise; the display of merchandise by "size selection"; the use of perimeter stockrooms adjacent to selling departments; and the adaptation to a store of the latest industrial material-handling techniques and devices. He believes that the costs of a store should be analyzed operation by operation and that great savings can be effected by the elimination of waste motion and antiquated methods.

But Mr. Fred's favorite idea, perhaps, is the strongly held view that a store's success is almost in direct ratio to its hippodrome qualities and that older customers as well as children like to shop in a lively, animated atmosphere. As a department store usually provides this on a bigger scale than one of its smaller competitors, he does not regard the big stores as doomed dinosaurs. He has enlivened Federated stockholders' meetings with fashion shows.

"A good store is like a big circus," he explains. "You can have one ring, or five or twenty. That is why a department store has it all over others in attracting people to come in and look around." He also believes a store should be exciting to those who run it. "Retailing is our life," he once said. "We enjoy its excitements. It is a life in itself full of challenge."

Showmanship combined with good merchandising helped the Lazarus store in Columbus grow to 196 departments sprawling over 32 acres of floor space and to do a business of more than $110,000,000 a year in Columbus, a city of 471,000. This monumental institution sometimes attracts 90,000 shoppers a day, does 60 percent of the local department-store business and for forty years has been the largest store in central Ohio. Its chief local competitor is its own three-level basement, "upstairs" from some entrances because of the sloping site. The store's garages park 2,800 customer automobiles and many shoppers come from 150 miles away. Two of its delivery routes are so long that the drivers make overnight stops.

A live alligator, brought back from Florida by an uncle of Fred, Jr., was a basement attraction at the Lazarus store until the reptile died after eighteen years of exhibition. It ate a lot of steak. For years the store had a raucous whistle that tooted a weather forecast at 3 P.M. daily. One toot meant "fair," two "rain," three "unsettled." Santa Claus early became a Lazarus property, with the store bringing the old gentleman into town with a parade. When an early electric automobile crashed into a show window, instantly up went a sign reading "Everything Comes to Lazarus." Once a year the store entertains fifteen to eighteen hundred customers more than eighty years old at a tea. The store auditorium is constantly in use for hobby shows, club meetings and similar gatherings, and a lighted blimp was employed to announce a change in store hours.

Dramatic exploits also turned Shillito's in Cincinnati from a moribund fifth-place store doing $4,000,000 business when the Lazarus family bought it in 1928 to the biggest department store in southern Ohio with sales of more than $90,000,000. Cincinnatians still talk of the service of Shillito's in the record 1937 Ohio flood. Food, blankets, gasoline and other merchandise, as well as drinking water, went from the store to refugees, and its staff fumigated, sorted and distributed thousands of garments donated for flood sufferers.

Telephone for the time in Cincinnati and you will be connected with a Shillito number, where it will be supplied along with an announcement of a sale or a suggestion that you support the local opera or some other civic enterprise. Shillito's sponsors a Junior

Town Hall at which high-school students argue questions like: "Should parents be held responsible for the delinquency of children?" or "Should eighteen-year-olds be allowed to vote?" The store gives space to a Craft Shop of the Handicapped, profits of which go to the local blind or crippled.

Behind the dramatics are generations of solid merchandising. The original Lazarus store was opened as a tiny men's-clothing store in Columbus in 1851, the same year that William Filene became a storekeeper in Boston. Fred, Jr.'s sidewhiskered grandfather, Simon Lazarus, an immigrant from Prussia, founded the store. He also served as the first rabbi of Temple Israel, the oldest Jewish congregation in Columbus. Temple Israel, in which his descendants are still active, incidentally has on its walls two bronze plaques, one expressing the thanks of members of the First Methodist Church, who worshiped there when fire destroyed their building, and the other from members of the Broad Street Presbyterian Church, who used the temple while their structure was remodeled.

Simon Lazarus started with $3,000. His store on South High Street was twenty by fifty feet. There was one clerk. The founder had four daughters and two sons, Fred and Ralph, great uncle of a later Ralph. When not in school, they helped in the store, sometimes breaking ice in the Scioto River for water to mop the floor.

First of many expansions came in the early sixties when an adjoining boot and shoe store was purchased for $3,500. In 1870, the Lazarus store, then one of sixteen local retail clothiers, became the first Columbus store to operate a delivery wagon. In 1877, the founder died and his two sons took charge.

Store advertising then emphasized "One Lowest Price" or "Strictly One-Price Store" and "Every Article Marked in Plain Figures." In 1887, the store added men's, women's and children's shoes. In 1888, on the occasion of the state fair and centennial celebration, the store closed at 10:30 A.M. and all the employees, numbering between thirty and forty, went to the fair in a body. Led by Fred and Ralph Lazarus and a brass band, they marched to Union Station and entrained for the fair grounds.

Ralph Lazarus wrote most of the store advertising in the nineties. "He would just sit down," a veteran employee once recalled, "and write on a piece of wrapping paper." The store at this period consisted of eleven ground-floor rooms with connecting doors. "Uncle Ralph" Lazarus, as he was known, had an office in an elevated cubbyhole in the center of the eleven rooms. This was equipped with a system of mirrors so arranged that by their chain reflection he could see every part of the store.

In 1891, the store expanded vertically with the moving of the tailor shop to the second floor; it was connected with the main store by a circular stairway. In another expansion the space between the store and the southwest corner of Town and High streets was acquired and a clock tower, a landmark for many years, was constructed atop the structure.

Merchandising at the turn of the century involved presents and premiums. A baseball and bat usually went with the purchase of a boy's suit. A man received a pair of suspenders with each suit. A purchaser of a pair of shoes expected a strip of tickets entitling him to free shines. Complaints were loud when the practice was stopped in 1903.

All employees, called associates then as now, wore nickel lapel buttons bearing their number. These buttons were required to be polished and in evidence at all times. Even floorwalkers wore large badges saying "Lazarus Floor Walker."

In 1903, Ralph Lazarus died. He had never married and shuddered at the thought of a woman secretary. The business continued under his brother Fred, with the latter's four sons, Simon, Fred, Jr., Robert and Jeffrey, all assuming responsibilities in the store as they grew up.

Nearly all of the founder Simon's sons, grandsons and great-grandsons have gone into the business. They all have been competent and successful merchants, but the most kinetic and peripatetic of them is Fred Lazarus, Jr. A childhood illness left him with a hand tremor but this did not deter him from starting in the store at age ten as a boy collar-salesman on Saturdays.

Until he and his three brothers began to take charge, the Lazarus store was little more than a men's clothing shop. Simon, the eldest brother, had a flair for employee relations and headed the store for thirty years. The younger brothers, Robert and Jeffrey, became notable merchandise and sales-promotion executives and then respectively heads of the stores in Columbus and Cincinnati. To Fred, Jr., was left finance and the freedom to consider bold innovations.

He cut short his education in his freshman year at Ohio State, where he was a straight-A student, to take the place of his dying uncle in the store, and soon induced his family to construct a new building and expand into the department-store field. He personally supervised the building of a five-story structure that is part of the present Lazarus store and termed its opening in 1909 the happiest day of his business career. He was then twenty-four years old. Since then he has supervised so many expansions that he can talk to architects and engineers in their own language.

Sales surpassed $1,000,000 for the first time in 1914 with a gross of $1,109,811. Several new departments were added then and later, one a notable book department under the late Mrs. Lulu S. Teeter, which became a center for Ohio literary affairs.

Though Lazarus sales mounted to $4,000,000 a year during World War I, its business still was exceeded by one Columbus store and equaled by another in 1920. That summer, Fred, Jr., visited New York and became convinced that the war inflation had run its course. Markdowns, greater than the profits of the previous year, were taken, especially on items like silk shirts, but the overpriced goods were cleared out. The store's 1921 gross of $5,773,000 was the largest in Columbus.

Fred, Jr., early developed a liking for travel and out of his trips have come many ideas. While visiting Europe, he once wandered into the Printemps store in Paris and noticed that all the dresses of one size, regardless of price, were grouped in single alcoves. The simplicity of it impressed him and he adopted the idea at once. Why should stores scatter garments of the same size all over a floor, perhaps even on different floors, simply because they are of a different price or a different make? After all, the customer had to determine one fact before all else—would the garment fit? With all dresses of one size grouped, customers often buy an item of better quality than they planned. Size selling is now used widely.

Out of Mr. Fred's interest in construction has come adoption of horizontal warehousing, the practice wherever possible of storing merchandise, except the bulky furniture, on the same floor level that it is sold. It places salespeople close to the stock and enables them to do work in slack hours that might otherwise require a separate staff in a warehouse. Errors in handling are greatly reduced.

One of the Lazarus family's most successful ventures was the purchase in 1928 for $2,500,000 of the John Shillito store in Cincinnati. Founded in 1830, this had the distinction of being the oldest store west of the Alleghenies. Mrs. Fred Lazarus, Sr., a native of Cincinnati, bought her wedding dress there and the family knew the store well. It had been the city's biggest store but after the death in 1925 of Stewart Shillito, a son of the founder, it was no better than fourth. Many departments were leased, merchandise was cheap and the building fifty years old.

Shillito's was rehabilitated with startling speed under Fred Lazarus, Jr., president for some years, and his brother, Jeffrey Lazarus, first general manager and then president. Leonard R. Minster, from another Cincinnati store, improved service and personnel. The store was cleaned up, rearranged, refixtured and, department by department, stocked with better merchandise.

In the first year of Lazarus management sales increased to $5,700,000 and in 1929 reached $6,500,000. While other large Cincinnati stores lost as much as half of their volume during the depression, Shillito's dropped only to $4,500,000 in 1932 and then began to rise steadily. For 1935, the volume was $7,300,000, more than it had ever been at the peak of the Shillito family's operation. The building was expanded and air conditioned and a customers' garage built. In 1939, sales passed $10,700,000 and Shillito's was definitely the No. 1 store in Cincinnati. At the end of World War II, sales were nearly $30,000,000 and were accounting for 33 to 35 percent of the Federal Reserve department-store figures for Cincinnati. Jeffrey Lazarus retired in 1965 after seeing Shillito's sales increase more than twenty-fold.

Shillito's and Lazarus do so well downtown that they have been slow to open branches. As of 1966, Shillito's had three, Tri-County, Western Woods and Kenwood. Fred Lazarus III, a son of Mr. Fred, was then chairman at Shillito's.

At the big Columbus store, Robert Lazarus, a gentle, asceticappearing Phi Beta Kappa graduate of Ohio State who has been active in countless civic enterprises, became president in 1947. He was made chairman in 1959 and was succeeded as president by his nephew, Charles Y. Lazarus, a Yale graduate who had started as a salesperson in the store in 1936. He is a son of the late Simon Lazarus. Robert Lazarus, Jr., became a vice president and general merchandise manager of the basement store in 1959. The first branch, Lazarus West, on West Broad at Georgesville, was opened in 1962. A much larger full-line branch, Lazarus Northland, was completed in 1964 in the Northland Shopping Center, site also of a Sears, Roebuck store, at Karl and Morse roads. Raymond Loewy–William Snaith designed both Lazarus branches. A full-line Eastland was planned for 1967.

Federated Department Stores, Inc., was born on a yacht in Long Island Sound one weekend in the summer of 1929. The craft belonged to Simon Frank Rothschild, president of Abraham & Straus, the big Brooklyn store. Guests included Fred Lazarus, Jr.; Louis Kirstein, general manager of Filene's in Boston; and Samuel Bloomingdale, head of Bloomingdale's, the big New York store. They had been associated with the Retail Research Association and the Associated Merchandising Corporation. They returned from the cruise with the first three agreeing to a proposal by Paul Mazur, the former Filene man who had become a partner in the investment banking firm of Lehman Brothers, that they share the risks of their businesses through a holding company to be set up by an exchange of stock.

The new company was incorporated in November and a majority of the stock of each company exchanged. Holders of each Lazarus share received nineteen-thirty-sevenths of a Federated share, an A. & S. share received two-thirds of a Federated share and Filene shares were traded evenly. Lehman Brothers, the investment bankers, were interested and first Arthur Lehman and then Mazur served as directors.

Bloomingdale's joined the group the next year on the basis of a share of Bloomingdale stock for three-fourths of a Federated share. Bloomingdale's and Abraham & Straus are curiously intwined in history. Just before the Civil War, the small Bettlebeck & Co. dry-goods store in Newark, New Jersey, employed three clerks. They were Benjamin Altman, Abraham Abraham and Lyman Gustave Bloomingdale. Each founded great stores, the first B. Altman & Co. in New York, the second Abraham & Straus in Brooklyn and the last Bloomingdale Bros., Inc.

The depression struck just as Federated was organized and it was October 31, 1931, before the first dividend was paid. They have continued unbrokenly since then. Until World War II's end, Federated continued to be simply a holding company, without authority, headquarters offices or formal work. Between 1933 and 1945, the number of stockholders increased only from 1,173 to 2,861.

A trip of Fred Lazarus, Jr., in 1941 to visit his son, Ralph, then an Air Force lieutenant at Ellington Field, led to Federated's becoming an operating company and to its expansion in Houston, Texas. While waiting for his son to come off duty, Fred. Jr., visited the local stores and discovered the largest to be Foley Brothers. This was founded in 1900 by Pat C. and James A. Foley with $2,000 borrowed from an Irish immigrant uncle. Since 1917, the store had been owned by the George S. Cohen family.

When Fred, Jr., found Foley's doing only a fourth of the business of Shillito's in a city as big as Cincinnati, he decided Federated should expand into Houston. At war's end Mr. Fred sold his Federated colleagues on building a store there. This required considerable departure from the original idea of Federated's simply acting as a holding company. He became Federated's president, and set up his headquarters in a small office over a bank across from Shillito's in Cincinnati. There were two secretaries, a telephone operator, and two men who began doing research on ways in which the stores could better share their most successful techniques. An early improvement was to expand the use of "revolving credit," whereby customers have a monthly credit balance and pay stipulated amounts each month. Today more than 60 percent of Federated's sales are on credit of various kinds. The office was soon moved to the top of Shillito's garage, where it remains. It became his command post for expansion, at a time when some retailers were retrenching in fear of a postwar depression.

While sites were being purchased for the Houston store, the owners of Foley's decided to sell. After several discussions, one of which lasted eighteen hours, Fred, Jr., worked out a plan which in 1945 gave Federated the Foley business and real estate in exchange for $3,250,000 in securities. As the real estate included a surplus store site, this gave Fred, Jr., the chance to turn real-estate salesman. He sold the extra site, which had been optioned at $1,250,000, to Woolworth's for $3,055,000, a matter of $2,000 a front inch, a record price even for busy Houston.[3]

This profit helped pay for a new $13,000,000 store completed in 1947 and embodying all of the Lazarus ideas of perimeter stockrooms, movable walls, size station selling, and scientific operation. A tunnel under Travis Street connected the six-story-and-basement store with a garage and service building. Packages of shopping customers reached their cars by a system of chutes and conveyor belts. Kenneth Franzheim was the architect and Raymond Loewy designed the interiors, including a luxurious Crystal Room. It was the first entirely new department store built in the country in almost twenty years.[4]

Even before the new store was completed, the Federated management increased Foley's sales from $6,500,000, the year before it was purchased, to $16,000,000. By 1950, Foley's sales passed $29,000,000. Max Levine, a Harvard graduate trained at Filene's, Abraham & Straus and Lazarus, became first president and then chairman at Foley's. Sales reached $50,000,000 by 1955. Four additional floors were added to the store and later branches were opened at Pasadena, Sharpstown and Alameda-Genoa. As of 1966, Milton Berman, formerly of Abraham & Straus, was president of Foley's. Stewart Orton, formerly of Shillito's and Milwaukee's Boston Store, was executive vice president.

With the advent of Fred Lazarus, Jr., as president in 1945, Federated abruptly changed character. All existing stores were enlarged and rehabilitated. The transformation at Bloomingdale's, under James S. Schoff and J. Edward Davidson, made it one of the most profitable Federated units. At Federated headquarters, operations, finance, research and acquisitions divisions were set up. Owen

C. Frost, son of the Filene executive, headed the list. Research was headed by Myron S. Silbert, co-author with Paul Mazur of *Principles of Organization Applied to Modern Retailing,* who earned the Legion of Merit as a Quartermaster lieutenant colonel in World War II. As treasurer, John Lebor took over financial and tax problems. Within a few years, the number of stockholders increased to more than ten thousand.

Federated attempted to buy the John Taylor Dry Goods Store in Kansas City but was outbid by Macy's. Halliburton's, an Oklahoma City store, was purchased in 1947 and sold a few years later. In 1948, Federated bought the well-publicized Milwaukee Boston Store, one of the largest in Wisconsin, along with three branches. Pat Maher, a Lazarus executive who as a boy had been a golf caddy for Mr. Fred, headed the Boston Store until his retirement. As of 1966, Peter G. Scotese was chairman and Ross F. Anderson, formerly of Macy's, was president.

Sanger Brothers, pioneer Dallas store, was purchased in 1951. It was founded in 1872 by Isaac, Lehman, and Philip Sanger, immigrant brothers from Bavaria who previously had had a succession of stores at the rail head of the Houston and Texas Central Railroad as it was built northward from Houston. On the basis of some of their earlier retailing, the store claims to date from 1857 "as an institution." Eli Sanger, a later member of the family, headed the local Civic Music Association for many years and gave it an office in the store. It was the first in the area to hire women as clerks and the first to expand to department-store status. It was long the biggest store in Dallas but, after passing from Sanger ownership, suffered from the competition of Neiman-Marcus in fashion and from Sears, Roebuck in hard lines.

Under Federated, the company expanded spectacularly, acquiring the local A. Harris & Co., and becoming Sanger-Harris, opening additional branches and in 1965 completing the first new downtown Dallas department store in thirty years. With an exterior marked by an arched colonnade and a great mosaic mural, it occupies almost a block at Akard and Pacific, far uptown from the old site. Branches are in Plymouth Park, Preston Center, Big Town, Highland Park and Oak Cliff Harris Center. Chief executives under Federated have been

Henry X. Salzberger, from Bloomingdale's; Ray Cummins, from Lazarus; and, since 1966, Weston P. Figgins, formerly a Federated vice president and earlier executive vice president of Woodward & Lothrop, Washington, D.C.

In 1953, the Federated Retirement Income and Thrift Incentive Plan, called RITI for short, was inaugurated. This is an employee retirement benefit program similar to that of Sears, Roebuck. The company makes an annual allocation in cash, which for some years has run around 6½ percent of each employee's earnings. This is used to buy Federated stock at various times during the year for the retirement income part. Employees may invest up to 5 percent of earnings in the thrift incentive part of the plan. On this part, the company's contribution for some years has averaged about 50 percent of the employees' savings. The accounts rapidly increase in value but could drop in a declining market. They are payable at sixty-five, or after twenty years' service, starting at fifty-seven; or at once in case of disability or death.

Burdine's of Miami, biggest department store in Florida, was acquired by Federated in 1956 in an exchange of stock with the heirs of W. M. Burdine, who launched it in 1898. With it were acquired four branches, new and colorful like the main store, in Miami Beach, North Miami, Fort Lauderdale and West Palm Beach. Federated built another in South Miami at the Dadeland Shopping Center in 1962 and bought land for one in Hialeah. Alfred H. Daniels, previously a Federated vice president and earlier an Abraham & Straus executive, became chairman and chief executive. He is a magna cum laude graduate of Harvard College, a Phi Beta Kappa and has an M.B.A. from Harvard Business School. Thomas C. Wasmuth became president in 1965. *Women's Wear Daily* estimated Burdine's sales for that year at between $70,000,000 and $75,000,000.[5] Wasmuth previously had been executive vice president of Rike's in Dayton, Ohio.

In 1959, Federated added Rike's, a store dating from 1853, in a legal "pooling of interests"; and Goldsmith's in Memphis, Tennessee, dating from 1872 and largest store in the area, for 200,000 Federated shares. As of 1966, David L. Rike was president and Roy

Eberhard, executive vice president, of Rike's. Walter L. L. Bergquist was president, Jack L. Goldsmith, chairman, and Edwin M. Marks, executive vice president, at Goldsmith's. Each store has two branches. In 1964, Federated by another "pooling of interests" acquired Bullock's and I. Magnin.*

The first of the smaller tightly-engineered Fedway stores was opened in Wichita Falls, Texas, in the fall of 1952. Others followed in Corpus Christi, Longview and Amarillo, Texas; Albuquerque, New Mexico; Tucson, Arizona; also Bakersfield and Pomona, California. Each was constructed at a cost of around $3,000,000 and provides full department-store stocks, charge accounts, parking and usual Federated services. The Tucson and Albuquerque stores each have a branch. Edward Watson, a Lazarus alumnus, heads Fedway.

Abraham & Straus in Brooklyn and Bloomingdale's in Manhattan, meanwhile, added branches and increased sales in the face of competition from all directions. Sales of the great Brooklyn store passed $100,000,000 in 1954 and $200,000,000, in 1963. It is second only to Macy's in the metropolitan area and has met changing conditions by building a downtown garage on the site of Namm's, long its rival, and opening branches in Hempstead, Garden City, Babylon, Huntington and Manhasset. Walter N. Rothschild, grandson of the founder, died of a heart attack October 8, 1960, while in White Sulphur Springs for a meeting of Federated executives. He was succeeded as chairman and chief executive officer by Sidney Solomon and as president by his son, Walter N. Rothschild, Jr.[6] Kenneth C. Richmond became vice president and treasurer. In 1966, Solomon, a graduate of Harvard who began his career at Filene's, received both a Tobé award and the gold medal of the National Retail Merchants Association for "distinguished" contributions to retailing.[7] Bloomingdale's added branches in Fresh Meadows and New Rochelle, New York; Stamford, Connecticut; and Bergen County and Short Hills, New Jersey. As of 1966, it had sales of more than $125,000,000. James S. Schoff was then chairman, Lawrence Lachman, president and chief executive officer, and Marvin A. Traub, executive vice president.

* See Chapter XVIII.

Federated's central office staff, originally seven men in 1945, grew with the recruitment of talent from many fields. Some executives moved on to head store divisions. Abe Fortas, long a legal adviser, a month after becoming a Federated vice president was appointed by President Lyndon B. Johnson to the United States Supreme Court. Howard W. Johnson, previously dean of the Alfred P. Sloan School of Management at the Massachusetts School of Technology, after a year with Federated as consultant and executive vice president in charge of management development, returned to Cambridge as M.I.T. president. He continued as a member of the Federated board of directors, to which General M. Gruenther, former Supreme Allied Commander in Europe, also was elected in 1945.

Vice President Myron S. Silbert of the original staff, who launched Federated's economic research, served until retirement in 1966. John F. Lebor retired after twenty years and was succeeded as finance officer by Richard L. Knight, previously with General Dynamics and General Electric. J. Paul Sticht, previously president of Campbell Soup International, joined Federated as executive vice president and director in 1960. A 1965 reorganization set up a four-man top management, Mr. Fred as chairman, Ralph Lazarus as president, Maurice Lazarus and Sticht as vice chairmen. It created new executive vice presidents for management development; finance, as of 1966, Knight; public affairs, Robert M. Fuoss, formerly editor of the *Saturday Evening Post;* and research, Herbert S. Landsman, formerly of R. H. White and Filene's. John Paul Jones, formerly general manager for organization development at Union Carbide, came in as vice president for organization development. William Miller, earlier a Time, Inc., and New York *Herald Tribune* editor, became public relations vice president.

Miss Rose Wells, who coined the phrase "total look" during thirty-two years of fashion work with Ohrbach's, in 1965 became Federated's first woman vice president after serving as fashion consultant. That year she directed a series of spectacular events, including a Paris couture copy benefit show at the home of Mrs. Clint Murchison, marking completion of the new 450,000-square-foot Sanger-Harris downtown store in Dallas. She began a series of multi-store fashion promotions with one in cooperation with Celanese in the spring of 1966.

But top leadership at Federated remained in the Lazarus family. Next in rank to President Ralph Lazarus as of 1966 was his younger brother, Vice Chairman Maurice Lazarus, a graduate of Harvard with heavy retail experience at Shillito's, Foley's and Filene's. And the influence of Mr. Fred, who learned to dance the samba at sixty-two, continues as chairman. He just travels a little less than formerly.

"It's poison to enforce retirement at sixty five," he remarked when announcing that Ralph would be chief executive officer. "That's a hangover from the depression. It's easy for a chief executive to maintain the compulsory retirement practice. He simply avoids making a decision. Meanwhile, people who reach sixty begin to drift and fade away. It is such a waste when business needs all the skill and sophistication it can get. I admit I am talking from a very prejudiced point of view."

If his sons have their father's vigor and share this belief, they will be guiding Federated until around the year 2000.

VIII

MARSHALL FIELD & COMPANY

Elegance for the Middle West

EVERY GREAT STORE is a showplace in its community but Marshall Field's with its elegance and its clocks has achieved and retained an attraction value for visitors to Chicago that probably is unmatched in any other city. Out-of-towners go to Field's before visiting the Art Institute, the Union Stockyards or the great museums. This is true of the famous as well as the ordinary traveler. The store's tooled-leather guest book includes the autographs of Prince Philip of England, Queen Marie of Roumania, Prime Minister Winston Churchill, President William Howard Taft, Crown Princess Martha of Norway, Eleanor Roosevelt and many others.

It is a sentimental store, where Hughston M. McBain, the sixth president, kept five red roses on his desk in memory of his five illustrious predecessors. It is also a resilient enterprise, which survived the Great Chicago Fire and since has surmounted difficulties that would have defeated a store of less stamina. It has doubled its sales in recent decades by divesting itself of wholesale and manufacturing interests and investing in purely retail expansion.

Under Gerald A. Sivage, its current president, the company had record sales of $306,034,046 and record earnings of $14,830,029 in the fiscal year ending January 31, 1966. A Field unit is within easy driving distance of anybody living in the big Chicago metropolitan area. There are branches in Evanston, Lake Forest, Oakbrook, Oak Park, Old Orchard (Skokie), Park Forest and River Oaks, Illinois, and in the big Mayfair shopping center at Wauwatosa, near Milwaukee, Wisconsin.

The company owns one of the finest stores in the West in Frederick & Nelson of Seattle. This has two attractive suburban branches, Aurora Village and Bellevue.

When built in 1907, the huge Chicago store at State, Washington, Wabash and Randolph streets, was "the largest store in the world." With over 450 departments in 73 acres of space on 13 floors, Field's still is one of the three physically largest stores in the world. Macy's of New York and Hudson's of Detroit boast only a few more square feet. The longest selling aisle in the world is in Field's basement; on the Wabash Avenue side it extends six hundred feet under Washington Boulevard into the Field's Store for Men across the street. Each December Field's displays "the largest indoor Christmas tree in the world" and issues handsome toy and fashion catalogs.[1]

Field's boasts more show windows than any other store and each is numbered to enable a shopper to be specific when asking for something displayed. As of 1966, it claimed the largest department-store restaurant operation in the world; the largest retail shoe operation under one roof; the largest china department, the largest year-round toy department, the largest book department in the United States; the largest imports of linen and one of the largest imports of women's fashions. Historically, Field's was the first to establish an underprice basement and to use the basement for selling. It was the first to offer a personal shopping service and was among the first to exchange goods and offer a delivery service.

What the Biltmore Hotel clock is to rendezvousing New Yorkers, the two Field clocks are to Chicagoans. Big enough to be visible for blocks, they have marked the State and Washington and State and Randolph corners since the turn of the century. Each is twelve feet six inches high, has minute hands more than two feet long, and weighs seven and three-quarter tons.

The store traces its history to 1852 when a young Quaker named

Potter Palmer, later famous for hotels and other enterprises, arrived in Chicago from Lockport, New York, where he had operated a small dry-goods store. He started a similarly modest store in Chicago on Lake Street. Palmer was a student of *Godey's Lady's Book* and saw the importance of the ladies as customers. Everything about his establishment was calculated to please them. His store had no whiskey barrel and pot-bellied stove. Instead there was an atmosphere of gentility. There was a tempting array of stylish shawls, laces and cloaks. There were price tags on them. Above all, there was acceptance, something new, even cordial acceptance, of the fact that women sometimes change their minds.

Four years later, Marshall Field, a twenty-one-year-old Presbyterian youth, also arrived in Chicago, from Pittsfield, Massachusetts. One of nine children, he had started life as a farm boy but had become a $4-a-week clerk in the store of Henry G. "Deacon" Davis at Pittsfield. There for nearly five years the shy, serious-minded, conscientious youth put in ten hours a day, six days a week. He swept the floor, dusted the counters and shelves, arranged the goods, and waited on the shrewd New England customers. Women liked him. He was polite and painstaking, with a good memory for names and faces—bolstered by a little book in which he made notes about the customers and their preferences.

In Chicago, through the help of his brother Joseph, Marshall found a job with Cooley, Wadsworth and Company, the largest dry-goods firm in the city. He saved half of his $400-a-year salary by sleeping in the store and buying nothing for himself except some overalls. Hard-working and single-minded he rose to a junior partnership and finally to a full partnership with Cooley and Farwell. The firm of Farwell, Field and Company—the first in which Marshall Field's name appeared as a partner—was formed in 1864, when Cooley stepped out of the picture. The next step came the next year, when Potter Palmer decided to retire from his store. He sold an interest to Field and one to Levi Leiter, Field's junior partner, and the firm of Field, Palmer and Leiter was launched.

Their first advertisement made it clear that they were "Successors to P. Palmer." The pioneer merchandising ideas which had made

Palmer's so popular formed a solid foundation for the new company and for the development of Field's own far-sighted convictions about successful storekeeping. "The best way to show a lady that the merchandise she purchased is worth the dollar she paid for it," said Field, "is to give her the dollar in return." He laid down as one of the company's rules: "What we write and what we say about our merchandise or service must be strictly, scrupulously, unfailingly the truth." Low prices, Field believed, could not do the trick alone. Nor could goods of the highest quality. There must be the personal touch—that atmosphere of honest, pleasant service that makes customers feel they are *special* customers and brings them back faithfully, year after year.

It worked then, as it does today. The ladies liked the courteous attention they received, no matter how small their purchases. They liked the three female clerks who were hired to make them feel more at ease when buying the elaborate lingerie of the period. They appreciated the distinction lent to the store's front entrance by the two men hired to sweep the street three times a day. They loved the goods-on-approval policy. Through the years some of them, of course, have taken advantage of it. There was the society woman who returned a cape on the day after a ball, maintaining that she had not worn it. It was such an expensive cape that the matter was brought to the attention of Field himself. He took her word for it—and found, after she had left with her refund, a lace handkerchief tucked into one of the folds of the cape. His comment was characteristic: "If she said she didn't wear it, she didn't wear it. But I guess we'd better send her handkerchief back to her."

Business was so good that by 1868 Field and Leiter decided to take Palmer up on his offer to rent them his palatial marble store building on State Street. The $50,000-a-year rental was breath-taking. So was the grand opening, which Chicago newspapers described as "A Dazzling Assemblage of Wealth, Beauty and Fashion." The main attraction was the first floor, the retail floor, with its walnut counters, frescoed walls, and—lit by splendid gas fixtures—its rich display of silks and satins, sable-trimmed cloaks, black and white astrakhans, Persian cashmere and point-lace shawls.

While the wholesale trade was an important part of the firm's business, he noted that it was the retail floor which drew the most ecstatic "Ohs" and "Ahs" from the ladies who swarmed into the store. Marshall Field was there to greet them, unobtrusively polite, his youthful shyness ripened now into dignity. A quiet-mannered, handsome man, he made his presence felt among customers and clerks alike.

Striding through the store one day, Field encountered one of his assistants arguing with a woman customer.

"What are you doing here?" demanded Field.

"I am settling a complaint," the man explained.

"No, you're not," said Field. "Give the lady what she wants."

This was done and the phrase became a motto for the store and the title years later of a book on its history.[2]

Representatives of Field and Leiter ranged far afield, visiting the fashion centers of Europe and buying high-quality mill products on the spot in England. "In 1871," recalled Prince Philip of England visiting Chicago long afterward, "Marshall Field sent his brother Joseph, to Manchester to open the first buying office abroad for any American retail store—and it's been going strong ever since."[3] Congress made Chicago a federal port of entry and the first direct Field and Leiter importations triumphantly arrived that year. Before it could be displayed disaster struck the whole city.

News of the fire sweeping Chicago roused both partners out of their beds. Field organized a brigade to hang wet blankets in the store windows while Leiter supervised the job of moving the most valuable merchandise to safety—to the lake front first, later to Leiter's home and a nearby schoolhouse. Luckily, somebody thought to hurry to the basement and fire up the furnace so the steam elevators would run, thus speeding the task of removing goods from the doomed store. For it was doomed, in spite of all the partners and their faithful employees could do. By morning nothing was left but smoking ruins and twisted steel. A significant notice was posted on a pole stuck in the rubble: "Cash Boys & Work Girls will be Paid what is due them Monday 9 A.M. Oct. 16th at 60 Calumet Ave. Field, Leiter & Co."

In two days Field found a new business site—a brick barn at State and Twentieth streets which had been built by the Chicago City Railway Company as quarters for its horses. Here the merchandise salvaged from the fire was arranged on pine counters hastily set up in the horse stalls. New orders arrived from New York in such quantity that bobtail horsecars were needed to help haul the goods from the railroad depot. In Field's opinion speed was vital. The big store that opened first after the fire would not only make money but would be doing an important service for Chicagoans. All but $750,000 of the firm's $2,500,000 loss was covered by insurance. Less than two weeks after the catastrophe the partners announced their new location, adding, "We sincerely thank our friends for their many kind expressions of sympathy and hope soon to renew our former pleasant business relations."

In the spring Field and Leiter moved to Market and Madison streets. It soon became clear that the ladies did not care to travel so far west to shop. State Street, rebuilt after the fire, was again Chicago's logical shopping center, and back to State Street Field and Leiter moved their store. Business continued to be excellent. Even the panic of 1873 failed to hurt the firm. Soon they were expanding their delivery system, which before had hardly existed, except when an errand boy occasionally carried packages to waiting carriages. Now, for $2 a week, boys were hired specifically for the purpose of making deliveries to residences within a few miles of the store. At first the youngsters went on foot, later on the cable cars. As the store and the city grew, the delivery boys were replaced by horse-drawn delivery carts. When an epidemic of distemper hit Chicago horses, the store used oxen for deliveries.

Today Field's corps of delivery men, more than four hundred strong and making about twenty-five thousand deliveries a day from store-owned trucks painted a special green, are trained to be good-will ambassadors. A Field deliveryman wouldn't think of barging right up a customer's steps with a Christmas sled or bicycle. He reconnoiters first, empty-handed. If the coast is clear he goes back to his truck for the gift; often he is requested to leave it with a neighbor. He knows which of the customers on his route have a new baby that may wake up screaming if he leans on the doorbell at nap time.

He is a regular Boy Scout when it comes to good deeds. Maybe he'll be called upon to climb up a house and open the window for a customer who has forgotten her key, or pack down snow in a driveway with his big truck tires to clear the way for the owners' car. Frequently he returns small children or pets who have strayed. One Field driver, seeing an elderly lady slip and fall on an icy street, promptly stopped his big furniture truck and rushed to her rescue. By the time an ambulance reached the scene the lady, wrapped in quilted furniture pads, was resting comfortably on the cushions the driver had pulled from chairs and sofas in his truck. Field's deliverymen are proud of their ten-million-mile no-accident record. Some of them have been on the same route for forty years.

In 1877 fire once more ravaged the Field and Leiter store on State Street. The Italian-style building which the Singer sewing machine people had put up for Field was destroyed, and with it $750,000 worth of merchandise covered by insurance. The Chicago *Tribune* reported: "The destruction of St. Peter's at Rome could hardly have aroused an apparently deeper interest than the destruction of this palatial dry goods establishment." Again the partners moved, to a vacant hall on the lake front. An offer from the Singer people to sell Field what was left of the store, plus the corner lot, was declined. Singer put up a new building and offered to rent it to Field; this too was declined and James Bolton, the Singer agent in Chicago, leased the structure to Carson, Pirie and Company. But Field changed his mind and wound up paying the Singer company $700,000 for it and giving Carson, Pirie $100,000 to relinquish its lease.

Field and Leiter took possession of their new store in 1879. There was a uniformed official greeter at the entrance. Clerks no longer shouted, "Cash! Come Cash!" The cash boys, scrubbed and brushed until they shone, now had numbers. Tense in their tight-fitting uniforms, they waited on a bench for their numbers to flash on a nearby board. There were still only two elevators, but they were fancy ones, and a splendid staircase led to the second floor. An impressive stock of carpets and upholstery occupied the entire third floor, while on the fifth three hundred women worked at making dresses.

Field and Leiter parted in 1881. Leiter, never an easy man to get along with, did not share Field's enthusiasm for the retail end of the business. Field proposed a figure at which either of the partners might buy or sell the business. He named $2,500,000, low for a business with sales of more than $24,000,000 the previous year. Leiter made up his mind to buy, only to discover what Field had already made sure of—that none of the key executives would stay with Leiter in case Field left. Leiter was cornered, and he knew it. "You win, Marshall," he said. "I'll sell."

At forty-seven, Marshall Field was one of the richest men in America. The country boy had made good in Horatio Alger style. Spare and erect in carriage, with cold blue-gray eyes, prematurely gray hair and ruddy complexion, he was a dignified, aloof figure who wore white gloves even in summer. Although he and his ailing wife lived with their two children in a mansion on Prairie Avenue, Field never cared for lavish ostentation. His tastes were simple, his friends few, his life—outside of the store—lonely and pathetically lacking in satisfactions that his wealth should have brought him. His wife, Nannie, spent more and more of her time abroad, trying to regain her health; she died in France in 1896.

The standards for even the humblest of Field's employees were high. Wages and praise were skimpy, but the prestige of working for Field's made up for these lacks. Field's had "tone," a quality which was recognized even in shoplifting circles. One shoplifter, an oldtimer who was nabbed repeatedly by the store detectives, was asked why she didn't sometimes work the other side of the street instead of concentrating so faithfully on Field's. The lady explained why. "I'm no jitney thief boosting cheap stuff," she said. "I work your store because you got all the best stuff in the city!"

Though Field's usual attitude toward his employees was one of awe-inspiring reserve, he could on occasion be surprisingly indulgent. Once two clerks playing with a heavy basket on wheels managed to send it careering down the aisle just in time to hit Field and knock him down. The clerks were struck dumb with horror. But Field's only comment was: "Boys, don't forget to be gentlemen." Again, when he happened on four clerks who had organized an impromptu quartet during working hours, he remarked: "Sing it again, boys, but this time just a little softer." It was his custom to arrive every morning at nine o'clock. He rode only part of the way in his carriage; the last few blocks he covered on foot. No morning passed without his making a tour of the store, during which his sharp eye noted mistakes and commendable performances alike. After conferences with his department managers he repaired to the wholesale store, where a similar routine was repeated. This system enabled Field to spot talented executive material among his employees.

The career of John G. Shedd is a case in point. As a clerk in the women's neckwear section, Shedd attracted Field's attention and approval through a method he worked out for keeping track of sales by sizes so that the store's buyers would have an accurate basis for their purchases. The method, when tried out, was a success, and Shedd advanced rapidly.

A man who worked his way up from office boy at Field's was Harry Gordon Selfridge, who later became a merchant prince in his own right in London. Selfridge, known as "Mile-a-Minute Harry," was a fountain of spectacular and imaginative ideas. As general manager of the retail store, he hired a window-display genius named Arthur Frazer away from a store in Creston, Iowa, and Field's show windows became world famous. Selfridge lit up the merchandise displays with more and more electric globes. He tripled the number of telephones in the store, and today the store handles more than a million telephone orders a year. He ripped out counters and piled up assortments of piece goods on tables in the middle of the first floor so that customers could paw through them. At his urging Field increased the newspaper advertising budget but advertising in Sunday newspapers was forbidden. Selfridge himself wrote a good share of the advertising copy; it was exuberant and eye-catching but also completely honest. Basement merchandise was described as "trustworthy" and "less expensive but reliable," out of deference to the store's more conservative partners, who shuddered at such words as "cheap" or "lower priced." Field's sold in the basement as early as 1868 but Selfridge made it a bargain center. Eventually the basement, which grew to be the largest single salesroom in the world, was known as the "Budget Floor."

It was Selfridge, too, who persuaded Field to open a tearoom on the third floor, arguing that many women cut short their shopping to go home or elsewhere for lunch. Customers were quick to appreciate this new convenience. In a year the tearoom was serving as many as fifteen hundred each day. Today Field's entire seventh floor is devoted to five restaurants—the Walnut Room, the Narcissus Room, the English Room, a cafeteria called the Crystal Buffet, and the Veranda ($1.25 in advance, limited menu, no tipping). Field's menus still include such specialties as the chicken pot pie which was featured on the opening day, back in 1890.

Selfridge took advantage of the Chicago World's Fair of 1893 to lure the Infanta Eulalia of Spain and other visitors from all over the world into Field's. At this time an admirer wrote a poem in honor of Field's, calling it "Cathedral of All the Stores." A Wabash Avenue addition to the store was completed that year. Later a new twelve-story building was erected north of the original store and spread over the remainder of the block to Randolph Street. This was advertised as "everybody's store," with low- as well as high-priced items available.

In 1904, Selfridge left Field's to run another store briefly in Chicago and to make and lose two fortunes in London before his death there in 1947. An earlier alumnus of Field's, a $23.08 a fortnight salesman named Montgomery Ward, by this time had founded the great mail-order house bearing his name and earned a great fortune. More recently, the late Fred Harvey, once a Field's basement merchandiser, built the biggest store in Nashville, Tennessee, while the late Hector Escobosa and Egil E. Krogh, executives of a Field's subsidiary, became respectively president of I. Magnin & Co. in California and Sibley, Lindsay & Curr in Rochester, New York. The influence of Field's has been felt throughout retailing.

Marshall Field, the founder, outlived most of his early associates. Golf was his only recreation. On New Year's Day of 1906, he played in the snow, using red balls, with his nephew, Stanley Field; his employee, James Simpson; and Robert Todd Lincoln, the Pullman executive who was the son of the Civil War President. The seventy-year-old merchant caught cold but insisted on making a trip to New York as planned. He developed pneumonia and died there on January 16, disposing of an estate of $120,000,000 in a shrewdly drawn will. The last months of his life had been brightened by a second marriage and shadowed by the mysterious fatal shooting of his son, Marshall Field II, officially termed an accident but later believed suicide. The merchant's funeral was attended by three thousand store employees. One of these, Pierre Funck, veteran of forty-three years who had been left a pension, was so affected that he made a daily pilgrimage to the Field grave, and died himself, apparently of grief.

The store remained as Marshall Field's monument. His grandson and great-grandson of the same name served on its board of directors as did his nephew, Stanley Field, until his death in 1964, but no member of the family has ever run it and the estate's interest has shrunk through the years. Executors of the estate of the fourth Marshall Field, who died September 18, 1965, sold 126,000 of his 177,000 shares at $51.50 a share in 1966 on the Midwest Stock Exchange for a total of $6,498,000.[4]

John Shedd, stepping into Field's shoes as president, took over by tearing down the original store and building a new one which would consolidate all units into one grand whole. The thirty-five acres of selling space in the main store were divided into more than 150 retail sections; a fabulous dome of multicolored Favrile glass, the biggest glass mosaic in existence, was designed by Louis Comfort Tiffany for the light well; a Belgian sculptor was commissioned to develop the central theme of the opening, the contribution of merchants to civilization. Once more Chicago was treated to the full dress of a Field opening. A few years later Field's leased the one remaining corner of the square block, that at Randolph and Wabash, and constructed there a twelve-story building to match the rest. And in 1914 the firm, spreading across the street, put up a twenty-one-story structure to house its famous Store for Men.

Two extraordinary doormen, first Eddie Anderson and then Charles Pritzlaff, the latter a former coachman, greeted Field's carriage-trade customers by name at the Washington Street entrance for many years. Charley in particular made a point of jotting down names and other pertinent details in a notebook. Among the famous names in Charley's book were those of Mrs. Potter Palmer, Grover

Cleveland and Theodore Roosevelt, Prince Henry of Prussia, Mrs. William McKinley, who came to Field's for her inaugural gown, Isadora Duncan, at that time an unknown dancer, and Hetty Green, the richest woman in the world.

Out of the services of these doormen developed Field's personal shopping service and the personal information service desk on the third floor, where courteous experts answer questions about Field's and Chicago, translate for those speaking foreign tongues, find hotel rooms, arrange sight-seeing tours, or just take messages.

It is practically impossible either to surprise or stump Mrs. Phyllis Weaver, head of this service. Somebody in Winnipeg, Canada, called up requesting a Willkie campaign button (years after the campaign) by next noon. The caller had bet he could find a Willkie button within twenty-four hours, and with the help of Field's he won his bet. Every day Mrs. Weaver and her staff are bombarded with questions, not only about where to find what at Field's, but on such historical points as who was mayor of Chicago during the fire. People often leave money at the Personal Information Service Desk to be passed on to some particular charity, and one man used to leave his alimony check there every week.

The shopping service started one morning when the doorman found a note on the Washington Street door, placed there before opening time and ordering a pair of baby shoes and a spool of thread. A LaSalle Street broker had thought up this effortless method of carrying out the shopping errands assigned to him by his wife. The doorman took care of the order himself, and when the broker's coach turned up again in the afternoon the package was ready and waiting. Evidently the broker spread the glad tidings among the other husbands, because from then on similar notes appeared with increasing frequency.[5]

The personal shopping service, with a staff of from 80 to 150 shoppers, averages more than three thousand purchases a day for customers with problems. Often they are complicated problems. There was the Milwaukee woman, for instance, who was going to spend Christmas in Europe and thought it would be nice to take a present for each member of her husband's family. The list of relatives turned out to be forty-seven names long and time was alarmingly short. Then the woman thought of Field's. She turned the list over to the personal shopping service, with a description of each of the forty-seven relatives, and when she boarded her ship in New York there were the forty-seven gifts, each labeled and ready for presentation.

All executives have made a great point of the public-service idea at Field's. During World War I the store was the headquarters for Red Cross and Liberty Loan drives; and when the steamer *Eastland* sank, with a death toll of 812 lives, the survivors were supplied with clothes and other necessities by Field's, and the store's employees worked all night making stretchers to carry the victims on Field trucks to a temporary morgue.

When Shedd retired in 1923, his place was taken by James Simpson, who had started out as an office boy at Field's. In an effort to pump new life into the wholesale part of the business, Simpson built the huge $28,000,000 Merchandise Mart. It was the largest commercial building in the world. Half the space was to be occupied by Field's wholesale and manufacturing divisions, and the rest was to be leased out to jobbers' representatives and manufacturers' agents. But depression was gripping the entire country, there was a dearth of tenants for the Mart, and the wholesale division kept on sinking. Even the retail store, for the only time in its history, lost money in 1932.

A. T. Stewart, John Wanamaker and Macy's years earlier had built up big manufacturing and wholesale operations only to abandon or reduce them. "Manufacturing is quite another business," explained Wanamaker once, "and a man had better attend to the business he knows." But because Field's wholesale trade had once been highly profitable, Simpson, by then the principal stockholder, and others clung to the idea of integration.

His successor, John McKinlay, who rose from cash boy to president of the store, struggled with the growing losses. Simpson, who was board chairman, could help but little. Chicago banks had given him the even greater task of salvaging something from the wreckage of the Insull utility empire. Year after year, retail earnings were almost wiped out by wholesale losses.

In 1935, James O. McKinsey, a noted management consultant,

was called in by the directors. Once professor of accounting and marketing at the University of Chicago, and a founder of the management-consulting firm bearing his name, he had improved the workings of several companies. Pointing out that wholesale had lost $12,000,000 in five years, he recommended that the losing operations be lopped off. He was put in as chairman, the first time an outsider had such a job at Field's, and McKinlay resigned.

In what came to be called "McKinsey's purge," domestic jobbing and eight hundred wholesale employees were dropped. Manufacturing operations were streamlined. But McKinsey was unfamiliar with retailing and Field traditions. When cotton and wool went down instead of up after he had made heavy purchases for the manufacturing division, he found himself in hot water with the directors. He died in 1937, a victim of worry and work as well as pneumonia. While it took more than a decade, virtually all of his recommendations were carried out, and employees who once derided McKinsey came to speak of him with respect. Frederick D. Corley, the president, became executive officer and continued in charge until retirement in 1943.

Hughston M. McBain, once an office boy for John Shedd and a Field's man since 1922, then became president. He was only forty but had had experience in every part of the business. At the same time, James L. Palmer, a native of Maine and a graduate of Brown University, became first vice president and second in command. Palmer had come to Field's in 1937 from the University of Chicago, where he was professor of marketing. He also had been an adviser to Sears, Roebuck and Co. and a number of other firms. The two worked as a team to regain Field's profits and prestige.[6]

One step was the opening of the "28 Shop," so called because of the 28 Washington Street address, the old carriage entrance of the store. Reached by a private elevator, each of the twenty-eight luxurious fitting rooms has a telephone, and there are facilities for serving lunch or tea in the shop. Here, in a luxurious setting of carpeting, hand-woven draperies, and subtle lights, today's equivalent of the carriage trade views and buys clothes ranging from simple daytime clothes and accessories to fabulous imports.

McBain and Palmer redecorated notable old departments, such as the Store for Men and the book department. Built by Marcella Hahner and Rose Oller Harbaugh, the latter pioneered book fairs and autographing parties in the department stores and has assured the success of many a book. Though its volume is not as great as the Doubleday or Brentano stores, its sales often have run more than a million dollars a year and it disputes Macy's for the honor of being the biggest in the department-store world.

McBain and Palmer modernized employee training. The store's girl elevator operators, who once numbered Dorothy Lamour, later of the movies, were sent to charm school, beginning in 1947. Instruction manuals, little changed since the days of the founder and John Shedd, were revised. A film on employee courtesy, titled *By Jupiter*, proved so successful that prints were sold to other stores. A pension plan paid for by the company was devised. It soon had assets of $26,000,000. With Social Security, this assures many retirees 60 percent of their salaries.

Public relations also received attention. A research firm was employed to determine what the customers thought of the store. Advertising and promotion were expanded. The store became the first to purchase a double-page color spread in *Life*. In local newspapers, a new "newspaper within a newspaper," called *Pace*, proved an effective vehicle for institutional advertising. In 1952, Field's centennial was publicized nationally. A match book promoting the 28 Shop received a 1953 award as the most distinguished example of that form of advertising in the department-store field.

All of the innovations combined to achieve an operation more profitable than many larger companies in the department-store field and enabled the store to solve long-standing financial problems. Rent was eliminated by the purchase of the store site from the Field estate. Half of the preferred stock was retired. Finally in 1946, the Merchandise Mart, a white elephant for most of its existence, was sold to Joseph P. Kennedy for $18,000,000. It was a good deal for both parties. The loss that Field's took materially cut the taxes that otherwise would have been paid in that prosperous year. In 1949, McBain and Palmer became respectively chairman and president. In 1953, the Fieldcrest Mills, last of the firm's textile manufacturing interests, were sold and McBain that year received the Tobé award in recognition of his contributions to retailing.

These transactions made available millions of dollars for expansion. Field's established suburban branches at Lake Forest and Evanston in 1928 and another at Oak Park in 1929. These were modernized and enlarged following World War II. More branches were built beginning in 1954.

Chairman McBain retired in 1958 and was succeeded as chief executive officer by President Palmer. On reaching retirement age in 1964, he was succeeded by Executive Vice President Sivage, general manager of the Chicago stores and a Field man since 1931. David W. Davidson succeeded him and Harry D. Perkins succeeded Davidson as senior vice president. As of 1966, the company had around fifteen thousand full-time employees and some eighteen thousand stockholders.

One of the most important ventures in the history of Field's was the purchase for about $6,000,000 of Frederick & Nelson, Seattle's largest department store. This was founded in 1890 by Donald E. Frederick, son of a Georgia farmer, and Nels Nelson, a Swedish immigrant. The store prospered during the gold rush to Alaska and a new store modeled somewhat on Field's was built in 1918. Nels Nelson died at sea and by 1929 Frederick, then seventy, was ready to retire.

As he admired Field's, which he often visited with his daughter, Frederick called at President Simpson's office. Finding him absent, the Seattle merchant picked up an envelope and wrote on the flap: "I will sell my business to Marshall Field & Company and to them only." After some negotiations, which at one point almost collapsed, the purchase was concluded on July 25, 1929. The staff was almost undisturbed, only treasurer Thomas Lewis going out from Chicago.

William H. St. Clair, a Frederick & Nelson man, became president, and was succeeded by Charles C. Bunker and then William S. Street, a native Californian who for some years was general manager at Field's. He retired in 1962 and was succeeded by Cornelius J. Byrne. Sales, which had been $12,000,000 in 1929 and dropped to half that in the depression, rose to more than $30,000,000 after World War II.

Five additional floors were added to the main store at a cost of $6,250,000, increasing the space 50 percent. Later, an adjoining parking garage costing $3,250,000 was constructed. John Graham & Co., Seattle, were architects for the main store addition and also the suburban branches in Bellevue Square and Aurora Village.

Frederick & Nelson's follows Field's customer-pleasing policies. Mrs. Kathryn Kavanaugh of Seattle, for example, made a trip to Eire and photographed her relatives and Irish scenes in color. On her return, she took the films to Frederick & Nelson to be developed. Somebody lost them. To keep her good will, the store had her list and describe the pictures, then commissioned Joseph Hollander, London photographer for the Fairchild News Service, to retrace Mrs. Kavanaugh's journey and duplicate her pictures.

IX

BRENTANO'S

"Booksellers to the World"

BRENTANO'S, INC., is one of the oldest and most respected names in bookselling. With 31,000 square feet of selling space and 250,000 volumes, its Fifth Avenue headquarters is New York City's largest bookstore. In the United States the only larger bookstores are the Cokesbury store in Dallas, 66,000 square feet, and Kroch's & Brentano's in Chicago, a former affiliate, with 40,000 square feet.[1] There is a Brentano's in Paris, France, once but no longer part of the firm, and a score of branches stretching from Boston to the City of Paris department store in San Francisco, and including The Pentagon in the District of Columbia, which are owned by the firm.

Since its purchase by the Crowell-Collier Publishing Company in 1962 from Nixon Griffis and others, Brentano's has had a remarkable revival and expansion. Leonard Schwartz, who joined the main store at seventeen as a stockboy, became president. This and all its branches became culture centers, selling paintings, statuary, prints and sometimes jewelry as well as books. Sales doubled in two years, reaching $4,850,000 in 1964 and $5,660,000 in 1965.

The Fifth Avenue store has been expanded upward, downward and laterally and now has entrances also on both West Forty-seventh and West Forty-eighth streets. Inside the Fifth Avenue air-curtain door is a Wall of the Muses. Here titles of poetry, music and the performing arts are arranged under the appropriate muse of ancient mythology. Books of epic poetry are under a sign CALLIOPE, MUSE OF EPIC POETRY. A series of Thursday-evening cultural events, including a recital of Japanese koto music, attracted hundreds to the remodeled store.

The firm owes its success to a combination of nostalgic friendliness, reminiscent of the tiny bookshop, and shrewd operation. New books cost less in quantity, the difference between 40 and 45 percent, or more, a margin which may mean profit or loss to a store. Hard-headed Brentano buyers disregard pressures of all kinds from publishers to order the quantity their intuition tells them is the optimum. Their intuition is sound and, by correctly estimated original orders, Brentano's usually enjoys maximum discounts. At the same time, clerks and branch managers, some of them women, know the tastes of many customers so well that books are sent them unordered and returns are few.

Leading writers of the day, visitors such as the King of Greece and notables as varied as the daughters of President Lyndon B. Johnson and Greta Garbo are among Brentano's shoppers. Through the years, is has managed to create about itself a blend of the romance and knowledge that its customers seek in the books it sells. It has maintained this unique fame and prestige despite fire, book clubs, bankruptcy and inroads on the time of the human race by motion pictures, automobiles, radio and now television.

The business was founded by an enterprising immigrant news vendor shrewd enough to supply sporting news ahead of his competitors. August Brentano was young, ambitious, and newly arrived from Austria in 1853 when he set up a newsstand in front of the New York Hotel. Newspapers and magazines at that time usually were peddled from door to door; but the hotelkeeper allowed Brentano this desirable space because he was handicapped by a withered arm.

Discovering that the hotel guests, who included visitors from abroad, were betting on the great English horse races, Brentano ordered newspapers from England and met the clipper ships bringing them at the dockside. The Atlantic cable was still in the future and

Brentano's newspapers made him first with the racing news. He prospered and moved his stand to a hallway of the old Revere House, at Broadway and Houston Street. Above the table, which offered some books as well as papers, he had an imposing sign reading "Brentano's Literary Emporium."

The John Heenan–Tom Sayers prizefight in England, in which an American and an Englishman fought a bloody thirty-five-round draw for the heavyweight championship, aroused so much interest that young Brentano sold great bundles of papers at $1 apiece, and became rich enough to open a real emporium in 1860. His store was a basement at first; seven years later it took up half the building at 708 Broadway. The other half was occupied by the Frohmans' tobacco business, conducted by the fathers of Charles and Daniel Frohman, famous theater managers.

Brentano's, because it catered to a cosmopolitan patronage and offered foreign books and periodicals unobtainable elsewhere, became a rendezvous for the fashionable hotel guests from across the street, and for "the carriage trade" from all over the city. By 1870, when August moved his store to an even better residential neighborhood, at 33 Union Square, next door to the Goelet mansion and just down the block from Tiffany's, Brentano's was already one of New York's landmarks. In the next two decades, the Union Square store acquired a reputation throughout the country. Sightseers came to gape at the browsers, who included Ralph Waldo Emerson, Lillian Russell, John Drew, Charles Dickens, James Russell Lowell, General U. S. Grant, and other socially important or wealthy customers.

August, by his enterprise and resourcefulness, created a successful business. His nephew, Arthur, who started in the store in 1873 and sold books from the floor for seventy-one years, made Brentano's an institution. He was fifteen years old at the time he first set foot in the store. A cholera epidemic in Cincinnati had killed his father, a sister and brother. His mother moved with the remaining six children to Evansville, where she had two brothers, and soon thereafter Arthur was sent to his uncle in New York to earn his fortune.

His first job was a paper route for the store, from Broadway to the East River. Later, because he did so well at it, he was rewarded with a route that reached to Central Park. He delivered papers morning and evening; during the day he sorted books and also delivered them, becoming so familiar with the stock that he was consulted by the customers in preference to the senior salesmen. The best sellers with which he dealt in those days were by such authors as Louisa May Alcott, T. B. Aldrich, Lew Wallace, Bret Harte, Mark Twain, and William Dean Howells.

A few years after Arthur's arrival at the store, his younger brothers, Simon and August Brentano, came from Evansville and were taken into the business. The store was open seven days a week, 9 A.M. to 8 P.M. All worked hard. In 1882, the three brothers bought out their uncle. August, Sr., by then an elderly man, wanted to retire and make a tour of the world. Afer extensive farewells, he got as far as Montreal, when nostalgia brought him back to the Union Square store. Until his death in 1886, he remained there, working at the cashier's desk.

Meanwhile, in 1884 Brentano's opened a Washington branch; and in 1887 Arthur went to Paris to open another branch. Three years later, in Paris, he married a California girl, Maria Louise Sepulveda Lan Franco. His best man was Robert Chambers, the novelist, and another friend at the ceremony was Whitelaw Reid, publisher of the New York *Tribune* and American Ambassador to the Court of St. James's.

Financial difficulties first afflicted Brentano's after the great business depression of 1893. Another disaster occurred in 1898. The Union Square establishment and all its stock were destroyed by a fire that started in the house next door, and the store had to be rebuilt. To straighten out their finances at this crisis, Simon Brentano sued his two brothers for dissolution of the partnership, and in 1899 the firm was reorganized. Simon became president. Charles E. Butler, president of the American Booksellers Association, who represented the publishers' interests in working out credit, became secretary; and Clive Mecklim, a veteran employee, was made treasurer.

Arthur, who hated office work, fled from financial statements and wanted to stay with his books, was named vice president. Arthur had never been to high school, a fact which embarrassed him all through his life. "I don't know a scrap of Latin or Greek," he once explained, "and for more than sixty years I have been in perpetual fear of being exposed." He learned French and German fluently, however, and through the books he handled gave himself a remarkable education. His courtly manners, his impeccable appearance—he always wore a navy-blue suit, starched collar, dark tie, and pince-nez—and his considerable knowledge made him a great favorite with the customers; indeed, in the store he became the good friend of many eminent men and women in art, politics and society.

He inaugurated the old and rare department, which became his special pride. As well as collecting fine old books of great value, the store was also offering a service at that time unique among bookstores—scouring the market to locate any publication requested, no matter when and where published, including privately printed pamphlets, books and periodicals in foreign languages, first editions, out of print, and other rare items. This service brought Brentano's orders from all over the world and gave it international importance in the book world.

Arthur Brentano once listed the two things that he liked most about his business: "Getting a nice library . . . good, solid, useable, permanent books," and "Making a good sale—getting those good, solid, useable, permanent books into the hands of an appreciative buyer." Arthur's idea of hospitality—that each customer should be greeted at the door and made welcome—was followed as long as he was alive.

A reporter for *Publishers' Weekly,* who interviewed this gentleman when he was eighty, remarked that Arthur Brentano was always at the door. For years the reporter had been visiting the store and talking to him without realizing it. "Brentano," he wrote, "had been as gracious, as friendly, as urbane, as kindly, as communicative when I bought nothing as if I were negotiating for the four Shakespeare folios."

Sales clerks hired by Arthur Brentano were carefully selected and instructed by him to maintain the store's tradition of boundless erudition and limitless, unhurried service. Laurence Gomme, long head of the old and rare department, recalled that, when he arrived from England in 1907 and applied for a job, Arthur subjected him to a lengthy test of his knowledge, manners, and grooming, then hired him at $12 a week. It was considered a distinction and rare privilege just to work for Brentano's.

In 1907, Brentano's, keeping up with the fashionable trend, moved again, this time to Twenty-seventh Street and Fifth Avenue. In this new headquarters, a great deal of literary history was made. "I can remember the wonderful store they had down there," recalled Bennett Cerf, the publisher, years later in the *Saturday Review*.[2] "There were originals of all the magazine covers in the side-street windows and the huge pile of periodicals from all over the world in the basement! Theodore Roosevelt came in one day and ordered the pigskin library that he took with him to Africa. The store had an indescribable glamour; the staff harbored some rare and congenial personalities." Mayor William Jay Gaynor of New York, Andrew Carnegie, J. P. Morgan, Henry Clay Frick, George Ade, Oliver Herford and other celebrities of the period congregated at the Twenty-seventh Street store. There an autographing party for Gertrude Stein was mobbed by her readers and nonreaders. The firm discontinued the sale of sheet music, newspapers and theater tickets but there were more books and magazines. Displays of art work for the covers of these by Charles Dana Gibson, Montgomery Flagg, Maxfield Parrish and others attracted a daily crowd.

When Simon Brentano died in 1914, Arthur became president. The sons of these brothers—Lowell and Arthur Brentano, Jr., joined the business. Since the elder Brentano continued to avoid administrative details and devoted himself to rare books, his son worked at retailing, store management and the development of branches. It was a period of expansion for the firm. Additional New York branches were established, and stores followed in Pittsburgh, Cleveland and Philadelphia.

An author and playwright himself, Lowell Brentano in 1918 took charge of the firm's publishing department after his graduation from Harvard, where he attained Phi Beta Kappa despite a serious congenital hearing defect. This part of the business previously had been directed by Volney Streamer and the late Temple Scott. From 1879 to 1881, Brentano's published a magazine of field and water sports;

from 1881 to 1882 it issued a chess monthly. In place of catalogs, announcements, and a monthly bulletin previously supplied to its customers, the store in 1907 started *Book Chat,* advertised as "a periodical which should be chained to the desk of every man in search of literary information." Subscription was first 25 cents, then $1 a year. *Book Chat* offered news about books and authors, notes written by prominent authors, answers to queries, scholarly information about old and rare books and manuscripts offered for sale at Brentano's; and, of course, announcements of the new books—including those in Spanish, Italian, German and French—which Brentano's stocked. South American literature and foreign Christmas cards also were advertised.

At the same time Brentano's published noteworthy books. It was the first to print the plays of George Bernard Shaw in America and the letters in the company's files attest to the fact that, even then, Shaw was a vigorous and unorthodox correspondent. Other Brentano authors included George Moore, Margaret Sanger, whose books on birth control were the subject of violent controversy; David Loth, Robert Briffault, Eugène Brieux, and Channing Pollock.

The Brentano family once went to meet the unpredictable Shaw when he landed in New York. An elaborate program was planned but the great dramatist remained only a few hours and sailed home the next day. Later in London, Arthur Brentano one day rushed in to his daughter, Rowena, and said, "Come, Lambie, it's time for lunch with Mr. Shaw." Rowena replied, "Papa, I'd rather stay here and knit if I may."

All Brentano departments were profitable as the main store moved northward again in 1926 to its present location. The new store, a journalist noted, had the "same admirable features" as the old with "The varied and enormous stock, the easily accessible galleries, comprehensive foreign department administered by clerks who understand the languages of the literature to which they are accredited, and the fascinating display of periodicals on the tables of the basement." The Bible, a steady seller at Brentano's, was stocked in several versions and a dozen languages. There were thousands of technical books.

Books of its own authors sold well and those by Sinclair Lewis,

F. Scott Fitzgerald and Anita Loos went by thousands to the customers. American tourists going to Europe read books from Brentano's in New York on the way over and from Brentano's store in Paris on the way back. In 1928, Arthur Brentano, Jr., told the convention of the American Booksellers' Association that the store had delivered as many as twenty thousand books to one liner. The firm's sales were more than $3,000,000 a year.

The stock market crashed the next year just as the first novel of a writer named Thomas Wolfe appeared. The book business was hit hard. With a huge inventory of expensive books, several new branches, and a big new main store, Brentano's was in serious financial trouble. Because it was one of the largest retail outlets for books in the world, publishers could not afford to see it go out of business. A publishers' committee took over the management.

Salaries were cut drastically, in some cases to as low as $7 and $12 a week, but employees continued loyally at their jobs. The American rights to the plays of George Bernard Shaw were sold to Dodd, Mead & Company. The remainder of the Brentano book publishing department went to Coward–McCann. At this point, Lowell Brentano left the firm, except for an interest in the Paris branch, and devoted himself successfully to his own writing. He lived until 1950, turning out plays, novels, motion-picture scenarios, anthologies and a final book, *Ways to Better Hearing,* inspired by his own lifelong struggle against deafness.

As the depression deepened, the business shrank further. All outlets except the main store in New York and the branches in Washington, Chicago and Paris, were discontinued. But even these economies were not enough. After the "bank holiday" in 1933, Brentano's was bankrupt. The Irving Trust Company was named receiver.

A savior appeared in the person of an urbane Brentano customer, Stanton Griffis, a partner in the investment banking firm of Hemphill, Noyes & Co. and a man of many other interests. He was chairman of the executive committee of Paramount Pictures and the Lee Tire & Rubber Co., and a director of Madison Square Garden. He had backed some Katharine Cornell stage productions and reorganized many corporations. He heard of the plight of Brentano's in the course of a bridge game on his yacht and promised to help. "I thought it would be amusing," he explained later, "to see what a hard-headed businessman could do in such a situation with a famous name like Brentano's as an asset."

On June 4, 1933, Griffis paid $150,000, only $72,000 of it in cash, for nearly all of the firm's assets. It had grossed $1,500,000 the previous year, listed assets at $745,983 and liabilities at $511,445. Three-year notes were signed for the remainder and book publishers assured Griffis liberal credit. He was joined in the purchase by Adolph Kroch, a leading Chicago bookseller, who acquired a 20 percent interest. After three years, Kroch was given the Chicago branch and bought out in New York. Merged later in larger quarters on South Wabash Street, Kroch's & Brentano's advertises as "the world's largest bookstore."

Griffis became chairman of the board of Brentano's, Inc., as the new firm eventually was titled. The courtly Arthur Brentano continued as president until his death in 1944 and his son, Arthur, Jr., remained as vice president and general manager. Some of Griffis's bookish Wall Street friends, Amos Tuck French, Winky Thomas and Bruce Ryan among them, came to work in the store for a time but Griffis himself remained so much in the background that fifteen years later a noted Broadway columnist breathlessly printed: "Has Stanton Griffis purchased the Brentano bookstores?"

While Griffis had counseled his friend, Arthur Brentano, Sr., against expanding earlier, the financier, when he took charge, believed on the basis of business trends that a chain of bookstores could be run something like the A & P, or even Woolworth's, and bookselling could profit from an application of similar large-scale merchandising. This seemed valid for a time. Under his regime, the business quickly began to improve. Thousands bought *Anthony Adverse* and *Gone with the Wind,* the heavyweight historical romances that were the best sellers of the depression. "Best sellers are the vitamins of the book business," explained Joseph Margolies, formerly Washington manager who then became vice president and chief buyer. "They bring in the customers who buy not only the best seller but a classic like *David Copperfield* for a niece or nephew."

Griffis amazed his publisher creditors by paying their notes after only six months, giving them a 35 percent return on their claims against the old company. The firm earned profits in 1937, operated at a deficit of $16,918 in 1938, and from the next year onward had profits through World War II.

A branch was reopened in Philadelphia. More branches were opened in the Washington area, including one on the concourse of the Pentagon Building. Under the management of Mrs. Virginia Ward it soon numbered the highest military brass as customers. A leased department established in the City of Paris store in San Francisco under Sybil Bardshar became the largest bookstore west of Denver. Lillian Friedman was promoted from there to be chief buyer for the firm. Several other branches were opened, including one at Waikiki Beach, Hawaii, to which Horace Hutchins was dispatched as manager after a hilarious hula-hula party.

World War II caused a boom in the book business. With gasoline rationed and television still in the future, some bought and read books to forget their worries. Brentano's sold twenty-eight thousand copies of Kathleen Winsor's *Forever Amber*. More bought books to help them qualify for commissions or to obtain jobs in war industry. Soaring taxes created a demand for the works of J. K. Lasser, Brentano's own tax adviser. Hundreds of copies of Professor Smyth's *Atomic Energy for Military Purposes* were sold. Governments bought books in quantity for instructional and propaganda purposes.

At the request of the Free French government, Brentano's returned profitably to publishing during the struggle. With French publishing plants in the hands of the enemy and the sale of their books banned in occupied countries, Brentano's produced paper-backed editions in French of the works of writers like André Maurois, Pierre Lazareff and André Girard. These were shipped by the thousands to North Africa, the French colonies and via the underground into occupied France.

The Brentano branch in Paris, at 37 Avenue de l'Opéra and extending through to Rue des Petits Champs, felt the tramp of Nazi soldiery. As the Wehrmacht marched into the city in June of 1940, the store executives, who were British subjects, fled by motorcycle and bicycle to the coast. The French employees remained until the

Nazis took over. But first an official of a German library walked in and placed an order for 6,000 books, including 349 assorted titles in Everyman's Library, a variety of art books, the unexpurgated *Lady Chatterley's Lover* and some expensive erotica. He paid 755,000 francs for his order and sent trucks to carry the books away.

After that the Nazis confiscated without payment all leather goods, stationery, fountain pens, guidebooks, dictionaries, encyclopedias, maps and atlases; and converted the premises into the official film and camera supply center for the Wehrmacht in Paris. The firm name on the windows was covered over with black paint; the fixtures and remaining stock were moved to the rear of the store and to the basement. In a period of almost five years, the converted photo shop, which was also a place where German soldiers could have their pictures taken or developed, made a profit of a million francs ($20,000). Deposited in a Paris agency, and left behind when the Nazis departed hurriedly, that money was turned over to Brentano's by the French government after the liberation.

When Arthur Brentano, Jr., who became president of the firm at his father's death, reached Paris on March 15, 1945, he found that, along with hundreds of pictures of German soldiers, in the cluttered-up basement and rear of the store approximately one-third of the previous stock remained—about twelve thousand books. The concierge and his wife, who had lived in the concierge apartment on the premises all through the occupation and had tried to protect what they could of Brentano's property, and the office secretary were also waiting for him. While they were all digging through the debris to clean up and refurbish the place, a truck arrived with a shipment of five hundred books; these had been ordered from London early in 1940, had been stored in a Paris warehouse during the German occupation, and were now being delivered per order.

To determine prices in the new inflated currency Brentano simply marked up each item 500 percent of its prewar price. That was in line with the inflated prices existing in other Parisian bookstores and also permitted the firm to buy books in France, where they were expensive, to restock the depleted shelves.

By great effort and much slashing of red tape, he managed to reopen the store on April 19, giving it the distinction of being the first American retail establishment in the city to resume business. The first customer on the day of reopening was an American sergeant who bought two Penguin books—*Walden* and *City of Beautiful Nonsense.* This Parisian shop, which since its beginning in the eighties has been a favorite meeting place for Americans traveling abroad, began to do a thriving business with European customers, too, filling the great demand for American technical books useful in rebuilding war-devastated areas.

Sales volume of Brentano's passed $4,000,000 in the years following the war but profits dropped and some branches failed to develop enough volume to sustain themselves. Beginning in 1948 the firm operated at a loss for three years. By this time the versatile Stanton Griffis was far away. During the war, he had embraced a chance to make history as well as sell books about it. He headed government missions to England, Finland, Spain, Portugal and Sweden, in the last stopping the export of vital ball bearings to Germany. He served as Red Cross Commissioner in the Pacific. He then became successively ambassador to Poland, Egypt, Argentina and Spain.

He wrote of Brentano's and bookselling as well as diplomacy, in an autobiographical volume, *Lying in State,* published on his return from Spain in 1952.[3] Among difficulties besetting a bookseller, he listed: the book clubs, which sell some current books at lower prices than the wholesaler can buy them; and the department store "loss leader," a method of attracting customers into the department store by selling items such as books at lower than cost. These practices, Griffis charged, have been promoted by publishers. "In no other industry," he said, "does the manufacturer go to such lengths and use such vicious means to destroy his outlets." Finally, in this list of forces that cut profits in the bookselling business, he mentioned unions. In the old days, he related, bright young intellectuals found the satisfaction of working in a bookstore to be payment enough, and so they worked for very little. At present, the unions "tell us what we should pay everyone in the business from the shipping clerk to the buyer." Years earlier, incidentally, Arthur Brentano and some other booksellers had protested the book clubs by refusing to sell the early selections of the Literary Guild. The gesture was abandoned when it was found that its only effect was to deprive the stores of more sales.

His investment in Brentano's, Griffis said, had brought him fun rather than cash. "I would spend sleepless nights of horror if I heard that any customer of Brentano's felt that we had made a profit on his purchase," he wrote. "We are in trade only for dignity, atmosphere and service." And to make this point even more emphatic, he added, "I am happy to have had the experience of high hopes and failure in the retail bookselling business."

But even as the diplomat wrote, his son, Nixon Griffis, was making the century-old enterprise again a profitable one. Like his father Nixon was a graduate of Cornell University, where he studied astronomy and became a boxing champion. After Army service and work at Hemphill, Noyes, he joined Brentano's in 1947 as secretary of the firm. In 1949, he became president and the next year, on the retirement of Arthur Brentano, Jr., became chairman of the board as well. Young Griffis was then thirty-two. Leonard Schwartz, who had been with the firm since 1937, except for war service, became vice president.

Changes involved both expenditures and economies. The Paris branch was modernized. At a cost of $100,000, the main New York store was refurbished and rearranged to do the same business in less space. The Waikiki Beach branch was sold and Horace Hutchins returned to take charge in Philadelphia. Several branches were closed. Machine bookkeeping replaced a hand ledger system with a reduction in cost and a gain in efficiency. Modern window displays were introduced.

Branches established for a time on the *Independence* and *Constitution,* new liners of the American Export Line sailing to the Mediterranean, proved reasonably profitable from a business standpoint and tremendously successful from a Brentano's morale point of view. The floating branches and libraries were managed each cruise by a manager or employee who had done an outstanding job in New York or Washington. Many cruise passengers, however, felt that their passage should include free library service, as it does on many liners, and the free voyages to Naples, Capri, Sorrento, Genoa and the Riviera came to an end.

Efforts were made to find merchandise that could be sold along with the books, magazines and stationery that are the backbone of the business. Sophisticated greeting cards by artists like Rosalind Welcher proved successful. So did games like Scrabble, which Brentano's discovered early; many purchasers were found for a $15 toy planetarium. Seashells, records, 16-millimeter films and rare postage stamps did not work out at the main store though stamp albums continued to be sold. More successful were reproductions of museum statuary which, in most cases, had been available previously only in the museums owning the Aphrodites, Han Dynasty horses and Egyptian Sacred Cats.

In 1953, Brentano's centennial year which passed without any special celebration, it all added up to give the venerable enterprise a modest profit on sales of $2,823,326. This was roughly a million dollars more than the volume from many more outlets a decade earlier. The unique commerce between Brentano's far-flung customers and its erudite employees continued.

Much of Brentano's durability is due to its employees, remarkable both for their learning and their loyalty to the enterprise. Scholarly George W. Stair, who formerly ran his own bookstore in Rockefeller Center, came out of retirement to head the rare-book and fine-binding department.

Customers of Brentano's include the famous, the learned and the eccentric. Most notable of all, perhaps, was twenty-three-year-old Dorothy Arnold, daughter of a millionaire. On December 12, 1910, she bought a novel from Ernest Dell, a salesman in the New York Brentano store. She then stepped out into the Fifth Avenue traffic and was never heard from again. Her family exhausted its fortune seeking her and the case remains New York's leading unsolved mystery.

Many of the names on Brentano's charge accounts have been the subject of books. They include the country's artistic, social, political and financial leaders, as well as scientists and specialists in every field. The firm's mail-order business is even more remarkable. It has a mailing list of seventy-five thousand persons living in every corner of the globe. To customers from Allahabad to Zomba, Brentano's importance rests not only on the forty thousand titles it keeps in stock, and on its long-standing ability to obtain others, but also on the fact that the United States for years after World War II was the only country where so many books were freely obtainable. The war's destruction of great libraries abroad, paper shortages, political and economic restrictions in other countries enhanced the value of American books. Also in many underdeveloped countries and those rebuilding after the war, there was a great curiosity about this country, especially about our technical skills. Brentano's, as the best-known American bookseller, became a kind of literary United Nations.

The Brazilian government, for example, ordered $8,000 worth of books to be sent to its embassies all over the world. One of the books listed in the order was out of print, and Brazil wanted a thousand copies. So Macmillan, the publisher, printed a special edition at Brentano's request.

Unless asked to do so, Brentano's does not attempt to guide or improve a customer's taste. An order for "60 feet of white books" to fit the decorative scheme of a customer's new apartment was filled without comment largely with volumes from Italy, where publishers favor such bindings. Attempts of pressure groups to censor or prevent the sale of books usually are ignored by Brentano's though titles likely to incite any important segment to riot are not displayed prominently.

Early in his career as a bookseller, Stanton Griffis refused to stock *The Truman Merry-Go-Round* by Robert Allen and W. V. Shannon because it was critical of Griffis as an ambassador. Drew Pearson reported the fact and the book received more notice than it would have otherwise. Since then the Griffis policy has been: "Brentano's believes that the condemnation of any given book should be determined by the courts and the publishers themselves, and not by the booksellers." Friends of Senator Joseph McCarthy were ignored when they attempted to stop Brentano's selling copies of a Senate report on his financial affairs; so were his foes when they protested display of an admiring biography of him.

When the store gave a window to *The Frenchman* by Philippe

Halsman, a French committee protested that the book was in bad taste and would give Americans "the wrong impression of Frenchmen." The author-photographer solved this problem by obtaining a letter from the French ambassador certifying that he found "the book delightful, in excellent taste, and fine for promoting good relations between the two countries." In the next printing, Simon & Schuster left out one of the more sexy photographs in the volume to be on the safe side.

While selling more copies of Rachel Carson's masterpiece on the sea than were initially printed, as well as hundreds of volumes of T. S. Eliot's plays, Brentano's also sold nine thousand copies of Dr. Alfred C. Kinsey's *Sexual Behavior in the Human Male*. Its female sequel, skimmed by countless magazine articles, was much less popular. Mention of this subject at Brentano's recalls two women customers. One with an accent asked a salesman to direct her to "Sex." He took her to the man in charge of the store's array of Havelock Ellis and similar volumes. Everybody was embarrassed. It seemed she wanted directions to the store across the street, Saks Fifth Avenue. At another time, a woman shopper stopped a Brentano employee and asked: "Do you have *Fun in Bed?*" As he was the store detective and unfamiliar with the writings of Frank Scully, he politely replied: "I manage to get along."

Sometimes the courtesy of the Washington staff costs it a sale. One day the embassy of a new and rather backward country telephoned frantically for a book on etiquette to be delivered within a matter of minutes. The distance was too great for this and the clerk asked discreetly what was the problem.

"Somebody left cards for the ambassador with P.P.C. written in the corner," said a desperate diplomatic voice.

"Oh," explained the all-knowing clerk, "that just stands for *pour prendre congé,* French for good-by."

"Thanks," gasped the relieved diplomat, "never mind the book."

X

MACY'S

The Strauses and the Biggest Store

MACY'S, THE WORLD'S LARGEST STORE, in Herald Square, and the ten other stores in its New York division, rang up $3,000,000 in sales one Saturday during the 1965 Christmas season, undoubtedly the highest single day's volume achieved in a metropolitan area by an individual department-store group. The store was in business eighty-six years before its first million-dollar day in 1944, but only thirteen more were required to reach a $2,000,000 day and just eight additional years for the new mark.

Since 1944, R. H. Macy & Co., Inc., has exploded from an organization of seven stores to a nationwide chain of fifty-two in six regional divisions. Between 1956 and 1965, Macy's volume jumped substantially from $398,261,000 to almost $670,000,000. During the same period, its earnings more than doubled to $15,432,000 from $7,634,000.

This gigantic expansion of Macy's was led by Chairman Jack I. Straus, whose family has supplied chief executives of the company for four generations. Other strong merchants—like Ernest L. Molloy, named president of the corporation in 1966; Donald B. Smiley, vice chairman and treasurer; and David L. Yunich, head of the New York division, whose eleven stores have played important roles in this program of retailing growth—helped to push Macy's into its present position. But perhaps the single most important fact in this success story is the remarkable relationship of Macy's and New York.

Macy's is the store that Manhattan built. To New York alone belong the polyglot of its tolerant crowds, its competitive nervousness, its din, its reflex response to the customer. New Yorkers are always mildly surprised to learn their city holds more Italians than Rome, more Jews than Tel Aviv, more Poles than Warsaw. Through the years, though, millions of these shoppers have become convinced that, no matter what they want, they can usually find it at Macy's.

Macy's is fabulous the way New York is fabulous. When an Oriental camel driver invited to America by President Lyndon B. Johnson showed up at the store, someone was available to talk to him in his native Urdu—one of the forty-two languages spoken by fourteen hundred bilingual Macy employees. Tourists visit Macy's just as they do the Empire State Building and the Statue of Liberty. Babies have been born on the premises and a young lady named Ann Macy Hettrich is growing up with a middle name to remind her of where she came into the world.

"The World's Largest Store" has been a Macy slogan since the store moved to Herald Square at Thirty-fourth Street in 1902. This boast was challenged by big John Wanamaker, Marshall Field and J. L. Hudson store buildings erected in later years, but Macy's added additions in 1924, 1928 and 1931 to bring its space to 2,157,330 square feet. Today no one questions the fact that this one store generates higher sales each year than any other.

Every solvent American pays his income tax on the pay-as-you-go plan devised by Beardsley Ruml, long treasurer and later chairman of Macy's. James P. Mitchell, who learned about labor as Macy's director of personnel and industrial relations, was appointed Secretary of Labor by President Dwight D. Eisenhower.

The impact of Macy's is everywhere. "Macy's basement" has passed into the language for any mob scene; "Macy's window" is well understood as the ultimate in public exposure. Traffic engineers say there is statistical truth as well as poetry in these slang expressions.

With an average of 150,000 shoppers a day, the human population per square foot has rivaled the pack of Hindu worshipers along the Ganges, and Macy's windows look out on the intersection of more transportation facilities than any other store enjoys.

A Macy shopper can buy anything from an iguana to a painting by Joan Miró, from a set of Tom Swift books to fresh Beluga caviar. Some nine hundred private-label items are on sale at prices 10 to 15 percent below comparable nationally-advertised brands.

Macy's security force of young men and women chosen for their resemblance to customers is deputized by the New York City police force. Macy's zealously protects their anonymity, even from its own sales staff. They patrol a different beat every day and are not even permitted to eat in the company lunchroom. Four Doberman pinschers (Mom, Red Star, Cash and Suzy) help watchmen guard the Macy treasure house at night.[1]

The store will go to almost any length to rectify an error. Once it mistakenly sent a Christmas gift to a Californian that had been intended for his grandchild in Boston. When Macy's received an irate telephone call from the Westerner on the day before Christmas explaining what had happened, executives searched around until they found a Macyite who was going to Massachusetts for the holidays. The gift was personally delivered to the child, beating Santa Claus by a hair.

Macy's bigness creates a number of small problems as tragicomic as the inability of the fat woman in the circus to tie her own shoelaces. Macy executives have had to use all their wit to cope with the unnaturally large size of the operation. Here is how some problems have been solved:

Problem: How to keep twenty-five thousand purchases a day moving smoothly to the basement for delivery or shipment?

Solution: Once a day a clerk slips a numbered block of wood down each of the nine main tubes and times their appearance on the conveyor belt in the basement. If they don't show up promptly, or if he detects a tell-tale thud, he calls for a professional akin to a chimney sweep who dons protective clothing and slides through the chute to the site of the trouble like a youngster going down the enclosed spiral slide of a fun house at Coney Island.

Problem: How to get over a million dollars in small cash to the bank every day?

Solution: An honest and infallible robot sorts, counts and wraps the change in an elaborately guarded cashier's room mined with secret alarm devices.

Problem: How to maintain the personal touch with hundreds of thousands of customers?

Solution: Customer letters are answered in the same style in which they are written. If Macy's receives a poem, it sends a poem back. Equally adaptable are the complaint adjusters. A woman who bet she could duplicate a $369 antique lamp for practically nothing if she had a picture of it was supplied a photograph. When a newlywed couple didn't get their bedroom set, Macy's sent a bed by special truck to the rescue. In fact, this particular emergency is so painful that the complaint department keeps a special bed in readiness for victims of misdelivered furniture. When the right bed is retrieved, the emergency bed is returned and sterilized for the next time.

Macy's 168 selling departments carry over 400,000 items, half of which didn't exist about a decade ago, and customers simply take it for granted that Macy's has everything. A battery of correspondents cope with letters like the one from the woman who wanted a sort of love seat, "something in which two could snuggle and have the luxurious feeling of being crowded yet not uncomfortable . . . strong and tasteful" or the one from the man who wanted a dead horse for eel bait. President Tubman of Liberia completely furnished his executive mansion from Macy's. Sailors of the U.S.S. *Argonne* once sent the store their 104-page Christmas list, an $8,730 order.

Personal shoppers assist customers looking for a pony, a prefabricated house, an antique chess set, a left-handed pair of scissors, or an elephant hunting rifle. When Macy's advertised Bob Froman's book *One Million Islands for Sale,* salesgirls had to explain that they were selling a book about islands, not the islands themselves. Its dress and coat shops offer high-style French and Italian originals but the emphasis is on inexpensive line-for-line Macy copies of the best from the fashion capitals of the world.

The New York division of Macy's boasts 46,500,000 sales transactions annually, including over 20,000,000 charges to customers' accounts. It has 1,500,000 charge accounts outstanding and issues more than 200,000 new charge plates a year. Other merchants throughout the world marvel at Macy's assortment, value and depth of stock.

To live up to its title as the biggest retailing competitor, Macy's has become one of New York's biggest retail customers. Thirty-six comparison shoppers disguised as typical customers spend as much as $250,000 a year in competing stores. If any identical item is sold for less, the Macy price comes down in twenty minutes flat. Competitive price reductions are posted on a big blackboard and in ordinary times there are some 890 a week. In a battle such as the one following release of many items from fair-trade pricing in 1951, prices may tumble several times a day or as fast as Macy shoppers can phone from their posts in other stores. During that field day for consumers, aspirin tablets, for instance, fell to four cents a hundred. Macy's may buy up the entire stock of a competitor running a limited-quantity loss-leader sale, but store policy forbids a wounded buyer from withdrawing a competitive item from the fray.

Macy's Bureau of Standards, the arbiter of the store's conscience, is unequaled in all retailing. Under laboratory conditions, 7,500 products are annually put through tests of fire, water, high pressure and simulated wear. A flunking mark means that the product—even a private-label item—cannot be sold at Macy's.

Among the 33,000 Macy employees throughout the nation are stylists, carpenters, nurses, chemists, researchers, traffic engineers and tax advisers. These specialists take their place beside the 17,000 salespeople on the firing line who serve 100,000,000 customers a year.

This, then, is Macy's. How did it become the biggest store in the lushest and toughest retail market in the world? Perhaps the best answer is simply the continuity with which the store has maintained three basic policies for over a century: (1) selling at fixed prices; (2) selling for less; (3) advertising vigorously.[2]

Macy's did not invent any of these policies, although all of them were radical when they were adopted. What its founder did was to stick with them as articles of faith through thick and thin and pass them on to successors who stuck to them too. The result of this persistence was not only a fabulously profitable business, but also the development of a new way of retailing, the department store, which was very soon to have many followers.

No such institution existed in 1858 when Rowland Hussey Macy scraped together the resources to start a small fancy dry-goods store with an eleven-foot front on Sixth Avenue near Fourteenth Street.[3] Nor did Rowland Macy himself, all of thirty-six years old, seem likely to create such an institution. A Nantucketer, he had spent what should have been his high-school years on a four-year whaling trip around the world on the *Emily Morgan*.

In 1844, he had started a little thread-and-needle shop on Hanover Street in Boston. It promptly failed, and so did another store in Boston. He made a profitable trading venture in Marysville, California, during the gold-rush days. Then he had another store in Haverhill, Massachusetts, which also did not prosper. Yet, through all these ups and downs, Macy was developing the philosophy of retailing which later made his big New York store a revolutionary influence.

What is known of Rowland Macy hardly adds up to the stereotype of a merchant prince. A stocky, bearded veteran of hard times, he was frugal (he refused to shade the lamps in the store because he was paying for the light) and his temper was hot (he once broke all the umbrellas in stock because a customer complained of a weak handle). He was known to flirt with the girls on buying trips to Europe, lunch long at Delmonico's, play billiards and get religion all over again at a Moody and Sankey revival meeting.

A surviving advertisement for the "Haverhill Cheap Store" might spell Macy's to any modern New Yorker. Headed by the Macy rooster, the very style of the ad is a radical departure from the tombstone formality of trade notices in 1852. It reads, in part:

Macy!!!

Haverhill Cheap Store!

Ever Onward!! Ever Upward!!

English, French and American

DRY GOODS

1. We buy exclusively FOR CASH!!!
2. We sell exclusively FOR CASH!!!
3. We have but one price, and that is named first! No deviation except for imperfection!

These are the three great principles upon which we base our business. Buying *exclusively* for cash, we keep our stock in constant motion and are having new goods from New York, Philadelphia and Boston *every day*. It also enables us to procure many of our goods under the market price, and our customers have the advantage of these bargains for this reason, viz: selling exclusively for cash, we have no bad debts on our books, consequently our good customers do not have to pay them in the shape of extra profits.

By adopting one price and never deviating, a child can trade with us as cheap as the shrewdest buyer in the country.

Possibly because of these principles, the Haverhill Cheap Store failed. In spite of its failure, Macy carried them to his New York store. There obscure changes in distribution were unwittingly creating more favorable conditions for them.

Pre-industrial retail channels were already cracking under the rising volume and diversity of goods pouring from factories—much of it merchandise which had formerly never been sold because it was made and consumed at home. The peddler and the general storekeeper could no longer supply the more sophisticated wants of the growing number of city wage earners. As more everyday necessities had to be bought, shopping became a recurrent chore for customers and they were ready to have it made easier. One store for everything with standard pricing and selling methods could draw patrons from a widening urban area.

Rowland Macy's bid for this dynamic market was unpretentious. On October 28, 1858, he offered ribbons, laces, embroideries, artificial flowers, feathers, handkerchiefs, cambric flouncings, hosiery and gloves on two long counters at 204-206 Sixth Avenue. His first-day sales were $11.06. A specialized shop confined to "fancy goods," an offshoot of the general dry-goods store, the store had the luck to occupy a central crossroads of the growing city. But possibly the most important influence on its spectacular future was Macy himself.

The most important influence on the character of Rowland Macy was that he was brought up a Quaker. In all his retailing ventures he adhered, as a matter of religious principle, to the one-price policy originated by George Fox in 1653. Many other merchants in the New World as well as in Europe had recognized the good business sense of the Quakers, but few merchants before the Civil War could resist the temptation to deviate from it. Implicit in the Quaker thinking were further Macy policies of "true value"—policies which were later to flower in the Bureau of Standards and the fight to sell for less in spite of restricting laws.

Macy had furthermore experienced the seamy side of the credit system, which was the biggest hazard in retailing in his time. Some say that his credit was so badly dented by his previous business failures that a cash policy was sheer necessity. Nevertheless, his early misfortunes with credit convinced him of the competitive advantage of dealing in cash. This was a saving grace during the period of rapid changes and alarms in which he lived.

There was also a fortunate bit of P. T. Barnum in this Nantucket Quaker. He wrote much of that modern-sounding advertising at Haverhill, and the promotional flavor in New York was a reflection of his own personality. By temperament he was fitted to reach out to the new middle-class customers and draw them to his store with informally written messages quoting actual prices to prove his claim of bargains. He was one of the first to use typographic devices to gain attention and spent a healthy 3 percent of sales on advertising at a time when well-established competitors were spending only 1 percent.

But the most dramatic part of the rise of Rowland Macy was the way in which he turned to good account the restlessness and impatience which had early marked him a ne'er-do-well by New England standards of storekeeping. As a young man he had gone whaling, enjoyed gold hunting in California and disappeared from sight on several occasions to engage in nonretailing ventures. Settled down in the New York store, he was to express his need for adventurous fields by taking on new lines of merchandise.

In his first year in business he took a flyer into gloves and hosiery for men, the nucleus of a men's furnishings business. He tried a small stock of towels and sheets and found himself in house furnishings. In 1860 he added a miscellany of "French and German fancy goods" including pocketbooks, tea sets, photograph frames, games, dolls and toys. Four years later came costume jewelry, in 1868 clocks and silver, and in 1869 baby carriages and kitchen utensils.

By 1872 he was scandalizing more conservative competitors by selling books, rocking chairs, garden tools and fancy groceries for picnics. If books for children, why not books for adults? If books, why not stationery and magazines? Soon came velocipedes, bathing suits, barometers and even a short-lived experiment with potted plants. Every year saw wider assortments of each line. It is no accident that he was in Paris hunting for new lines when he died in 1877, leaving an estate of $300,000 to $500,000.

At the time of Rowland Macy's death, there was no doubt that his store was a department store. Among the characteristics of such a store, Macy's filled the bill in these respects.

1. Its volume was large. From $90,000 during the first thirteen months, sales rose to $1,612,788 by 1876.

2. It sold a wide diversity of merchandise in a variety of departments, including white goods, linens, curtains, laces and embroideries, corsets, ladies' underclothing, smallwares and notions, ribbons, silverware, hosiery and furnishings, ladies' ties, furs and parasols, fancy goods, jewelry, toiletries, boys' and youths' clothing, house furnishings, toys and dolls, books, stationery, albums, worsteds and worsted embroidery, china, glass and crockery, soda fountain preparations and candy, kid gloves, millinery, flowers and feathers, ladies' and children's shoes, cloaks and suits, black dress goods and silks.

3. It was organized by departments, each with its own buyer completely responsible for selection of merchandise, amount of stock and profits. Meanwhile, bookkeeping, cash handling, marking and personnel were centralized.

4. It was directed to the woman customer.

5. It was drawing customers from faraway Brooklyn and enticing others by mail order.

6. It offered delivery service, planned the first store lunchroom in America and opened a writing room with the daily papers. Macy's liberal attitude toward the customer and a concern for making shopping convenient presaged further developments in the direction of the "free" services.

The department store Rowland Macy left behind him was already committed to most of the policies for which Macy's has an international reputation today. In addition to competitive, low and fixed prices and aggressive advertising, he left a lasting aversion for extravagant quarters. Quaker and Nantucket simplicity ruled against the marble palaces competing storekeepers were building. Macy's at Fourteenth Street expanded into a labyrinth of nearby buildings which were not primarily designed for retailing. The big store on Thirty-fourth Street is efficient and spacious, but seems designed to give the shopper the impression that overhead is not adding unnecessarily to prices.

Macy was the first great merchant to employ a woman to run what has since aptly been called "a woman's business." In 1860 he engaged Margaret Getchell, a pretty and bright schoolteacher from Nantucket, who was a distant relative, to preside over his cash drawer. She rose to bookkeeper and in 1866 became the store's first general superintendent. Macy not only relied on her aptitude for figures to keep his books, but also generously attributed a large part of his success to her accounting and administrative talent.

Macy even became involved in her social life. When he learned that she had lost her heart to a good-looking young salesman she had seen visiting the store, he connived to bring them together at parties. The upshot was that Abiel T. La Forge took a job in the store to be near its cashier, married her, and wound up as a partner in the business. Appropriately enough, the La Forges lived over the store and Margaret continued to lend a hand when she could spare time from her growing family. Abiel La Forge's pride in Margaret's ability and his respect for her opinion were all that a career wife could wish. "She is the Superintendent, having full charge of the entire business," he boasted in a letter to his sister. "As we sell a million dollars' worth of goods a year and have nearly 200 employees, her position is a very responsible one."[4]

Finally, Macy planned for his own succession so well that his store survived the biggest hazard of a one-man business. Realizing that his son, Rowland, Jr., was unfit for business, Macy shifted increasing responsibility to two junior partners, La Forge and Robert Macy Valentine, the son of his youngest sister. They bought out his estate at his death, but the well-loved La Forge succumbed to tuberculosis. Valentine survived La Forge just long enough to buy out his share and bring in a Macy relative and employee, Charles B. Webster.

Webster had neither extensive funds nor retail experience, but he solved the first problem by marrying Valentine's widow and the second by bringing in a brother-in-law, Jerome B. Wheeler. But, when Webster proceeded to interest himself in a lady employee whom he insisted on promoting to positions for which she was unqualified, Wheeler objected to this breach of store discipline. Webster, in turn, objected to Wheeler's growing interests outside the store. Thanks to its solid foundation, however, Macy's continued for the next ten years to grow with the times, although it did not break any new retailing ground.

When Webster finally broke with Wheeler and bought him out in 1887, he was able to turn for new blood to a great merchant family named Straus, which has had a unique association with Macy's that remains unbroken to the present day. Lazarus Straus, the head of this remarkable line, was a well-to-do cultured Jewish grain merchant of liberal principles who left his farmlands in Bavaria following the uprisings of 1848. Two years later, his wife—who was also his cousin—and four children followed him to the United States. Unlike most immigrants, he by-passed the melting-pot cities to start a modest little store in Talbotton, Georgia.

During the Civil War, the Strauses were Confederate sympathizers —one of them in fact attempting unsuccessfully to bring arms to the blockaded Southern states. Following the war they moved north to Philadelphia and then to New York to form the wholesale chinaware importing firm of L. Straus & Sons.

The family association with Macy's began in 1874, when L. Straus

& Sons established leased departments to sell china, glassware and silver. At that time Macy's was the largest New York customer of the Straus concern and the arrangement was a logical one.

Under the Strauses, Macy's china and crockery departments grew until in 1888 they accounted for nearly 18 percent of the company's sales and returned the highest profit in the store. It was the first to feature bargain sales and public exhibitions. To the china department, too, goes the credit for introducing Macy's famous odd price policy—$3.98 instead of $4.00—to make the customer feel she is getting a bargain.

Webster offered the Strauses a partnership in 1888 and joined with them in 1893 in acquiring a half interest in the Brooklyn store thereafter called Abraham & Straus, an interest which they later sold. Webster finally disposed of his remaining half interest in Macy's to the Strauses.

Isidor Straus, the oldest son of Lazarus Straus, was a typical patriarch: confidant, dignified and reliable. He watched the store's finances and developed the operating system required to keep a growing business under control. His hobby was foreign exchange and his idea of recreation was advising his friend, President Grover Cleveland, on currency reforms.

In his autobiography, Isidor Straus analyzed his own personality when he said: "Possibly at times I was subject to an acute sensitiveness and caused, I confess, many nervous anxieties. To take things calmly, always to be optimistic and not forbode troubles, which in many cases I admit prove imaginary, is a happy faculty, but I am not ready to say likely to lead to success."

Younger brother Nathan, on the other hand, was enthusiastic, gregarious and popular. He endeared himself to employees by wandering around the store whistling "There'll Be a Hot Time in the Old Town Tonight" and thought up most of the stunts and promotions which kept Macy's name before the public. A natty dresser, he loved horses and amused himself with Tammany politics and spectacular philanthropies like the free milk fund. Nathan was so visible, in fact, that most New Yorkers thought he ran the store singlehandedly.

Under this well-balanced team, Macy sales inched slowly upward from about $5,000,000 in 1888 to $10,800,000 in 1902, the year of the move uptown. There were no radical departures from previous policies, but assortments and lines grew steadily as the middle classes filled their gaudy parlors with the first luxuriant fruits of mechanization. Selections from the long lists of products the Strauses added every year afford a provocative backward glimpse into the days of bloomer girls and bicycles built for two: 1889, oriental rugs, engraved stationery, buggy whips; 1890, brass beds, rowing machines; 1891, bicycles; 1892, diamonds, Tokay wines; 1893, oil paintings, fancy groceries; 1895, amateur photographers' supplies, sleighs; 1897, firearms; 1898, wallpaper, pianos, talking machines; 1899, cocktail shakers.

Progress was slow because Macy's was not the only big store in New York. During this period, many other stores were also vying for the privilege of supplying almost all of the customers' wants. While none of them equaled Macy's assortments and few even tried to compete with Macy's low cash prices, their success proved that many customers were still willing to pay for additional convenience and service.

Macy's competed on service as well as it could. Like other stores, it adopted the "satisfaction guaranteed or your money back" principle, as a steadily rising rate of returns testified. At the close of the century the store was teaching purchasers of bicycles how to ride, installing ovens and ranges and packing the provisions the wealthy bought for their yacht trips. In order to dramatize a delivery service that required hundreds of horses to serve customers lured into Macy's from New Jersey and Long Island, Macy's imported two Mercedes horseless carriages, the first European automobiles to come to America, which attracted attention but made few deliveries.

It became increasingly clear that a great store could no longer make do with the makeshift quarters which were now spread on both sides of Sixth Avenue—to the confusion of shoppers and to the profit of at least one merchant, who encouraged the public to think he was part of Macy's. Furthermore, trade was on its historic march uptown and Macy's would have to downgrade its merchandise or upgrade its address. Isidor's sons, who were already in the business, campaigned successfully for a new building uptown.

The choice of Macy's present location at Thirty-fourth Street and

Broadway, a crossroads which has gained in importance over the years, was at the time a radical leapfrog over the competition in the movement of New York retailing. It was particularly alarming to Henry Siegel, a Chicago merchant who had just pushed the center of shopping gravity northward by building Siegel Cooper New York on Eighteenth Street. Through agents, Siegel bought up a little over a thousand square feet of the strategic Thirty-fourth Street and Broadway corner, paying $375,000 for it. Then he offered it to the Strauses for only $250,000 if they would sell him the unexpired lease on their old Fourteenth Street store and with it the custom of shoppers used to the location.

The Strauses refused to pay tribute. They instructed their architects to build around the little corner—which is still, incidentally, unoccupied by Macy's—and used the $250,000 they had ear-marked for its acquisitition to acquire land to the west, on which a twenty-story building was erected in 1924. The new land was first used to house the store's generating plant, which had been planned for the north side of Thirty-fifth Street on the site of the Pekin and the Tivoli, New York's famous brothels.

Over a half century of hard usage and architectural progress has not outdated the nine-story store the Strauses opened in 1902. It was the first to install a vacuum-cleaner system for removing stale air, pneumatic tubes for transporting cash, and escalators with flat steps instead of inclined ones with cleats against which riders had to brace their feet.

The new building put Macy's in a position to compete on service as well as price. The Strauses also sought new ways to dramatize Macy's low cash prices. To dramatize the advantages of cash, Macy's adopted the "6% cash policy," which soon became more than an idle slogan.

Macy's virtually guaranteed to sell merchandise offered in charge-account stores at 6 percent less. Socks that sold for $1 in other stores became 94 cents on Macy counters in a clever adaptation of the store's traditional odd pricing to accentuate the new policy. New York's bargain-hungry crowds took Macy's at its word, calling lapses of the price challenge to the attention of the management in such numbers that it became necessary to hire a small army of clerks to verify the claims. From this beginning was born the comparison-shopping department.

With the opening of the new store, Macy's launched its own answer to the inconvenience of carrying cash. Customers who traded regularly at Macy's could deposit their money with the store and draw against it as they made purchases. To the surprise of competing merchants, the Deposit Account system worked. Thousands of housewives transferred their secret savings from the grocery budget into Macy's Bank, since the store was destined to get the money in the end anyway. This system remained in effect until 1960, when the number of charge purchasers became such a preponderance of Macy's customers that a conventional charge-account arrangement was adopted.

The store's fight against fixed prices began early in the century when an association of book publishers sought to maintain retail prices and contended that Macy's underselling process lowered the value of their copyright. Macy lawyers charged that the book publishers were a trust under the Sherman Act and sued for damages. Meanwhile, secret agents ranged the country to buy up popular titles and in one case at least secured copies from the author, who told the publisher he was buying the copies for his own use.

In 1913, after nine actions in federal and state courts, the Supreme Court of the United States vindicated the Macy contention. A photograph of the $140,000 damage check the publishers paid Macy's is still one of the store's prized exhibits. A similar lengthy dispute with the Victor Talking Machine Company ended its attempt to control prices by licensing instead of selling its Victrolas.

But price-fixing measures gradually were passed by more and more legislative bodies and Macy's had no choice but to obey them. It increased its emphasis, however, on items manufactured to its specifications and sold under its own brands. Some of these date from the days of Rowland Macy, who had the store make its own cigars. Housewives began to be encouraged to buy Supre-Macy towels, Lily White canned goods and Red Star articles of many kinds.

Chairman Straus minces no words in his frequent attacks against price-fixed merchandise. "Quality stabilization is a high-sounding phrase," he says. "So was fair trade. Both are propaganda phrases. Do not be misled by either one of them. Read the small print on the package. What such legislation contains is restraint of trade and that is injurious to a free economy and therefore damaging to consumers."

Macy's advertising and public relations departments, now headed by John A. Blum and Eleanore Bruce, have always attracted many men and women of talent. Kenneth Collins, who first advertised the Macy Bureau of Standards, moved on to a series of executive posts. William H. Howard became executive vice president of the big store and later joined Young & Rubicam.

A 1948 Macy Christmas advertisement headlined, "Oh, Darling—You Shouldn't Have!" and written by Barbara Collyer was chosen by Julian Watkins as one of the hundred greatest advertisements. Most remembered of all is Bernice Fitz-Gibbon, a forceful ex-teacher of English from Wisconsin. For Macy's, she coined "It's Smart to be Thrifty," a slogan that is even painted on the store roof.

A widely-publicized "feud" between Macy's and Gimbels, its Herald Square neighbor—similar to the one that Fred Allen and Jack Benny used to engage in—has drawn great consumer interest and generated additional sales for both stores. The two stores occasionally vary the battle with friendly gestures. In 1946, they buried the hatchet long enough to adopt a well-publicized uniform outdoor decorating scheme for Christmas. Seven years later, Gimbels called attention to Macy's flower show with an advertisement which trumpeted, "Does Gimbels tell Macy's? No, Gimbels tells the world!" Macy's responded politely with a thank-you: "Nobody but nobody said it more prettily than Gimbels." In 1955, each of the retail giants temporarily posted signs on their buildings directing shoppers to the other's store.

Macy's started its Thanksgiving Day parade in 1924 and, with the exception of two war years, it has been an annual event ever since, heralding the arrival of Santa Claus in New York. The parade is a two-mile panoply of celebrities, bands, six-story balloons and majorettes. Over a million people crowd the line of march to get a glimpse of the fabulous characters and some 67,000,000 more watch the parade on national television. It has inspired a popular motion picture, *Miracle on Thirty-fourth Street,* and a musical, *Here's Love.*

During the early part of the twentieth century, Macy's growth paralleled that of New York City. Sales climbed steadily to $17,300,000 at the outbreak of World War I. Inflation, as well as a war-detonated explosion in consumer expenditures, pushed Macy's sales to $35,800,000 by 1919, the year the store was incorporated.

In the speculative years following World War I, the Strauses expanded by buying a controlling interest in Toledo's La Salle & Koch Company in 1923 and Atlanta's then ailing Davison-Paxon four years later. In 1929 they bought L. Bamberger & Co. of Newark, a store founded in 1892 by Louis Bamberger and notable for its pioneer radio broadcasting. In 1945, they bought O'Connor Moffatt & Co. of San Francisco, and in 1947 the John Taylor Dry Goods Store in Kansas City.

Macy's Parkchester store in the Bronx was one of the first department-store experiments in decentralizing to follow its customers to the suburbs. Although a branch store in Syracuse that carried only best-selling items failed in 1940, Macy's New York has since opened branches in White Plains, Jamaica, Flatbush, Roosevelt Field, Huntington, Bay Shore, Albany and New Haven. And its big Queens unit—a 300,000-square-foot store-in-the-round surrounded by twin parking helixes—is one of the most novel approaches to store construction in history. Still other units are on the drawing boards.

In 1922, Macy stock was offered to the public, but the Straus family retains control through a declining stock interest which now amounts to less than 20 percent. Allocation of the leadership within the family seems to have followed the law of primogeniture. Isidor, the eldest son of Lazarus, was the head of Macy's until he refused to enter a lifeboat of the sinking *Titanic* ahead of women and children in 1912. A bronze plaque in the store pays tribute to the memory of him and his wife, who died at the same time.

His sons, "Mr. Jesse" and "Mr. Percy," had already taken over running the store. Their younger brother, Herbert, and the two sons of Nathan Straus, while they contributed in other ways, never overcame the head start of the legendary pair. Whenever the slightest disagreement arose in public, Jesse and Percy would retire behind locked doors until one of them could emerge with the traditional pronouncement, "My brother and I have decided."

A disagreement between Isidor's sons and Nathan Straus led to a friendly sale of the latter's interests to his nephews Jesse, Percy and Herbert. For a time Jesse held the top post at the store and then the leadership descended on his eldest son, Jack.

Jack Straus, moreover, is not the only Straus at Macy's these days. His only son, Kenneth, a World War II infantry veteran and a well-known fire buff, is merchandise vice president of the New York division for men's wear. His cousin Edward, son of Herbert, is president of Macy's shopping center subsidiary, Garden State Plaza Corporation. And Edward's brother John is vice president in charge of Macy's New York drug and cosmetic manufacturing and marketing.

Jack Isidor Straus, who has been the number one man at Macy's since he was named president in 1940, was only two years old when he performed his first official act for the store. That's when he held a silver trowel in his hands at the laying of the cornerstone of Macy's Thirty-fourth Street store.[5]

A tall, slim, quiet man whose accomplishments as an amateur jazz pianist have won him wide admiration among his friends as well as from his teachers, Eddy Duchin and Teddy Wilson, Straus was imbued with retailing principles and philosophy from the days of his youth when he sat around the breakfast table listening to his father and uncles discussing merchandising.

"The image of Macy's," he says, "has been built on providing a wide assortment and many services to our customers. We intend to continue offering a variety of merchandise and whatever services are necessary in order to maintain this traditional retailer image. The bull's eye of our target is the middle income group."

Straus joined the famous Macy training squad after his graduation from Harvard and worked in such jobs as a main-floor stocking salesman and a clerk at the handbag counter before moving into management positions. His father taught him that merchandising is the most important aspect of department-store retailing, a lesson he has never forgotten. Employees call him "Mr. Jack," following the old Macy tradition of referring to members of the Straus family in this manner.

As soon as people he meets at parties or other social occasions learn of his affiliation with Macy's, they usually take the opportunity to voice whatever complaint they may have about the store, no matter how minor. Straus was finally forced to get an unlisted telephone number because of the many calls he received at all hours from people who wanted to complain directly to the top man.

Nevertheless, the Macy chairman makes it a point to investigate every complaint that is brought to his personal attention. "First," he believes, "it's important to straighten out the complaint itself. Then a particular complaint might indicate a weakness in our setup to be eliminated which we might have otherwise overlooked."

One area of Macy's operations that occupies much of Straus's thinking is customer service. "Somebody has got to get religion on this matter," he tells his associates. Straus is a constant battler against the deterioration of service that takes the form of poorly informed personnel, clerks who pay no attention to customers, failure to take care of complaints the first time, etc. Walking briskly through his flagship Herald Square store, he urges, encourages and otherwise pleads with Macy staffers to end "the age of the goof-off."

"We're a service business," Straus says. "We can have the greatest merchandise, the greatest displays, the greatest buyers and the greatest foreign operation. But without service, we're nothing."

President Ernest L. Molloy, a native of Cambridge, Massachusetts, has been a Macyite ever since his graduation from Harvard College in 1929. At Harvard he was a pitcher on the baseball team. Like so many others in the company who have risen to high positions, he started his retailing career on the famous Macy training squad at the Herald Square store. From there, he succeeded to a series of managerial posts and developed a distinctive merchandising philosophy.

"Trends are all right for the lazy and self-satisfied merchandisers," he believes. "But if the trend is downward, I suggest tearing up the charts and setting out to create demand."

To Molloy—who was president of Macy's California division for fourteen years before acceding to the presidency of the corporation—the development of a fashion image is one of the key functions of a successful department store.

"The most significant thing in retailing today," he says, "is the growth of fashion in virtually everything. In 1956, high-priced ready-to-wear constituted fashion. Today it is pervading not only all price ranges of apparel, but every room in the house, fully coordinated and highly colorful."

The President of the New York division is David L. Yunich, a short, chunky former minor-league catcher. The eleven stores of this division stretch from midtown Manhattan to New Haven, Connecticut, and do almost half the volume of the entire corporation.

Yunich, who played baseball for three-and-a-half years with teams in the Cincinnati Reds' farm system and once said that he took a 400 percent cut in his salary to become a retailer, joined Macy's as a $35-a-week trainee after receiving his degree from the Harvard Graduate School of Business Administration. He moved quickly up the organization chart, becoming president of the Bamberger's New Jersey division in 1954 and president of Macy's New York in 1962 when he was forty-five years old.

Among the retailing fraternity, Yunich has built a reputation for his pragmatic application of theoretical merchandising ideas. Perhaps his most impressive accomplishment has been the development and application of the "equal-store" concept, which he introduced first at Bamberger's and then at Herald Square.

Under this concept, two separate but equal organizational lines are established in the store—the buying line and the selling line. Buyers are responsible for planning, purchasing, pricing, distributing and promoting goods, while department managers are in charge of sales, service, customer contacts and presentation of these goods. Buyers can concentrate on their primary role of scouring the market and obtaining the best possible merchandise without being held responsible for selling conditions in widely-separated branch stores.[6]

The equal-store operation is termed by Yunich the third phase of department-store operation. "The first was the store itself," he says, "followed by the branch store which regarded the downtown store as the mother hen."[7]

As now in practice at Macy's, there is no longer any distinction between the downtown and the branch stores; each has equal status in the hierarchy. "In each of our stores we have a very knowledgeable group," he notes. "There is no second team."

Yunich believes that "there is nothing wrong with retailing which cannot be solved by efficiency and leadership. New forms of retailing have sprung up to meet the explosive growth of population and the challenge of competition has been sounded. The weak will fall and the strong will survive. It's really a matter of leadership."

The other division presidents of the Macy corporation are Herbert L. Seegal at Bamberger's New Jersey, Rolland A. Maxwell at Davison's, Michael Yamin at La Salle & Koch, James M. Lundy at Macy's California and Thomas W. Johnston at Macy's Missouri-Kansas.

One tangible symbol of Macy's unwavering faith in its future survival is its five-pointed Red Star trademark, originated in 1862, used on everything from delivery trucks to letterheads and derived from a lucky star seen at sea by Captain Rowland H. Macy. Since 1918 it has also been the symbol of the Soviet Army. Because of that, many have urged Macy's to stop using it as a label and a cable address. But Macy's feels that this is not at all necessary, since the store had the mark first and intends to have it last.

XI

THE FOOD GIANTS

Supermarkets, the A & P and Its Rivals

THE SUPERMARKET, the ingenious retailing innovation that changed the food-buying habits of literally tens of millions of American shoppers, was developed in its present form by an employee of a food chain who couldn't sell the idea to his bosses.

The innovator was Michael Cullen, a man who foresaw in the late 1920's that grocery stores, usually clerk-served and occupying less than two thousand square feet apiece, could not fully meet the needs of the populace in a changing society. Anticipating the further growth of the automobile industry, he recognized that most of the then-existing groceries were scattered throughout heavily-populated urban areas and relied entirely on foot traffic or on-street parking facilities.

Cullen's idea was to develop five-thousand- or six-thousand-square-foot self-service stores on a cash-and-carry basis, surrounded by an equal amount of parking space and located outside the high-rent district. Loss-leader and low-markup merchandise would be surrounded by high-profit items, mass displays of groceries would be featured in the aisles and newspaper advertising on a major scale would boost traffic and promote volume by making customers aware of what these stores offered.

Self-service food selling *per se* was not Cullen's invention. The

Piggly Wiggly stores, started in 1916, used self-selection as a principal feature. Drive-in markets for quick service developed in California in the 1920's. What Cullen did, however, was to take these ideas, add his own concepts about grocery selling and fuse them into a large, integrated market, a supermarket.

When his company wouldn't buy this idea, Cullen quit his job and opened what is generally accepted to be the first supermarket, King Kullen's, in Jamaica, New York, on August 30, 1930. The extent of this revolution in marketing can be seen in Cullen's immediate success. Two years later, the King Kullen Grocery Company, Inc., was operating eight markets with grocery sales of $6,000,000 annually and total sales of almost $9,000,000.

Today supermarket merchandising—in which gross markups average about 22 percent—has become the predominant method of selling grocery products throughout the United States.[1] In 1965, 71 percent, or $43,500,000,000 worth, of grocery stores' volume of $61,100,000,000 was done in supermarkets, compared with 26 percent, or $6,400,000,000, of the $25,000,000,000 volume in 1948.

The news of King Kullen's operating technique quickly spread throughout the country. Although there had been chain stores in other merchandising categories before this—some of them dating back centuries—here was the first effective application of the supermarket-chain principle. Soon a few other small and large food chains and independents began to open supermarkets and these were followed by the entire industry.

Half of the grocery volume in 1965 was done by the food-chain companies operating four or more store units. Another quarter of the sales was accounted for by voluntary groups of independent grocers jointly sponsored by a wholesaler. Some 18 percent came from cooperative stores—owned by grocers who jointly operate their own wholesale organization—and the remainder by independent grocers.

Supermarkets, many of which carry as many as 7,000 items and encompass about 17,000 square feet, do the overwhelming bulk of the nation's grocery business in a relatively small number of stores. Only 11 percent of the 241,000 grocery stores can be defined as supermarkets—a complete, departmentalized, at least partially self-service store containing grocery, meat, dairy and produce departments with a minimum area of 4,500 square feet and minimum annual sales of $500,000.

When it comes to supermarkets, though, there is one company which not only has more than any other but whose name is also known everywhere as the symbol of a food chain. That name, of course, is the A & P.

The A & P, as shoppers know The Great Atlantic & Pacific Tea Company, Inc., is the world's largest food retailer and one of the greatest exponents of chain-store operation. Its annual report for 1965 reveals that its profits were a bit more than one cent on the dollar—that is, earnings of $52,339,276 on volume of $5,118,-977,802. Only eight other companies in all American business had larger sales that year.

What is the A & P? To Americans who visit them at the rate of about 6,000,000 a shopping day, it is 4,625 unpretentious stores, approximately 80 percent of them supermarkets, so devoid of frills that they are simply machines for selling food. Though the stores are few in the West, and not to be found at all in fifteen states, into their cash registers go about eight cents of every dollar of retail food sales in the country.

The A & P is also the largest food-processing plant in the country at Horseheads, New York, and a cheese warehouse at Plymouth, Wisconsin. It is twenty-eight big bakeries turning out bread and cakes, nine coffee-roasting plants, four salmon canneries in Alaska, a fresh milk plant in Pennsylvania, a buying organization in South America, two laundries for washing uniforms and a print shop just for the printing of its private labels. Around three hundred of these are registered with the Patent Office.

The A & P is also research which has developed the big-breasted "chicken of tomorrow" and is continually working to improve its turkeys and hogs. It is a meat-purchasing empire which buys around 2½ billion pounds a year. It is the biggest user of eggs, 250 million dozen a year, both for sale and as ingredients in its cakes.

The A & P is 133,000 employees, from clerks who mark cans and packages in stores to traveling auditors who report to headquarters in New York's Graybar Building, where statisticians analyze and chart the figures.

The huge organization was started by George Huntington Hartford, a shrewd Yankee from Augusta, Maine, who in 1859, when he was twenty-six, was employed by George F. Gilman in a New York hide and leather business.

Tea then retailed in New York at $1 a pound. Hartford convinced Gilman that this could be reduced to 30 cents by eliminating middlemen. Gilman abandoned hides and leather and the two formed The Great American Tea Company, a partnership which promised "to do away with various profits and brokerages, cartages, storages, cooperage and waste, with the exception of a small commission paid for purchasing to our correspondents in Japan and China, one cartage, and a small profit to ourselves which, on our large sales, will amply repay us."

Initially they sold tea on the docks of New York directly to consumers. Their first shop at 31 Vesey Street in New York resembled something from the Arabian Nights. A gigantic capital T, blazing with gas lights, illuminated the store's vermilion-red-and-gold front. Strings of red, white and blue globes festooned the windows. Inside the store, tea bins were painted red and gold, the cashiers' cages were built in the shape of Chinese pagodas and a green parrot stood on a stand in the center of the main floor. A band played on Saturdays, often far into the night.

To advertise the store, eight dapple-gray horses pulled a tremendous red wagon through the city streets. A prize of $20,000 was offered to anyone who could guess the combined weight of team and wagon. All kinds of premiums were given away—dishpans, china, crockery and colored pictures of babies. "This is the day they give babies away" was one of the song slogans used to attract customers.

New Yorkers swarmed to the store. Hartford and Gilman gradually added spices, coffee, soap, flavoring extracts, condensed milk, baking powder and other staples. Wherever possible they applied the same middleman-eliminating purchasing they inaugurated with tea.

They added more stores. There were five by 1865 and there were eleven in 1869 when the partners adopted the more grandiloquent name The Great Atlantic & Pacific Tea Company. Hartford envisioned a chain of stores that would reach from coast to coast as the just-completed Union Pacific Railroad linked the two seaboards. The older name was preserved until 1964 in a subsidiary which operated tea and coffee truck routes in forty-nine cities.

By 1876, there were sixty-seven A & P stores, all with the familiar red-and-gold façade, all conventional grocery stores with charge accounts and delivery service. They were operating as far south as Baltimore, as far north as Boston and as far west as St. Paul. A comic advertising card a little later listed twenty-five stores in New York and five in Brooklyn.

Gilman retired in 1878 to a life of luxury in Bridgeport, Connecticut, and left Hartford to run the stores. He was soon joined by two of his five children. These were his sons, George Ludlum Hartford and John Augustine Hartford. A third son, Edward, became an inventor and did not enter the business, and there were two daughters.

George, the eldest, born November 7, 1864, and named for his father, started to work at fifteen. Plump and short, he was first employed in 1880 as an office boy to fire the boiler. After two weeks, he took the place of a cashier who quit, strangely enough because he thought the business might fail. There were then 110 stores and George counted and banked the cash from all of them. This came in by express, sometimes as much as $55,000 a day.

Keeping tab on the money aroused his interest in economy. Hearing that baking powder was only alum and sodium bicarbonate, George set a chemist mixing the ingredients behind a screen in the Vesey Street store. This brought down the price of baking powder and was the start of the company's own manufacturing operations.

John Hartford, eight years younger than his brother, went to work cleaning inkwells and sweeping floors in the Vesey Street store in 1888, all of sixteen years old and fresh out of high school. His salary was $5 a week, and his mother, as frugal as his father, charged him $1 for board and made him bank another $1. When he received a $2 raise, his mother increased his board bill. Soon he was clerking and also buying and handing out premiums, then an important lure.

In the panic of 1907, John's gift for strategy was credited with literally saving the business. He was sent to withdraw the company funds from a bank on which there was a run. Finding many depositors already in line, he asked the first, a little man who had been there all night, how much money he had in the bank.

"Four hundred and forty-seven dollars and ninety cents," he replied. "All I have in the world."

"I'll give you $450 for your place," John said. "Get back in line and maybe you'll get your deposit, too."

As it turned out, John Hartford salvaged the A & P thousands of dollars and the little man who had been at the head of the line also collected his deposit in full, he later learned, becoming probably the only one actually to double his money in a panic that caused even J. P. Morgan some trouble.

At this time, A & P headquarters were moved to Jersey City, New Jersey, not far from Orange, where the Hartford brothers grew up and their father was mayor for twelve years without salary.

Cash and carry, one of the biggest innovations in A & P history, was introduced in 1912 by John Hartford. At this time there were four hundred stores, but charge-account paper work, thousands of delivery horses and wagons and premiums limited profits. The success of a New Jersey grocer named Henry Cole with some cash stores caused John Hartford to think along this line. He proposed to his father and brother that they open "economy" stores to be staffed by one man, to be run without charge orders or premiums and to sell at low profit aimed at large volume. They thought it a crackpot idea.

He persisted, however, until he persuaded them to let him open just one to prove his point. They invested $3,000, and to really test it John opened his store on West Side Avenue in Jersey City, around the corner from the company's biggest money-making store. The economy store didn't even have a name but the customers rushed in when they saw its bargains. In six months the regular A & P store was out of business, and the economy store was in to stay.[2]

For the next two years John opened economy stores at the rate of one every three days. By the end of 1915, there were one thousand A & P stores and each establishment was laid out exactly alike so customers could find things in the same location in any store. John often remarked he could go blindfold into any store and find a can of pork and beans.

The company borrowed $5,000,000 to finance the new stores and the sales volume more than doubled to $75,000,000 in 1916. The father then turned the business over to George and John to run as a trust for themselves, their two sisters—Mrs. William B. Reilly and Mrs. A. G. Hoffman—and their brother and, as they died, the heirs of these. Perhaps the most famous of these heirs is Huntington Hartford, the well-known art connoisseur and patron. In 1917, the founder died at eighty-four. The trust, incidentally, was not dissolved until after George L. Hartford died in 1957.

"Our one desire," the sons wrote later in an instruction book for store managers, "is to perpetuate A & P as a great public service, to have it stand forever as a monument to the integrity, perseverance and human understanding of the man who founded it, George Huntington Hartford." When the Chicago Merchandise Mart years later established its Hall of Fame of Retailing, the father of the A & P was among the first four elected, along with Marshall Field, Frank Woolworth and John Wanamaker.

Under the sons, the A & P became an even bigger integrated business empire. Among the new subsidiaries organized were the Quaker Maid Company (later named the Ann Page division), processing and packing more than forty products, many bearing the Ann Page label; the White House Milk Company, with milk-processing plants in Wisconsin; and the Nakat Packing Corporation, America's largest canner of Alaskan salmon and operator of an Alaskan fishing fleet. Meanwhile, the American Coffee Corporation hired thirty coffee-purchasing agents in Colombia and Brazil, and the company's agents attended tea auctions in India and Ceylon. Cigarettes later became an important profit item for the stores.

Departments for the sale of meat, now the most important single item in A & P volume, were added in 1925. That year also saw the company expand into Canada, buy group insurance for its employees, and decentralize its operations into geographical divisions, of which there now are five. Under them were unit offices and stores.

John Hartford was the merchandising genius of the A & P, while his brother George looked after the financial end. But both realized the importance of decentralization in a business as large as theirs and had each division run virtually like an independent corporation.

Each division was given a president, treasurer, director of sales, director of purchases and director of operations. Each unit had a similar group of specialists. Except in finances, each unit and store manager was free to run his business as he wished within overall company policy. New York continued to keep directly in touch with stores and units through traveling auditors, who inspected stores and their records and reported directly to headquarters.

Sales passed the billion-dollar mark for the first time in the fiscal year ending February 28, 1930. The number of red-fronted stores reached an all-time peak the next year with a total of 15,709, the record number in the company's history. Sales then topped $1,000,000,000 and earnings were more than $30,700,000.

In the next quarter of a century or so, the A & P abandoned almost three-quarters of the stores it owned in 1930, but its total volume during this period increased more than fourfold. The average A & P store also boosted its annual sales from about $68,000 to approximately $1,135,000.

During the 1930's, the A & P was big but not beloved. Because of its bigness and success, it was one of the most unpopular of companies. In part, this was the result of the temper of the times. In part, it was due to disregard for public opinion on the part of the management. Like all mass buyers, the A & P drove hard bargains with its suppliers through allowances and discounts which then were legal. Competitors who were hurt by this, middlemen who were bypassed and others complained to the government. Bills having the principal aim of hampering or destroying the A & P were introduced in Congress and in state legislatures.

While all chains had expanded, the A & P growth had been the most phenomenal. At the same time, the A & P had done nothing to explain itself to the communities in which it operated. While the "A & P Gypsies" were on the radio and the company's advertising appropriation had been increased from $2,000,000 to $6,000,000, this still amounted to less than $8 a week per store.

Expansion had been so rapid that all sorts of men were A & P managers. "We went so fast," John Hartford once explained, "that hobos hopping off freight trains got hired as managers." While instructions from headquarters insisted that the stores give sixteen ounces to a pound and mark and sell goods at correct prices, there were complaints of short change, short weight and "selling the broom." In the last instance, a broom was leaned against the checkout stand and its price added to each check as if the patron had purchased it. If this was noticed, the checker would simply apologize. It was an accusation against every chain food store.

The company left its gathering troubles to its lawyers. They succeeded in having an early North Carolina anti-chain-store tax declared unconstitutional in 1928 but several setbacks followed. One came in 1931 when the United States Supreme Court, in upholding an Indiana chain-store tax, ruled that chain stores could lawfully be taxed differently from independent stores. Another came in 1936 when John Hartford sat in a Washington, D.C., courtroom and saw A & P store managers convicted of short weighing chickens in forty-eight out of fifty cases.

A stickler for complete honesty with customers, he spent the next six weeks personally signing forty-six thousand letters to A & P employees warning against any recurrence of this. At least one executive was fired for tolerating stock gains in his stores. In a case of a different sort, he heard of a New York City manager helping a butler cheat the woman for whom he worked. John Hartford required complete restitution and sent an apology and his personal check to the customer, who had not known that she was being cheated.

Regarding his employees, Mr. Hartford—a slim, gray-haired, impeccably dressed executive—once said that "no man can be asked to do better than his best. If he does his best, he will do a little better than he thinks he can and usually a little better than others think he can."

He thought constantly of his customers too. John Hartford's merchandising philosophy was summarized with these words: "We would rather sell 200 pounds of butter at a penny a pound profit than 100 pounds at 2 cents a pound profit."

Under his leadership, customers were encouraged to write their complaints to headquarters. John Hartford personally investigated many of these. A letter from a mother about the hours her son worked in an A & P store in Virginia, for example, led to the discharge of a store manager. Stores were forbidden to sell anything below cost. While the A & P continued its lone-wolf policy of not joining trade associations, it began to make contributions to some and eventually joined various state chain-store councils.

Although the A & P was not the first food chain to latch onto the supermarket idea in the early 1930's, it eventually became the leading proponent of this method of distribution. The company was also a pioneer in the self-service sale of cellophane-wrapped meat and was an early user of packaged produce.

An important development in the company's promotion program was the conversion in 1937 of a giveaway "menu sheet" to a full-fledged women's service magazine. In a contest, two customers received $1,000 each for naming it *Woman's Day*. While other retailers had attempted and abandoned magazines, *Woman's Day* was a success from the start. It expanded from the thirty-two pages of the initial issue to as much as two hundred pages. The bulk of the advertising was naturally from A & P suppliers, but makers of sewing machines and similar items also advertised.

Woman's Day was sold by the company in 1958 to Fawcett Publications, Inc., which had printed it for the A & P. It is now sold in other stores as well as the A & P.

Also in 1958, a year after the death of George Hartford and seven years after John Hartford died, the A & P corporate organization was simplified. The New York A & P, which had been owned by the trust established by the founder, was merged into the Maryland A & P, the holding company for all A & P companies and subsidiaries. This recapitalization extended voting rights for the first time in 1959 to the general public, which previously had had access only to nonvoting common and preferred stock. Nevertheless the John A. Hartford Foundation still owns the controlling interest in the company.

After World War II ended, the A & P was slow to take on two of the merchandising ideas that advanced throughout the supermarket field. The first was the increased use of supermarket space to sell nonfood items.

From small areas in the back of supermarkets, high-profit departments selling health and beauty aids, baby needs, housewares, toys and apparel spread throughout the store. Rack jobbers, or merchandisers, emerged whose sole function was to develop and run these nonfood departments in food stores. By 1965, for example, 71 percent of all grocery stores sold health and beauty aids. While many of these items are sold at A & P stores, the company has not developed them to the extent of some other food chains, which used their nonfood departments as the nucleus of their emerging discount-store divisions.

The other major postwar development at supermarkets was the use of trading stamps. Though trading stamps have had their ups and downs in the past—as chains have taken them on or dropped them because of varying and changing estimations of their overall value—they have frequently served as important traffic builders for food stores. Sperry & Hutchinson, the Green Stamp pioneers, is an example of the many stamp companies that have evolved; in 1965 it had profits of $23,169,000 on $339,610,000 sales.

After most of their competitors had acted, A & P brought in Plaid Stamps, owned by the E. F. MacDonald Company, to stores at a number of their divisions. Some later dropped them but many of its stores still give Plaid Stamps, and stamp-saving customers eagerly await the merchandise they have won by filling up the required number of stamp books.

Beginning in the early 1960's, many of the top management men in the company's "old guard"—men who had been trained by the Hartfords—announced their retirement. In 1963, Ralph W. Burger, who had followed John Hartford into the presidency, retired at the age of seventy-three. Three years later, three division presidents in their sixties and seventies left the firm. And, later in 1966, John D. Ehrgott, with A & P for forty-nine years, resigned as chairman at the age of seventy.

The senior executive of A & P now is—like "Mr. John" and "Mr. George" Hartford, who each had only three lines in *Who's Who*—quite reticent about himself. Byron Jay, president and chief executive officer, is a native of Detroit who started with A & P as a clerk in 1927 at $35 a week after receiving an M.A. from the University of Michigan. His rise in the company was rapid and steady, and included such posts as unit head in Louisville, Kentucky, and executive vice president of the Middle Western division.

Melvin W. Alldredge, chairman of the giant chain, also started from the bottom in the same year as Mr. Jay. Born on a farm in Posey County, Indiana, he joined the A & P at the age of sixteen as a part-time clerk. During his long career with the company, he served also as a store manager, unit head, president of the Central division, vice president, executive vice president, president and vice chairman.

The five A & P regional divisions are now headed by veteran employees of the company. For example, heading the largest division, the Eastern with over 1,100 stores, is William J. Kane, once a part-time clerk and store manager.

J. Gordon Christian, Jr., a native of Richmond, is the boss of the ten-state Southern division with more than 850 stores. William T. Price rose through the ranks to the presidency of the 600-store Atlantic division. And William E. Ayres, another former clerk from Syracuse, New York, is president of the Central division with over 600 units.

The other division is the Middle Western, based in Chicago and under the presidency of O. Philip Nyquist. This division, which recently consolidated with the former Central Western division, controls about 1,100 stores.

The A & P is one company that has kept out of the real-estate business. George Hartford's short-term lease with many options helped it meet the 1929 crash without entangling real-estate commitments. But the concern has long since abandoned the short-term lease in favor of contracts averaging twelve years with five-year renewal options.

Though temptations have been great, the company keeps only a few weeks' inventory in its supply lines and has avoided speculation in commodities. "If we are in the grocery business," John Hartford often said, "let's stay there. If we want to speculate, let's sell out and go on the stock exchange."

A remarkable feature of A & P operation is its accounting system, one of the best in the world. Every item stocked is numbered and recorded. Costs are calculated to tenths and hundredths of a cent. Even electric-light bills are figured to the last cent. Percentage profits are worked out regularly. A unit vice president knows exactly how much stock each of his stores has on hand and what their percentage of profit and wastage is. Store returns are analyzed and compared. Economies in one store are immediately passed on to others.

Weekly figures reach division headquarters on the following Tuesday. There they are consolidated and sent to New York. Headquarters in the Graybar Building on each Thursday knows the condition of the company as of the preceding Saturday in some detail.

If clerks use large paper sacks when small ones would do, the accountants can detect it in the added costs. The A & P attempts to sell 100 percent of everything it buys. Shipments are planned to prevent spoilage and loss. Handling is swift and painstaking. In the stores, every empty carton is salvaged and wooden boxes are also saved for reuse or return.

A & P managers and executives are remarkable for their alertness and loyalty. Their achievements in emergencies have been notable. When the Kaw River in 1951 flooded the company's warehouse in Kansas City, Kansas, food trucked overnight from Chicago and St. Louis enabled the sixty A & P stores in the area to stay open and feed the flood refugees. To attract and keep the type of men it likes, the A & P has a national personnel department, training courses of many kinds and employee benefits as generous as any in the retail food field. These include wages which are among the highest in the industry, Christmas food baskets, hospitalization, group insurance and a noncontributory pension plan.

Some former A & P men have established businesses of their own and many hold important posts with other chains. Lansing P. Shield, who rose from clerk to general auditor with A & P, became president of the Grand Union chain. Roger M. Laverty rose to be president and general manager of the big Fitzsimmons supermarket chain in California. Sherwin Harris became president of the Mary Lee Candy Company of Cleveland. W. A. Coleman headed the Humpty-Dumpty chain in Oklahoma.

All look back at their A & P experience with nostaligc pride. As one says: "The most profitable thing I ever did was work for them, not in money but in education."

The second-largest supermarket chain is Safeway Stores, Inc., headquartered across the continent from the A & P, in Oakland, California. With 2,128 food stores and 45 Super S discount stores throughout the United States and overseas, Safeway had sales in 1965 of almost $3 billion and earnings of close to $50 billion.

Safeway had its start in 1915 when Marion Barton Skaggs bought an 18-by-32-foot grocery store in American Falls, Idaho, for $1,088 from his Baptist minister father. At the age of twenty-seven, Skaggs already had experience in food retailing but this was his first opportunity to put his own theories into practice.

Right from the start, Skaggs did away with the cracker-barrel, pot-bellied-stove approach. He built wall-hugging shelves, kept his aisles clear and refused to stack merchandise too high for easy reach. All sales were cash and carry. The company quickly prospered and became the Skaggs United Stores.

In 1926, the 428 Skaggs stores were merged into Safeway. Safeway had come into existence earlier that year when the name was adopted by the Sam Seelig Company, a firm with stores in California and Hawaii, following a contest. By the end of the year, the consolidated companies had 766 stores.

It was 1931 when Safeway reached its peak in number of store units. From this level of 3,527 stores, the total declined as small stores were closed with the growth of larger supermarkets in conveniently-located suburban areas.

Safeway's volume topped $1 billion in 1947 and $2 billion ten years later. Since 1957, the president of the company has been Robert A. Magowan, a former Macy's executive and son-in-law of Charles A. Merrill—the Merrill of Merrill Lynch, Pierce, Fenner & Smith and the man who put the Safeway corporation together in 1926.

With 70,000 employees, stores ranging in size up to 33,000 square feet and average weekly sales per store of $25,000, Mr. Magowan heads a massive organization. Yet he describes Safeway's goals in the simplest of terms:

"Serving customers better, of course, is the key to success. But part of the challenge is in finding ways to do it."

The third of the Big Three supermarket chains is the Cincinnati-based Kroger Company. Here too a company was built from the ground up and, as in so many other instances in food retailing, the giant corporate complex began with the hopes of one man.

The man here was Bernard H. "Barney" Kroger, the son of German immigrants, who began working in 1873 as a drugstore clerk at the age of thirteen. Jobs on a farm, as a coffee and tea salesman and as the manager of a small grocery store followed.[3]

When he was twenty-three years old, Barney Kroger struck out on his own with a seventeen-foot-front store. His investment was $372, to which he added $350 lent by a friend, B. A. Branagan. The name he chose for his bustling little market was The Great Western Tea Company.

Kroger was the kind of a man who worked in his store until midnight and then woke up at 4 A.M. to blend and roast his coffee and tea in the back room. He lived on a shoestring to save the money to open more stores—and owned four only two years after going into business.

When asked then how he operated his "chain" of stores, Kroger replied: "Simply duplicate and reduplicate what was demonstrated to be a successful thing. If a policy succeeds in one neighborhood, there is no reason why it should not succeed elsewhere."

By 1893, Kroger owned seventeen stores. At the same time, he built up wagon routes—later supplanted by truck routes—to serve the surrounding countryside. Mail-order customers were developed in such places as the mining areas of Pennsylvania and West Virginia.

In 1902, the name of the company was changed to the Kroger Grocery and Baking Company. Two years later, Kroger bought a meat-store chain and began adding fresh meat to his grocery stores—despite the fact that the personnel problems of integrating butchers with grocery employees in those days were formidable.

Kroger's concern expanded throughout the Midwest and then the South. Stores were later opened on both coasts. Barney Kroger sold all his stock in the company in 1928, thus preserving his assets from disaster in the market crash the following year. The chain, nevertheless, continued to operate 5,575 stores in 1929.

During the first four years of the depression, sales fell 28 percent. But the company weathered the storm and along with the other food and nonfood chain organizations went on to fight successfully the anti-chain crusade that was proceeding apace through the legislatures and the courts in the 1930's.

The growth of the Kroger Company between 1956 and 1965 has been strong and steady. Its sales have risen from $1,500,000,000 to more than $2,500,000,000 and its profits have almost doubled from $17,000,000 to $31,000,000.

In 1965, the company owned 1,459 big supermarkets with over 23,000,000 square feet in 24 states. Its annual sales per food store amounted to $1,666,619. In addition to the supermarkets, there are also 25 huge distribution centers and 180 well-stocked drugstores.

The Kroger Company today is under the leadership of Jacob E. Davis, a former prosecuting attorney in Pike County, Ohio, who has been with the company since 1944. Mr. Davis succeeded Joseph B. Hall in the presidency, after Mr. Hall was named chairman of the board. Mr. Hall later became chairman of the Federal Reserve Bank of Cleveland.

The development of the A & P, Safeway and Kroger is paralleled by the rise of many other giant food chains. A roster of these names could include such firms as Acme Markets and Food Fair Stores of Philadelphia, Winn-Dixie Stores of Jacksonville, the Grand Union Company of East Paterson, New Jersey, First National Stores of Somerville, Massachusetts, and Waldbaum, Inc., and H. C. Bohack & Co., Inc. of New York City.

All of these stores have long since passed through the pine-table and warehouse phase in which they relied on price appeal alone. They have also upgraded their merchandise and added new lines.

The food giants today are at the stage where—despite the self-selection features of their stores—a number of services are constantly being added to attract and hold more customers. This appears to be an important thrust of supermarket merchandising in the decade of the 1960's—one that is receiving more and more attention from merchandisers everywhere who are seeking to capture a greater portion of the consumer's fickle food dollar.

XII

RICH'S

"The Store That Married a City"

RICH'S INC. of Atlanta for many years has been the biggest department store, both in sales volume and physical size, south of Philadelphia and east of the Mississippi River. It sells everything imaginable for the adornment of a person or the furnishing of a home. Its main store is actually four stores in two buildings, each occupying two city blocks.

One building houses a fashion store for women and children and a store for men. Connected with this building by a four-story glass-enclosed Kublai Khan—like bridge over Forsyth Street, is a huge store for homes, and beneath both is a basement store. Each of the four stores has its own restaurants, entrances, restrooms, and escalators, or elevators. Adjacent to the store for homes is Rich's six-level self-park garage, enlarged to handle 1,250 cars at a time and 6,500 per day.

"Do you go by Rich's?" a woman once asked an Atlanta bus driver. He thought for a moment of the ramification of the store's twenty-nine acres of floor space.

"Madam," he replied, "I go by Rich's, under Rich's, through Rich's, and around Rich's."

In addition to this huge and unique construction, Rich's as of 1966 had five branches circling Atlanta, each occupying 1.98 to 5.62 acres of ground. For the twelve months ending January 30 of that year it had profits of $6,600,000 on record sales of $131,000,000, roughly $151 for every resident of metropolitan Atlanta, a very high per capita figure for a department store. In the face of able competition in 1964 it sold $135 worth of goods for every square foot of its vast selling space in Atlanta. The average sale per square foot for Associated Merchandise Corporation member stores that year was $115. Rich's has accounted for 59.9 percent of the Atlanta area big-store business reported to the Federal Reserve Bank.

Over 13,000,000 people visit Rich's each year. This is more than the combined population of Alabama, Georgia and Florida. An average day brings crowds of 50,000 to 75,000 and the busiest days 85,000, or the population of a city the size of Augusta, Georgia. Such a crowd spent $2,500,000 the day after Thanksgiving in 1965.

Headed during the years of its greatest growth by an engineer, a rarity in retailing, Rich's has made notable advances in stock control and the mechanics of storekeeping. At the same time, in the tradition of the Rich family, it has achieved even greater advances in human relations with its employees, customers and the community. The store is married to Atlanta.[1]

The business was founded by Morris Rich, one of four brothers who immigrated as youths to the United States from Kaschau, Hungary, just before and during the Civil War. In America all of the brothers speedily became clerks, peddlers and store owners. Only twenty years old but with six years of work as a clerk and peddler behind him, Morris rode a bay horse from Albany, Georgia, to Atlanta, where his brother William in 1865 had started a wholesale-retail dry-goods business. From William, who soon moved his own business to Nashville, Tennessee, Morris borrowed $500 and established a tiny dry-goods store on Whitehall Street. It opened on May 28, 1867. His brothers, Emanuel and Daniel, joined him as partners a few years later.

His first move to make his store attractive was a simple one. Whitehall Street, then little more than a country lane, was always ankle-deep in dust or mud. Young Rich laid down a row of planks which permitted ladies to alight from their carriages and enter the store without spotting their high button shoes or ruffled skirts. Inside, a salesman rushed forward to take the shopper's parasol or umbrella. This was in the tradition of Southern hospitality and customers liked it.

In a day of haggling, he began with fixed prices. This did not deter him from granting liberal credit or from trading calico and candles for sorghum, cotton and shelled corn. Another early-adopted policy was that of permitting customers to return goods without question. It is now publicized as "You make your own adjustment at Rich's."

This is interpreted so liberally that several million dollars' worth of goods, $15,660,000 in 1964, for example, are returned each year. The store that year had a 13.5 percent return rate as compared to a 9.7 percent AMC store average. Adjustments are made in the departments involved and it is not necessary for customers to seek out a bureau of adjustment or complaint department.

An analysis of a year's returns once revealed that the store had refunded the price of an unused pair of women's button shoes thirty years old, an unworn man's shirt ten years old and a dead canary! Also included was a suit inaccurately altered by the wife of the sad but resigned gentleman who returned it, who explained that his wife had not liked the work of the alterations tailor and had unhappily sought to improve upon it.

In addition, some fifteen customers presented goods for credit or exchange which were not even bought at Rich's. In such cases Rich's customarily points out that the store does not carry these lines. Invariably the customers brightly reply, "But I never shop anywhere but here." Facing such a delicate impasse, Rich's clerks accept even these items and requested adjustments are made.

There also was a lady who dropped in to explain that the wedding cake she had ordered had been yellow inside, and not white, as specified, a fact which caused her some sorrow, even though the cake had been excellent, the wedding party had eaten of it heartily and the bridesmaids had taken away the traditional slices to put beneath their pillows. The lady received another cake, white inside, and went away unaware that she had made history by becoming the first person ever to eat her cake and have it too.

Rich's, known in Atlanta as The Saturday Banker, in 1964 cashed

$35,000,000 in checks exclusive of those presented for partial payments on accounts. Most of this "business" was done on Saturdays when Atlanta's banks are closed. For identification Rich's requires a driver's license, one of their own Charga-Plates or some sort of identification issued by the person's employer. This service is open to all callers—customer and noncustomers. The bad-check loss on $35,000,000 was $53,129, approximately .15 percent.

With men like Lucian W. York, David H. Strauss and members of the Rich family as executives, the store grew steadily through the years. York was a colorful figure who rose from bundle wrapper to general manager. As a boy, he had been ticket taker in an Atlanta theater and all his life collected autographs of stage folk who became his friends. Any parade of minstrels or show people was likely to turn into Rich's and wind up in York's office. Long before a cow named Elsie became an attraction, York filled Rich's with living Georgia animals, including possums and goats, to advertise a harvest sale. For another occasion, the store became a Chinese palace. He inaugurated an annual sale on the anniversary of Whitney's cotton gin and on this day for years Rich's sold more cotton goods than any other store.

Emanuel Rich died in 1897 and Daniel Rich in 1920. The founder, Morris Rich, lived until 1928 but some years previously yielded his responsibilities to his nephew, Walter Henry Rich, a shy and kindly man who visited each department of the store daily for forty-five years and was one of Atlanta's best-loved citizens.

In 1901, the partnership was converted into a corporation with the number of stockholders gradually increasing to more than three thousand. In 1907, construction of a new building on Whitehall Street made Rich's the largest store in Atlanta. An expanded mail-order trade and an economy basement opened in 1910 increased volume. But Rich's was placed on the defensive in 1918, when its carriage-trade rival, the Chamberlin-Johnson-DuBose Co., moved into a new building.

Rich's answered the challenge with a still bigger building, completed in 1924 a few blocks west at Broad and Alabama streets. Other important stores moved from Whitehall Street at this time but instead of following Rich's to the west moved north to create a new shopping center along historic Peachtree Street. There were many who said that Rich's new location was a mistake.

With greater space, larger stocks, more help and increased expense, the store did only one-tenth more business and was left with a burdensome inventory. At this time, York, the general manager, died of a heart attack. As a final ominous note, Macy's was buying the rival Davison-Paxon store and Sears, Roebuck and Co. was building a $3,000,000 branch in Atlanta.

In this crisis, Walter Rich turned for help to Frank H. Neely, a mechanical engineer without retail experience but who at forty already had a remarkable background.

Neely was born in Augusta, Georgia, into a family which for generations had run largely to preachers and teachers. His grandfather had been the former and his father the latter. Neely was not quite five years old when his school-superintendent father died, leaving nine children, of whom the future engineer was the youngest. He had a rough time of it, being farmed out to various relatives, who were deeply chagrined because the young orphan had no liking for school. He was generally regarded as a sweet but backward child by all except a doting sister at Cedartown, Georgia, who kept urging him into regular school attendance. The arrival of some new farm machinery at a nearby farm brought the boy, along with others, to view it. Fascinated, he went home and said, "I am going to Georgia Tech to be an engineer."

A relative in Atlanta took him in and sent him to summer school to cram for entrance examinations. With no Latin to trouble him, young Neely sailed right through and at sixteen was entered as a freshman at the Georgia School of Technology. He graduated at twenty with highest honors and the mathematics medal.

Neely was one of the first Southern graduates to be hired by the Westinghouse Electric Company. The starting wage was $40 a month. After three successful years in its Pittsburgh shops, he reversed the flow of Southern technical graduates and came home, setting himself up in a small office as consultant on scientific management.

About the same time he married his childhood sweetheart, Rae

Schlesinger, and she began to apply the sort of scientific management which an intelligent and doting wife can provide. She kept him on an even keel and directed his enormous store of energy and ability. Once she insisted he spend the rent money to pay his membership fee in the American Society of Mechanical Engineers and attend its annual meeting. His articles were published in the association's journal. One of them, explaining a system he had worked out to increase candy production by a new conveyor-belt arrangement for wrappers, attracted the admiring attention of the late Frederick W. Taylor and Henry Laurence Gantt, who pioneered scientific management in American industry. The three became friends, and Gantt was a frequent guest in the Neely home until his death. Neely developed a passion for Gantt's charts and invented many of his own, applying them to the reorganization of the Fulton Bag and Cotton Mills, which had seven large plants in the South. He had been in charge of these for a decade when Walter Rich offered him the job of general manager.

"I've never worked a day in a store," Neely objected. "I'm too old to learn a new business. Besides you can't pay me enough." Thinking to end the matter, he asked for a salary roughly equivalent to that then paid the President of the United States.

"When can you come to work?" countered Rich. Thus Rich's in 1924 gained the distinction of becoming the first department store ever to be run by a mechanical engineer. Neely's impact was felt almost immediately. For that year, the store had net sales of $5,450,000. They were more than a million greater the next year.

One of Neely's first moves was to eliminate time clocks and have workers simply sign in for a record of being at work. He urged executives to worry less about this sort of thing and to spend more time training and encouraging their employees. "Habits of industry," he quoted Gantt, "are far more valuable than any kind of knowledge or skill, for with such habits as a basis, the problem of acquiring the knowledge and skill is much simplified. . . . The general policy of the past has been to drive; but the era of force must give way to that of knowledge, and the policy of the future will be to teach and to lead, to the advantage of all concerned. . . ."[2]

Looking about for executive help, Neely found in the store a young man, a graduate of the University of Pennsylvania's Wharton School of Commerce, who had worked at Bamberger's in Newark. He was Richard H. Rich, a grandson of the founder. A son of a daughter of Morris Rich, he had adopted his mother's surname legally after a family discussion at the suggestion of his uncle, Walter Rich, to insure preservation of the name into the third generation. Born and bred in the department-store brier patch, so to speak, he demonstrated intelligence and ambition.

About this time an eager young man from Georgia Tech presented himself at Neely's office. Always a patsy for anybody from his alma mater, Neely saw him. The young man said he was writing a thesis on the subject of department stores and was interested in whether a store in Rich's location could succeed. This caused Neely—also a seeker in the same market—to quiver in his chair and to peer intently at the young face before him, seeking some hint of leg pulling. There was none, and Neely went on to sweat out the study, leaning on it as a sort of augury. When thesis writer Ben Gordon graduated with an A-plus on a thesis which proved that management could make Rich's location more desirable than any other, Neely hired him fast.

Following the death of Walter Rich in 1947, Neely became president and two years later chairman of the board of directors. At this time, Dick Rich became president and Gordon executive vice president and general manager. They continued as a three-man executive team until Gordon left in 1955 to become president of City Stores Company. He later was named president of Stern's in New York and became a vice president of Allied Stores.

He was succeeded by Harold Brockey, who had moved from Chatham, New Jersey, to Atlanta in 1950 to become general merchandise manager of the store for homes. He was elected a vice president in 1954 and senior vice president and general merchandise manager for the entire store in 1955. He was named executive vice president in 1958 and became Rich's fifth president in 1961. At that time, Neely became chairman of the executive committee and Dick Rich, an impeccably tailored gentleman who likes to drive open cars, was named its third board chairman and chief executive officer.

To meet the challenge of Macy's mass buying, Rich's joined the

Associated Merchandising Corporation. This linked the store's buying with more than a score of big stores in other cities but kept the Rich slogan: "Atlanta-born, Atlanta-owned, Atlanta-managed."

Rich's refers to itself as a Southern institution and manages to create in its customers a feeling that they are privileged, dues-paying members. For many years a large share of its advertising has been institutional, identifying the store with the history of the state, its historical figures, colleges, artists, singers, musicians, the PTA, motherhood and so on. The advertising runs not only in Atlanta newspapers but in many others across the state.

When a hotel fire took 121 lives in Atlanta one weekend in 1946, the copy about a Georgia industry that had been prepared for the store's Monday-morning institutional advertisement struck Neely as inappropriate. He undertook to write something else.

After watching him crumple and throw away several drafts, Mrs. Neely, who is the author of a book of poetry, made a suggestion.

"Why not," she said, "just print the Twenty-third Psalm?"

This was done with the comforting phrases set within a black border. Only "Rich's, Inc.," in small italic type in a lower corner identified it with the store. When Atlantans recall the fire, they also recall this advertisement.

One of the stories told in the trade relates that an Atlanta competitor, attending a retail convention in New York, was asked the secret of Rich's success. "All they do," he said, with a wry face, "is stand on the corner and wave that blankety-blank Confederate flag."

But there is more to it than that. Bernard F. Gimbel, merchant prince in New York, spent some days in Atlanta as the guest of Robert W. Woodruff, head of the Coca-Cola Company. Gimbel cased the town thoroughly. A small dinner in Gimbel's honor was attended by Dick Rich, who suffered through seven courses with courage comparable to that of the Spartan youth whose vitals were being gnawed by a fox. The report was around that Gimbel would there announce that he was moving into Atlanta. After dinner, in an off-the-record talk, Gimbel praised Rich's highly and restored Dick Rich to a normal blood pressure by saying, "We don't care to come into Atlanta and buck competition as efficient and thorough as Rich's."

Rich's stumbles, of course, at times. A branch opened in Knoxville, Tennessee, in 1955, with radioactive atoms cutting the ribbons, for example, proved a disappointment, and was sold in 1961. Branches in shopping centers around Atlanta, however, have added importantly to sales and earnings. These begin with the Lenox and Belvedere Centers in 1959. A Cobb County Center store was added in 1963. North DeKalb County and Greenbrier Center stores followed in 1965.

The store operates the largest private automatic branch telephone exchange in the South. This system includes 1,115 internal stations and 120 outside lines. It is the approximate size of the central exchange for a town the size of Hawkinsville, Georgia (population 3,500). At peak periods, 17 operators handle a switchboard system which receives between 12,000 and 15,000 calls per day.

Rich's painstakingly identifies the store with the life of the city and state, for richer, for poorer, in sickness and in health. In the twenties cotton plunged. Rich's offered to take up to five thousand bales from Georgia farmers at a price well above the market, and did take what came in—a few hundred bales.

In 1930, Walter Rich picked up his morning paper and read that the city council had failed to find the money to meet the teachers' payroll. He telephoned the mayor and suggested that the administration issue scrip to the teachers, which Rich's would cash at full value with no obligation that they spend any of it with them. The city accepted with an alacrity exceeded only by the joyous pedagogues'. Rich's paid out $645,000 to teachers and held the scrip on faith until the city repaid it. The teachers and their families naturally think of Rich's as being more than just a commercial institution.

The Sunday before Labor Day in 1945, Dick Rich had the store's safe opened to provide nearby Fort McPherson with money to pay off a large detachment of troops who had arrived on Saturday afternoon to be discharged on Sunday morning. The fort's funds were in vaults time-locked until Tuesday.

Long before Britain's Sir William Beveridge was advancing his idea of service that commentators described as "from the cradle to the grave," Rich's had it in effect. When the youngsters are old enough to be brought along on shopping tours, Rich's has a nursery —sound-proofed, air-conditioned and decorated—waiting for them, with a registered nurse and staff. Germicidal lamps, which glare witheringly at all germs, are a part of the equipment.

The Rich Foundation gave radio station WABE-FM to the Atlanta public-school system. The schools use it daily for instruction, musical programs, lectures and announcements for which it is not possible to assemble the entire student body or class groups. The store provides four trips to Washington for the annual 4-H Club Leadership Conference. A savings bond is awarded to the best English student in each Atlanta public school. The Agnes Scott Freshman Award to the top freshman is also contributed by Rich's.

Rich's gave a building to Young Harris College, in North Georgia, and set up a foundation, through which a $250,000 building was erected at Emory University for a school of business administration, $100,000 was given to Georgia Baptist Hospital, and many other gifts were made. These have included an industrial engineering laboratory and an electronic computer center for Georgia Tech, and a wing at St. Joseph's Infirmary.[3]

Rich's provides headquarters for the three hundred garden clubs of Greater Atlanta and their ten thousand members. The traffic to Rich's is heavy. Fashion shows (many of them benefits) and lectures on homemaking, beauty and interior decorating lure adults. Periodic supershows called "Fashionatas" have New York models and scenery. They are produced by Sol Kent, fashion director.

A shopping service does more than remind citizens of anniversaries, birthdays, and special dates. The young ladies on the staff assist with weddings, help plan entertainments and offer suggestions on how to dress and how to decorate tables, rooms or lawns for these occasions. Each year hundreds of weddings in Georgia are planned by Rich's, down to the wedding cake out of the store's fine bakery.

The store does not neglect its ten thousand employees. As much attention and research are lavished on them as on customers. A forty-hour week was in force long before federal laws required it. So was the five-day work week. Rich's was the first Southern department store to institute them. There has long been a clinic, primarily for employees, where a registered nurse and staff furnish medical attention in the event of injury or illness, as well as advice on matters of family health. Executives are supposed to visit the clinic at least once a week for a rubdown and sunlamp treatment. All employees for years have been protected by a hospitalization and sick-benefits plan. A credit union, four employee cafeterias and a Christmas-bonus plan which includes every regular employee are a part of the program.

New sales employees receive two or three days' instruction before meeting the public and wear green training badges when they begin to sell. All are coached as to their appearance, manners and attitude. The store has a Junior Executive Training Program, known as JET for short, in which young men and women, some fresh out of college and others selected from the store, train for management jobs.

As of 1966, Rich's had 398 employees with 20 years service; 66 with more than 30 years; and 22 with more than 40 years. As the anniversaries of these employees roll around, an orchid is pinned on the ladies and the men are given ties.

The late Walter Rich wanted a store without any fear or awareness of big brass, and the store has none. "We can't expect our employees to be friendly to customers unless we lead a friendly existence ourselves," says Neely. The result of an absence of the big-brass atmosphere is a feeling, on the part of the employees of the store, of "belonging" and of pride in their job and work.

Perhaps the greatest tribute to Rich's was expressed in an address by Preston S. Arkwright, a president of the Georgia Power Company. After recalling that of twenty-three dry-goods stores in Atlanta in 1867, only Rich's survives, he said: "In all Atlanta, there is not a single human being who speaks ill of Rich's."

XIII

F. W. WOOLWORTH CO.

"World's Greatest Variety Chain"

IN THE SPRING of 1966, F. W. Woolworth Co. shareholders for the first time in their history did not meet in Watertown, New York. They gathered instead in San Francisco, headquarters of one of the company's nine regional organizations. Chairman Robert Campbell Kirkwood, who rose from "learner" to chief executive of the oldest and biggest variety chain, reported there on the company's record $1,443,322,466 sales and $73,001,321 profits of the previous year. The shift of scene was formal recognition of the fact that the company has grown to one vastly different from the "five and dime" chain created in 1879 by Frank Winfield Woolworth, an upstate New Yorker who spent his boyhood near Watertown and began his career in retailing there. It was also a belated concession to Lewis Gilbert and other stockholders who oppose meetings in remote places.

Americans could be sure of three things about Woolworth stores during the founder's lifetime and long after his death in 1919. They were modest, downtown red-fronted structures. They had the whole corporate name across the front. They carried no items priced higher than ten cents, or fifteen cents in the West. These are now only nostalgic memories.

The dime price level was fractured as early as 1932 and rose steadily in the fifties and sixties. To serve an affluent America and to maintain its leading position in the fast-growing mass-distribution chains (as Kirkwood prefers to refer to the so-called variety industry) some very large Woolworth stores now stock as many as forty thousand items, a few as costly as caviar, television sets and diamonds.[1] Newer Woolworth stores are big and more likely to be in a suburban shopping center than downtown. They are likely to be of a color other than red, perhaps of aluminum or glass. The name is usually abbreviated. The company's department stores, launched in 1962 with one on the edge of Columbus, Ohio, and nearly all in or adjoining shopping centers, are called "Woolco." It owns the Harvest House Cafeterias and its Kinney Shoe Corporation factories and stores continue under that name.

Frank W. Woolworth is in the Retailing Hall of Fame in Chicago and the distinctions of the company bearing his name are many. It has paid uninterrupted dividends since incorporation. It trains its own executives and all promotions are from within the organization. The more than 2,100 stores of the U.S. company serve all fifty states and Puerto Rico. Its downtown store in Denver, Colorado, expanded in 1963 to 174,000 square feet overall, is claimed to be the largest variety store in the world. The British Woolworth Company, in which the parent company as of 1966 owned a 52.7 percent interest, has more than 1,100 additional stores. There also are Woolworth stores in Canada, Mexico, the West Indies, Ireland, West Germany and Rhodesia. In 1965, a joint-venture Tokyo Woolworth company was set up to operate in Japan, Korea and Southeast Asia; and Woolworth Española, S.A., was established in Madrid under Thomas H. Gato, who had headed Woolworth stores in Cuba until their confiscation by Fidel Castro.

More than a million Americans a day eat at Woolworth lunch counters or in Woolworth restaurants, some of which are handsomely furnished, candle-lit places of considerable charm. The company is the country's largest commercial purveyor of foods prepared and served on the premises. In this field it competes successfully not only with its variety-chain rivals but with thousands of drugstores and restaurants. As of 1966, H. W. Bode, vice president of restaurant operations, was buying annually food for 19,475,000 hamburgers, 6,100,000 turkey dinners, 6,900,000 slices of apple pie and 130,000,000 cups of coffee.

Woolworth's is also the leading retailer of items such as greeting cards and dolls, as well as pocketbooks, phonograph records and pets of all kinds. It is an important seller of candy, Christmas ornaments, brassières, girdles, panties, hair nets and growing house plants. It is geared to take quick advantage of sudden fads. When the hula-hoop mania hit the country in 1958, Woolworth sold four million in five months. There was similar success later with records of the British Beatles and the more recent "Batman" fad.

It all grew from modest beginnings. Frank Winfield Woolworth was born April 13, 1852, on a farm in the town of Rodman, Jefferson County, New York. The family was of English descent and the name was an Americanization of a British place name, Woley or Wolley, and the Colonial progenitor, Richard, a weaver, was known both as Wooley and Woolworth. Frank, his younger brother, Charles, and their parents later moved to another farm near Great Bend in the same county.[2]

One of his teachers, Emma Penniman Otis, remembered Frank as a tall, thin, somewhat frail but nimble-witted and persistent boy. "Frankie was a bright pupil," she recalled long afterward, "and never gave me the least trouble. He was inclined to be sober-minded, not at all prankish, and always had his lessons." His schooling ended at sixteen and he worked five years on the farm. He had no aptitude for this and hated it.

In the depression year of 1873, he escaped by becoming a clerk, at first unpaid, in the Augsbury & Moore dry-goods store in Watertown. On his initial day, he appeared in a flannel shirt and was sent home to put on a white one and a collar and tie. He developed a flair for dressing the windows and, after an interlude with another store, advanced to $10 a week. He then married a neighbor, Canadian-born Jennie Creighton, a young seamstress.

The store, which had become Moore and Smith, with Perry R. Smith buying out Augsbury, offered a table of five-cent items in 1878. They sold so well during the county fair that young Woolworth became convinced that a store devoted to nothing else would prosper. With $300 credit from Moore and Smith and some money borrowed from relatives, he opened "The Great Five Cent Store" in Utica, New York, on February 22, 1879. The location was poor and it was a failure.

Undaunted, he opened another in Lancaster, Pennsylvania, on June 21, 1879, just ten days after closing in Utica. It was a success and doubly so after he added a counter of ten-cent merchandise. Enlarged and remodeled several times, this is the oldest Woolworth store. Stores at Harrisburg and New York were not successful but one at Scranton, opened in 1880 with Frank's younger brother, Charles Sumner Woolworth, as manager, was and the chain was launched.

Frank Woolworth liked the red color of the A & P stores and from the first painted his stores the same hue. The gold lettering was his own idea. He opened more stores and took in as partners or managers his cousin, Seymour Knox, and other relatives; also Watertown friends and men encountered by chance, such as Harry Albright, the postman who delivered mail to the store in Lancaster. Meanwhile his brother, Sumner, bought Frank Woolworth's interest in the Scranton store and together with Fred Kirby, a friend from Watertown, began two separate chains. While they minded the stores, Woolworth searched for merchandise in New York and Europe.

By 1895, there were twenty-eight stores and sales were more than a million a year. Five years later, there were fifty-nine stores and sales of more than $5,000,000. The chain became a New York corporation, F. W. Woolworth & Company, on February 16, 1905, with Woolworth as president. Carson C. Peck and C. P. Case were vice presidents. The fifty thousand shares of $100 preferred stock were offered at par to store managers and other employees. It carried 7 percent interest payable quarterly. The fifty thousand shares of common stock went to Woolworth and a few New York and Chicago executives. A regional organization was set up in 1908. The British company was started in 1909 with two stores in Liverpool.

Woolworth in 1912 took the lead in merging his and five other five-and-ten chains to form the F. W. Woolworth Co. Included were the stores of S. H. Knox and Co., headed by his cousin Seymour Knox, the stores of his brother, Sumner, those of Fred M. Kirby and Earl Charlton; also the stores of W. H. Moore, his old employer in Watertown, and for sentimental reasons the place was made the headquarters of the new company.[3] Through Goldman, Sachs & Company, $6,000,000 of $15,000,000 par preferred stock and $7,000,000 of $50,000,000 par common stock were sold to the public. They were offered at $101.50 and $55 respectively but soared to $109 and $80.75 the same day on the New York Stock Exchange. The new company had 611 stores. Frank Woolworth had slightly more than half the stock. He became president and the other four founders, vice presidents. The company had profits of $5,414,798 on sales of $60,557,767 its first year.

The famous Woolworth Building was completed the next year. Designed by Cass Gilbert and constructed by Thompson-Starrett, this 792-foot edifice wrested skyline honors from both the Metropolitan Tower and the Singer Building, previously claimants of the distinction of being the "tallest in the world." Woolworth's own office was an array of marble and Napoleonic relics on the twenty-fourth floor. He had personally paid the $13,500,000 construction costs. President Woodrow Wilson, recently inaugurated, pressed a telegraph key to light the building for the first time. His old friends from Watertown were present and it was perhaps the happiest evening of Frank Woolworth's life.

Because of his age and illnesses, he turned direction of the company over to Vice President Peck but resumed it when Peck died of diabetes in 1915. Woolworth died himself in New York on April 8, 1919, five days short of his sixty-seventh birthday. There were then 1,081 Woolworth stores with annual sales of $119,000,000. He left an estate, largely in company stock, of more than $27,000,000 to his widow, who died May 21, 1924, and four daughters or their children. One granddaughter was a wistful and beautiful girl named Barbara Hutton, who wrote poetry and married seven glamorous men.[4] Long after selling all her Woolworth stock, she was still known as a Woolworth heiress.

Buying and selling for cash; buying direct from manufacturers;

minimum selling costs, including low wages for sales help (though no lower than many other stores at the time); open displays on the counters and selling for low prices were part of the founder's formula for giving the customer more for his money.

He was generous with his executives and associates, treating many of them like the sons he never had. "At least a hundred men—buyers, heads of departments, managers," according to his biographer, John K. Winkler[5] became millionaires through their association with him. These included all who took part in the 1912 merger; C. P. Case, the early vice president; and Hubert Templeton Parsons, who rose from bookkeeper to general manager and became president on the death of the founder.

Stores were opened in Cuba in 1924 and in Germany in 1927. In 1931, the 1,081 Woolworth stores had sales of $282,000,000. Parsons retired in 1932 and was succeeded for three years by Byron D. Miller, who had been a builder of the British company. Charles W. Deyo, who had started as a stockman in an S. H. Knox store, became president in 1935 and later chairman of the board.

He raised store price levels to 20 cents and then more to continue paying higher wages to store personnel when NRA was declared invalid. He was so successful generally that directors waived the compulsory retirement to have him lead the company through World War II. He was succeeded in 1946 by Alfred L. Cornwell, who had started as a "learner" in Worcester, Massachusetts, and in 1954 by James T. Leftwich, who had started as a bookkeeper.

Profits continued, especially in the British company, and sales rose but the years after World War II presented many problems to the Woolworth organization. Population shifts made many downtown stores with long leases unprofitable.

All of these problems began to be attacked. The company was among the first of all variety chains in moving into the suburbs and in adopting self-service. President Leftwich launched an expansion and modernization program. To finance it $75,000,000 was borrowed from the Equitable Life Insurance Company and $35,000,000 more from various pension funds. A Finance and Policy committee, which included Leftwich and three directors, Allan P. Kirby, Seymour H. Knox and Fremont C. Peck, all sons of figures in early Woolworth history, spurred innovations.

They were stepped up further under Kirkwood, who became executive vice president in 1954, president in 1958 and, while continuing as chief executive officer, chairman in 1965. An urbane, friendly man with a gift for showmanship (a picture of him shining the shoes of the office shoeshine man on the latter's forty-fifth anniversary went around the world), he had been a Woolworth man since going to work in the Provo, Utah, store as a "learner" after graduating from high school there in 1923. He was manager of a store in Denver when twenty. He also managed stores in Sheridan, Wyoming; Mitchell, Bismarck and Grand Forks, North Dakota; and Des Moines, Iowa.

Lester A. Burcham, who was made president at fifty-two on January 1, 1965, also has spent his entire business career with the company, beginning as a "learner" in the Woolworth store of his home town, Lancaster, Ohio. The first store he managed was in Bellefontaine, Ohio, and he managed three stores in Cleveland, Ohio, when he went to executive positions in the Cleveland and Philadelphia Regional Offices. In January, 1963, he became executive vice president, after being appointed vice president in 1958.

Other top executives as of 1966 included Frederick L. Chaplin, board chairman of the British company; Alan B. Munro, vice president and managing director of the Canadian company; John S. Roberts, executive vice president. Other vice presidents included John E. Stromenger, merchandising; Walter E. Saunders, construction; Robert W. Young, personnel; Edward F. Harrigan, public relations; Harry B. Fogerson, real estate; James R. Webb, treasurer; Keith L. Sumner, expense; Henry R. Wilson, international; W. Robert Harris, sales promotion. Lester F. Davis was in charge of the Woolco Department Stores and Clifford O. Anderson was president of Kinney Shoe.

Regional vice presidents were: Harry E. Davidson, New England; Charles M. Dale, New York; John W. Lynn, Mid-Atlantic; C. Milburn Purdy, Southeastern; Richard I. Dale, East Central; James

E. Pierce, North Central; C. Walton Backhaus, Midwestern; Frank C. Kirkbride, South Central; and Hubert P. Smith, Pacific.

Hundreds of old Woolworth stores have been closed, expanded or moved to better locations. Bigger and bigger stores have been opened, a great many in suburban shopping centers. One was opened in the great Ala Moana center outside Honolulu in 1959. Self-service has become the rule rather than the exception. Clerks are in the aisles with the customers in newer Woolworth stores. Recruitment and training of employees has been made systematic and professional.

From a notorious nonadvertiser, the company has become an important user of newspaper space, often full pages in color, and of television and radio time. Its first network show was a Sunday-evening "Woolworth" musical hour over CBS in 1955. It has published some catalogs. Local managers are encouraged to take part in community activities and some have won awards for such service. The annual report lists contributions to youth organizations.

But the greatest changes have been in the merchandise. Few retail companies have ever upgraded entire lines of merchandise so dramatically. There is now a wealth of fashionable wearing apparel as well as better-grade household appliances and other items. A customer may buy a Java temple bird or an air conditioner.

A chain of competitive mass merchandising Woolco Department Stores was started and at the start of 1966 there were eighteen in the United States and nine in Canada with more scheduled to open at the rate of approximately thirty each year. Various forms of credit are offered in Woolco Department Stores. At the same time the company battled discount competition in Akron, Ohio, and elsewhere with frankly discount Worth Mart outlets. And in mid-1966, the company announced the beginning of a franchising program whereby other retailers would be authorized to use the Woolworth name and sell its merchandise.

XIV

THE J. L. HUDSON COMPANY

Detroit's Colossal Store

A YOUNG MERCHANT named Joseph Lothian Hudson was one of thousands of retailers to whom the panic of 1873 was a cruel blow. He was then twenty-seven years old and, in partnership with his father, was running a small men's clothing store in the lumber town of Ionia, Michigan. Soon after the failure of the Jay Cooke banking house in New York, the sawmills stopped in Ionia and Hudson's customers could not pay their bills.

The father died that year, partly from worry, but young Hudson struggled on until 1876. He went bankrupt, losing a flour mill and some timberland as well as the store that year to pay his creditors sixty cents on the dollar. He then started all over as an employee in another store.

Twelve years later, by remarkable enterprise, he owned a bigger store in Detroit. Even more remarkable, he looked up all the creditors whose claims had been erased by the bankruptcy proceedings and paid them in full with compound interest. Such action is rare enough at the present time. In 1888 it astounded the business world. The amazed creditors showered him with gifts and praise.

"We sent today by American Express two cases containing a clock and mantel ornament which we ask you to accept as indication in some small degree our sincere respect and esteem," wrote David T.

Leahy of E. H. Van Ingen & Co., New York. "Especially we have wished to make known to you our appreciation of your high sense of commercial honor as shown by your payment—in a quiet and unostentatious way—of principal and interest of debts forgiven to you by your creditors many years ago and indeed almost forgotten by them. Your failure was an honest one that left no stain upon your reputation. You could have found plenty of plausible reasons for not paying when you became able to. You chose the high and manly course. . . . Our best wishes for a merry Christmas and a happy and prosperous New Year."[1]

This letter is cherished today in the great Detroit department store of The J. L. Hudson Company, headed since 1961 by another Joseph Lothian Hudson, a grandnephew of the founder. The integrity that it memorializes is one of the reasons that Hudson's and its branches have sales of more than $300,000,000 a year.[2]

Hudson's downtown store has forty-nine acres of floor space and its twenty-five stories make it the tallest department store in the world. Its four basement levels also make it one of the deepest. In space under one roof, it is second only to Macy's Thirty-fourth Street. When Ford, Chrysler and General Motors work overtime Hudson's downtown volume, about 40 percent of its total as of 1966, sometimes exceeds that of Macy's Thirty-fourth Street.

Hudson's and Macy's, incidentally, have the largest switchboards among retail customers of the telephone company. Hudson's leads on trunklines and Macy's is ahead on extensions. Only the Pentagon, Metropolitan Life, Union Carbide and a few others have bigger boards.

Hudson's closest retail competitor in Michigan is its own Budget Stores. The two-level operation in the downtown store boasts one of the largest budget volumes in the world. Additionally, it has budget operations in its Northland, Eastland, Westland and Pontiac branch stores; and total Budget Stores in Lincoln Park, Madison and Dearborn. Hudson's is the largest store in the Associated Merchandising Corporation buying group.

One reason for Hudson's success is the completeness of its assortment of merchandise. In an institutional advertisement, it once boasted carrying 553,921 items "A to Z—from antimacassars to zippers, aspirin to zwieback. An African mask to Zeurcher cheese." Detroit's biggest bookstore, biggest drugstore and biggest toy store are all Hudson departments. Even a tiny department for dog owners offers canine candy, deodorants, dog books, leashes trimmed in gold, traveling boxes and supersonic whistles.

The drug departments, which employ thirty-six registered pharmacists, offer fifty thousand items. To serve Detroit's polyglot population, clerks speak fourteen languages and its stock includes ancient and exotic remedies as well as the sulfas and antibiotics. On the shelves are camomile flowers from Hungary, agar-agar from Japan, orrisroot from Spain, and oils from everywhere, including Turkish rose oil that sells for $16 for a few drops or $720 per pound. In addition, the store sells commodes, wheelchairs, canes, crutches, back rests, bed trays, sun and heat lamps, surgical garments, hearing aids and almost any sickroom article.

There is heavy emphasis on related selling. Hudson's is the No. 1 outlet for items like Simmons mattresses. But along with a mattress Hudson's likes to sell everything related to it, such as bedroom furniture, bedding, pajamas, nightgowns, bedroom slippers and even an alarm clock. Hudson's encourages home building with a planning center and often sells every item that goes into the home when it is built. At least half of all Wayne County brides are registered with Hudson's Bridal Registry and Xerox copies of their wishes and purchases for them go daily to all branches to avoid duplication of gifts. Numerous weddings are outfitted even to flowers and tickets for a honeymoon trip. There are whole floors for boys and girls and there is also a barbershop for children, where they ride a tiger or car while having their hair cut.

Also a factor in Hudson's success is the care with which it recruits, trains and keeps happy its 16,000 employees. The store has pioneered importantly in the development of buying and inventory controls and the use of business machines. It also lures 100,000 customers a day with year-round promotions, which include a Thanksgiving Day Santa Claus parade that is several years older than Macy's. It has a liberal returned-goods policy.

Most important of all in the growth of the big store has been a continuity of able, civic-minded management. When J. L. Hudson, the founder, died unmarried in 1912, he left the store to his four nephews. Richard H. Webber, who had been his uncle's companion since the Ionia days and who had risen to vice president in the store, then became president. He later became chairman and honorary chairman of the board, serving more than sixty-five years. His younger twin brothers, Joseph L. and James B. Webber became directors of merchandise and vice presidents, the latter dying in 1960. Youngest of the four, Oscar Webber, a Phi Beta Kappa graduate of the University of Michigan, began in the store as cash boy and advanced to president and chairman.

Six-foot Joseph L. Hudson, Jr., who at twenty-nine succeeded Oscar Webber as president in 1961, is a retailer by both inheritance and training. His grandfather, William H. Hudson, was a brother of the store founder who worked with him in Ionia. The young store head was born July 4, 1931, in Buffalo, New York, where his father, Joseph L. Hudson, was treasurer of the Adam, Meldrum and Anderson department store which absorbed an early Hudson men's store there.

He first worked for the Detroit store as a stock boy and receiving dock hand during summers while attending Yale, where he earned a letter as goalie on the hockey team and graduated in 1953. He then joined the store as an executive trainee, worked in the employment office, toy department and the downtown basement, now called the budget store. He served two years in Germany as an artillery lieutenant and on his return in 1956 became assistant to the general manager and a director.

The next year he was made vice president and general manager. He received the 1960 Distinguished Service Award of the Detroit Junior Chamber of Commerce for his civic activities and in 1965 was general chairman of the United Foundation Torch drive, a cause to which the store contributes around $400,000 annually. When he became president he was succeeded as vice president and general manager by Arizona-born Frank A. Colombo, who had joined the store as an honor graduate of Harvard in 1939. At the same time, Read Jenkins, store manager, and W. E. Simmons, upstairs merchandising, were named senior vice presidents. In addition to these, other directors as of 1966 included J. W. Paynter, financial vice president; F. J. Wilton, vice president and merchandise manager; Foster Winter, vice president, real estate and civic affairs; A. B. Perlin, Jr., vice president and general counsel; and Dexter H. Ware, vice president and director of personnel. Other vice presidents were C. E. Blanton, J. D. Coulter, E. D. Fisher, J. W. Harms, W. F. Randolph, R. B. Regan and H. K. Wallstrom.

During young Hudson's first five years of leadership, more than $6,000,000 was spent modernizing the downtown store and the suburban expansion program was stepped up. He expanded the store's interest in art, put in his office a canvas by his friend Enrico Donati, and opened a contemporary gallery in the downtown store selling paintings at $500 to $50,000. For this the store in 1966 paid $85,000 at auction for a Miró, a record for the work of this painter.[3] Though young Hudson is a Presbyterian who does not smoke or drink coffee, he installed a fine wine shop—the first sale of alcoholic beverages in the history of the store. Since 1956, it has also had a second Hudson. After graduation from Yale, his younger brother, J. Gilbert Hudson, joined the staff and a decade later was divisional merchandise manager for boys', sporting goods, camera and luggage departments.

President Hudson has resisted numerous overtures from interests of all kinds proposing merger or sale of the company or that it become a unit of one of the big chains. The store continues family-owned as well as family-managed. As of 1966, it had 170 stockholders, some living in England, but all members of the Hudson family or families like the Webbers into which they have married.

Joseph Lothian Hudson, the founder, was born, the third of seven children, on October 17, 1846, in Newcastle-on-Tyne, England, where his father, Richard Hudson, ran a small tea and coffee business. In 1853, the father migrated to Canada and found a job with the Grand Trunk Railroad at Hamilton, Ontario. Two years later the family followed. At thirteen young Joseph got his first job, as a telegraph messenger. He also worked as a grocery boy-of-all-work at $5 a month in Hamilton. In 1860, the family moved to Grand

Rapids, Michigan, where the father had another railroad job. Young Joseph worked on a fruit farm and managed to finish eight years of school. In 1861, the family moved again to Pontiac, Michigan.

There Joseph Hudson, now fifteen, met and went to work for Christopher R. Mabley, who was then running a small men's clothing store with sales of about $25,000 a year. The first month he paid young Hudson $4; this was doubled the next month and the youth showed such an aptitude for the business that, after five years, he was drawing $500 a year and board. The Mabley store volume rose to $100,000.

Mabley was a flamboyant personality who soon became one of the best-known merchants in the country. He was a pioneer in the then new field of men's ready-to-wear. This barely existed before the Civil War but when uniforms of Union soldiers began to be made by machine, it developed rapidly. Mabley was a big advertiser. He bought display space in newspapers and plastered fences and barns with his name. For a time, every fifth purchase made by a customer was free. He conducted pie-eating contests as publicity stunts and even raffled off horses, which he stabled in his show windows. Usually in partnership with somebody else, Mabley opened stores in Cincinnati, Baltimore, Toledo, Detroit, and elsewhere to build the largest retail clothing business up until that time. The Cincinnati store survives as Mabley & Carew.

In addition, one of Mabley's many ventures was a store in Ionia, Michigan, in partnership with Hudson's father. In 1865, the elder Hudson bought out Mabley's interest and induced nineteen-year-old Joe to take over the management. It had attained a volume of $40,000 a year when the panic of 1873 struck.

With this store bankrupt, young Hudson again became an employee of Mabley, this time as manager of his Detroit store while he went abroad for a vacation. Hudson did so well that he was rehired at $50 a week and given 10 percent of the profits. These amounted to $2,500 at the end of six months. Mabley then gave him a quarter interest and a guarantee of $7,500 a year for three years.

At the end of this time in 1881, Hudson went into business for himself. The first venture was in Toledo, Ohio, but within the year he opened a men's and boys' clothing business in Detroit on the ground floor of the old Detroit Opera House on the Campus Martius, not far from the present store site. Within a few years Hudson was prosperous enough to pay his old Ionia debts. He also opened branch stores in St. Paul, St. Louis, Grand Rapids, Cleveland, Sandusky and Buffalo. By 1891 he had eight stores doing a total volume of more than $2,000,000 a year and was the largest individual buyer and retailer of men's clothing in the country.[4]

Business troubles following the depression of 1893 caused the sale or liquidation of all the stores except the main one in Detroit. This was Hudson's favorite enterprise. In 1884, he formed a partnership with Campbell Symington and took over space in another building to sell furniture, rugs and carpets, draperies and curtains. There was expansion in 1887, and in 1891 he moved into a new eight-story building at Farmer and Gratiot streets and added more departments.

"He'll never make a go of it!" said Hudson's friends. The location was considered too far uptown and the fact that a Presbyterian church had occupied the site previously was deemed an ill omen for a commercial enterprise. But the store was successful. In 1895, it was incorporated as The J. L. Hudson Company.

In 1905, he shortened store hours with the comment, "It has been shown we can produce with the same labor in eight hours what we used to produce in twelve." An addition was made to the Farmer Street building in 1907 and in 1911 a ten-story building was constructed on much of the Woodward Avenue side of the block. Though all of this frontage was not obtained until 1923, the store began to take on its present appearance.

As his nephews assumed responsibilities in the store, Hudson gave more of his time to other activities. One of these was helping a niece's husband, Roscoe B. Jackson, and his partners, Howard E. Coffin and Roy Chapin, launch the Hudson Motor Car Company. Incorporated on February 24, 1909, the company was named for Hudson, who supplied most of the modest capital and became chairman of the board. The firm started with $15,000 in cash; models, patterns and dies valued at $25,000; and subscriptions later paid in cash aggregating $58,990. It proved incredibly successful. On the next July 3, the first Hudson car, an efficient four-cylinder twenty-horsepower model priced at $900, rolled forth. Within a year, four thousand had been sold. There was a profit of $587,355 the next year. This increased to $822,000 in 1912 and after Hudson's death earnings were as much as $21,000,000 in a single year. The company merged with Nash-Kelvinator in 1954 to create American Motors, Inc. Hudson also had another connection with the automobile industry. A daughter of his sister, Mrs. William Clay, married Edsel Ford.

Three times in his career, J. L. Hudson assumed large indebtedness when under no obligation to do so. The preservation of the Third National Bank of Detroit was one example. Following the panic of 1893, banks were shaky. The Third National Bank, of which Hudson was a director but not a large stockholder, was ordered to close in 1894. Such was J. L. Hudson's reputation that the Comptroller of Currency appointed him receiver. Hudson called the stockholders together, and announced that, if they raised as much as $1 among themselves, he would see that the $300,000 needed would be secured. In the final accounting, Hudson put up half the cash, helped pay off the depositors and re-established Detroit's confidence in its banks.

Hudson was perhaps the foremost philanthropist of Detroit and gave not only of his money but of his energy and personal direction. He was a humanitarian of rare quality, not only in the sense that he aided hospitals, orphan asylums, churches, scientific research, Y.M.C.A. work and innumerable charities, but he went out of his way to aid unfortunates.

A murderer who had served out his sentence came to Hudson with an idea with which to rehabilitate himself. Hudson said, "Your idea needs publicity. We'll go over to the newspaper editor and talk to him about it." Afterward, the editor asked Hudson why he walked over to the newspaper office with the felon, when he could just as well have called up or sent a note. Hudson answered: "I wanted to help the man regain his self-respect. I wanted to show that I was willing to walk with him and be seen with him publicly."

Hudson played an active role in his city's political affairs. Though he served in many appointive positions, he never accepted any salary. His own personal interests were of secondary importance. Two rival lighting companies were fighting the city's attempt to establish a municipal lighting plant. Hudson held stock in both of the private companies—and operated, in addition, his own plant for his own use. Hudson turned over his own plant cost figures to Mayor Hazen S. Pingee and the city voted to establish its own lighting plant as a result. Hudson was later named Detroit's first public lighting commissioner.

He founded, directed, and for many years practically supported Detroit's Municipal League, a nonpartisan body devoted to the general public's interest and local government affairs.

The store had sales of nearly $3,500,000 a year when the founder died in 1912 on a vacation trip to England. This was considered remarkable but the spectacular growth of Detroit and the enterprise of the publicity-shy Webber brothers (they were never interviewed and posed for few group pictures), multiplied this many times. While the average department store turned its stock four times a year, Hudson's turned its seven times. Sales grew from $4,000,000 in 1913 to almost $66,000,000 in 1929. When the depression hit Detroit hard,[5] Hudson's sales slipped to $31,500,000 in 1933. They then surged back, passing $170,000,000 with the opening of Northland, and have increased every year since 1955, despite some dips in Detroit's economy. The president of one competing firm committed suicide in 1957.

Many selfless, devoted executives have contributed to this growth. Some have spent their entire careers in the service of the big store. William T. Petzold, a parcel boy on the original staff, worked eighty-two years for the store, becoming secretary and treasurer. His son, Herman G. Petzold, for many years basement-store manager, was a vice president and general manager when he died in 1954.

Very important contributions were made by the late Carlos B. ("Pop") Clark, whose pride for thirty-three years was that he was "controller of The J. L. Hudson Co." Clark was a leader in formation of the Controllers' Congress of the National Retail Merchants Association and received this organization's first gold medal for distinguished service. As chairman for years of its taxation committee, he was the first to propose that individuals should be given credit for "earned" income on their tax returns and that corporations should be allowed reasonable deductions for contributions to charities. Congress adopted both. He left his mark on the operating systems not only of Hudson's but of many other great stores.

Physical expansion continued. Air conditioning was installed gradually. A regular cycle of interior modernization was adopted by the store's architectural staff with increasing emphasis on open displays and greater facilities for self-selection. In 1945 the old Sallan building at the corner of Woodward and Gratiot was demolished to make way for a twelve-story addition. Completion of this made the Hudson store a full block square. In 1946, two additional stories were added to the Grand River end of the building. In addition, the mezzanine floors in both the Woodward and Farmer buildings were enlarged.

All of this gave the store a ground area of 420 by 220 feet and a building containing 51 passenger elevators, 17 more for freight and 2 escalator systems. The building contains 5 restaurants and an employees' cafeteria. There are 705 fitting rooms, believed the most of any store, scattered over 10 floors. There is a store hospital, considered one of the finest industrial hospitals, with 4 doctors, 4 nurses, a laboratory technician, and 6 visiting nurses who make regular calls upon employees who are ill. The hospital also includes a silence room where employees may relax during their rest periods.

Suburban shopping centers came under consideration as Detroit began to share the traffic congestion which its products have created. The Webbers decided to build three centers to be known respectively as Northland, Eastland and Westland after a survey by the Detroit *News* revealed that 50 percent of the city's suburban residents did not come downtown to shop. A subsidiary company was organized and the first of these, Northland, twelve miles to the northwest, was completed in 1954 at a cost of $25,000,000.

With 1,317,030 square feet of roofed space, this was 25 percent larger than any previous suburban shopping development. Hudson's Northland branch store, managed by Dick Schroeter, a former University of Detroit football player, was located at the center of the development and is adjoined by 108 stores, shops and restaurants. Surrounding all is a paved shoppers' parking lot providing space for more than 11,000 automobiles and offering all of the stores an equal chance at customer traffic.

Northland stores had sales of $134,000,000 in 1965. Designed by Vienna-born Victor Gruen, the center combines beauty and efficiency. All truck delivery is underground. Colonnades, malls, covered walkways, modern art and flowers make the center attractive. Planted were 1,500 shade trees, 625 flowering trees, 1,900 evergreens, 18,000 ground-cover plants and 23,000 bulbs. Harold Gluckman and Alfonse Rapaczak of Hudson's display department painted a mural 500 feet long for the branch store. Fountains, statuary and other art objects by Gwen Lux, Lily Saarinen, Marshall Fredericks, Richard Hall Jennings and others adorn the malls. Miss Lux's "Totem Pole," a dramatic abstraction, is a favorite meeting place for shoppers.

Hudson's Eastland, east of the city, was completed in 1957 by its subsidiary, Shopping Centers, Inc., headed by Horace Carpenter, Jr. The Hudson branch there is surrounded by 74 stores and shops. Westland, a glass-enclosed mall-type center, was completed in 1965 at a cost of $10,000,000. It houses a Hudson branch and 50 stores 20 miles west of downtown Detroit. In 1966, a 96.5-acre site was purchased for Southland. Meanwhile, Hudson battled discount competition with "budget" branches in Dearborn, Lincoln Park, Madison, Oakland and Pontiac, the last growing into a full department branch.

Hudson's has the tallest flagpole in Detroit, rising 125 feet above the 24-story tower, to a height of 522 feet above the ground. The gold-leaf ball at its top is two feet in diameter. The flag flies every business day and downtown Detroiters watch it intently. Let it be a foot or two below the top of the pole, and several persons will telephone the store. Let it be ripped by a sudden gale and there will be more calls. A new flag goes up about every two months.

This interest in flags led the store to have "the largest flag in the world." The first big flag was made to order by Annin & Company of New York and unveiled on Armistice Day in 1923. It measured 90 by 230 feet and covered 8 floors of the big Woodward Avenue side of the store. The flag was displayed at least every Flag Day, decorated the U.S. Capitol in Washington on Flag Day in 1929 and was shown at the New York World's Fair. It was replaced by one still larger in

1949. Made in Detroit by the George P. Johnson Company, this is of wool and measures 104 by 235. It was given a new 50-star field in 1960. The stars are 5½ feet high and the stripes are 8 feet wide. The flag weighs 1,500 pounds and requires 6,240 feet of nylon rope.

In a long-remembered public-relations project, Hudson's designed a county flag for each of the eighty-three counties in Michigan. Then the store had the flags made up of fine material and presented them in ceremonies at county seats. Hudson's then published a book, distributed it free to libraries and other educational institutions, with pictures of each flag and a brief history of each county.

Probably no event of the holiday season other than Christmas itself is more keenly anticipated by youngsters within a hundred-mile radius of Detroit than Hudson's annual Thanksgiving Day Parade. Some 300,000 people watch it. Hudson's display staff, which creates and builds the huge and colorful floats, tries to visualize its work with the eyes of the youngsters it tries to please. Over twenty-five floats, one thousand marchers and more than a dozen bands take part in the huge spectacle, which has wound its way down Woodward Avenue every year since the 1920's with the exception of a brief lapse during World War II. It is a Detroit tradition; so much so that it is considered to be the official start of the holiday season.

Christmas at Hudson's means a Santa Claus awe-inspiring in his authenticity on a big golden throne in true North Pole surroundings. It also means ingenious animated windows and the world's tallest department-store building decked inside and out with trees, lights and decorations of a hundred different kinds. The Hudson Carolers, an employee singing group, appears daily during December on the selling floors, and ends the season with a Christmas Eve television show.

Art and music have always had a prominent place in Hudson's activities. School children have been entertained at symphony concerts and store musical organizations have made tours. Since the early days of radio, a daily hour of music has been sponsored on WWJ, Detroit's oldest station. The store's art department is the largest in any department store. For a "Michigan on Canvas" art project, Hudson's in 1946 employed ten leading artists at a cost of $75,000 to paint, without restrictions, scenes about the state. The artists were Arnold Blanch, Aaron Bohrod, Adolf Dehn, John DeMartelly, David Fredenthal, Joe Jones, Doris Lee, Carlos Lopez, Ogden Pleissner and Zoltan Sepeshy. The ninety-six canvasses which they produced, depicting automobile making, lake freighting, mining, agriculture and similar subjects, were exhibited in thirty showings and won Hudson's notice in *Life*[6] and many other publications. They are now displayed at Greenfield Village.

Hudson's advertising at times has lashed out at discount houses with long lists of branded merchandise offered at competitive prices "plus the advantages of the many services offered by Hudson's . . . plus the security of knowing that Hudson's stands back of every piece of merchandise it sells." Most of the store's heavy volume of promotion, however, is of a dignified and an institutional character. Besides heavy newspaper space—as much as forty-eight pages come in an issue of the Detroit *Free Press*—Hudson's also used a metropolitan shopping news, radio and television.

During Detroit's 250th anniversary celebration in 1951 Hudson's bought newspaper space to publish twenty-five biographical sketches by Dr. Milo M. Quaife, local historian, saluting prominent Detroiters. The store also changed all of its Woodward Avenue windows to historical dioramas of the highlights in Detroit's history. They were presented to the Detroit Historical Museum, where they now circle the entrance hall. The store also has erected bronze tablets at points of historic interest about Detroit. Several Detroit guides and histories have been published by the store and distributed gratis. Hudson's shoots off fireworks in the Detroit River. It gives a trophy to the first ocean-going ship to reach Detroit each year. It has authors sign books. It has sponsored Stock Market Forums with Merrill Lynch, Pierce, Fenner and Smith, Inc., and baseball coaching "clinics" with the Detroit Tigers.

The store's fame rests also on the loyalty and service of its employees. When John Thomas Williams, a Hudson doorman, died in 1961, a Detroit *Free Press* editorial saluted his "scrupulous alertness, tireless politeness and genuine friendliness to every customer."[7] This spirit extends to the handling of telephone and mail orders, and the faithfulness of its delivery men. Some of this is the reaction of well-trained and loyal employees. Mostly, it is the result of planning. Hudson's has a plan for nearly every contingency. For example, parcel-post shipments are speeded up by recording of their addresses by Dictaphone. If it begins to rain, a whole lot of things happen. The main-floor superintendent notifies the switchboard. The operators call several departments and tell appointed girls, "It's raining." By the time the first wet customers come in, extra umbrellas have been set out and there is extra help in the raincoat department.

The store has a charge account with Detroit's largest taxi company to provide a ride home for customers who become ill while shopping.

Through its personal shopping service the store serves many customers far from Detroit. Among these is the family of an American missionary in Bombay, India. For more than twenty years, the store has been outfitting the husband, wife and three children.

Hudson's has 500 delivery trucks, painted a distinctive green. Large trucks shuttle goods from the Woodward Avenue store to the delivery center a quarter of a mile away to three substations. Others fan out daily from these for points as far away as forty-five miles. The 280 men who man these trucks drive 4,500,000 miles a year, deliver 8,000,000 packages, and are among Hudson's best salesmen.

Hudson drivers have started countless cars on cold mornings for ladies in distress, pulled cars out of mud with their trucks. They regularly find and return lost dogs and children. They've started the fire on a cold morning when grandmother was home alone, then stopped to check it later. They've been slugged and robbed. They've hidden their day's receipts from would-be robbers. One had his face pushed through the glass of his truck by a bandit.

A weeping but thankful mother once called the store. She had been away when the driver arrived at the house, to be met by her young sons, one holding a revolver, the other some bullets, belonging to their dad. The driver took the pistol and got the next-door neighbor to step in and take over until mother returned.

A driver named Joe Krul had the most unusual adventure. It was just another busy pre-Christmas Saturday when he started on his package delivery route. Before completing his second stop, things happened. He heard a plane's motors close above. Then the thunder of a tremendous crash, just one street away. While his "jumper" ran to pull the fire alarm, Joe dashed to the scene. He stopped short. A big DC-3 cargo plane lay with it shattered nose buried in a home, a mass of smoke and flames. Women were yelling, "Save her!"

Joe looked up and saw a woman on the second floor of the shattered house, just staring, shocked. "The house was tilted over, so I ran up the side to the porch, grabbing onto the bricks that were shoved out," said Joe. He kicked the door in, dragged the woman out and passed her down to waiting arms. Then he leaped free of the collapsing porch. Wringing wet, dirty with smoke, his knees shaking, Joe called the store, headed home to change uniforms. Then he went back to work delivering his packages.

New Hudson employees, who are often chosen on the basis of aptitude tests, are indoctrinated with the store's ideals by tales of exploits like these and the Hudson Creed. This reads:

I believe in Hudson's because into its makeup have gone the finest thoughts of those at its head.

I believe in Hudson's because back of every piece of merchandise which crosses the counter, there is something which says to the customer, "If not satisfactory, this may be returned and full value given therefor." Furthermore, each and every piece of merchandise is the best that can be produced at the price.

I believe in Hudson's because I am putting into it myself—the best that is in me.

My faith is not alone a faith in the store, the organization—it is a faith in the ideals of men, those who are responsible for this great house of industry.

And so I stand inspired with the blazing truth that I am taking an active part in building, through honest effort, one of the greatest institutions in this broad country—Hudson's, Detroit.

XV

SEARS, ROEBUCK AND CO.

The World's Biggest Retailer

SEARS, ROEBUCK AND CO. became the world's biggest retailer in 1964. In that year its net sales soared 12.2 percent to $5,740,034,700 while those of the A & P, the previous champion, dropped 2.1 percent to $5,079,564,000. In the fiscal year ending January 31, 1966, Sears sales rose another 11.3 percent to $6,390,000,372. Both gains were double the national average. No retailer had ever before sold so many items in such quantities.

Even more remarkable, Sears usually earns on its huge volume a larger percentage of profit than the average department store, specialty shop or food store. Its growth and its rate of return on investment year after year have rarely been equaled by any big retailer. As of 1966, its common stock was the most popular retail investment of the mutual funds.[1]

Why has Sears been so extraordinarily successful? There are two alliterative answers, one: "Bargains, brains and ballyhoo."[2] Chairman Austin T. Cushman, who became chief executive officer in 1962 three decades after joining Sears as a part-time salesman in Oakland, California, explains in more dignified words. "Men, merchandise, methods and money," he says are responsible, "and men come first."

To these can be added motivation. Most Sears employees are well chosen and trained. Their salaries and benefits are considerably above average. They bring to their jobs loyalty and competitive spirit. If bandits rob a Sears store, employees are likely to chase and capture them. This is what happened to two gunmen who held up a Sears mall store at Troy, Michigan, north of Detroit, soon after it opened in 1965 as the biggest Sears store in the country.[3] Dallas-born Crowdus Baker, who became the ninth Sears president in 1960, and many other executives played football. They tackle their tasks as they once did runners on autumn afternoons. Stock-exchange quotations on both Sears stock and that of its great rivals, Montgomery Ward and J. C. Penney are posted three times a day in the lobby of Sears' South Homan Avenue headquarters in Chicago.

Most Sears employees act as if they owned the company. They do own a large part of it. As of the start of 1966, the fifty-year-old Sears Profit Sharing Fund, in which 172,393 employees then participated, was the biggest owner of Sears stock, 35,417,956 shares—23.2 percent of those outstanding. These were then worth $2,337,585,096 and the fund had other investments of $314,590,632. No other retailer has anything approaching this, and attitude studies of Sears employees by outside organizations on an anonymous basis repeatedly have shown that 95 percent of them would rather work for Sears than for any other company.[4]

Sears began as a mail-order seller of watches and jewelry and later general merchandise to farmers. Eugene Talmadge, several times governor of Georgia, won votes by earnestly assuring rural audiences: "Your only friends are Jesus Christ, Sears, Roebuck and Gene Talmadge." President Calvin Coolidge, a chief executive known for his thrift, was a customer.[5] President Lyndon B. Johnson, at the wedding of his daughter Luci, recalled that the wedding ring he gave her mother in 1934 was one for which he paid Sears $2.50. Today the company sells nearly everything to everybody and often on credit. One-fourth of America's families have Sears charge accounts, and credit sales accounted for 57.7 percent of its record 1965 volume.

In an exact reversal of the situation in the late twenties, about 25 percent of its huge volume comes from its famous catalogs and about

75 percent from its hundreds of retail stores, usually found alone or in shopping centers with ample parking space at the edges of cities. These are in every state, as well as in Puerto Rico, Latin America, Spain and, through Simpsons-Sears, Ltd., in Canada.

James W. Button, president of Simpsons-Sears and earlier a buyer and merchandising executive in Chicago and New York, on the death of George H. Struthers in 1966 was named vice president in charge of merchandising, the No. 3 post in the Sears hierarchy. The executive in this post directs fifty-one buying divisions, also the retail and catalog sales-promotion divisions and their supporting staffs. The buying divisions, forty-five in Chicago and six in New York, buy centrally from some twenty thousand suppliers and have branches in other cities and abroad.

The typical flow of merchandise is from a large manufacturer to a small retailer. Sears, on the other hand, is a large retailer dealing primarily with small or medium-size manufacturers, and its method of buying is different from that of most competitors. Instead of passively shopping the offerings of various manufacturers, Sears takes the initiative in product development; testing; design; cost, inventory and quality control; and all phases of production management, sometimes including financing. Sears develops specifications for the items it wants, locates a manufacturer to produce the goods, then typically tenders him a long-term contract for deliveries of merchandise over an extended period of time. The goal is to schedule production for maximum plant efficiency, hence lowest unit cost.

The more than 140,000 items now sold by Sears include mink stoles and sculpture priced as high as $39,500. With the exception of food, liquor and automobiles almost any article can be bought from Sears. While no automobiles are sold, the company does a big business in automobile supplies, including tires made by Michelin of France, and there are big Sears automobile service centers at Hicksville, Long Island, and many other points. From selling automobile insurance, Sears' Allstate subsidiary has moved into casualty, health, commercial, life and fire insurance.

No other company is as close to the heart of suburban and rural

America. No company has been more astute in forecasting future social trends and adapting its operations to capitalize on them. It has been largely responsible for making American living standards uniform. It has brought city refinements to farms. It has helped create a great hemispheric market for manufacturers. No company has had to overcome more bitter prejudices in attaining success. No retail operation has about it a greater wealth of humor, lore and legend.

Sears men give the principal credit for Sears stature to three remarkable executives, General Robert E. Wood, Julius Rosenwald and the founder, Richard Warren Sears. The last was born December 7, 1863, at Stewartville, Minnesota. His father was a farmer-blacksmith who lost all his money in a stock farm and died when Richard was fourteen. To help support his mother and three sisters, the boy learned telegraphy and went to work for the Minneapolis and St. Louis Railroad.

The turning point in his life came in 1886 when he was twenty-three and earning $6 a week as agent for the railroad at its North Redwood station. This served Redwood Falls, Minnesota, a county-seat town, two miles to the south. In an effort to increase its small freight business there, the line allowed its agent special rates and he dabbled in selling coal and lumber and also in buying and shipping meat and fruit.

Opportunity knocked when a local jeweler refused to accept a C.O.D. express shipment of watches. It was then a common practice for wholesalers to send unordered goods to retailers and when the "mistake" was discovered to offer it at half price. But the Redwood Falls jeweler would have none of these watches. So Sears opened up the box, made a deal with the shipper to buy them at $12 each, and began to sell the flashy gold-filled timepieces himself.

While similar watches retailed for $25, Sears priced most of his for $14. He sold watches to his neighbors. He sold watches to the train crews. Finally, he sent sample watches to his brother agents up and down the railroad and they began to sell for him. In six months, he made about $5,000 and left the railroad to start the R. W. Sears Watch Company first in Minneapolis and then in Chicago, where Montgomery Ward had been in the mail-order business since 1872.

The railroad later gave the green frame depot building in which Sears started business to the Redwood County Historical Society. Fire destroyed it in 1961.

While the watches that Sears sold were attractive and low priced, some came back for repairs. He also found that he could cut his costs by buying movements and cases separately and assembling them. So, on April 1, 1887, he advertised in the Chicago *Daily News* for a watchmaker who could furnish his own tools. The applicant who received the job was Alvah Curtis Roebuck. He had been born January 9, 1864, in Lafayette, Indiana. At twenty-three, he was earning $3.50 a week and his board running a watch-repair shop in a delicatessen store in Hammond, Indiana.

Thus began a famous alliance. Roebuck was a tall, unusually thin man, whose black suit and high collar caused some to think of him as a Methodist minister. He was gentle and unaggressive. Sears at the time was a handsome, mustached restless young man of ingratiating personality, boundless optimism and incredible energy. Of Sears, an admiring banker once said: "He could sell a breath of air!"

In addition to watches, the firm sold jewelry and diamonds, the last available on installment payments. Every article was "warranted exactly as represented," some of the watch movements were guaranteed for six years, and anybody dissatisfied could have his money back. A small catalog was printed and the wares advertised in magazines. A branch was established in Toronto.

Sears had a doubt early in 1889 as to the permanence of it all. At twenty-five, he sold the Chicago business for $72,000 to what became the Moore and Evans Company. For $2,950, he sold Roebuck and another employee a half interest in the Toronto branch and a little later for $5,190 the remaining half. Sears talked of becoming an Iowa banker and, in his mother's name, did invest $60,000 in Iowa farm mortgages. But in a few months he returned restlessly to the mail-order jewelry business.

As he had agreed not to do business under the Sears name for three years, he reopened in Minneapolis under his middle name as The Warren Company. But in 1891, Sears invited Roebuck to rejoin him and on April 6, 1892, the business was incorporated as A. C.

Roebuck, Inc. Of 750 shares, Roebuck held 250; Sears 499 and his sister, Eva Sears, 1. Sears was president; Roebuck secretary-treasurer, and the three made up the board of directors.

In addition to jewelry, silverware and pistols were sold. On September 16, 1893, the three-year ban on the name having expired, the firm became Sears, Roebuck and Company.

An enlarged catalog of 196 pages, nearly all written by Sears, appeared at this time. In addition to watches, jewelry and firearms, it offered sewing machines, furniture, dishes, wagons, harnesses, saddles, buggies, bicycles, shoes, baby carriages, musical instruments and a little clothing. Prices were guaranteed "below all others" for the same grade of goods and anybody unhappy with his purchase was assured his money back. In two years, the catalog was enlarged to 322 and 507 pages respectively, despite a serious business depression. To obtain better shipping facilities, the firm returned to Chicago.

Roebuck worried about the chaotic nature of the business. There was little system in filling orders. Sears sometimes advertised items without adequate stocks. Net sales increased from $276,980 in 1892, to $388,464 in 1893 and $393,323 in 1894 but profits did not increase and the firm's debts grew. This was too much for Roebuck's stomach and nerves. He insisted on selling his interest. Sears paid him $25,000 and looked for another partner.

Roebuck allowed the firm to use his name and continued for a time as the salaried head of the watch department. He then formed a company which made stereopticons, motion-picture projectors, and later typewriters for Sears, Roebuck and others. In 1925, he sold out for $150,000 and entered the real-estate business in Florida. When this boom collapsed, he returned to Chicago and in 1933 again went to work for the company that bore his name.

He was employed in writing a history of the beginnings of the company in 1934 when a manager asked him to make an appearance at one of the company's retail stores. The event was a success; some customers traveled a hundred miles to shake his hand. The next year, he was made a Kentucky colonel. He sometimes named Sears leaders and the money they made, punctuating each with "He's dead" and concluding: "Me, I never felt better." He continued happily to greet visitors in Chicago and to visit stores until his death at eighty-four in 1948. His contemporaries amassed great fortunes, but poor Roebuck outlived them all.[6]

The partner that Sears sought, meanwhile, walked in the door in the person of Aaron E. Nusbaum. He had made $150,000 from an ice-cream concession at the Chicago World's Fair in 1893 and had invested some of it in a firm making pneumatic tube systems. He hoped to sell Sears one of these, and the firm eventually installed an elaborate one, but he first found himself talked into investing in the company. More important, Nusbaum brought in his brother-in-law, Julius Rosenwald, who had been supplying some men's clothing.

The son of a Jewish peddler from Westphalia who established a clothing business in Springfield, Illinois, Rosenwald learned the business from the bottom up. He served an apprenticeship with his uncles who ran Hammerslough Brothers in New York. In 1885, he and a cousin started the manufacture of men's suits in Chicago, and in 1890 he married Nusbaum's sister Augusta. In 1891, their first son, Lessing, was born.

When the firm was reincorporated under Illinois law on August 23, 1894, with a capital of $150,000, Sears held 800 shares, representing $80,000. He was still president. Nusbaum and Rosenwald each held 350 shares worth $35,000. Nusbaum was treasurer and general manager. Rosenwald was vice president. But Sears sold more of his shares to the two until on April 12, 1898, each of the three partners owned 500 of the firm's 1,500 shares.

With his partners expertly handling phases of administration that bored him, Sears had more time for the advertising and selling, for which he had an extraordinary talent. The addition of rural free delivery to the mail service in 1896 helped the firm. Sales soared from $800,000 in 1895 to $11,000,000, a volume greater than Montgomery Ward, for the first time, in 1900. But it was not a happy partnership. Sears and Nusbaum were different types. Sears, for example, issued suggestions rather than orders and believed in praising employees. Nusbaum thought criticism more effective. He also refused to commit himself on important matters.

The crisis came in 1901. Sears demanded of Rosenwald either that he join him in buying out Nusbaum or that the two brothers-in-law buy the Sears shares. It was an agonizing decision for Rosenwald. He was bound to Nusbaum by many ties. His wife was Nusbaum's sister. It was Nusbaum who had brought him into the firm. On the other hand, the business had been built largely on Sears' understanding of the American farmer, his needs, his hopes, his suspicions. Neither of the other partners had this understanding.

Rosenwald sided with Sears. Nusbaum agreed to sell his third interest for a million dollars and at the last minute demanded a million and a quarter. Sears and Rosenwald were furious but agreed. By 1903, the full amount had been paid and Sears and Rosenwald were free to deal with other problems.

The country storekeepers and their friends opposed the mail-order business with slander and calumny as bitter as any in the history of commerce. The goods were denounced as shoddy. They were said to arrive damaged and late. In the race-conscious South, it was rumored that Montgomery Ward and both Sears and Roebuck were colored.[7] When Rosenwald included Negroes in his philanthropy, the rumors began anew. Under the pressure of local merchants, many newspapers refused to sell advertising to the mail-order houses and joined in the derision at their operations.

Where a storekeeper also was the postmaster, it took courage to accept the delivery of a Sears catalog, buy money orders in the firm's name and later pick up the merchandise all under his scornful eye. A man ran for mayor in Warsaw, Iowa, on the pledge that he would discharge any municipal employee buying from a mail-order house. In some small towns, children were given ten cents each or admission to movie theaters for every mail-order catalog that they produced. The catalogs thus collected sometimes were burned publicly, the only authentic "book burnings" in American history.

The net effect may have been to advertise the mail-order houses, to move the curious surreptitiously to send off orders. In the 1903 catalog, the firm offered to send goods without the name of the shipper appearing and promised to keep "every transaction with us strictly confidential." It countered the charges that its executives were colored by publishing their photographs.

There was also persuasive propaganda, both planned and fortuitous, in behalf of the company. Customers were invited to visit the firm when they came to Chicago. In the course of a tour, a visitor lost a $5 bill. Richard Sears gave him another. A village committee seeking funds to build a new church were told by a local merchant to write to "Rears and Soreback." They did and to the merchant's chagrin received $10.

An Ohio customer complained that the brake on a Sears bicycle ridden by his son had failed. In a pile-up into a tree, the boy's leg had been broken, a local doctor had set it improperly, and the boy seemed destined to become a cripple. Richard Sears had the boy brought to Chicago at company expense. A famous surgeon reset the leg and the boy recovered.

As the company's operations became systematic and the goods of better quality under Rosenwald's influence, there were more satisfied customers. In 1905, these were encouraged to make customers of their neighbors. It was one of Dick Sears' most successful ideas. In return for premiums in proportion to the resulting purchases, customers were asked to distribute catalogs to twenty-four friends. This was first tried in Iowa and produced such a flood of orders that the whole country later was "Iowaized."

That winter saw the firm move into a new $5,600,000 plant constructed for it by the Thompson-Starrett Company on a forty-acre site at Homan Avenue and Arthington Street on Chicago's West Side. Railroad sidings eliminated much of the trucking previously required. In the new quarters, order gradually came out of chaos. Unfilled orders no longer lay around for weeks.

A remarkable "schedule" system of handling orders was worked out by Otto C. Doering, operations superintendent, and others. The mail was weighed as it came from the post office in the morning and hourly during the day to give the departments an idea of the work ahead. The first automatic mail openers ever devised slit letters at the rate of twenty-seven thousand an hour. Girls removed remittances, checked catalog numbers, typed out order forms, stamped a scheduled shipping item, and shot them by pneumatic tube to stockrooms. From these, items moved by conveyor belts and gravity chutes to assembly points. There they were packed and dispatched by mail, express or freight. Some heavy items were sent direct from factories. Though filling and shipping an order involved twenty-seven steps, orders for a single item began to be filled in one day and mixed orders, involving goods from several departments, moved out in two days. As there was a different-colored form for each day of the week, delayed orders were detected quickly. Henry Ford studied the Sears operation before setting up his famous automobile assembly line.

All of this required money. At the suggestion of one of Rosenwald's boyhood friends, Henry Goldman of Goldman, Sachs and Company, the firm was incorporated in New York on June 16, 1906. Lehman Brothers and Goldman, Sachs and Company underwrote the sale of $10,000,000 in 7 percent preferred stock and $30,000,000 in common stock of the new corporation in return for $500,000 cash and $5,000,000 in common stock. The preferred was marketed at $97.50 a share and the common at $50 a share.

Sears and Rosenwald received $4,500,000 each in cash in exchange for their previous stock. The latter advanced $90,000 to some senior employees to enable them to buy stock. The preferred, all retired by 1924, was listed at once on the New York Stock Exchange and the common was traded there beginning in 1910.

Timing of the recapitalization was fortunate. The year 1906 was one of prosperity. Sales of Sears, Roebuck for the year were more than $50,000,000, an increase of a third over the previous year. But, in the fall of 1907, the Knickerbocker Trust Company closed in New York and a business panic followed. Sales of Sears, Roebuck for the fiscal year ending June 30, 1908, dropped nearly $10,000,000 to $40,843,866 and profits dropped 37 percent to $2,034,796.

Dick Sears, who had been traveling in Europe with his ailing wife, returned and urged increased advertising and promotion as a means of meeting the crisis. In earlier years, he had spent 9 to 13 percent of sales profitably on advertising. For the fall of 1908, he suggested going as high as 17 percent. Rosenwald opposed increasing advertising or any other expense on the ground that customers simply didn't have the money to buy more goods. When two of Sears' own appointees, Louis Asher, the general manager, and J. Fletcher

Skinner, the merchandise manager, reluctantly agreed with Rosenwald, the founder resigned as president on November 21, 1908.

He took no further part in the company's affairs though he was board chairman for a time and continued as a director until November 26, 1913. He had worked such long hours and at such a furious pace that his health, as well as that of his wife, was impaired. He spent his last years at Waukesha, Wisconsin, and died there in his fifty-first year on September 28, 1914, leaving an estate of $25,000,000 and a legend as a "Barnum of merchandising."

Under Rosenwald, who became president and later chairman of the board, the company entered a period of calm growth. Prosperity returned. Farm income increased. The company's first mail-order branch outside Chicago was established by Elmer L. Scott on Lamar Street in Dallas, Texas, in 1906. Dallas has been important in Sears business ever since. Others followed in Seattle and Philadelphia. The start of parcel-post service in 1913 proved a great boon. Dubious patent medicines and electric belts vanished from the catalog. This became bigger but less flamboyant. It began to include automobile and electrical items, including telephones. A thirteen-year-old boy named Charles Franklin Kettering bought one of the latter to dismantle and started his inventive career. From 1908 to 1911, an auto, the high-wheel Sears Motor Buggy, was sold at $445 to $495.[8]

More attention was paid to the development of reliable sources of supply. A testing laboratory was started to insure the quality of materials. One of the early laboratory men, Donald M. Nelson, later rose to executive vice president of the company, and during World War II headed the War Production Board. While on a hunting trip, Dick Sears had noticed a $150 cream separator in a farm kitchen. He thought one could be made to sell at $50 and found a manufacturer able to do so. Thousands of separators were sold. This became the pattern for many other ventures. When what was desired could not be bought, Sears invested in manufacturing facilities. This happened in the case of farm implements, pianos, stoves and many other items.

During World War I, Rosenwald became a $1-a-year man for the government and left Sears, Roebuck in the able hands of Vice President Albert Loeb, as *de facto* president. This gentle and able lawyer had been with the company since drawing the documents for Rosenwald's purchase of an interest in the firm and contributed greatly to its success.

While serving as chairman of the committee for the purchase of noncombat supplies, Rosenwald drew no salary from the company and allowed it to sell to the government only at cost. But he took along some Sears, Roebuck catalogs when he made a tour of American camps and hospitals in France as a representative of Secretary of War Baker and the Young Men's Christian Association. Farm boys in hospitals found the catalogs a voice from home. As the only civilian in a party of generals in the course of this trip, Rosenwald once introduced himself as "General Merchandise."

The most dramatic service of Rosenwald to the firm came in 1921. In the fiscal year ending June 30, 1919, Sears sales reached a record $234,242,337 with profits of $18,890,125. A 40 percent stock dividend was declared. The next year, sales rose to $245,-373,418 but profits dropped to $11,746,671. Prices of farm products began to tumble. Corn fell from $2.17 to 59 cents a bushel. Other prices followed and Sears was caught with millions of dollars' worth of merchandise bought at high prices. Many small mail-order houses failed. Lehman Brothers, Goldman, Sachs and Company and four Chicago banks loaned Sears, Roebuck $50,000,000 on notes but this was not enough. Despite a reduction in the number of employees from 21,652 in 1920 to 18,144 in 1921 and other economies, the firm operated in the latter year at a loss of $16,435,469.

On December 29, Rosenwald pledged $20,000,000 of his personal fortune, $4,000,000 in cash, to aid the company. He gave the firm fifty thousand shares of its stock and paid the cash as down payment toward purchasing its Chicago real estate for $16,000,000 if necessary. The cash enabled Sears to meet its bank debts. The stock rose eight points on the news. John D. Rockefeller, Jr., telegraphed his praise to Rosenwald and C. W. Barron, the publisher, wrote: "I do not know of anybody in the United States in the mercantile line who today is held in higher esteem or sounder regard than you and your great enterprise." Business improved, profits the next year were

$5,435,168, the debts gradually were paid and common stock dividends were resumed in 1924.

Two important new executives joined Sears that year. To become president, Rosenwald brought in Charles M. Kittle, executive vice president of the Illinois Central Railroad. While working in Washington, Rosenwald had been impressed by the ability of rail executives to handle large affairs. Before settling on Kittle, Rosenwald had asked an employment agency to list the ten most outstanding railroad vice presidents under fifty years of age. At the same time, he added a new vice president, Robert Elkington Wood, a retired Army general with whom he had become acquainted in Washington and who lately had been working for Montgomery Ward.

Kittle was without previous experience in merchandising but did not shrink from bold decisions. He supported the building of additional mail-order plants in Kansas City, Atlanta, Memphis and Los Angeles. More important, he and General Wood in 1925 took the company into the retail-store business, beginning with one in the corner of the Chicago mail-order plant. In that year, Sears' sales of $258,318,000 came 95.5 percent from mail order and 4.5 percent from retail stores. The latter figure grew steadily and from 1931 onward accounted for more than half of the firm's volume. Kittle did not live to see this. He died January 2, 1928.

General Wood was then picked as president by Rosenwald, still the largest stockholder despite huge gifts to philanthropy. Two older vice presidents, who may have expected the post, then resigned. They were Otto C. Doering, operations, and Max Adler, merchandising. The latter became interested in planetariums and built the Adler Planetarium on the Chicago lakefront in 1930 at a cost of some $600,000. Adler was succeeded by Donald M. Nelson and Doering by the chairman's son, Lessing Rosenwald.[9] In 1932 on the death of his father (who left $17,415,500 after giving away $63,000,000) the latter became chairman and on his retirement in 1939 was succeeded by General Wood. Replacing him as president were Thomas J. Carney, who died in 1942; Arthur Barrows, who retired four years later; and Fowler B. McConnell, who thirty years earlier had started to work as a Sears stock boy. But until his own retirement in 1954 in favor of Vice Chairman Theodore V. Houser, a veteran merchandiser, it was General Wood who led Sears. In 1955, he became the first living person elected to the Retailing Hall of Fame in Chicago.

He brought to Sears a background of colorful military experience. Born in Kansas City, Missouri, on June 13, 1879, he studied engineering at West Point, where he was graduated in 1900. After service as lieutenant of cavalry during the Philippine insurrection, he worked for a decade on the Panama Canal, handling supplies both for the Canal and the Panama Railroad. He retired in 1915 but returned to active service during World War I, became a brigadier general under his old Panama chief, Major General George W. Goethals, who was a Quartermaster General, and earned the Distinguished Service Medal as well as British and French decorations.

In 1919, Wood became vice president in charge of merchandising at Montgomery Ward. One of the first to see clearly the changes in American life heralded by completion of the Lincoln Highway and the increasing number of automobiles, he urged the establishment of retail stores to which farmers could drive. He also interested himself in the sale of automobile tires and put Ward far ahead of Sears in these though the general volume of the latter was greater than Ward's.[10] But differences with the president of Ward, culminating in a letter suggesting he resign, sent Wood to Sears. Four years later, incidentally, Houser, who was Wood's eventual successor as chairman, joined the Sears organization after spending ten years at Ward's. He entered merchandising after studying electrical engineering at Iowa State College.

While a retail organization was built, new lines of merchandise were added and old ones improved. What Wood and Houser had done for automobile tires at Ward's, they also did at Sears. In 1925, the Sears product was inferior and Ward outsold Sears in tires, 2,000,000 to 700,000. Wood drew specifications for a greatly improved tire and contracted with Goodyear to make it. Cash prizes totaling $25,000 were offered in a contest to name the new tire. One of the 937,886 entrants, Hans Simonson, an art student of Bismarck, North Dakota, won $5,000 for the name "Allstate." In 1929, Sears sold 4,300,000 Allstate tires, 3,000,000 of them in retail stores, and was far ahead of Ward. Goodyear gave Sears such favorable terms that the contract drew a Federal Trade Commission complaint and was a factor in the passage of the Robinson-Patman Act. The complaint came to nothing but the law caused Goodyear to cancel the contract and Sears returned to smaller tire makers.

The Allstate brand was applied also to automobile supplies and accessories and in 1931 to automobile insurance. The last proved one of the most successful Sears ventures. Carl Odell, a Chicago insurance broker who handled some of General Wood's policies, suggested to him that the cost of automobile insurance could be cut by selling it by mail. With Odell as an officer, the Allstate Insurance Company was organized with $700,000 from Sears. Within a year, it was operating profitably.

In addition to selling by catalog and at booths in Sears stores, Allstate added branches and agents. In 1952, it began to write comprehensive personal liability and in the next few years commercial and residential fire insurance and, through the Allstate Life Insurance Company, life insurance, beginning in 1957.[11] Commercial liability, personal health and group health and group life policies were added. A California Allstate subsidiary finances new cars and runs a building and loan association. During 1965, Allstate collected $799,145,938 in casualty and fire insurance premiums and $660,443,270 in auto premiums. Life insurance in force as of the year end totaled $4,386,000,000. Judson B. Branch, who began as a salesman in 1934, became president of Allstate in 1957, and on retirement of Calvin Fentress in 1966 also chairman.

Everything, of course, was not a success. A notable failure was a line of high-fashion gowns styled by Lady Duff-Gordon. She gave each a name and one was called "I'll Come Back to You." This was prophetic, for every dress sold of that style was returned. The sale of groceries, a catalog item for years, was abandoned in 1929 in the face of A & P competition.

Then there was the *Encyclopaedia Britannica*. Because Julius Rosenwald golfed with Horace Everett Hooper, one of the proprietors who brought the venerable reference work to America, Sears first marketed a "handy volume" edition and then in 1920 bought the enterprise. When Sears needed money after the 1921 depression, it was sold back to Hooper with a loss to Sears of $1,848,000. But in 1928, Sears purchased control of the *Britannica* and attempted to make a success of it, until 1943 when it was given to the University of Chicago. The *Britannica* was too costly and sophisticated for Sears customers. Five years later it began to publish a simpler and less expensive work. It also launched the Sears Readers Club, which offers best-selling volumes in low-cost editions.

The firm committed some egregious errors in establishing its retail stores but mistakes were corrected rapidly. Retail stores presented problems of display, merchandise selection, store layout and personnel that did not exist in mail order, but with the aid of outside experts, like Alvin E. Dodd, these were gradually solved.

Retail-store managers at first reported to branch mail-order plant managers who often had little understanding of the problems involved. A committee of Sears executives, composed of T. V. Houser, J. M. Barker and E. J. Pollock, and an outside firm of consultants in 1930, worked out a more workable form of organization. While preserving central buying and fiscal authority in Chicago, this called for both retail and mail-order plants to report to territorial executives. The depression delayed adoption of this but under Vice President Barker, formerly an assistant professor of civil engineering at Massachusetts Institute of Technology, it eventually was carried out.

The stores proved so profitable and inventories were so well controlled that Sears came through the depression thirties, with a loss only in 1932, when the company was in the red $2,543,641. Salaries were cut 20 percent. The next year there was a profit of $11,249,295 on mail-order sales of $120,334,000 and retail business of $167,860,000. Totals for both rose steadily, with the exception of 1938, but the retail grew at a greater rate.

World War II, which saw many Sears factories converted to war work and some of its hard goods available on priorities, slowed Sears growth only a little. Sales soared past the billion-dollar mark in 1946 and two-billion in 1948. By then, Sears had eight thousand suppliers turning out goods to its specifications and one thousand of them had been doing so for more than twenty years.

With the 1942 opening of a retail store in Havana, later expropriated by Fidel Castro, Sears started expansion into Latin America. As a young army officer in the Canal Zone, General Wood had invested profitably in a Panama City hardware store back in 1905 and realized the possibilities.

World War II interrupted the expansion program and it was not until 1947 that a big store was opened in Mexico City. Others followed in Guadalajara, Monterrey, Tampico, San Luis Potosí, Mérida and Puebla. Stores were opened two years later in São Paulo and Rio de Janeiro, Brazil. A crowd of 120,000 persons, including Papal Nuncio Carlo Chiarlo, who blessed the establishment, attended the opening of the latter. The first of six stores in Venezuela was opened in Caracas in 1950. Units followed in Peru and Costa Rica (1955), El Salvador and Panama (1956), Puerto Rico (1957), and Nicaragua (1965). In 1965, Sears had sales of $115,394,249 from forty-six stores and eighteen sales offices in the ten countries.

All Latin American stores of the company are staffed almost entirely with nationals of the country and the bulk of their merchandise is manufactured locally to specifications from Chicago. Local customs are respected to the extent of closing some units from 2 to 4 for the traditional afternoon siesta. Sears is the largest advertiser in Mexico.

Sears moved into Canada in 1952 as a 44.3 percent partner of the eighty-year-old Robert Simpson Company, Ltd., the second-largest retailer in Canada. Each invested $20,000,000 in a new company, Simpson-Sears Limited, formed to sell by mail in Canada and through retail stores to be located at least twenty-five miles distant from the five big Simpson department stores. The new firm paid $48,000,000 for the existing Simpson mail-order business and facilities. New stores were built at Ottawa, Vancouver, Hamilton, Moose Jaw, Kitchener, Calgary and elsewhere. In 1965, Simpson-Sears had sales of $351,708,203 from 26 retail stores, 4 catalog order plants, and 344 catalog sales offices.

Without counting Simpson-Sears establishments, Sears in 1966 had

786 retail stores, 11 catalog order plants, 1,294 catalog sales offices and 58 telephone sales offices. Of the stores, 178 were of the "A" type, a Sears designation for a complete department store with at least 100,000 square feet of selling space; 350 were medium-size department stores carrying extensive assortments of general merchandise; and 258 were hard-lines stores carrying major household appliances, hard lines, sporting goods and automotive supplies. All retail stores have catalog order desks.

A lot of Sears growth in the sixties came from the expansion of soft goods and the successful introduction of fashion lines in women's and children's apparel. Women were cultivated in many ways. In 1963, Mrs. Claire Giannini Hoffman, daughter of the founder of the Bank of America, became the first woman on the Sears board of directors. Forty percent of the business that year was in soft goods. Letitia Baldrige, formerly Jacqueline Kennedy's social secretary, was employed to advise on teenage merchandise.[12] In 1966, Lillian Jaffe, buyer of better furs for Sears, was chosen "Man of the Year" by the industry.

While Sears stores receive an increasing amount of their merchandise from nearby sources, store managers can buy only from a Chicago-approved list of items. On the other hand, no buyer can require a Sears manager to stock anything.

Public relations, advertising and employee relations became vital as the business grew gargantuan. Though not the primary target of the anti-chain-store and fair-trade-law agitation of the thirties, Sears operations were affected by both. The fair-trade measures caused the company to emphasize its own brands even more. Except for a few popular and well-advertised items, all fair-trade items were eliminated from the Sears catalog. The anti-chain-store pressure impelled the company to systematize its public-relations activities in a department, headed in 1966 by William F. McCurdy, a divisional vice president, and to identify itself more strongly with the communities in which it operated.

"Business must account for its stewardship not only on the balance sheet," said General Wood, "but also in matters of social responsibility." Sears' first community activities naturally were in agriculture.

As early as 1912, Julius Rosenwald gave $1,000 to each of the first hundred counties to employ a professional farm advisor. Learning that many of its farmer customers were part-time trappers who had trouble marketing their furs, Sears in 1924 started a raw marketing service without profit to the firm. Trappers sent in their furs and received money or merchandise as they wished. More than seven million copies of *Tips to Trappers,* a booklet by "Johnny Muskrat," were distributed. The Sears Roebuck Foundation has supported education, youth activities, community improvement and—with the American Medical Association—has helped many communities obtain medical service.

The company's newspaper advertising, which amounted to but $480,000 in 1925, has increased greatly. By 1945, this had grown to $11,130,000. In 1965 it reached $90,000,000 and in 1966 it passed $100,000,000. In the space, often with colored ink, Sears advertised not only its retail-store offerings but often its purchasing in the locality. A page in the Dallas *Morning News,* for example, pointed out Sears had four thousand employees in Dallas, and Sears merchandise sources included more than one hundred Texas factories in thirty cities and towns of the state. Space in the Rochester *Times-Union* explained Sears spends $11,000,000 a year for "fine merchandise produced in the Rochester area by Rochester craftsmen" and listed twenty-four local suppliers. In addition, Sears advertising utilizes circulars, radio and television and magazines, including full pages in *Reader's Digest* and *Life* prepared by Ogilvie & Mather, Inc., in Chicago. Marvin C. Lunde, Sears national retail-sales promotion and advertising manager, advocates "news value" and "use value" in advertising.

The ubiquitous catalog, which is really two large and three smaller catalogs a year, appears in eleven regional editions edited to appeal to sectional interests. Contents may vary and some prices may vary because of freight rates. Because of difference in climate, some items given space in one edition may be omitted in another. Items like diamonds and corsets appear in all, but heavy woolen union suits and maple-syrup equipment are found only in the northern editions.

Biggest of the catalogs are the two general catalogs issued for the spring and fall seasons. Each contains about 1,700 pages, weighs more than 5 pounds, and lists over 140,000 items. A poll of customers found that the most popular cover ever to grace the big book was a landscape by George Inness. For the 1934 edition, the late Edgar A. Guest, the famous Detroit poet, wrote a poem especially for the company titled "The Catalog." There also are two midseason catalogs of about 400 pages each, a summer book and a winter sale book; and a Christmas gift book of around 500 pages which appears in October. The catalogs cost from 40 cents to $1.95 each and up to 11,000,000 copies of each are distributed.[13]

The expense of printing and mailing some 60,000,000 catalogs a year is so great that much thought has been given to cutting their cost and increasing their attractiveness. In the early days, customers were asked to pay postage and it was sold briefly at $1. Free but judicious distribution proved the most effective. Anybody can ask for one and, in most cases, if he spends $25 in two catalog purchases in six months will receive the next one without asking. The firm once toyed with the idea of letting noncompeting outsiders share costs. In 1931, Chevrolet and the Curtis Publishing Company were allowed to buy catalog pages at $23,000 each in a short-lived experiment. From 1903 to 1923, Sears did its own catalog printing. In recent years, R. R. Donnelley and Sons has done the printing and binding under great secrecy with prices set into type only at the last minute.

Color printing, lightweight but improved paper and high-quality photography have improved the attractiveness of the catalog. From modeling for its pages, beauties like Joan Caulfield, Norma Shearer, Susan Hayward, Gloria Swanson, Elyse Knox and Anita Louise moved to Hollywood. Some seven hundred persons, mostly in Chicago and New York, produce the catalog, art and copy. This must comply with the frequently revised two-hundred-page *Advertising Guide* and is a model of accuracy, simplicity, taste and forceful salesmanship in print. Exaggerated claims and unrestrained superlatives are forbidden. "Sweat" is preferred to "perspiration." For hard work, the word is "pants." For dress, it is "trousers." The catalog itself explains: "Our descriptions are simple, honest, straightforward statements of facts." There is always the line: "Satisfaction Guaranteed or Your Money Back." When Julian Watkins, an authority on the subject, in 1939 chose "The 100 Greatest Advertisements," one was the Sears, Roebuck catalog.[14]

The catalog moves customers to telephone or send in orders by the thousands, as many as 100,000 a day to the Chicago catalog-order plant before Christmas. Each 100 pounds of mail contains approximately 3,500 orders for about $12 each, or $42,000 in business for each 100 pounds of mail. Most letters contain only order blanks but some are chatty missives informing the firm of the customer's health and activities, asking for advice on all sorts of problems, or even ordering a mate. There is a legend that at least one such order was filled satisfactorily. A plea from a Montana rancher fell into the hands of a spirited girl clerk who was weary of Chicago. They were married and continued to buy from Sears, Roebuck. The catalog of "Shears Robust and Company" figured pleasantly in the hit musical show *Finian's Rainbow*.

Good employee relations began with Richard Sears, the founder. He was chary of using first names but was as considerate of his associates as of his customers. He did not summon men to his office but went to their desks. His approach was "What do you think?" or "Will you?" and he was quick to praise good work. The company began to publish an employee house organ, *The Skylight,* in 1901.

Scott, who rose from Sears' office boy to general manager, eliminated night and Sunday work, common in the early days, and began systematic employee training around 1904. Scott opened and managed the Dallas branch until 1913. After differences with Rosenwald, he then resigned and devoted the remainder of his long life to welfare work, adult education and civic cultural activities. He was one of Dallas's most beloved citizens at his death there in 1954.[15]

Rosenwald also was concerned with employee welfare. Some of his activity was on the negative side. Of the sixty-two pages in a manual for new employees, twenty-eight were taken up with the evils of drink, the futility of smoking, the desirability of morality, diligence and thrift. He chased saloons from the neighborhood and the nearest put up a sign "First Chance."

But The Savings and Profit Sharing Pension Fund of Sears, Roebuck and Co. Employees, one of the company's greatest distinctions, was set up by Rosenwald on July 16, 1916. A stockholder, Mrs. Joseph T. Bowen, had suggested something of the sort to him in a letter a year earlier and he had been impressed by a plan started by the Harris Trust and Savings Bank of Chicago. It has since grown to be the largest fund of the sort not only in retailing but in all industry. Changes in it have only increased benefits for the employees.

To this fund, Sears employees of a year or more can contribute 5 percent of their annual salary but no more than $500.

Sears' contributions are figured on a sliding scale based on the company's consolidated net income before Federal income taxes and dividends. The percentage rises to a maximum of 10 percent on net income of $250 million or more. The maximum has been contributed for many years. Fund members are divided into four groups: Employees with less than five years of service; employees with more than five and less than ten years of service; employees with ten or more years of service; employees over fifty years of age with fifteen or more years of service. The company's contribution increases for each succeeding group. In 1965, the company contribution ranged to $2.80 for every dollar contributed by employees over fifty, with fifteen or more years of service.

Withdrawals can be made for emergencies. An employee, upon completing five years of service, who leaves the company for any reason receives his part. Many oldsters pile up sizable amounts.

Meanwhile, in 1931 a central personnel department was established in Chicago and it was decreed that no employee of five years standing could be fired without its approval. Under Clarence B. Caldwell, a former store manager who rose to vice president in charge of personnel, systematic training programs, involving manuals, films and job rotation, were evolved. Promising college graduates, sometimes six hundred a year, began to be hired systematically. Since 1955, Sears has made a systematic effort to hire the handicapped for certain jobs and to aid them in other ways. Snack bars in forty Pennsylvania stores are run by the blind. W. Wallace Tudor succeeded Caldwell as vice president in charge of personnel when he retired in 1956.

With an expanding organization and a rule that those earning $10,000 or more must retire at sixty-three, promotions are frequent at Sears. Regular estimates are made of future requirements. For senior assignments, these are made as much as five years in advance. The retirement of one senior supervisor may result in the promotion of fourteen persons.

Chairman Houser, termed "the greatest master of mass merchandising" by General Wood, was chief executive officer for four years, spending part of nearly every day systematically talking to distant Sears executives by telephone. He retired in 1958 and died in 1963. He was succeeded by Ohio-born Charles H. Kellstadt, who previously greatly expanded Sears' southern territory business. Practically "living" in the company airplane, he served as president 1958–1960 and as chairman from 1960 until May 4, 1962, when he retired and was succeeded by Austin T. Cushman, previously vice president in charge of the Pacific Coast territory, where he directed all retail and catalog operations in nine states.

Territorial vice presidents as of 1966 were Gordon M. Metcalf, Midwest; Charles A. Meyer, East; Lucien E. Oliver, South; Arthur M. Wood, Far West; and Alfred I. Davies, Southwest.

President Franklin D. Roosevelt suggested that the best way to convince the Kremlin of the superiority of the American way of life would be to bomb the Soviet Union with the Sears, Roebuck catalog. Something like this has been done. The Sears chapter of the first edition of this book was translated and published in both the Russian and Polish editions of *Amerika Illustrated,* the magazine published by the United States Information Agency for circulation behind the Iron Curtain.[16] The U.S.I.A. sends copies of the catalog regularly to the libraries of its overseas outposts. It may have had some effect. When Mrs. Nikita Khrushchev, wife of the Soviet Premier, visited San Francisco in 1959, she appeared at a Sears store before it was open. Roe Goisch, the manager, let her in and Titana Lysick, a Sears secretary who had been born in Siberia, translated for her and helped her shop. In an hour and a half, she bought a dozen of the best nylon stockings, many toys for her grandchildren and an armload of infants clothing, and paid cash—about $100.[17]

XVI

LANE BRYANT

Maternity and Special-Size Fashion Pioneer

"MATERNITY DRESS, size 32, Amerika," wrote a young woman in Poland on an envelope. With only this address, her letter reached New York and was delivered promptly as the writer intended to the Lane Bryant store on Fifth Avenue at Fortieth Street, opposite the stone lions of the Public Library.

Most of the company's business is now fashion apparel for women with fuller figures and other hard-to-fit sizes, but Lane Bryant is such a synonym for maternity that the post office could hardly have done otherwise. No other company in the world does as much business in maternity wear or does it so widely.

The story of the enterprise starts with the birth of an indomitable girl named Lena Himmelstein in Lithuania, then part of Czarist Russia, in 1879. Her mother died ten days after her birth. As a child in the home of her grandparents, she witnessed cruel Russian persecutions. At sixteen, she gladly accepted the invitation of some distant relatives to accompany them via steerage to America.[1]

They delayed telling her that they were bringing her along as a prospective bride for their son. When she met the young man for the first time in New York, Lena wept. Rather than marry somebody she did not love, she joined her sister Anna, who had preceded her, and went to work at $1 a week in a sweat shop.

This was in Lispenard Street, where negligée and lingerie manufacturing was just beginning. "We made beautiful lingerie for fast women," the immigrant girl later recalled. Within four years, she learned to speak English, learned machine sewing, and advanced to the then high wage of $15 a week.

She gave this up to marry a man she did love. He was David Bryant, a young Brooklyn jeweler. Evenings she helped him in his store and they made brave plans for the future. But soon after their son Raphael was born on February 3, 1900, the husband became ill. Six months later he was dead of tuberculosis.

As the expenses of his illness wiped out the store, his twenty-year-old widow was left with only a pair of earrings set with small diamonds, his wedding gift, with which to face the future. She pawned the diamond earrings for enough money to make a down payment on a Singer sewing machine and turned again to sewing as the only possibility of keeping her son with her and at the same time earning a living.

In a small apartment on West 112th Street, which she shared with her sister Anna, the young widow set up working quarters. It was the bicycle and shirtwaist era. The feminine ideal was the hippy and busty Gibson girl drawn by Charles Dana Gibson. Her waist was so tightly corseted that bosom and hips were accented. To achieve the popular hour-glass figure many women wore bustles.

The Gibson girl could buy blouses and skirts in stores of the day but her dresses had to be made for her. If she was wealthy, they were imported from Paris. If she was in modest circumstances, she made them herself. If she was in between, she had her clothes made by seamstresses working either in her home or theirs.

Mrs. Bryant's skill and instinctive love for fine things attracted an increasing number of customers. Women came in carriages for her negligées and tea gowns made from delicate laces and fine silks. But there were difficult days. She delivered the finished articles herself and sometimes had to spend hours waiting for customers to pay. The diamond earrings had to be pawned more than once for the purchase of materials and supplies. She worked with her young son on her knee. One day while her attention was distracted he pushed his finger beneath the swiftly moving machine needle. For a time it was feared that the finger might have to be amputated.

In 1904, the year that New York opened its first subway, young Mrs. Bryant moved to 1489 Fifth Avenue. This was between 119th and 120th Streets and only a short walk from Mount Morris Park, where there was a playground for her son. For $12.50 a month, the household of three rented the first floor of a new six-story building. They lived in the rear and used the front room as a shop, hanging garments from the gas fixtures.

Enough trousseau finery was made to cause the place to be known as a bridal shop. An early sign misspelled it "bridle." But Mrs. Bryant soon earned more than a neighborhood reputation for fine work of all kinds, especially for women of unusual proportions. She estimated lengths by eye, ignored tape measures and patterns, kept few records but turned out better-fitting garments than many of her customers had previously worn. More carriages began to arrive at the door and the earrings made fewer trips to the pawnshop.

Into the modest shop one day walked an attractive young woman for whom Mrs. Bryant had previously done some sewing. After exchanging greetings, the customer announced: "I am going to have a baby, Mrs. Bryant. What shall I do?"

For an instant the young widow thought that her visitor was asking medical advice but this was not the case.

"You make all kinds of things," continued the visitor; "can't you make me something that will be both pretty and practical and in which I can entertain at home?"

While the Empress Eugénie had been recorded as having worn a maternity dress in Europe, such a garment was unknown in New York in 1904, but Mrs. Bryant met the challenge. She created a comfortable and attractively concealing tea gown by the simple device of an elastic band attaching an accordion pleated skirt to a bodice. The result was the famous No. 5 maternity gown, so called because later it was given this number on a price list.

The first purchaser was grateful and enthusiastic. She was happy to pay $18 for the gown and praised it to her friends. She volubly told them about the ingenious little widow who made it. More expectant mothers ordered the tea gowns.

Word of Mrs. Bryant's talent and popularity reached the big downtown stores and two of them offered her jobs. But she preferred independence and the opportunity to rear her son. Her sister had married, and her new brother-in-law offered to lend the young widow $300 with which to open a bank account and to use as working capital for the purchase of fabrics.

Formalities required that Mrs. Bryant appear in the ornate quarters of the old Oriental Bank at 182 Broadway. She was so unaccustomed to the grandeur of the surroundings and the awe of having so much money that she filled out the deposit slip not as Lena Bryant, but as *Lane* Bryant.

Thus was born Lane Bryant. The young widow was at first too timid to rectify the mistake and later grew to like the euphonious name. She used it when she opened a new shop in a loft at 19 West Thirty-eighth Street, a few yards off Fifth Avenue. There she employed a dozen girls. Mrs. Bryant was still not free from financial worries. She increased her balance in the Oriental Bank to $400 just in time to see the institution close in the financial panic of 1907. She eventually recovered the money. In the meantime the diamond earrings again served as collateral. But, despite the unbusinesslike methods, the little business grew.

Romance flowered again for Mrs. Lane Bryant soon after her move to Thirty-eighth Street. Through mutual friends, the twenty-seven-year-old dress creator had met a handsome young engineer named Albert Malsin. He had also been born in Lithuania and they had many common interests. After being graduated as a mechanical engineer by the Polytechnic Institute at Gothen, Anhalt, Germany, Malsin emigrated to America and became associated with an engineering firm that constructed amusement parks all over the world.

Albert Malsin and Mrs. Bryant were married in 1909 and he adopted her young son, who henceforth was known as Raphael Malsin. For a time, the engineer continued his work. Mrs. Malsin, however, soon began to wear her own maternity clothes. Three children, a daughter and two sons, were born to the couple within the next four years.

At first of necessity, and later because he saw great possibilities, Malsin took an increasing role in his wife's unique enterprise. While she continued to design the dresses, he took charge of the business and began systematically to develop and expand it. Where his wife had worked without patterns and measurements, he instituted engineering exactness. Where she had set prices at sometimes the first figure that came into her head, he installed cost accounting.

To handle the financial end of the Lane Bryant business, which had grown to more than $50,000 annually, Malsin in 1910 enlisted the services of an astute friend, Harry Liverman. For his task, Liverman had a remarkable background. As a youth he had sailed from England to Australia to seek his fortune in the gold mines. There he took part in civic affairs and served as both city counselor and acting mayor of Leonora, Western Australia. En route there after a vacation in England, he stopped off in New York and decided to remain. His varied business experience and calm judgment proved invaluable to the Malsins.

One day Malsin and Liverman went walking and chanced to pass Crocker's, a store devoted entirely to the sale of mourning goods. This was possible because of the then rigid observance of mourning and a death rate that would now be considered high.

"This is a country of specialization," said Malsin, calling Liverman's attention to the mourning-goods store. Liverman agreed. They decided that Lane Bryant should specialize. The obvious first choice was maternity wear, to which the business already owed most of what success it possessed. Bridal finery was dropped.

The firm took the revolutionary step of designing maternity dresses for street wear. Up until this time expectant mothers had nothing appropriate to wear outside of their homes and few ventured abroad in the daylight.

At the same time the earlier maternity gowns and dresses for indoor wear were varied and improved in construction. In addition to the original elastic, drawstrings, snaps, hooks, buttons and other devices were employed to adjust the garments to changing figures.

To obtain maternity dresses in quantity, Lane Bryant abandoned on-the-premises manufacturing and began to create a unique phase of New York's remarkable women's clothing industry. By mechanically cutting dozens of identical dresses at once and employing high-speed sewing methods, this industry began to produce dresses at lower costs than ever before. By 1910, it was large enough to support a newspaper and *Women's Wear Daily* was founded. Since then the manufacture of women's clothing has become the biggest industry of the biggest city and its products have made American women the best-dressed women in the world.

At a time when any kind of ready-to-wear dress was a novelty, the manufacture of maternity dresses presented more problems than the average contractor cared to face. More material and more work were required for a maternity dress than for an ordinary dress. Some also believed the maternity business would never be great.

Lane Bryant overcame these objections by supplying designs, patterns, materials and, in practically all cases, by actually financing the contractors. Only then did the unique maternity wear begin to flow from the factory to the store. Once educated to the merits of the dresses, the suppliers helped work out more improvements.

One stumbling block remained. This was the refusal of newspapers, in keeping with the prudery that then existed, to accept advertisements for any kind of maternity clothing.

It was not until a memorable day in 1911 that the New York *Herald* accepted a Lane Bryant advertisement for maternity dresses. The copy read:

> Maternity wardrobes that do not attract attention. It is no longer the fashion nor the practice for expectant mothers to stay in seclusion. Doctors, nurses and psychologists agree that at this time a woman should think and live as normally as possible. To do this, she must go about among other people, she must look like other people.
>
> Lane Bryant has originated maternity apparel in which the expectant mother may feel as other women feel because she looks as other women look.

Response to the advertisement was astonishing. More customers appeared than ever before. Malsin, Liverman and a boy working in receiving and packing had to help the two saleswomen wait on the eager throngs. By closing time, the store's entire stock of maternity dresses for street wear had been sold for $2,800. Mrs. Malsin, who was at home with her children, could hardly believe the figures when they were relayed to her.

Lane Bryant's fame for maternity wear and also its regular advertising date from this day. The business doubled within a year and was moved to still larger quarters in the same block at 25 West Thirty-eighth Street.

As expectant mothers were still shy and embarrassed customers, the side-street location was an advantage to the store. Some sensitive women even took pains to leave their carriages a block away and to hold veils over their faces as they entered the premises. Mail-order customers often insisted that their maternity dresses be sent in plain wrappings.

Mail business even in 1910 was large enough for publication of price lists illustrated by simple line drawings. A 1911–1912 winter catalog of thirty-two pages was the first bound publication distributed.

Though other garments were made, maternity wear accounted for the bulk of the business and a 1916 advertisement announced: "Society should not be abandoned by the mother-to-be. She needs the stimulus of the Opera, the Theatre, and other social functions."

The year 1916, which saw a woman elected to Congress for the first time, also saw the business incorporated as Lane Bryant, Inc. Employees of the store subscribed to 25 percent of the capital stock. The company expanded its advertising from New York newspapers to *Vogue, Woman's Home Companion* and the *Ladies' Home Journal.*

World War I, like other wars, increased the birth rate. Young men marching the "long, long trail" of a popular song of the day and their wives wanted heirs. Lane Bryant's maternity business soared and the company's sales passed $1,000,000 for the first time in 1917.

As a natural expansion of maternity activity, Lane Bryant early developed and has continued a large business in simple and elaborate layettes. When twins or triplets arrive, the additional layettes are free.

Maternity dresses for street wear were no sooner established than restless Albert Malsin, who always kept a T-square and a drawing board on his desk, turned his engineering talents to another specialty. Maternity clothing was a fine thing but its possibilities were limited. Not all women became mothers and those who did so required maternity clothes only at a few intervals in a comparatively brief period of their lives.

Engineer Malsin began to study women's figures and found, as Shakespeare had observed four centuries earlier, that they came in an infinite variety. He began to chart feminine curves with the same thoroughness with which he earlier had planned the curves of scenic railways in amusement parks all over the world.

As a research tool, he invented a flexible yardstick for figure measurement. This device was of soft metal alloy which could be bent and twisted by slight pressure to conform precisely to the curves and angles of the human body. Springs held the metal in place while a tracing or other record was made. Release of the springs straightened the metal.

With this yardstick, Malsin measured the figures of 4,500 Lane Bryant customers. In addition, he obtained from a large insurance company the body measurements of more than 200,000 women policy holders. He also studied population figures as to sex and age.

Malsin found that nearly 40 percent of all women were larger in some or all of their dimensions than the perfect thirty-six figure idealized by designers and artists. They were entirely healthy, normal and attractive women. Nature and inheritance simply had chanced to endow them with more flesh than their slenderer sisters.

Here were both the challenge and the opportunity that Malsin was seeking. Stouts were stout all of their lives and many became stouter as they became older. At the time, there was no ready-made clothing for women of larger sizes and most made-to-order clothing actually seemed to accent the size of the wearers. Some had even written letters to Lane Bryant begging that clothing be designed for them.

"Won't some ingenious man please take pity on us poor stout women?" read a typical appeal. "It seems as if some way should be found for us to walk into a store and buy comfortable and also stylish clothes as easily as our slimmer sisters do."

Malsin recognized the need and Mrs. Malsin began to design

clothing especially for women requiring larger sizes. Dresses began to be made in a wide range of sizes to meet the needs of the three general types of stoutness that Malsin's research charted. These were the stout over-all type, the full-busted but normal-hipped type, and the flat-busted but large-hipped type.

As a crowning psychological stroke, a size system was adopted which allowed a woman who requires a 42 elsewhere to fit comfortably into a Lane Bryant 40. More important, colors and lines were chosen which minimized the wearer's silhouette. Lane Bryant's designs for larger women borrowed both from the "height, slenderness and airy grace" of Gothic cathedrals and camouflage of World War I.

> Camouflage is not the exclusive property of war [explained a company catalog], but has been used for years in architecture, in landscape gardening, in house furnishings and in the making of clothes. In camouflaging ships, for example, the idea was not to make the ships invisible, as many supposed, but to deceive the eye of the submarine observers as to the ship's size, its course and its speed.
>
> Likewise, broad eaves are used to make a narrow house appear wider, and a striped wallpaper is used to make a ceiling seem higher. By the same principle, if correctly applied to the designing of one's clothes, the wearer may be made to appear smaller or larger, taller or shorter, as may be desired. Lane Bryant stout garments are not merely large sizes; instead, they are especially made with lines that create the optical illusion of slenderness.

So novel was the idea of styles for fuller figures when introduced by Lane Bryant that both manufacturers and customers were at first incredulous. The store had to finance its initial orders. Some of the customers thought that "stretched" maternity garments were being offered. Many 1916 advertisements headed "Appearing Stout Is Merely a Matter of Clothes" were required to convince shoppers that a distinct new line was being created.

Half sizes were first developed to eliminate excessive alterations for the average woman—this means the average American woman, who is actually five feet five or under. The half sizes are distinguished by the fact that the shoulders are cut narrower, waistlines are shorter, hips fuller, and skirts shorter. The sleeves are fuller through the upper arm. They are generally young styles and close in fashion and styling to regular misses-size dresses.

In addition to negligees and dresses, Lane Bryant gradually added extra sizes in foundation garments, suits, blouses, sweaters, skirts, shoes, hosiery, both cloth and fur coats, gloves, sportswear and bathing suits until literally everything for the larger woman came to be stocked. Gloves are available in sizes up to 9½. Shoes are offered in sizes to 11, and in width to EEE. Even tent-size umbrellas are offered.

A salesman once attempted to sell a Lane Bryant executive a stock of reducing pills for sale to the store's stout customers.

"If these women reduced," objected the executive, "they wouldn't need our clothes."

"Don't worry," answered the salesman. "These pills don't work." Whereupon he was shown the door.

But even without pills Lane Bryant records indicate that larger American women are becoming more slender. Of the company's 38 to 60 sizes, 46 was long the largest seller. By 1950, it was 44 and 42 and 40 close seconds. Diet and activity have been responsible.

The introduction of each of these articles in special sizes presented all the difficulties that had been overcome in maternity wear. Manufacturers were reluctant to manufacture them. Large-size coats and dresses demanded a great deal more material and work than the same articles in usual sizes. The knitting of extra-size hosiery and the making of large shoes actually required expensive additional machinery. In the case of almost all of these items, it was necessary for Lane Bryant to create an industry.

When fashion and artists like John Held emphasized the slender, flat flapper figure in the twenties, Lane Bryant's service to fuller figures became doubly welcome. By the time of Albert Malsin's death in 1923 the store's larger-size sales had passed its maternity business in volume, despite steady increases also in the latter, and accounted for more than half of the $5,000,000 annual business at that time.

With such a background of success with the special-figure problems, it was only logical for Lane Bryant later to turn its ingenuity to two other important feminine groups with challenging figure problems of a different sort. These are tall women and chubby girls.

The average height of women in the United States is 5 feet 3⅙ inches. Thirty-six percent, however, are taller than 5 feet 4 inches; 20 percent are more than 5 feet 7 inches; and there are enough six-footers to compose several tall-girl clubs.

Women of the latter groups are taller than most of the men with whom they come in contact and must dress carefully not to appear too towering. Dresses and accessories expressly designed to solve their problems are stocked by the Lane Bryant "Over Five Seven Shops," under George T. Palley, son-in-law of the founder. These operate in Lane Bryant stores. For the tall customers there are even suitably long necklaces, earrings and umbrellas.

The chubby customers are young girls and teenagers who are plumper than their companions. The plumpness is usually a temporary condition but while it lasts may be a grave problem to sensitive youngsters. For these Lane Bryant established the first special department in which sizes were determined not by age but by measurements. Here attractive dresses and coats designed to minimize weight are available, along with underwear and other articles in special chubby sizes. These range from 8½ to 14½ for girls and 10½ to 16½ for teens.

A Chubby Club is also sponsored by Lane Bryant. The members have a newspaper, style shows of their own, and meet at intervals for special events. The discovery that other youngsters have the same problems gives members confidence and poise. The newspaper carries encouraging accounts of famous actresses and singers who outgrew their girlhood chubbiness.

The Lane Bryant special-size business has increased so amazingly through the years that it and the subsequently developed related departments account for 95 percent, and maternity garments for only 5 percent of the company's annual sales, which reached a record $135,673,218 in the fiscal year ending January 31, 1966. There has been a similar shift in the company's mail-order business.

In 1919, the stout catalog had fifty-two pages and the maternity catalog seventy-six pages. By 1950 the stout catalog had grown to one hundred pages while the maternity had dropped to thirty-six pages. Each issue of the latter goes on request to 175,000 prospects while each issue of the catalog of stout apparel is sent to 1,850,000 regular mail customers. Norma Shearer of motion-picture fame, incidentally, was once a model for the Lane Bryant catalogs.

As business increased and the modern wholesome attitude toward maternity developed, the Lane Bryant stores gradually emerged from side-street upstairs operations to Main Street locations.

When Harry Liverman succeeded Mr. Malsin as president after his death in 1923, Lane Bryant had stores in Manhattan, Brooklyn, Chicago and Detroit. Customers elsewhere were served by mail. Stores were established in Philadelphia and St. Louis in 1925 and in Baltimore in 1926.

Lane Bryant, in 1928, purchased two Midwest groups of stores, Newman Cloak & Suit Company and Benton's Coat & Cloak Company. These were combined as the Newman-Benton Stores and integrated by opening in them Lane Bryant departments selling maternity and special-size clothing. Other stores of this type have been added until now there are fifteen.

As of 1966, there were well over one hundred units of retail shops in all divisions of the company—sixty-seven of them operating under the Lane Bryant name. A dozen others in its discount-department-store division centered in Harrisburg, Pennsylvania, operated under the Town & Country name.

Mail-order operations were shifted in 1941 from New York to Indianapolis, where modern quarters provide four acres of floor space. There six hundred workers handle the mailing of some 8,500,000 catalogs a year and fill an average of eight thousand orders a day. For maximum speed, only right-handed girls are employed for this work. Lane Bryant's more than $20,000,000-a-year mail business is the sixth largest and the company boasts the most modern retail electronic mail-order plant in America.

Under the imaginative leadership now of Raphael Malsin, whose birth was a factor in the start of the business, the Lane Bryant company has recognized increasingly its obligation not only to its customers, but to its employees, to its stockholders and to the general public.

President Malsin is probably the only head of a retail company in America who is a member of both Phi Beta Kappa and Sigma XI, honor society distinctions which he earned at Yale. He was a secretary of the late Arthur Brisbane, famous Hearst journalist, and worked as a newspaper reporter on the New York *Mail* and *Evening Journal* before joining Lane Bryant in the merchandising office. He later became advertising manager and then general manager. He served with the Lend Lease administration in North Africa during World War II, is trustee of a hospital and is active in numerous civic organizations.

The five thousand employees of Lane Bryant for years have participated in a profit-sharing plan (they were among the first). This involves the annual distribution of a share of the company's profits before taxes. Employees share on the basis of length of service.

After one year, all employees are covered by an Employees Security Program, which consists of life insurance, Blue Cross hospitalization, major medical, surgical, health and accident insurance; all costs are borne by the company. Employees also participate in a company-financed pension plan. The pension fund, with assets of over $11½ million, guarantees a minimum of $600 a year to retired workers in addition to their Social Security benefits. Employees of stores acquired by Lane Bryant are given pension credit for half of their previous service.

Employees may continue their education under the Albert Malsin Scholarships. These are administered by the company's Twenty-Five Year Club. The company contributes $100 to the club as each member joins and the organization raises additional funds through contests and benefits.

After World War II, all Lane Bryant stores served as collection stations for maternity and other clothing for the devastated areas of Europe. Tons of clothing were collected and forwarded through various organizations to grateful women in a dozen countries.

Many Americans have vivid memories of aid from Lane Bryant in time of disaster. When explosion and fire devastated Texas City in 1947, the fifty-eight mail-order customers of Lane Bryant there received direct and through the Red Cross an offer to supply free new clothing to any whose wardrobes had been destroyed. The same offer was made to customers in Danville, Indiana, and Coatesville, Indiana, when tornadoes struck those communities. Some customers accepted in each area and scores wrote warm letters of thanks.

The company has done much to assure its customers that parenthood is a normal and even an amusing experience. There is a lounge for "expectant fathers" in the New York store. The firm's public-relations department, headed since 1946 by Jerome Klein, has given prizes for novel birth announcements.

Scientific prenatal care has been publicized by Lane Bryant since 1914. The company now mails free to expectant mothers a bulletin prepared by the Maternity Center Association titled *Stork Facts.* It explains the necessary care from the third month onward. Thousands of doctors give this bulletin to their patients. Lane Bryant also distributes booklets with titles like *Dear Well Rounded, Very High Fashion* (a primer for the tall girl) and *What's My Size?* It provides twice a year a two-hour program for women's clubs.

The Lane Bryant Annual Awards, $1,000 to an individual and $1,000 to an organization, "for distinguished volunteer service," have been presented since 1948. A third $1,000 award for volunteer work in the international field is presented every few years. Among the judges for these have been President John F. Kennedy, Norman Thomas, George Romney and Supreme Court Justice William O. Douglas.

Senator Paul H. Douglas of Illinois, in an address at presentation of an award to the Citizens' School Committee of Chicago, praised the company for "going back into the communities to search out and to recognize the groups of men and women who struggle unselfishly and without hope of reward to make our life better. . . . These awards may inspire others to start and to carry on similar works of unselfish citizenship." The awards earned an American Public Relations Association award for the firm.[2]

Such activities combined with conscientious service have made

Lane Bryant a world-famous institution and increased the company's business far beyond the dreams of its founder.

Mrs. Malsin, a modest, gray-haired grandmother too small to wear any Lane Bryant garment, lived to see her modest venture become a great enterprise. Though her sons had directed the business for years, she still had an office in the New York store when she died at seventy-two of a heart attack on September 26, 1951. After bequests to her sister and twenty-one charitable and educational institutions, her will divided her $1,909,648 estate, $1,795,034 of it in Lane Bryant stock, equally among her four children.

XVII

J. C. PENNEY COMPANY

Merchandise Chain in a Modern World

JAMES CASH PENNEY, a twenty-seven-year-old son of a minister, and two partners opened a tiny cash dry-goods store in Kemmerer, a frontier town in the southwest corner of Wyoming, on April 14, 1902. For his third, Penney, who ran the store, invested his $500 savings and a borrowed $1,500. His partners offered to lend him this amount at 8 percent but Penney found his home-town bank in Missouri would let him have it at 6 percent. Thriftily and characteristically he obtained the money there.

He named the store the Golden Rule, and remembering his Baptist father's admonitions undertook to deal with the local coal miners and sheepherders in accordance with the Biblical injunction: "Therefore all things whatsoever ye would that men should do to you, do ye even so to them."

Nearly all local trade was on credit at stores owned by the mining companies. Failure was predicted for Penney's store. It was only one room, twenty-five by forty feet, and off the main street. Penney and his young wife lived in the attic overhead. Their furniture was made from packing cases. Water had to be carried from a Chinese restaurant a few doors down the street.

With his wife as his only clerk at first, Penney went ahead

undaunted. By liberally distributing handbills in advance and by staying open from sunrise to midnight, they made first-day sales of $466.59. Thereafter, the store opened at 7 A.M. on weekdays and 8 A.M. Sundays and remained open as long as there was a miner or sheepherder on the street. Sales for the first year amounted to $28,898.11.

From this small beginning grew the great J. C. Penney Company, a chain of department and junior department stores that in 1965 racked up record profits of over $78,000,000 and sales of almost $2,300,000,000. In that same year, the company was able to sell millions of dollars' worth of merchandise every day by dealing with over 100 million different customers.

Penney today has 1,669 stores containing a total of 47,600,000-square feet. Its stores range in space from 2,500 to 250,000 square feet and in annual sales from about $120,000 to over $13,000,000. And its modern computer programming gives up-to-date, pinpointed control of both its fashion and staple merchandise.

For years, Penney has been the nation's largest seller of women's hosiery, sheets, blankets, cotton dresses, work clothes and men's underwear. More recently, it has spruced up its assortment of fashion merchandise, adding designer dresses and young-minded sportswear. It has done this by doffing its former T-shirt and coverall image and marching out in the direction of fashion merchandise.

From the beginning, profit-sharing has been a keystone of the company's operations, with managers and store employees sharing in the earnings they have helped to generate. There are year-end bonuses for everyone. For many years, there was a $10,000 limit on all salaries at Penney but this has long been done away with.

The Penney Company has made such an impact on the public that its customers sometimes actually petition the firm to locate a store in their neighborhood. One unit in National City, California, for example, was opened in 1954 in response to a petition circulated by Mrs. A. H. Bolen, who had been a customer before moving there. About this time, a rancher drove fifty miles to the Penney store in Buffalo, Wyoming, and spent $910 outfitting his ten children.

The Penney merchandising philosophy was set forth recently by

William M. Batten, chairman, when he said: "We are in the distribution business for any and all kinds of goods and services the great mass of people want. We will sell them anything for themselves or for their homes, in any way convenient to them, and for cash or credit, as they wish."

Many of the company's present policies trace back to the founder and his early associates in the little store that he opened in Wyoming in 1902. At that time James Cash Penney had a variety of experience behind him.[1]

He was born the seventh of twelve children on September 16, 1875, near Hamilton, Missouri, on the mortgaged farm of his father, an unsalaried Primitive Baptist minister. While keeping the farm, called Bluegrass for the Kentucky the parents had left, the father also bought and mortgaged a house in Hamilton to let the children go to school.

The family was poor. From the age of eight, Jim ran errands for money to buy his clothes. A number of childhood incidents made indelible impressions on him. For example, Jim learned a lesson in thoroughness one Sunday when he shined his self-bought $1 pair of shoes only in front and a neighbor named MacDonald called attention to them. Five boys of the MacDonald family later worked for the Penney Company, two becoming members of the board of directors.

When he was ten years old, Jim was in the pig business—at which time he learned a lesson in public relations after neighbors protested the odor. His father made him sell them at once, before they were fat enough for full value. Jim collected $60 and deposited it in two banks, lest one fail.

On graduation from high school, Jim began to grow watermelons on part of the family farm. When the county fair opened, he took a wagonload of watermelons to a spot just outside the entrance. He was doing a brisk business when his father ordered him home.

"You're disgracing the Penneys," said the minister. "Folks selling inside the fair pay for the privilege."

"But I wasn't inside the fair," Jim protested. "I was on the outside."

"Exactly," his father told him. "You were getting trade away from others without paying for the privilege." Jim never forgot this lesson in business ethics.

The boy's enterprise convinced his father that he had the makings of a merchant and a job was obtained for him at the J. M. Hale & Brother general store in Hamilton. The owner didn't need anyone at the time, but he took Jim on as a favor to his father.

Jim then went to work for Hale in 1895 for $2.27 a month. Though timid at first, he soon became a good salesman. In addition, he swept floors and sidewalks, sorted, dusted and kept the stock in order. He studied the stock so thoroughly that he could close his eyes and tell the grade, weight and price by the feel.

Jim's success in the store was a comfort to his father in the last days of his life. Shortly before he died, he said: "Jim will make it. I like the way he's started out."

Jim worked so hard at the Hale store that in three years' time his salary was raised to $300 a year. But he was also wrecking his health and a doctor warned him to get outdoors and out of Missouri. "Go to Denver at once," advised the doctor. "Otherwise you'll become a consumptive."

Jim did so. He worked briefly for two Denver stores, then went north to the small town of Longmont, where, with his entire savings of $300, he bought a butcher shop.

Longmont's leading hotel was his best customer. One day Jim's meat cutter told him that the hotel cook threatened to stop buying from them because they had neglected to send him a bottle of whiskey each week.

Jim bought the whiskey, sent it over and then, on second thought, regretted it. He remembered that, in Kentucky tradition, his grandfather and great-grandfather, although preachers, had each kept whiskey in their cellars. But his father had broken with that tradition. The more Jim thought about it, the more convinced he became that it was wrong to bribe the hotel cook. The following week he told the cook as much and promptly lost the hotel business. Not long afterward the shop failed.

Flat broke, Jim looked for another job. He found one at $50 a month with T. M. Callahan, who, with a partner, Guy Johnson, owned several stores in and around Longmont. On the strength of his $50 salary, the most he had earned until that time, on August 24, 1899, he married Berta Hess, who also had been sent to Colorado by a doctor.

It was with the backing of Callahan and Johnson that Penney opened his store in Kemmerer, which then had a population of one thousand. He did so well there that when his partners decided to end the partnership in 1907 he was able to buy the Kemmerer store and two others for $30,000.

By this time Penney was the father of two sons and hoped to have a chain of six stores. He thought he could do it with $75,000. "It's shooting at the moon," he told his wife. She assured him he could do it and Penney agreed. "If I can find the right men for partners. Men who are capable of assuming responsibility, men with indestructible loyalty rooted in confidence in one another."

After interviewing fifty candidates, he found one such partner that same year in Earl Corder Sams, a restless man from Simpson, Kansas. Sams worked first as Penney's clerk in Kemmerer, then managed a store for him in Cumberland and, in his third year with Penney, became a partner in a new store opened in Eureka, Utah. Sams became increasingly important in the company's affairs.

Penney's goal increased to a chain of twenty-five stores. He then had fourteen and his expansion program was based on this plan: Enable a store manager to accumulate enough capital out of his earnings to buy a one-third partnership in a new store, provided he had trained another man to manage his former store.

Penney believed he had no right to be in business unless he could save his customers money on everything they bought. He confined his stores to small communities, refrained from expensive locations, had no fancy fixtures, and handled only merchandise that created a general demand. This merchandise was piled on tables where customers could see and touch it, there was one price for all, cash was paid and purchases were carried home. If customers were not satisfied, they could return the merchandise and get their money back.

Penney prices in 1910 were unbelievably low. Children's underwear sold for as low as 7 cents, ladies' fancy cloth coats cost $2.98, men's heavy cassimere suits were $4.98 to $6.90 and men's ties retailed for 15 cents.

In 1910 the fourteen Penney stores had gross sales of $662,331.16. Penney then had eight partners, all of them small-town men who had started with him as clerks. He had given up management of the Kemmerer store and set up headquarters in Salt Lake City, Utah.

Soon after this move, Penney and his wife planned a long-postponed wedding trip to Europe. But before they could leave Mrs. Penney developed pneumonia and died.

Penney plunged into his work and opened twenty additional stores in rapid succession in eight Western states. Finally, still beset with grief, Penney went to Europe alone. When he returned he changed the name on the stores from the Golden Rule to the J. C. Penney Company.

Another change was made in 1913, when the company was incorporated under the laws of the State of Utah. Ten thousand shares of common stock with a face value of $10 each were issued. These were nonassessable, carried no dividends and were all issued to Penney as trustee.

Preferred stock, however, was issued to each of the partners in proportion to their individual store interests. Dividends were paid to the preferred stockholders on the basis of the earnings of each store.

By 1914, the chain had extended to 48 stores, and registered sales of $3,650,293.75. A central buying office was established in New York that year and Penney visualized a national chain with perhaps as many as 500 stores. Two years later there were 127 units doing an annual business of $8,428,144. When Penney went to the annual convention of partners in Salt Lake City in 1916, he nominated Earl Corder Sams as his successor. On January 1, 1917, Sams became president while Penney was elevated to chairman.

During World War I, when Penney headquarters were moved to New York, the government had imposed heavy taxes on business. One of the first things President Sams had to do was to find new sources for borrowing to finance the rapidly expanding company.

New York investment bankers did not approve of the Utah articles of incorporation and to win them over Sams and Penney agreed to change the preferred stock to a common issue. A board of directors was authorized to issue a limited amount of this stock for public sale to meet tax burdens.

This change satisfied the bankers and expansion went on with tremendous strides. Hundreds of new stores opened. In 1923 Penney bought the store from his first employer, J. M. Hale & Brother, in his home town. It was reopened as the five hundredth Penney store.

The company expanded further in 1927-1929 with the purchase of 54 stores from F. S. Jones and Company, 20 stores from Johnson-Stevens Company and 113 stores from the J. B. Byars Company and the J. N. McCracken Company. All of these were in the West and Middle West. Their acquisition pushed the number of Penney stores past 1,000.

At the end of 1929, there were 1,395 stores and the company reported record sales of $209,000,000 and more than $12,000,000 in profits. Penney stock was listed on the New York Stock Exchange beginning October 23, 1929, just six days before the stock market crashed and the depression got under way.

Sales dropped to a low of $155,271,981 in 1932 but even then there were earnings of $5,082,672. Recovery began for the company the next year. With 1,466 stores, 7 fewer than in 1932, sales soared to $178,773,965 and profits more than doubled to total $14,235,638.

Florida bank failures and a decline in the value of Penney stock at this time were a blow to founder Penney's personal fortune. He successfully met the crisis by again drawing a salary from the company for a time and by borrowing from five New York City banks.

The Penney Company was one of the first to recognize the strength of the anti-chain-store movement. From 1927 onward, the company directly and through trade associations fought anti-chain measures in courts, before legislative committees and in public forums. This activity was redoubled when Representative Wright Patman of Texas introduced his "death sentence" anti-chain bill which would have imposed additional taxes of $63,912,000 on the company at a time when its earnings were $13,739,160 a year.

As the first opposition witness at 1940 hearings of a Congressional subcommittee considering the bill, President Sams traced the history of his company and asked defeat of the measure for these reasons:

1. It would destroy the Penney Company or any other similar company.
2. It would destroy the finest field of opportunity that has ever existed in retailing for the young ambitious man born without family means.
3. It would add to the cost of living for every American family of limited means and would lower the American standard of living.
4. It would deal a staggering blow to the entire economic life of this country and would be especially destructive to the smaller cities and towns for the benefit of the larger cities.
5. It would hurt and tax this entire nation for the protection and enrichment of a small minority group of self-interested middlemen and of another small minority group of ill-advised marginal retailers.

Scores of witnesses, including spokesmen for farm, labor and consumer groups as well as the chains, followed Sams to Washington to condemn the bill and it was killed in committee.[2] No more states have enacted anti-chain legislation, and some of the earlier measures, such as those that were in force in California and Utah, have been repealed.

Proposals for mergers of Penney with Montgomery Ward and then Sears, Roebuck were considered seriously when the mail-order giants moved into the retail-store field but negotiations came to nothing. There seemed no way to transfer good will and trained personnel.

Although Penney has historically leased most of its stores, a flexible policy of ownership is presently followed where savings in occupancy costs can be achieved over leasing. The stores owned by the company are financed internally, as are the warehouses owned by J. C. Penney Properties, Inc., a wholly-owned subsidiary.

In 1965, 32 new stores with 3,200,000 square feet were opened, most of which contained large hard-goods departments. At the same time, 55 existing units were modernized and enlarged and 15 smaller stores were closed.

In 1960 the average new Penney store measured about 40,000

square feet. Five years later, the new stores constructed averaged 86,000 square feet—and 11 of them exceeded 110,000 square feet.

The prototype of the "new" Penney department store is the 195,000-square-foot shopping center unit in King of Prussia, Pennsylvania. This two-level facility has 32 major departments, 238 separate subdivisions and parking in the plaza for 9,000 cars. Among the services offered in this store are a snack bar, an optical shop, a beauty salon and a portrait studio.

Penney deals with 7,000 merchandise suppliers throughout the world. But, unlike some other large chains that have a financial stake in many companies that manufacture their goods, Penney has no monetary interest in any of its resources.

There are presently Penney stores in operation in 49 of the 50 states in the union. California has the largest number of these stores with 159 and Texas is next with 138. There are Penney stores in Levittown, New York, and Levittown, Pennsylvania, in Anchorage, Alaska, and Honolulu, Hawaii, in the suburbs of Chicago and in downtown Denver.

It was in 1958 that a 150-page report following an intensive, internal two-year study of their company convinced Penney officials that sweeping merchandising and operational changes had to be made. The most serious problem found was that 96 percent of Penney's volume was in soft lines. This heavy preponderance of apparel and home furnishings meant, according to one vice president:

"We had no browsing areas for men while their wives shopped, like paint and hardware departments. We had nothing to attract the kids, like a toy department. We realized we needed to tend more toward the one-stop shopping idea."[3]

While soft goods still predominate at Penney, hard lines—also with Penney private labels—are very much in evidence. In those stores with hard-goods departments, the ratio is 70 percent soft lines to 30 percent hard lines.

Another recent innovation has been the use of door-to-door salesmen to sell carpeting, curtains, drapery and furniture coverings. More than a hundred Penney stores have this home service available.

While Penney store buildings vary greatly, Penney men and women are usually the same everywhere—rarely flashy but always hard-working and trustworthy individuals who are assets to their stores and communities. Their company trusts them. The more than $2 billion that flows into its cash registers each year is largely cash or the equivalent and managers bank it locally. But no Penney employee is bonded. While a Penney man goes wrong now and then, the loss is much less than the cost would be to bond all who handle money.

A "Penney type" man, besides liking retailing, must know how to be helpful to people and treat them fairly. He must know how to make money and build a business. He must know how to make a place for himself in any community where he may be sent.

The company has some 62,500 "associates"—the word "employee" isn't used at Penney. To train them and keep them abreast of new sales techniques, Penney uses sales courses on teaching machines that can be circulated from store to store.

Just like all other employees, the top Penney executives have started at the bottom. Earl Sams, as noted, began as a clerk in the original Kemmerer store. After managing several other stores, he served as president from 1917 to 1946. He was then named board chairman until 1950, when he died at sixty-six, leaving an estate of $9,340,468.

J. C. Penney retained the chairmanship of the company he founded until 1946. He took the post again after Sams died and held it until 1958, when he relinquished it to Albert W. Hughes.

Hughes's history with the company is typical of a successful Penney executive. When he was a young man, he tutored Penney's sons in Latin at the Hill School in Pottstown, Pennsylvania, and quickly decided that retailing would be more exciting than teaching a dead language. He began in a store at Moberly, Missouri, and later managed stores in Utah and Georgia. Later he became head of the personnel department in New York, was elected a vice president of the company in 1937 and was named president in 1946.

William Batten, now the chairman of the board, first worked for Penney in 1926 while attending high school in Parkersburg, West Virginia, his birthplace. He washed windows, worked in the stock-room and then sold shoes. After graduation from Ohio State University, he joined Penney in Lansing, Michigan, in 1935, as a shoe salesman. He became assistant manager of the store and then joined the personnel training department in New York. Batten moved up the ranks to presidency in 1958 and the chairmanship in 1964—and now spends the bulk of his time concentrating on long-range planning and corporate affairs.

The president of the company is Ray H. Jordan, a Missourian whose Penney career began in 1930 in Picher, Oklahoma. He moved up through various positions to executive vice president in 1959 and president in 1964. Jordan is responsible for day-to-day operations.

Linking headquarters and store managers are five zone and fifty-nine district managers. These men spend most of their time visiting stores to counsel with managers on problems of all kinds, to detect new customer tastes, and to help train store personnel. Zone and district men meet for a fortnight in New York each December. There are also quarterly district meetings for managers, who, in turn, meet frequently with their department heads and clerks. There is free discussion at all levels—which Penney executives regard as a great source of company strength.

The store manager is the key man. He hires and trains his own help. If he runs a store in the Southwest, this may include such things as giving Spanish lessons. He decides what to do about advertising and supporting local causes.

The store manager at Penney orders most of his merchandise from lists and samples sent him by headquarters but is not required to accept anything he thinks unsuited to his climate or his customers' tastes. He can choose which central office training, promotion and advertising aids best fit his needs. Ninety percent of the advertising expenditure is usually in newspapers but managers can use other media if they like.

Penney has a retirement plan into which employees can deposit from 3 to 10 percent of their salaries. The company adds several times this amount, based on its profits, and even if the employee deposits nothing he has an account in the plan if he qualifies. The money can be drawn out in time of need or when the worker retires or leaves the company.

Fashion as well as value is now stressed in Penney apparel. Cashmere sweaters and other quality items are now offered as part of a general trading-up policy. A semiannual publication, *Fashions and Fabrics*, reports fashion news and forecasts trends for the home sewer. Fifty thousand copies of this magazine are given away to home-economics teachers and others as part of the company's public-relations program. This program also includes the circulation of motion-picture films on Penney operations to schools and colleges.

Most Penney buying is done in New York, although buying offices in Dallas, Miami and Los Angeles cover the ready-to-wear and similar industries in those areas. While the company once owned its own corset and brassière factory, everything is now purchased, partly in the open market but primarily from manufacturers with whom buyers work closely to plan articles of definite quality to sell at predetermined prices. The International Silver Company, for example, created silverwear of a special pattern for both the Penney twenty-fifth and fiftieth anniversaries.

In recent years, the company has taken steps to upgrade its hard-goods lines to the same prominence as its apparel and home furnishings. Some of the country's leading durable goods manufacturers—like the Hotpoint division of General Electric Company, the Goodyear Tire & Rubber Company and the S.C.M. Corporation—now produce merchandise under Penney's own private labels.

All of this, says Chairman Batten, is a part of the company's basic strategy: "The broadening of merchandise assortments to include a greater representation of hard goods . . . and two, the introduction of services such as charge accounts and catalog shopping to make shopping at Penney's easier."

Credit, which was only introduced at Penney in 1958 and against the wishes of the founder, now accounts for one-third of the company's total sales. And catalog selling, which began in the Midwest when Penney bought the General Merchandise Company of Milwaukee in 1962, was extended into the Southeast in 1965.

Penney's goal is to have a nationwide catalog service, *à la* Sears, Roebuck and Montgomery Ward, by the early 1970's. By 1965 it was well on its way to this goal with 453 catalog centers in its stores, the launching of a 40 percent expansion program at its Milwaukee catalog distribution center and the consolidation of its catalog and retail charge accounts on one computer system for single billing its customers.

At the time it acquired General Merchandise, Penney also bought that firm's two Treasure Island discount stores. It has since opened three others and uses this division as a merchandising laboratory where ideas are tested for possible absorption into other areas.

In 1964, Penney moved its executive headquarters and buying offices from an eighteen-story building on Manhattan's west side to 1301 Avenue of the Americas. The move to the building that was then named the J. C. Penney Building was another symbol of the changing face of and dynamic activity currently under way at the Penney Company.

Penney leases thirty-one of the forty-five floors in the building and utilizes 850,000-square feet. Twenty-five hundred company employees made the move following the completion of the largest lease of commercial office space in real-estate history.

The Penney building is a single sheer tower set back more than thirty feet from the building line, thus creating room for a spacious landscaped street-level plaza and a second, sunken plaza offering access to lower-level shops. Pedestrian walks on side streets bring the total plaza area to nearly 30 percent of the entire site.

Penney has set aside twelve merchandise floors on which a huge assortment of goods is displayed for evaluation by its buying staff. Display and storage facilities, many of which are automatic, provide easy access to a wide range of sample merchandise. In the shoe department alone, there are racks capable of holding forty to fifty thousand pairs of shoes.

Inside the building too is Penney's highly-regarded and well-equipped product-testing laboratory, its Merchandise Testing Center. The extent of the equipment there can be seen from its electronic testing section, where machinery in use is similar to that utilized in government space installations. It even has its own closed-circuit television station that can broadcast signals in both black-and-white and in color.

A complete data-processing center is located on the thirty-eighth floor. Here computers quickly translate sales information received from the Penney stores into stock orders and statistical reports.

All of these twentieth-century tools are necessary, says Chairman Batten, for Penney's future development. "If we are to continue to grow and prosper," he believes, "then our methods must change, our merchandise mix and customer services must adhere more closely to mass market demand and the environment in which our customers shop must be on rising levels of convenience and taste comparable to those which they are achieving in their daily lives."

The Penney Company has held abortive acquisition talks in recent years with the Diners Club Inc., and Channing Financial Corporation. Although neither of these deals worked out, the company continues to be interested in broadening the scope of its operation, particularly in the area of new services.

Though over ninety years old, founder Penney continues to work a full day, often through the lunch hour, in his New York office. In 1953, he received the Tobé award for his contributions to retailing and an honorary degree from the University of Missouri in recognition of his aid to agriculture. Among his gifts to the university have been an experimental farm and a herd of 225 prize Guernsey cattle worth $750,000.

The white-haired founder is less active than he used to be but still spends some time each year visiting Penney stores and lecturing to Rotary Clubs (he joined in 1942) and other groups, to assure them that America is still the land of opportunity. Whenever asked what made the Penney Company such a success, he replies: "Unquestionably the emphasis we have laid on human relationships, toward the public on one hand by careful service and in giving the utmost values and toward our associates on the other hand." And he emphasizes to his audience his belief that "chain and variety stores are only on the threshold of their development."

There is still a Penney store in Kemmerer. It is better located, more attractive and bigger than the one in which everything began and it now does about five times the business of the founder in his remarkable first year.

XVIII

BULLOCK'S AND I. MAGNIN

Glamour Pioneer of the West

BOASTFUL CALIFORNIANS spend their increasing wealth in all manner of stores, but they take the greatest pride in the spacious and beautiful establishments of Bullock's, Inc. and I. Magnin & Co. At these stores, fashion, décor and service are combined with a high degree of elegance to offer the most pleasant of shopping experiences.

The warmth of Bullock's relationship with its customers is, perhaps, best illustrated by the grade-school composition of a little Los Angeles girl named Janice McCoslar. When she and her schoolmates were asked to list what they liked best, Janice wrote: "1. Birthdays. 2. Bullock's. 3. Home. 4. School." The store heard about it and sent Janice a doll. Her mother acknowledged this with a note ending: "Anything I buy from now on until the year 2000 will be from Bullock's."

Both Bullock's and Magnin stores are noted for dignity and taste. Advertising is restrained and often entirely institutional. The store buildings are famous in architectural circles for their adaptation to the sunny climate, the luxury of their interiors and the prescience with which provision was made for automobile traffic in a state which now leads all others in automobile registrations.

The eight Bullock's stores and eighteen Magnin stores had sales in

1965 of almost $230,000,000—some $154,000,000 for Bullock's and the remainder for Magnin. They dominate the middle-and upper-income market in their areas and their labels are worn by status-conscious women everywhere.

Bullock's has made its name known among retailers all over the world for its decentralization of authority and its "unitization" of merchandise. Under unitization, merchandise is divided into separate units according to type, use, proportion or price line. Each unit is the responsibility of a buyer, of which there are approximately 500. To keep abreast of customer desires, each buyer-manager is required to spend at least two hours a day on the floor actually selling merchandise.

Chairman Walter W. Candy, Jr., defines the unitization system this way: "We tell the buyer, 'It's your store. Make a profit and you'll get part of it.' "

Each of the sixty buyers at a typical store has her own open-to-buy, hires her own sales force and fights desperately against possible encroachments by buyers of the same merchandise from other Bullock's stores. An executive once said about one of his buyers, "She'd rather let a train roll over her than tell another Bullock's buyer where she got a hot item."

A Bullock's veteran believes that the word "unitization" is to merchandise what the word "penny" is to the American monetary system. Both are the least common denominator.

As a part of this highly unusual department-store decentralization program, a management committee runs each store. It usually consists of three or more merchandise managers, a general superintendent who takes care of store maintenance and, in some instances, a publicity director.

The company is named for John Gillespie Bullock, a Canadian of Scotch ancestry who brought to his business all the Scotch virtues of energy, frugality and integrity. He was born on January 14, 1871 in Paris, Ontario, and his father, a railroad employee, died two years later. When he was eleven, the boy went to work for $2 a week delivering groceries for Munn & Co., a tiny local store.

"We kept open until midnight Saturdays," he recalled years later, "so Mother used to come down and fetch me, so I wouldn't be afraid of walking home in the dark." All his life he treasured a picture of the little store and a penny notebook in which he wrote orders.

He moved on to Rheder's, a dry-goods store that was the largest in town, but at twenty-five he was not earning enough to marry. So, when two uncles who were mining in the West wrote back about the wonders of California, his widowed mother staked him to a railroad ticket to Los Angeles and loaned him $150.

His sister packed some food for him and he reached Los Angeles in January, 1896, with all of the $150 intact. He deposited this in the Citizens National Bank and drew it out at the rate of $1 or $2 a week while he read newspaper advertisements and looked for work.

"It was a time of unemployment and I walked the streets in vain until late in February," Bullock once said. "Then I read in a newspaper that a bankrupt stock was to be sold the next day in a store at Broadway and Fourth. I was there early but the man in charge said he needed no more help. Still I waited around with the crowd for the store to open. It was soon filled and the front door had to be locked until some of those inside left by a rear door. I went in that way and told the man it looked like he could use me. I was hired—at $12 a week."

Bullock's employer in the busy little forty-foot store was Arthur Letts, who had purchased the bankrupt stock for $8,167 with borrowed money. In September when Bullock was beginning to do some of the men's-wear buying, Letts hired another Canadian as cash boy. He was fifteen-year-old Percy Glen (Jack) Winnett, a short youth in short pants who had come to California from Winnipeg with his parents. By then there were twenty-six employees at the Broadway store, which later became the keystone of Broadway-Hale Stores, Inc.

Letts pioneered odd-cent prices in Los Angeles and it was the job of the new $2-a-week cash boy to handle the pennies. He was short a penny one day and was scolded, an experience that he never forgot.

Bullock spurned offers of jobs with a bakery and another store. He was soon making $75 a month and married his Canadian sweetheart. Winnett advanced from errand boy to wrapper in the men's furnishing department when Bullock became the buyer. Between packages,

Winnett worked behind the counter and learned what he could from Bullock. Both learned from Letts.

Born in Holdenby, a village in Northamptonshire, England, in 1862, Letts had been apprenticed at fourteen to the dry-goods, or drapery, business as it was known in England. He worked in London long enough to pay his passage to Canada and informed his parents of his departure only when he was aboard ship. He arrived in Quebec in 1883 and went to work for $7 a week for Robert Walker & Sons in Ontario. He married in Toronto in 1886 and moved to Seattle, Washington, just before fire destroyed the business district there in 1889.

Afterward, he opened his first store in a tent and stocked it with women's wearing apparel and men's furnishings. This store went bankrupt in the panic of 1893 and, after paying his creditors 35 cents on the dollar, Letts moved to Los Angeles.

As soon as the Broadway venture really began to prosper, Letts, like J. L. Hudson in Michigan, looked up the creditors in his bankruptcy and by 1905 had repaid them in full. When some of them were hard hit by the San Francisco fire the next year, he sent out additional checks for 6 percent interest on his debts for twelve years.

As the Broadway store grew, Letts made Bullock superintendent and gave him the responsibility for all hiring. Young Winnett succeeded Bullock as men's-furnishings buyer after five older men had failed in the job. He later bought women's and children's knit underwear and hosiery.

As the salespeople disliked bothering with the complicated sizes, he found the children's end neglected and returns high. He established a children's section and placed a woman in charge with firm instructions not to leave her post in order to sell any women's garments. Her attention and specialized knowledge made the section a great success and convinced Winnett of the merit of what later became unitization—a term that he coined.

The big opportunity came for Bullock in 1906. Eastern merchants had planned a department store at the northwest corner of Seventh and Broadway. With the steel framework for seven stories erected, the death of one stopped the venture and E. T. Earl, the builder, offered the unfinished structure to Letts. It was three blocks outside the shopping area at that time but appealed to Letts as an alternative site for his Broadway department store if he could not renew the lease there on favorable terms. He signed a fifty-year lease with Earl, who completed the building.

To utilize the new structure until the time that it might be required for the Broadway store, Letts gave Bullock $250,000 and the task of establishing an additional store. Winnett, who at twenty-six held an important merchandising job, asked to be allowed to join the new venture and Letts somewhat reluctantly consented. A third executive from the Broadway, William A. Holt, also went along.

They planned to call the new store Bullock's Department Store but Winnett argued for a shorter name like Macy's and it was shortened to Bullock's. Bullock was made president and Winnett vice president and general manager of the new company. Letts gave them complete freedom to operate on their own.[1]

They set up an office in the Lankershim Hotel across the street and hired a staff of four hundred, who sat on beds as they were interviewed. H. M. Bigelow, who had just sold his general store in Grundy Center, Iowa, walked in and was employed as floor manager. Buyers were sent to market.

On the night of March 2, 1907, Letts and the public saw the new store at a nonselling preview. Thousands crowded through the brightly lit buildings to listen to bands play on the lower floor and to see a pony show in the roof garden. In later years, Easter services were conducted in this roof garden.

But rain, something of a rarity in Los Angeles, fell when the store opened for business on March 4 and customers were few. "You could shoot a cannon through the aisles without hitting anyone," recalls Winnett. Those who came found a beautiful store, singing canaries and violets. Bullock's has given away violets every March 4 since then. Customers unable to get downtown that day sometimes ask for and receive the free flowers by mail.

Unexpectedly, the finer-quality merchandise sold more rapidly than the inexpensive goods. Buyers replaced their stocks with better goods and the "mistakes" were cleared in the first of the August sales.

Bullock's was opened as a strictly cash store but within a few months established charge accounts and devised a coat of arms marked SUPREMA REGNAT QUALITAS, Latin for "Quality reigns supreme."

Troubles came when the panic of 1907, started by the failure of a bank in New York, hit in October. Two other Los Angeles stores that were started at the same time as Bullock's did fail but Bullock's struggled ahead. The store's six immaculate horse-drawn delivery wagons were sent out whether there were packages in them or not. Some shelves were filled with empty cartons and one floor was closed off.

Nevertheless, Bullock and Winnett counted sales of $1,310,725 in 1907, $1,511,650 in 1908, and operations became profitable. Letts, meanwhile, renewed the Broadway store lease and decide to continue both stores. Bullock's sales reached $2,031,408 in 1909 and $4,746,024 in 1912. In that year began expansions which eventually spread the big store over a good portion of the Broadway, Hill, Sixth and Seventh Street block. A street dividing the block, called St. Vincent's Court after a college once on the site, was bridged.

Bullock's also grew in character and prestige. While other stores were advertising $25 men's suits for $15, Bullock's startled the community by offering $15 suits for $15. Thousands laughed but they bought the suits. The store's policy of continual but dignified advertising was born. Bullock's was one of the first stores to use color in newspaper advertising and claims the distinction of publishing the first "three-dimensional" store advertisements, a series in the Los Angeles *Times* that had to be read with colored glasses.

A customer was once so moved by Bullock's annual Christmas institutional pages that she decided to embroider a sampler of it. So the store obligingly had the engraver make proofs of it on nylon, rayon and cotton and sent all three to the lady.

Bullock kept on his office wall the motto: "The ideals of this business must not be sacrified to gain." Like many other executives he gave every employee a copy of Elbert Hubbard's "Message to Garcia." A reminder from Winnett said that "Nothing much counts in the retail game until somebody sells somebody something."

The aspirations of Bullock and Winnett were best expressed,

however, in "The Bullock Ideal," written by Holt, the first advertising and publicity director and a graduate of Stanford University. Reprinted thousands of times in employee manuals, annual reports and elsewhere since its first appearance as an institutional advertisement in 1912, it reads:

> To build a business that will never know completion but that will advance continually to meet advancing conditions
>
> To develop stocks and service to a notable degree
>
> To create a personality that will be known for its strength and friendliness
>
> To arrange and co-ordinate activities to the end of winning confidence by meriting it
>
> To strive always to secure the satisfaction of every customer.

These words were backed by deeds, since there was little that Bullock's would not do for a customer. In his usual wing collar, Bullock was once at the door bidding customers good-bye the evening before St. Patrick's Day, when a lady expressed her regret that she had found no clay pipes for an Irish party planned for the next day in Santa Monica. He noted her address, had the city scoured for clay pipes that night and had them delivered to the amazed customer in Santa Monica.

One Saturday at 11:30 P.M., a night watchman answered the phone in Bullock's. A customer complained tearfully that a set of chinaware, purchased as a golden wedding gift, had not arrived and that the anniversary was the next day. The watchman called an executive who called a packer. The executive delivered the china himself on Sunday morning in time for the celebration.

During a holiday season, a Bullock's employee overheard a conversation about how a doll and a toy truck which a widowed mother had purchased to come from Santa Claus had been delivered too early and had fallen into the hands of the children. Without charge, the store sent some more toys as coming from Santa Claus.

A motorcycle messenger was dispatched once 150 miles to Trona with an evening dress required by nightfall. A special trunk required by a customer was delivered to him, also by messenger, in Paris, France. Southern California's growing population, especially the segment connected with the movie industry, greatly appreciated such service.

Sales reached $7,000,000 in 1918 and Bullock's increased its buying facilities by becoming a charter member of the Associated Merchandising Corporation. Volume passed $10,000,000 the next year, and soon after Letts died in 1923 sales were running at more than $22,000,000, a year.

To finance the purchase of the store from the Letts estate, the bank in which Bullock had deposited his mother's $150 when he first arrived in Los Angeles was happy to extend him a credit of $6,000,000. A new corporation, Bullock's, Inc., was organized and $4,000,000 in bonds and $4,500,000 in preferred stock were subscribed in an hour in the first public store financing in California.

On September 26, 1929, Bullock's Wilshire was opened in a beautiful new building, fronting three hundred feet on Wilshire Boulevard at Wilshire Place, that cost $6,000,000 to build. It quickly became a high-fashion showplace and established a new shopping area. Sightseers still come to view its pink marble foyer, its style shows, its glass-walled porte cochere rear entrance and its ceramic birds for sale at $1,350 a pair. One of the many features of this store is a children's barbershop patronized by the sons and daughters of many Hollywood notables.

Investors in the new company received dividends from the start. Though sales dropped from a peak of $27,000,000 in 1930 to a low of $18,000,000 in 1933, Bullock's earned profits all through the depression. Bullock's Palm Springs was opened in that California desert resort in 1930 and Bullock's Westwood in 1932.

One of the happiest days in the life of John Bullock came in 1930 when he returned with his daughter to his birthplace of Paris, Ontario. Henry Rheder, the merchant for whom he had worked as a boy, and the Board of Trade gave a dinner in his honor. Mayor Stewart, once a schoolmate of Bullock, presided. Present even was Mr. Penman, the big mill owner whom Bullock as a boy never hoped to know socially. A scroll was presented to the local boy who had made good. Solemn toasts were drunk: "His Majesty the King," "The President of the United States," and "John G. Bullock."

Bullock died of a heart attack on Sepember 15, 1933, leaving an estate of $2,587,559, mostly in the stock of his store. Mrs. Bullock presented two sets of bells to the Little Country Church of Hollywood in his memory. A bronze bust of the founder, the work of Helen and Holger Jensen, stands in Bullock's Downtown with a plaque: "This memorial testifies to our love for a friend and our loyalty to a leader whose spirit still lives and to whose ideals this business remains dedicated and devoted."

His successor both as president of Bullock's and as a local civic leader was the tireless P. G. Winnett, who had shared the responsibility for the store from the first. Bullock's famous Collegienne shops, where women young in years or ideas find everything conveniently gathered, for example, were started because of the interest of his own daughters in such merchandise.

To finance the modernization and expansion of the downtown and branch stores, Bullock's increased its capital in 1945. The common stock was split three-for-one and 237,775 additional shares were sold. Eighty thousand shares of a new issue of 4 percent preferred stock were sold at $103. Bullock's received a total of $13,515,334, used $6,640,757 to pay bank loans and retire the previous 5 percent preferred stock, and had new capital of $6,874,577 for additional facilities.

The bulk of this went into a new Bullock's Pasadena branch, widely acclaimed for its beauty and revolutionary architecture. Planned by architects Wurdeman & Becket, the building is a merchandising machine specially designed for the best functioning under Bullock's unitization of the sixty individual shops of the branch. "Inside and out," said one observer after the opening of the showplace on September 10, 1947, "it looks more like a club than a store—and a rather expensive club, at that."[2]

On the topmost of the three levels is a terrace café called the Coral Room. It provides a fine view of the mountains and is the scene of a daily fashion show. The middle level contains a series of men's shops which can be reached without passing through the lingerie and other feminine areas on the same floor. On the bottom level are the home-furnishing shops and service facilities. These include two motor-court lobbies with "will call" desks to which packages are dispatched by chute and conveyor belts from wrapping stations in the building. The place is so much the domain of the motorist that there is only a single entrance for pedestrians.

President Winnett became chairman of Bullock's in 1950 and was succeeded by his son-in-law, Walter Candy, a highly affable, outgoing retailing man. With the exception of three years of war service as a commander in the Navy, Candy, a native of St. Louis and a graduate of Princeton, had been with the firm since joining Bullock's Wilshire as a merchandise manager in 1935.

Another key executive at the company for many years is Mahlon E. Arnett. A soft-spoken but perceptive merchant, he joined the concern in 1929 as chief accountant and rose in the ranks to the most senior positions at Bullock's.

With the I. Magnin & Co. merger in 1943, Bullock's acquired one of the best-known women's specialty-store organizations in the world. It was founded by Mrs. Mary Ann Magnin, a tiny energetic woman of unerring taste in high fashion. Born in Scheveningen, Holland, she married Isaac Magnin, a Dutch wood carver, in London and together they migrated to San Francisco. There Magnin became a decorator and, fearing that he might be hurt at his work, Mrs. Magnin in 1876 opened a shop.

She began by making and selling fancy baby clothing and notions. Later she made trousseaus. She moved her business from shop to shop as the fashionable retail trade centers shifted and acquired an exclusive clientele who relied on her for the latest and finest gowns and accessories from Paris.

The name Magnin became a synonym for elegance and its showings of new models by designers like Christian Dior, Pierre Balmain, Jacques Fath, Molyneaux and Balenciaga were soon important events for California society. As the business grew with California, Magnin's became the largest buyer in the high-priced wholesale dress market and acquired exclusive West Coast representation of some of the greatest names in fashion. It earned profits continually except in 1906, when earthquake and fire destroyed the San Francisco store, and 1932.

"People want more than 'thank you' in this world," said Mrs. Magnin as she explained her quest for the finest in apparel. She yielded management of the business to her sons beginning in 1903 but continued to interest herself in its affairs. A remarkable personality, she lived on in the St. Francis Hotel, celebrating her birthday each April with a big party, until she died there on December 15, 1943, at the age of ninety-five.

A few weeks later, President Winnett of Bullock's and two of Mrs. Magnin's sons, E. John and Grover, who had entered the business around the turn of the century, quickly worked out the merger. Magnin stockholders received one Bullock's share in exchange for three and a half shares of the stock of their company.

Hector Escobosa, a well-known fashion expert of Spanish descent, was chosen to head Magnin on the retirement of Grover Magnin at the end of 1950. Though a native of San Francisco, Escobosa had been for some years executive vice president and general manager of Frederick & Nelson, the Seattle department store owned by Marshall Field & Co. When Escobosa died in 1963, the Magnin presidency went to William P. Keeshan, who had been a merchandise manager at Bullock's Wilshire store.

Bullock's-Magnin was involved in one of the hottest proxy battles of 1964 over a proposal to merge it into Federated Department Stores, Inc., the country's largest group of department stores, with eighty-seven stores in thirteen regional divisions. The merger went through as scheduled, but not before many acrimonious words were spoken by the two contending forces and were duly reported in the financial pages of newspapers across the nation.

On one side was Mr. Winnett, who vehemently opposed affiliating his company with Federated—the organization that includes Abraham & Straus in Brooklyn, F. & R. Lazarus in Columbus and Filene's in Boston and had record sales of over $1,330,000,000 in 1965. The largest individual stockholder of Bullock's-Magnin, Mr. Winnett at first said that his opposition to the linkup between the two companies, which had been sought by Federated seventeen years earlier, was based on sentiment.

But before the four-month fight ended in July, 1964, he expressed many other reasons for opposing the merger besides pride in the company he had helped to create. These included his firm's earnings record, better than Federated's, its high book value and, most important, his fear that the autonomous unitization system that had been developed by Bullock's would be sacrificed.

On the other side were eleven of the twelve Bullock's-Magnin directors, headed by Mr. Candy and cheered by Ralph Lazarus, president of Federated. They cited the higher market price of Federated common stock even at the proposed 1.4-to-1 share exchange ratio, the greater dividend income their stockholders would receive, the promise they had received of complete autonomy and the strength of the entire Federated corporation that would be available to Bullock's.[3]

Two other key points were made by Mr. Candy and Mr. Arnett in their proxy statements and in their travels around the United States to make their views known to newsmen and security analysts. They cited the greater geographic diversification of an investment in Federated and the broader marketability that would be provided in shares of the national department-store company.

When the sound and the fury ceased, 70 percent of the shares (slightly more than the required two-thirds) were voted for the merger and Bullock's-Magnin Company was made a division of Federated in August, 1964. Mr. Winnett quickly retired from active management and became a consultant to Bullock's—although he still, at the age of eighty-five, visited a company store each afternoon.

A management reorganization then took place, with Mr. Candy elected chairman of Bullock's-Magnin and Mr. Arnett named president. Two operating divisions were also established. The Bullock's division was put under the leadership of Frank Gillett, who had risen from a basement shirt salesman to vice president for merchandising. Mr. Keeshan retained the presidency of the Magnin division and Eric M. Stanford, a veteran employee of the San Francisco store, stayed on as executive vice president.

Bullock's-Magnin opened its first "fashion square," in Santa Ana, in 1958 on forty-five acres of what had been orange groves. As opposed to the conventional shopping centers, Bullock's fashion squares—there are now two and a third is under construction—are controlled-environment centers where quality "shopping" goods, not convenience items, are sold. At Santa Ana, for instance, there are an I. Magnin store and twenty-nine other quality retailers in addition to the Bullock's store.

In 1965, Bullock's Downtown made an informal study to determine whether its customers preferred to "find 'n flee" or "browse 'n poke." The results: 60 percent in favor of the latter method whereby they could look around the smartly-fixtured store at their leisure.

Chairman Candy believes that, in any future expansion of his company, the standards that have previously existed must continue to prevail. As he says, "We stand for fashion and unexcelled service. This is our niche in retailing and we're going to keep it that way."

XIX

NEIMAN-MARCUS

The Pride of Texas

THOUGH SHE HAD LIVED in Washington, D.C., for many years, Mrs. Lyndon B. Johnson on January 20, 1965, wore to the five inaugural balls marking the start of her husband's new term as President a gold-colored evening dress purchased from Neiman-Marcus of Dallas. It had been designed to order in New York by Texas-born John Moore. Her daughters, Luci and Lynda, also danced that evening in gowns from the famous Texas store. No special salesmanship was involved. Mrs. Johnson has had a Neiman-Marcus charge account since her student days at the University of Texas and had worn a Neiman-Marcus dress to her husband's inauguration as Vice President. He had given friends hats from the store.

When Luci Baines Johnson and Patrick J. Nugent were married August 6, 1966, in the most spectacular wedding in White House history, Neiman-Marcus supplied her gown and trousseau, the Adele Simpson–designed yellow silk dress of her mother and the pink dresses of the twelve bridesmaids. Mrs. Priscilla Kidder of Boston, who made Luci's white organza gown, was present to help with the train. As friends of the Johnsons, Stanley Marcus and his family were among the 700 wedding guests.

Considerable salesmanship had been employed by the store, however, in outfitting Mrs. Dwight D. Eisenhower with a pink Nettie Rosenstein gown and a Hattie Carnegie suit for the 1953 inaugural festivities. The story of the gown and the suit began three years earlier. While on a European buying trip, Stanley Marcus, the eldest of three brothers who now run the store, was introduced to General Eisenhower at Supreme Headquarters in Paris. Marcus expressed his admiration for the General and recalled the latter's residence in Texas.

"I hope you win the nomination," said the merchant as he departed. "If you are nominated, I hope you win the election. As you were born in Texas and served in Texas, I hope you'll remember there's a store in Texas that would like to dress Mrs. Eisenhower for the inauguration."

General Eisenhower laughed and nodded. When the votes were counted, and the Eisenhowers were deluged with proposals of all kinds, Marcus reminded the general of the conversation in Paris and submitted a number of sketches. Mrs. Eisenhower chose the Rosenstein number. While Neiman-Marcus issues amber-inked releases to the press almost daily, others announced this news adequately.

To Miss Kay Kerr of Neiman-Marcus' New York office, Mrs. Eisenhower wrote: "I have so many things for which to thank you—your patience, your courtesies, your helpfulness, your excellent opinions and judgment. . . . I can imagine what difficulties were imposed upon you where fittings were concerned by my nasty cold. . . . That you accomplished so much under handicaps is a tribute to your patience and efficiency. . . ."

One reason Neiman-Marcus does a business of more than $55,000,000 a year from comparatively small quarters in Texas is its talent for showmanship. It has an ability to get abroad and even to create news that earns word-of-mouth and printed notice that is the envy of competitors. For example, when a fortnight's strike of pilots threw American Airlines' hostesses out of work, the store hired forty of them as models and salespeople. They earned their money and spent much of it in the store. Neiman-Marcus garnered two pages in *Life* and newspaper notice throughout the country.[1]

Behind this sort of thing, the Marcus family has built a foundation of solid merchandising, extraordinary service and day-to-day promotion appropriate to the warm climate, easy living and chauvinism of the Southwest. This appeals alike to the Texans of legendary wealth and to their less rich sisters who like to have the same label in their coats. Neiman-Marcus has more than five thousand charge customers who spend more than $2,000 a year with the store, but the average of all its 200,000 charge accounts is only about $250 a year, and it has been the average accounts that have accounted for most of the store's increased sales in recent years.

The store was founded by three remarkable individuals, Herbert Marcus; his sister, Carrie; and her husband, A. L. Neiman. Herbert and Carrie had been born in Louisville, Kentucky, and had moved to Hillsboro, Texas, where a brother had a grocery, and thence fifty miles north to Dallas. There Herbert sold women's shoes and was promoted to boys'-department buyer for Sanger Brothers. Carrie followed him and became an assistant buyer at A. Harris & Co. When Al Neiman, a promoter of department-store sales from Cleveland, conducted a sale at the latter store in 1905, he met Carrie and they were married.

At this time, Herbert Marcus, married and the father of a newly born son named Stanley, demanded a raise at Sanger Brothers, then the largest as well as the oldest of Dallas stores. The raise was granted but only for $1.87 a week. He quit and joined Neiman in opening an advertising agency in Atlanta, Georgia.

They succeeded so well with this that two years later they had the choice of selling it for $25,000 cash or trading it for Coca-Cola stock and a Missouri franchise for the soft drink. They spurned the latter, which quickly became worth millions, took the $25,000, returned to Dallas and started Neiman-Marcus. This once caused son Stanley to remark that the store was founded "on bad business judgment."

The actual capital was $22,000 from Neiman and $8,000 from the Marcuses. Herbert was then twenty-nine and Carrie twenty-three. The trio rented at $9,000 a year a two-story building at Elm and Murphy streets and spent $12,000 on red mahogany fixtures and luxurious carpeting. Neiman was an able financial man. Marcus was a born merchant who even in his last blind years could accurately judge the quality of leather by its feel. Carrie Neiman's contribution was the most important of all—unerring taste and a shrewd judgment of style.[2]

To avoid merely duplicating existing Dallas retail operations, they undertook to make Neiman-Marcus a specialty store of style and quality for customers who did not need to haggle over pennies. Carrie Neiman spent $17,000 in New York for an initial stock and in the fall of 1907, with a page of the *Dallas News,* the new firm announced:

> On September Tenth will take place the formal opening of Neiman-Marcus Co., the South's finest and only exclusive ready-to-wear shop, the most elegantly equipped storeroom in the South. . . . It shall be the policy of Neiman-Marcus to be at all times leaders in their lines and to give buyers in Texas something out of the commonplace. . . . With these aims in view, exclusive lines of high-class garments have been secured, lines which have never been offered before to the buyers of Dallas. . . . We will miss a sale rather than have a garment leave the establishment which is not a perfect fit. . . .

Carrie Neiman and Herbert Marcus were ill on opening day, the latter with typhoid fever, and failure of the Knickerbocker Trust Company in New York precipitated a national business panic the next month. Nevertheless, within a few weeks the stock of "demi-costumes, modish waists, dress and walking skirts, better coats and millinery" was sold. There was money from cotton and also from oil in Texas even in 1907. Within three years, Carrie Neiman was making buying trips to Paris. In addition to women's clothes, the store began to sell accessories, infants' wear, girls' clothing and eventually men's wear and many other items.

In 1913, the firm had a $20,000 profit on a $380,000 sales volume despite a fire which destroyed the store. Neiman-Marcus then moved east to its present site at Main and Ervay streets but not without difficulty. The owner declined to sell but was agreeable to a ninety-nine-year lease on condition that a building costing at least $100,000 be erected. As the firm's capital amounted only to $80,000, Al Neiman sold five blocks of stock at $10,000 each to New York manufacturers. One of these had held its stock through the years and seen it increase to $700,000 in value. With additional funds borrowed, the firm built a $192,000 structure.

By 1916, Neiman-Marcus customers were becoming familiar with names like Callot Soeurs, Lanvin, Revillon Frères and Martial and Armand. Sales reached $1,260,046 in 1918 and $2,191,911 in 1919 as more oil fields were discovered in Texas. The Marcuses began to take larger roles in civic affairs.

Herbert Marcus, whose formal schooling ended at fifteen, helped raise money to launch Southern Methodist University. He gave Miss Hockaday's School for Girls $100,000 for a fine-arts building and served as a trustee. He helped found the Southwestern Medical Center. He helped bring grand opera to Dallas. He owned canvases by artists as noted as Renoir and Sir Thomas Lawrence. He encouraged his sons in similar tastes.

Neiman-Marcus's reputation was built by the free-spending customer. Perhaps the most famous was Electra Waggoner Wharton Bailey Gilmore, heiress to land and cattle fortunes, who bought as much as $20,000 worth of merchandise in a single day—and returned the next day for another $20,000 she'd forgotten. The store continued on its luxurious way during the twenties and sales reached a peak of $3,600,000 in 1929, but the firm had gone through a crisis the previous year.

After twenty-three years of married life, Al and Carrie Neiman were divorced. Marcus bought the former's interest in the firm and Neiman moved to New York. There he remarried, founded his own merchandising firm, Neiman Associates, and outlived both his former partners. Though he became blind in 1946, Herbert Marcus continued active in the store almost until his death from hypertension at seventy-two in 1950. His sister, by then "Aunt Carrie" to many, died three years later.

Stanley Marcus, Herbert's eldest son, who joined the store as a floor man in 1926 after earning a master's degree in business administration at Harvard, stepped into many of Neiman's duties. In 1928, he became secretary, treasurer and a director, also merchandise manager of the sports shop. The next year he was promoted to merchandise manager of all apparel divisions. In this role, he met

Mary Cantrell, a pretty buyer in the store's sportswear shop. In 1932, he married and retired her. "Mr. Stanley," as he was soon known in the store, became executive vice president in 1935, and, after the death of his father, president.

As they grew up, his three brothers also joined the store, Edward becoming executive vice president; Herbert, Jr., taking charge of men's wear; and Lawrence, in charge of the expensive second-floor women's shop with the title of vice president and secretary. As of 1966, executives also included Norman W. Bramley, formerly of Brooks Brothers, senior vice president and treasurer; Miss Mary Lloyd, senior vice president in charge of personnel; George Baylis, Jr., formerly of Bonwit Teller, senior vice president and general merchandise manager; Chris Stritzinger, formerly of the Associated Merchandising Corp., senior vice president and sales promotion director; Robert M. Jeffrey, vice president and controller.

According to the organization chart, "Mr. Stanley" is supposed to deal only with top executives in the store but actually he deals with everything and everybody. It was "Mr. Stanley" who first believed the store could attain national stature. In his first year at work, he started weekly fashion shows. He began to advertise Neiman-Marcus in national fashion magazines when such advertising was almost unknown. Many of the store's dramatic promotions have been his ideas. In addition to everything else, he personally has sold more than $5,000,000 worth of fur coats.

The two sides of Stanley Marcus's personality make him both an intellectual and a hard-driving merchant. His library includes works on art, china, brass, silver. He collects primitive masks and sculpture and is a serious student of typography. The time-consuming business of retailing has not prevented him from serving as president of the Dallas Art Association, a trustee of the Dallas Museum of Fine Arts, president of the Dallas Symphony Orchestra and an overseer of Harvard University. He is also a fellow of the Pierpont Morgan Library.

In the role of merchant, Stanley himself admits he has difficulty in delegating authority. During the day, he's all over the store, looking into everything, even running his finger along a counter in search of dust. He works himself and his staff hard. Wherever there's a customer who might be interested in Neiman-Marcus merchandise, Stanley believes in going to the customer. In fact, Stanley Marcus once flew a fashion show to Australia and continued around the world with it. A show was toured through Mexico and South America. Women in Detroit have been subjected to the temptations of a Neiman-Marcus fashion show, and when Stanley once heard of a woman in St. Louis who wanted a fur coat, he took the coat to her. The Neiman-Marcus fur staff travels eighty thousand miles a year and shows its collection in forty-two cities.

During the depression, the store lost money for two years. Though it was in 1930 that the great East Texas oil field, biggest the world has ever known, was brought in, there still weren't enough big spenders even in Texas for Neiman-Marcus to grow large with just the expensive lines of its early years. Some of this "new" oil went for as low as ten cents a barrel, and while it served to cushion the money panic that was about to paralyze the rest of the country, the store could no longer depend exclusively on high-priced merchandise.

It was during these depression years that Neiman-Marcus decided to split its personality and cater to the moderate income as well as to the wealthy. New lines of lower-priced, though well-edited, merchandise began to appear back to back with glamour apparel. When the Prudential Insurance Company balked at Stanley's request for a loan, on the basis that Neiman-Marcus was too "frothy" and catered too much to the big spender, Stanley was able to show Prudential that the bulk of the store's sales actually were made to the "upper masses" rather than to the "upper classes."

The store went after the under-$20,000-income group in earnest. This policy increased sales between 1942 and 1953 almost five times. Not even a 1946 fire, which destroyed much valuable merchandise scheduled for pre-Christmas sale, slowed up Neiman-Marcus's progress. The store's first suburban branch, a $2,000,000 Preston Center store, was opened in 1951. A $5,000,000 expansion of the downtown store was completed in 1953. A Houston branch was acquired with purchase of Ben Wolfman, Inc., in 1955 and a $1,000,000 expansion there was completed in 1959. In that year, the store offered 133,800 of its 598,800 family-owned shares to the public at $19.50 a share. The $2,600,000 offering was snapped up in a day and within a week the stock was selling for $21.

A $4,000,000 branch was opened in the Ridglea area of western Fort Worth in 1963. A new $4,000,000 North Park store with twice the floor space replaced the Preston Center branch in 1965. That autumn, the Neiman-Marcus Greenhouse, a $2,000,000 spa for improving the health and beauty of thirty-six women able to spend $750 a week or $1,500 a fortnight for its luxurious services, was opened at Arlington, midway between Dallas and Fort Worth. Plans were drawn in 1966 by Guy Obata, famous Japanese-American architect, for a new $6,000,000 suburban store in the exclusive Post Oaks area of Houston.

An unusual promotion was the Neiman-Marcus cookbook, *A Taste of Texas*, produced by Marihelen McDuff and Jane Trahey in 1949 when they were respectively in charge of public relations and advertising of the store.

They asked notables to contribute their "favorite or most tantalizing" recipes. Many did so. Paul Gallico, the writer, retorted with a letter saying he was planning to start a store and would like Neiman-Marcus to send him free "your favorite or most successful pieces of merchandise" and particularly "a fur evening wrap for a small blonde woman, about size 14, solid gold cuff links, a fine rod and reel for deep sea fishing, a pair of diamond and sapphire clips. . . ." The editors published his letter as a recipe for "Specialty Store à la Gallico." Six printings of the book have been sold.[3]

In a year when Tiffany's Christmas catalog listed a $20,000 bauble as its most expensive item, Neiman-Marcus advertised an emerald and diamond ring at $30,000. This lavish sort of advertising is based confidently on past customer performance. A Christmas advertisement portrayed an actress wrapped in yards of mink, wearing a diamond bracelet and a satin and black lace nightie. Gift-hunting husbands were advised to "send $21,173.75" and the merchandise shown would be wrapped and delivered—minus the actress. The items were sold, though it took three different husbands, in New York, Colorado and Chicago, to foot the bill.

"His" and "Her" Beechcraft airplanes, respectively a seven-passenger $149,000 job and a four-place $27,000 craft, were featured in the 1960 *Christmas Book*. Two years later a genuine Chinese junk made in Hong Kong was offered F.O.B. Houston at $11,500. Eleven of them were sold. In 1965, there was an Aegean cruise for ten on a chartered yacht "for 25 golden days and starlit nights" at $145,802. But there are many lower-priced items, a few under $5.

Service of a de luxe kind is as much a tradition as the unusual and expensive merchandise. Neiman-Marcus employees are well treated and well trained and, in the words of late author George Sessions Perry, "are to ordinary clerks as statesmen to politicians."[4]

Stanley Marcus takes great pride in his sales personnel and fashion models. He was furious when their morals were aspersed by U.S.A. *Confidential*, a book published in 1952. Suit for $7,500,000 was instituted against authors, publishers and printers of the book. The publishers and printers made public apologies in coast-to-coast newspaper advertising, and in letters to Neiman-Marcus employees. The offending material was removed from later printing. The suit was unprecedented, in that in a single suit it incorporated claims for damage against the individual, damage against an entire class and damages against others as well.

Neiman-Marcus employees have a pension plan open to all over twenty-five and with the store for two years. The various benefits amount to about 23 percent of the payroll dollar. In big or little crises, the employees respond with enthusiasm and ingenuity. When a customer wanted rice dyed to match the bridesmaid's dresses, it was done. When a jubilant football fan fell afoul of the law after a Texas-Oklahoma game, the store posted $250 bail for him and charged it to his account.

Employees performed miracles after a five-alarm fire swept most of the main store early on December 19, 1964, a Saturday, at the height of the Christmas shopping season. Damage was more than $10,000,000. President Johnson telephoned to express his sympathy. Wedding dresses for ten brides, some being married that day, were destroyed.

The store rented a suite in the nearby Statler-Hilton Hotel and at once began to fit them in gowns flown in from Houston and trucked from Fort Worth. One wedding was scheduled for 4 P.M. At 2 P.M. a wedding gown arrived at the hotel by truck from the Neiman-Marcus store in Fort Worth. A fitter measured the bride-to-be and the dress there and at 2:22 P.M. rushed it off to the Preston Center branch. There three seamstresses made the alterations in an hour and the fitter at 3:40 P.M. delivered it to the church, where the bride was waiting in her underclothing. The wedding began on time. So did the other nine. The bride in one was Ginny Lou Martin, a Baylor University senior chosen by *Glamour* as one of the ten best-dressed students.[5]

Despite the fire, which was covered by insurance both for damage and the December 19–January 15 interruption of business, Neiman-Marcus had sales of $49,381,122 and earnings of $1,370,873 for the year ending January 31, 1965. In the face of intensified competition from Sanger's, Sears, Roebuck and others, sales rose to $54,668,090 and earnings to $1,540,811 for the year ending January 31, 1966.

While Neiman-Marcus resorts to many ways of publicizing the store, Stanley Marcus believes in the use of newspaper advertising for pure hard selling. He has seen to it that the store's newspaper advertising is outstanding. Zula McCauley, Neiman-Marcus's first advertising director, set the pace for the distinctive copy and layout that have characterized its advertising ever since. Stanley is convinced color advertising in newspapers is here to stay, and the store uses a great deal of it. Neiman-Marcus will introduce a new fashion color theme by means of such advertisements as a huge black cat sipping a dish of golden cream against a honey-colored background. Stanley's interest in topography, acquired at Harvard, has led him to take a special interest in the appearance as well as the message contained in any advertisement the store runs.

For some years Neiman-Marcus has used an editorial-type column captioned "Point of View" as an effective part of its advertising. It is one of Stanley's ideas and is reminiscent of the personally penned advertising of John Wanamaker long ago. It was written for some years by Warren Leslie, a former newspaperman who won fame as a novelist. It appears several times a week as part of the daily Neiman-Marcus advertising in the Dallas *Morning News*, and often fails to mention any merchandise in the store. Instead it may discuss a new movie or devote itself to personality sketches, humor or any issue of the day. Stanley Marcus used advertising space on January 1, 1964, following the assassination of President Kennedy in Dallas, for a much-discussed message titled "What's Right With Dallas?" He defended the city against critics but urged more "fair play" for legitimate differences of opinion. He used the space a year later for a New Year's message of thanks to all who helped the store after the December fire.

One of Neiman-Marcus's big promotional achievements is the annual presentation of the Neiman-Marcus Awards—the fashion "Oscars" for "distinguished service in the field of fashion." Instituted in 1938, the presentation is the climax of a five-day celebration which includes fashion shows, lively Western-style parties and sometimes a Champagne Ball. The store also takes this opportunity to present what it deems The Ten Most Prophetic Fashions of the Year.

Awardees have included internationally famous personalities. Madame Helene Lazareff of Paris, editor of *Elle*, and Dr. Francis Henry Taylor, director of the Metropolitan Museum of Art, have shared honors with Norman Hartnell of London, dressmaker to the British Royal Family; Hattie Carnegie, Elsa Schiaparelli, Lilly Daché, Adrian, Anne Fogarty, John Frederics, Jacques Fath, Emilio Pucci and others. Awards also have gone to Henry Dreyfuss, the industrial designer; Pierre Balmain, the editors of *Vogue, Harper's Bazaar, Life, Look, Mademoiselle* and many others.

Some years the store added a Consumer Award for Personal Fashion Discrimination, the first being presented to Mrs. Leland Hayward. It also has gone to Gloria Swanson, Dolores del Rio, Princess Grace of Monaco, Dinah Shore, Rosalind Russell and Greer Garson, the last a resident of Dallas.

More important have been the "Fortnights" devoted to promotion of the products of a country or a region. These involve infinite planning, the obtaining of official and community cooperation, and the investment of thousands of dollars by other interests as well as the store. Stanley Marcus chanced to visit Nordiska, Stockholm's leading department store, in 1955 when it was holding a French

Exposition. A French chef was preparing food. There was French décor and French merchandise. On his way home, Stanley stopped in Paris and visited the Comité des Foires, which stages French fairs and expositions throughout the world. He arranged for one for Neiman-Marcus in 1957. It was the first held in America.

Twenty buyers scoured France for merchandise for the event. Nine months before the event, Stanley Marcus invited Dallas leaders to lunch and obtained their cooperation. The Dallas Museum of Fine Arts exhibited French paintings. The Memorial Auditorium showed French tapestries. Theaters showed French films, night clubs booked French entertainers, civic clubs booked French speakers. Advertising supplements in *Vogue* and the Dallas *Times-Herald* advertised the event.

The Mayor of Dallas and French Ambassador Hervé Alphand officially opened a round of gala balls and festivities. Some two hundred French visitors came by Air France charter, the first to land at Dallas. They included the Mayor of Dijon, an eighty-year-old priest; businessmen; industrialists; designers; artists; models; authors and actresses. The French Fortnight was so successful that before it was over British interests asked the store to do one for Great Britain the following year.

It did so and what had been planned as a one-time event became an annual one. For the British Fortnight, the Old Vic Repertory Company was brought to Dallas for performances at the State Fair Music Hall. A South American Fortnight followed in 1959 and an Italian one, actually a whole month, in 1960. For this the store imported an opera company from Palermo, Italy. The Fortnight was American in 1961, Far Eastern in 1962, Swiss in 1963, Danish in 1964, Austrian in 1965. Dr. Bruno Kreisky, Foreign Minister, visited and spoke in Dallas for this. In 1966, the store Fortnight returned to France to celebrate the tenth anniversary of the Fortnight programs. Many other stores now stage similar events but none are as successful in enlisting the help and support of their communities for them. In addition to profits, they have earned an array of foreign decorations and honors for Stanley Marcus and suggestions that he be appointed an ambassador.

He has been personally responsible for the discovery and promotion of two unusual products. One is vicuña. Even New York stores cannot provide the fabulous vicuña coats in the Neiman-Marcus manner. Probably no instance of Stanley's astute merchandising has made such retailing history as his promotion of vicuña. He has publicly had to deny that the store invented the precious fleece—stating that it was traditional garb of ancient Inca royalty. However, it was Stanley who brought vicuña from Peru, realizing that the expensive little cousin of the camel was an ideal article for a store whose customers are both wealthy and residing in a warm climate. Now even Peruvians buy their vicuña coats in Dallas. According to one South American customer, the Neiman-Marcus tailoring is infinitely superior.

While in India in 1961 seeking merchandise for the Far Eastern Fortnight the following year, Stanley Marcus found something even rarer—shahtoosh. Each May, the ibex goats which live only in the Himalayan Mountains, rub their necks on the high rocks. The natives gather this precious hair and it is woven into a delicate fabric that is called shahtoosh. This is so fine that it can be pulled through a ring.

Neiman-Marcus translates it into scarves, neck pieces, a man's robe and a woman's dressing gown, the last two priced at $1,500. As of 1966, the store is the only one in America to have it. Because Stanley Marcus discovered the precious fabric and has ordered all that is available in India, he has been called the "King of Shahtoosh."

XX

L. L. BEAN, INC.

Sporting Goods by Mail from Maine

MOTORISTS FOLLOWING U.S. Highway 1 through the "Down East" section of Maine come eighteen miles north of Portland to the old village of Freeport. It is a pleasant tree-shaded community of 4,055 which was famous in early Maine history as the place at which documents were signed giving the state its independence from Massachusetts.

Freeport is now famous as the home of L. L. Bean, Inc. This unique firm sells annually more than $3,000,000 worth of sporting goods to hunting and fishing enthusiasts all over the Western hemisphere. To it have been promptly delivered letters addressed merely "Bean, Maine" and "Mail order sporting goods house in a small town in Maine." Signs encountered five miles out lead the traveler to a store and offices on Main Street and huge frame buildings to the rear housing workrooms, warehouses and a printing establishment.

Regardless of the day or hour, you will find the place open and somebody on hand to sell you a hunting or fishing license or any of several hundred items for the sport, dress or comfort of hunters and fishermen. This twenty-four-hour service is an example of the consideration of customer needs that has enabled Leon Leonwood Bean, who was ninety-three in 1965, to build this remarkable business deep in Maine and to stamp his colorful personality on it.

"We have thrown away the key to the place," the bronzed booming-voiced founder explains. "A lot of our customers drive up from New York and Boston. Many leave right after work and are so eager to start hunting or fishing that they drive all night. This often brings them through Freeport in the middle of the night or even on Sunday. Where else can you get a hunting or fishing license on Sunday?"

Hundreds of places sell nonresident Maine hunting and fishing licenses but L. L. Bean, Inc., is one of the two top outlets. The firm collects the usual twenty-five-cent fee on each, but more important is the traffic it brings to the store.

"Only about one person in twenty-five who comes in for a license goes out without buying something else," says Bean. "When they leave home, they don't worry about being short something. They say: 'We can always get it at Bean's' " And they can.

The store stocks all the four hundred items offered in the famous Bean mail-order catalog, plus several hundred more that are being tested to see whether they merit space in it, and finally items like ammunition which cannot be sent through the mails.

The merchandise ranges from twenty-cent shoe laces to $340 canoes. The catalog says "Bean's Chamois Cloth Shirt is the shirt Mr. Bean uses on his fishing and hunting trips." It is probably the most popular sportsman's shirt. The firm is the largest outlet in the United States for the famous Hudson's Bay Company's woolen blankets. There are scores of sporting accessories. But the backbone of the Bean business is in its own boots and shoes. These are stitched by sewing machines or made by hand in Freeport. In fact, the enterprise grew out of a special hunting shoe devised and made by Bean on a financial shoestring.

Bean was born October 13, 1872, on a farm near Greenwood, Maine, an Oxford County town that no longer exists. He was the fourth of six children, five boys and a girl.[1] The family is descended from the Scottish Highland Clan MacBean, sometimes spelled MacBeane, which has a dagger and a wildcat in its coat of arms. Three brothers came to America and their descendants shortened the name to Bean. George Warren Bean, a Union soldier in the Civil War, died a Confederate prisoner and is buried at Andersonville, Georgia. His second son, Benjamin Warren Bean, was the merchant's father.

"My father lived on a farm," Bean once recalled, "but he was really more of a hunter and trader." Lennie, or L. L., as he became known, inherited both of these interests. When he was eleven, and the family moved to Milton Plantation, his father gave him the choice of going to a fair at Norway, Maine, or using the money to buy five muskrat traps the boy had been wanting. Young Bean settled for the traps. When he was thirteen, both parents died. He grew up with relatives at South Paris. His first big business deal was transacted at sixteen. L. L. went hunting and shot a good-sized buck. An empty-handed hunter offered him $12 for it. With the money Bean bought some bread and salt pork and a pair of mittens, returned to the woods and went trapping in earnest. When he came out three weeks later, he was carrying five sables, plus a wildcat and most of the twelve dollars.[2]

In 1912, after many jobs and ventures, L. L. became a partner of his brother Guy in a small clothing store in Freeport. It was just across Main Street from the present location of the firm. Some old newspaper advertisements attest that they sold overalls and shirts at thirty-nine cents each and some handkerchiefs at one cent apiece and ten cents a dozen. They once attracted a big crowd by closing the place up mysteriously for some days and then having a big sale.

Bean eventually bought out his brother, and the latter, who was one of the few Democrats in Maine, became Freeport postmaster. As his brother was the biggest user of postal service in Freeport (70 percent in 1934 and 85 percent in some later years), Postmaster Guy Bean put the post office on the first floor under the L. L. Bean office. It moved in 1962 to a new building two blocks east on Main Street but a rent-free substation continues in the space. In consequence, Bean's merely drops packages down a chute to mail them, an arrangement also enjoyed by the big mail-order houses in Chicago, but exceptional in a place the size of Freeport.

L. L. was so much more interested in hunting and fishing than in shopkeeping that the clothing store kept going only through the tolerance of his creditors and customers. Then in his forties, Bean was considered an easygoing failure until he began to discover business opportunities as well as personal happiness in his sport.

His success began when he came home with sore feet one day from a hunting trip. Woodsmen's shoes were then heavy and stiff. After being wet, they dried into torturing shapes. Bean sought something more comfortable. Next time out, he tried wearing rubber overshoes and three pairs of wool socks.

He found this comfortable, but at the end of a day's hiking had a "flat-footed" feeling. The wool socks also were not substantial enough for tops. He remedied the first by contriving an inner sole with a steel arch. Instead of the socks, he had Ted Goldrup and Dennis Bibber, local cobblers, cut and sew leather tops to the rubbers. He tested the new hybrid shoes in the woods and found them light, waterproof and comfortable. Thus was born Bean's famous "Maine Hunting Shoe."

When some of his friends also liked the shoes, Bean borrowed $400 from the local bank and began to have them made in the basement of his store. By way of advertising he sent holders of hunting licenses a single blue-sheet circular showing the shoe and describing it as "designed by a hunter who has tramped the Maine woods for the past eighteen years." Orders came in and a pair of these shoes were in the first parcel-post package mailed from Freeport when the service began in 1913. A tag on each guaranteed absolute satisfaction. Ninety of the first hundred pairs came back. The rubber had been too light and had torn away from the uppers. Bean made good on all and the shoe was improved.

By 1915, he had moved the business across the street. The clothing store faded out and, with stationery resplendent with ducks and fish in color, Bean became a manufacturer of "leather and canvas specialties." As he sold more and more shoes, he began to add related items, of similar quality and utility, starting with socks. While his formal education had included only grammar school and a short commercial course, he described his goods with persuasive simplicity.

With some patented improvements more than 1,500,000 pairs of the Maine Hunting Shoe have been sold. General Matthew Ridgway, a regular Bean customer, wore them in Korea. Rear Admiral Donald Macmillan, a native of Freeport, outfitted an Arctic expedition with them. Supreme Court Justice William O. Douglas has hiked in them. Big-game hunters like Richard Sutton have worn them all over the world. U.S. Marines took them to Iceland.

Fame of the shoe led the government to employ Bean as a consultant and contractor during World War II. By inducing the Army to use boots with twelve-inch instead of sixteen-inch tops he lightened the burden of many a soldier and saved millions in costs. He also designed for the Navy a nonskid boot for wear on aircraft carrier decks that could be removed quickly in the sea.

"For hunters who go just before the first snow," explained a catalog note on the Maine Hunting Shoe, "it is next to impossible to find footwear that is adaptable to both bare ground and snow hunting. For bare ground, its lightweight cushion inner-sole keeps it from drawing feet, while the crepe rubber sole keeps it from slipping. Outside of your gun, nothing is so important to your outfit as your footwear. You cannot expect success hunting big game if your feet are not properly dressed. The average hunting shoe weighs about four ounces more than ours. As big game hunters walk about seven miles (or 18,480 steps) a day they lift 2310 pounds more than necessary."

Bean's sales passed the $100,000-a-year mark in the early twenties and attained $1,000,000 for the first time as the business celebrated its thirtieth anniversary in 1937. Spurred by important notice in national magazines[3] and the spread of the shorter work week, which gave more men leisure for hunting and fishing, the business doubled again in less than a decade.

With growth came an increase in number of employees to more than one hundred, and incorporation in 1934.[4] L. L. became president and treasurer, and with his sons, Carl and Warren, and his son-in-law, Jack Gorman, formed the board of directors. By 1966, two grandsons, Tom and Leon, had been added to the board, along with long-time employees Shailer Hayes and W. E. Griffin. During this period adding machines, cash registers and mechanical letter openers were added to the office, and the factory expanded crazily on many levels. A profit-sharing plan for employees was added in 1953.

The friendly informality that charmed customers like Presidents Calvin Coolidge and Franklin D. Roosevelt, Babe Ruth and many other notables was preserved. Bean's twice-a-year catalog has grown to 104 pages, many of them in full color. Two 32-page circulars also are mailed. The printing requires 225 tons of paper a year and the more than 400,000 copies of each adds up to the biggest circulation of any Maine publication. But it is still the strangely indexed, fascinating hodgepodge of early days. In addition, L. L. uses space advertising in *Field and Stream, Outdoor Life, Sports Afield* and many other publications.

The effectiveness of low-pressure selling is well understood by the astute Down Easter. Typical was this catalog statement: "While it is impossible to find any knife that is 100 percent perfect for all purposes, we think this knife comes nearest to anything on the market."

A big-game hunter, under the influence of one edition, wrote Mr. Bean: "Your catalogue is a dangerous book. A sportsman can no more pass it up than a drunkard can pass up a saloon."

Bean's "Toter and Deer Carrier," a stretcherlike contraption with a single bicycle wheel suspended from its center, is one of the products of L. L.'s fertile brain. Bean's Field Coat, with a game pocket that lets down to serve as a waterproof seat, is another—described by gunners who previously had to sit on a frosty log as one of the greatest inventions since the wheel. Whatever Mr. Bean can't test in action himself he turns over to friends or employees to test.

Almost every item offered is presented as "Bean's." Despite the fact that some of the merchandise is clearly identified in print as having been made or conceived by other manufacturers, it is still labeled "Bean's" as long as Bean approves of it and sells it. This has never seemed in any way inconsistent to L. L. or to his customers. The Hudson's Bay blanket is one of the very few items allowed to fly under its own flag.

Bean fosters a sense of neighborliness between his customers and himself, whether by mail or in direct conversation. An impressive number of celebrities have visited the store and stopped to chat. Ted Williams, Jack Dempsey, Lauritz Melchior, the late Kenneth Roberts and the late Mrs. Eleanor Roosevelt have been among the many who have stopped by on vacation trips to Maine. Famous autographs are to be found in Bean's letter files. But they remain in their alphabetical niches. Bean makes no capital of names in selling his merchandise.

"They're just customers," he says, "just customers. Sportsmen are more interested in the product than who uses it."

Sportsmen who climb the stairs to Bean's factory salesroom are exposed to the same temptations and organized chaos the catalog reader undergoes. In spite of the sales staff, it's often necessary in a rush season for customers to wait on themselves. They're encouraged to prowl around and bring the load to one of the girl cashiers. When a cashier checked over one sportsman's order, she noted that the red hunting cap for which he'd written a sales slip was missing. The man pointed to his head. The girl glanced up and said: "That one's soiled. Let me find another one for you."

"No," replied the customer. "I got this one here last year and somehow forgot to pay for it. So I just included it in this batch."

Bean personally guarantees everything he sells and his policy of satisfying every conceivable complaint is remarkably liberal by any retailing standard. Bean feels sportsmen deserve extra attention and shrugs off any losses. He knows of only one customer who intentionally tried to gyp him—and then for only $3. "But the man wasn't a sportsman," he adds quickly. "He was a cook in a logging camp."

Largely to save himself time in answering questions, Bean in 1942 wrote and published a small book, *Hunting-Fishing and Camping;* into 196 pages, he packed a world of practical advice based on his own game bag. This has included, incidentally, thirty-six deer, two moose, one bear and a caribou, as well as all sorts of small game and fish ranging from brook trout to tuna.

"To my mind," he wrote, "hunting and fishing is the big lure that takes us into the great open spaces and teaches us to forget the mean and petty things in life." He advised on what to wear, what to carry, where to go in Maine and how many to include. "A perfect trip," he warned, "may be ruined by one person who does not fit. I recommend small parties, not over four. Two make a good party."

"No one should enter the big woods without being posted on Chapters 3, 13, 14, 15, 16," warns Bean. These, respectively, are How to Dress a Deer, Safety Rules, Signals for Hunters, How to Use a Compass and How to Find a Lost Hunter. He also included advice on bobcat hunting and camp cooking recipes. The initial printing sold out promptly at $1 a copy. Since then nineteen additional editions have been published, each revised to map the previous year's kill of deer and bear in Maine, and more than 131,000 copies sold.

Customers like to trade ideas with the receptive Bean, and frequently send him suggestions for improving one product or another. Some of the ideas he has adopted include a fur-lined bottle holder that enables a bottle to be tossed about without breakage, and a decoy with a removable head which permits more lifelike attitudes.

Bean's Yankee honesty and frugality are persuasive factors in his phenomenally successful business. He reminds customers that the price of leather is high, and that he can repair worn hunting shoes at a fraction of the cost of a new pair. He also urges impulsive fishermen to trim down their shopping list.

"Nine flies are all anybody needs for brook trout, six for Atlantic salmon, six for bass," Bean says flatly. Of these latter he adds: "If bass won't take one of these, they aren't rising."

However, not all his customers take this sage advice. A man in Baltimore still insisted on buying $236.50 worth of flies.

The wife of a sportsman also once came in to see Bean, saying she had a complaint. "Mr. Bean," she announced, "you are keeping my husband poor!"

As a final word of caution, Bean reminds customers that "We think it best to state that C.O.D. charges are high and are paid by the customer. (A $2 C.O.D. has a 60-cent postal fee.)"

The 65,000 square feet of the place are spread through a maze of annexes and different floor levels. The arrangement is actually not as inefficient as it seems at first glance and the hillside location permits trucks to deliver to the upper as well as lower floors.

Behind the apparent chaos in the office is also a systematic and highly profitable operation. Prices are arrived at by a simple markup. As the firm makes a large portion of its wares this results in prices that are competitive with any retailer offering the same merchandise. With a few exceptions everything is shipped postpaid. As the business, 80 percent mail order and 20 percent in the store, is for cash, there is little bookkeeping.

The catalog is printed on the premises but the presses are owned by Alexander R. Fowler of Falmouth, the printer. When not busy with Bean work, he cuts down the overhead with printing for others. Bean sends a catalog to anybody who asks for it, but unless an order results within a year a second request must be made to obtain another. If something is ordered, the name is kept on the mailing list for three years, or six more catalogs.

Incoming orders are handled somewhat as at Sears, Roebuck and Co., with whose executives Bean has several times exchanged ideas. With a single typing, a girl fills out an address label for the shipment, three copies of the order (one to go to the customer), and a name and address card to be checked against the mailing list. A staff of girls works full time correcting the mailing list.[5]

One winter day when the New York Telephone Company needed forty pairs of snowshoes for its repairmen in an upstate emergency, Bean's got them off within an hour. Nearly all orders are shipped the day received. The around-the-clock operation and the over-the-post-office substation location facilitate this.

The Maine Legislature passed a law in 1962 requiring businesses to close on Sunday but the Freeport Town Meeting exercised its local option and voted three to one that Bean's be allowed to remain open. Because the salesroom is continuously open, it serves as the fire alarm reporting center for Freeport. Fires are reported on a special telephone there and the answering clerk dials the appropriate signal into the alarm system to muster Freeport's volunteer firemen.

One mailing-room employee is a member of the volunteer fire department. "I've got to change levels eight times and go through five corridors, nine doors and two flights of stairs when the siren blows," he says. However, he adds, he still gets there faster than the butcher up the street who's about the same distance away. Customers aren't always so agile. In the small hours of the morning, a sportsman somewhat under the influence lost his way. He was found next day peacefully asleep under an overturned stack of hunting pants.

Parking facilities were greatly enlarged by the purchase and razing of an adjoining building in 1963. In one fortnight that summer cars from forty-eight of the fifty states used this new convenience while their owners visited Bean's.

In 1964 net sales soared past $3,000,000 for the first time. Among the sales were orders from a blind fisherman who had the Bean catalog translated into Braille for his use. At the request of the woman who translates for it, the company now advises her of the new items or changes in each catalog so she will not duplicate parts already put into Braille.

A factor in the increased sales has been a women's department first opened in the Freeport store in 1954. While the catalog already contained some feminine items, including ladies' long underwear, the fall issue that year was sprinkled with ladies' sweaters, boots, stockings, shoes and coats. Bean's wife is an expert at fishing and he has observed more and more women, especially young wives, accompanying their men on hunting and fishing expeditions. Men encourage this because they can get away oftener. And Bean thinks this is a very fine thing both for domestic happiness and the Bean business.

Playboy once presented one of its "playmates of the month" clad only in Bean's chamois-cloth shirt.[6]

Among the letters that Bean cherishes is one from a Minneapolis man, saying: "Enclosed find check for which please send me one Bean's Pack Basket one Pack Basket cover. Outside of my wife, this is the handiest piece of equipment a man could take to the woods." The same year, a customer named Otto Loeffler wrote: "For several years Miss Jean Hulbert, 606 Oakmont Ave., Erie, Pa., and Otto Ford Loeffler, 305 Poplar St., Erie, Pa., have been receiving your semi-annual catalogues. . . . Effective today, kindly remove Miss Hulbert's name from your mailing list, because she is Mrs. Loeffler now. The common interest in the items listed in your catalogue helped greatly to bring us together."[7]

Bean's prescription for success is: "Sell good merchandise at a reasonable profit, treat your customers like human beings, and they'll always come back for more."

Just how much more they come back for is evidenced by an order received from a man in St. Mary's, Pennsylvania. The sportsman wrote that it would take "too damn long to fill out the list he wanted," and instructed Bean to send him every item in the catalog on pages 8 through 64 inclusive!

XXI

OHRBACH'S, INC.

"A Business in Millions, a Profit in Pennies"

HIGH STYLE AT LOW PRICES has been the announced goal of countless retailers of women's apparel, but none have achieved it more convincingly than Ohrbach's, Inc. Its slogan, "A business in millions, a profit in pennies," is a literal statement of its success. By faithful adherence to an economical, low-markup operation devoid of frills, the firm has expanded from small beginnings on New York's Fourteenth Street to six stores in the New York and Los Angeles areas. In 1954, moreover, Ohrbach's stunned the retailing world by transferring its headquarters store to the Thirty-fourth Street store formerly occupied by McCreery's, and thereby coming into head-on conflict with the Herald Square and lower Fifth Avenue department and specialty stores.

The firm was founded by Nathan M. ("N. M.") Ohrbach, a cheerful, early-rising, self-made merchant who for decades personally opened the doors of his store each morning. A man who doesn't smoke and drinks only rarely, he has worked for years at an ultramodern kidney-shaped desk in a glamorous book-lined office with paintings by Thomas Gainsborough, John Constable and Thomas Benton lining the walls.

The Ohrbach's credo of merchandising was once expressed succinctly by the founder: "The housewife likes to feel that her favorite stores are not selling to her—they are buying for her. She is paying for a service, simply defined, to locate in the markets of the world those items which will best serve her wants, requirements and pocketbook."

Ohrbach, who built what has been called the Rolls-Royce of low-margin retailing, was born in Vienna, Austria, on August 31, 1885. The Strauss waltzes were being composed there at the time, but the pleasures of the Hapsburg capital were not for the Ohrbachs. When Nathan was two, his parents took their share of the family's few kronen, derived from a toll gate and a small salt mine thirty kilometers from the city, and migrated to America, without improving their fortunes.

Nathan and his three brothers grew up in Brooklyn. He attended elementary schools there and DeWitt Clinton High School. At fourteen, he went to work for $3.50 a week "running errands and sweeping out" for J. M. Tobias, a wholesale coat and suit house. By the time he was seventeen, he had been a traveling salesman. He was also briefly a Coney Island lifeguard and a delivery boy for Macy's.

At twenty, he became a buyer and "assistant to the president" of the First Co. of Jersey City at $25 a week. He was also a buyer for Berlin's in Brooklyn, Erich Brothers in Manhattan, and Brager's in Baltimore. By 1907, his prospects were bright enough for him to marry Matilda Kane of Brooklyn, a sister of two of his business acquaintances.

In 1911, he opened a small specialty shop, Bon Marché, Inc., of Fulton Street in Brooklyn and later one in Manhattan on teeming Fourteenth Street between University Place and Fifth Aveue. He also acquired some small stores in Pennsylvania towns. All sold low-priced ready-to-wear clothing in small quarters but managed to attract crowds with a table of fast-moving merchandise just inside the door. This later became a basic Ohrbach sales tactic.

By 1923, he had saved some money and had spent eighteen of his thirty-eight years in retailing. This experience convinced him that success for a retailer lay in either of two different directions. One was in providing customers with every imaginable service and charging them accordingly. The other was in cutting services to bare essentials and sharing the savings thus effected with the customers. Like several other famous merchants, he chose the latter course.

He then interested Max Wiesen, a dress manufacturer, in joining him in a new store to sell ready-to-wear—in the form of job lots, seconds, manufacturers' overstocks and irregulars—in large volume at low prices. Each invested $62,500 in a partnership and Ohrbach made a careful search for a high-traffic location accessible both by subway and surface transportation.

After considering many possibilities, he settled on a narrow fire-gutted structure on Fourteenth Street not far from his own small shop. Across the street to the north was Union Square, where orators of all political and economic persuasions voiced their world-saving dreams. A few yards to the east and across the street was "S. Klein, On the Square," Sam Klein's famous cash store that within a few years was to claim to be the largest women's wear shop in the world. To the west were several other big stores.

The site chosen by Ohrbach was historic ground. In the nineteenth century it had been the home of General Bronson Winthrop, law partner of Henry L. Stimson. On March 4, 1903, Adolph Zukor opened a penny arcade there, and the first motion pictures were shown in penny machines. The pennies rolled in so fast that a small car mounted on a track was required to haul them to the basement, where a shooting gallery also contributed to the profits. On the second floor, Zukor built the world's first nickelodeon. To entice New Yorkers upstairs, he made the steps of glass, installed an electric-lighted waterfall underneath them and called the place Crystal Hall.

It continued in business for two decades until it was badly damaged by fire a few months before Ohrbach decided to make a store of it. The partners spent $70,000, more than half their capital, repairing the place over a period of many weeks.

The two floors and basement were stocked with dresses to sell at $1 and coats at $5. Ohrbach, then and later, contended that there was nothing wrong with pricing items in round, or even, figures.

"In the early days of the cash register," he once explained, "the odd price was developed by retailers as a method of compelling clerks to ring up sales. If an item sold for $1, and the customer gave the salesperson a dollar bill, the clerk might hand over the merchandise and put the dollar bill elsewhere than in the register. But if the item sold for 95 cents and the customer presented a dollar bill, the salesperson would be much more likely to ring up the sale on the register in order to get the necessary change. In certain lines, women's gloves, for example, the odd price has become firmly established in customer's minds, but I unhesitatingly brand the general worship of the odd price as rank foolishness.

"I believe strongly that every retailer should experiment in this matter of odd prices. Profits in retailing are made in pennies, and the difference between profit and loss in more than one store might be found by refraining from throwing away profits in the form of smaller markups due to the fanatical worship of odd prices." Incidentally, with sales taxes, in effect in many states and municipalities, pushing most sales prices above the even dollar marks, odd pricing is even less appealing to retailers now that it was in 1923.

A "grand opening" was scheduled for October 4, 1923, for the new store. A huge sign announced "Ohrbach's, a bonded word for savings. . . . More for Less or Your Money Back." Ohrbach and his brother-in-law, Jack Kane, were at work in the store the evening before the opening when they recognized Sam Klein, the patriarch of the "On the Square" store, peering through the door.

They invited him inside for what proved to be the only meeting of Ohrbach and Klein—rivals until Klein's death many years later. Klein, a poor Russian immigrant who had made a fortune with pushcart methods, shook hands and looked around with amusement. "Such long counters," he said. "Such high ceilings! It's a joke!" He took his leave and announced: "I'll give them just seven months!"

Klein proved completely wrong about Ohrbach's. The opening-day crowds overwhelmed the store's fifty employees. A score of persons were cut and bruised and the police were summoned. Additional merchandise had to be rushed in that night to fill the bare racks.

The store was a success from the start. In 1924, sales amounted to

$1,600,000 and profits totaled $119,000. As business grew, the original frontage of twenty-seven feet was expanded by taking over adjoining buildings.

A "Miracle Day" sale, a duplicate of the opening-day event, was held at the end of every month for the next three years with coats, suits and dresses that were not selling drastically reduced in price. Then, however, an internal crisis threatened the store. Wiesen and Ohrbach disagreed over how the business should be run. When Wiesen refused for a time to sell out, Ohrbach leased quarters nearby and announced plans for a second store (all earlier Ohrbach stores by then had been sold, one of them to his brothers). The move brought Wiesen to terms and in January, 1928, he accepted $650,000 for the interest which had cost him $62,500 less than five years earlier.

At this time, Ohrbach abandoned special sales and undertook to make everyday a sale day. He then personally coined the slogan, "A business in millions . . . a profit in pennies." Ohrbach's markups were lower than the typical department store's and his prices reflected this difference.

He also added men's and children's furnishing and accessories. Most important, he began to "trade up" his women's merchandise and to offer garments of a higher style and quality than had been previously available regularly in the neighborhood. This caused some other merchants there to call the store "the fancy pants of Fourteenth Street."

At this time, he also formalized his policies of no price advertising, a minimum sales force, no alterations, no deliveries, cash and carry and no special sales periods.[1] This helped Ohrbach's open a branch in Newark and pass triumphantly through the depression, even earning 16 percent on invested capital in 1932. A few years later, Ohrbach's wrested the Fourteenth Street sales leadership from S. Klein by a margin of many millions.

Ohrbach's today is a bargain-hunter's paradise. Its management has blended daring buying and merchandising with conservative operations policies—and in so doing has wooed women of all income levels into its doors.

"A customer," says Ohrbach's manual for its employees, "may

state that she has seen an article like ours for less in a competitive store. When this happens, call your department manager at once. Someone from our comparison department will shop the article to determine whether the quality and workmanship are equal to ours. If the customer is proven right, our item is marked down. If the customer has paid the higher price, she is given a rebate for the difference.

The company has always operated under the philosophy that the customer is a lot smarter than many merchants suspect. Once as an experiment Ohrbach put one hundred handbags on sale at a low price—ninety-two of high quality and eight shoddy purses. At the end of the day, he discovered happily that four of the six bags left were the "dogs."

At Ohrbach's, there are probably more women's coats sold each year than at any other store in New York City, if not the nation. Vice President Sydney Gittler is known in Europe and on Seventh Avenue as the "coat and suit king" for the styling ideas and merchandise volume he has been able to create during his long tenure at the store.

Some of Ohrbach's low markup is made possible by its buying methods. As most ready-to-wear, however, is produced on the same sewing machines by members of the same union, the International Ladies' Garment Workers' Union, the possibilities in this direction are limited. Nevertheless, the store has developed special resources and often induces manufacturers to make additional runs of their products at trimmed prices without labels or under an Ohrbach label. The company buys as much as $45,000 worth of a single suit style at a time, compared with the $1,500 worth that another store might purchase.

The real economics, however, are in the store's selling operations. Fair-trade merchandise is avoided entirely. "The more billing, the less cooing" has been Nathan Ohrbach's explanation for no charge accounts. Selling is semi-self-service. This enables Ohrbach clerks to cover more customers and racks than clerks in stores where the merchandise is less open.

One favorite story of the Ohrbach's people tells of the genteel lady who was caught up in a crush around a glove table and was pushed squarely into another woman. "Oh, I do beg your pardon," she said sweetly. "I simply could not help myself." The other woman looked down at her and muttered, "If you're so damn polite, why aren't you shopping at Altman's?"

There is no alteration service at Ohrbach's. If garments don't fit, customers must alter them or find a seamstress to do it. There is no delivery service but packages will be wrapped for mailing if the customer desires. Employees, who in other stores receive discounts of as much as 25 percent, get only 10 percent at Ohrbach's.

Ohrbach's low markup policy is a firm one. An executive of the Newark store, who once telephoned with the suggestion that the price of umbrellas be increased because it was raining, received a severe lecture from Nathan Ohrbach. Any change in price is supposed to be downward but, unlike the situation in the vast majority of stores, there is no calling attention to this when it occurs.

"Promotion is like taking dope," asserts the founder. "You use one dose of it and you have to have another and another and another. The only price that matters on an item is the price for which it can be bought. The people who advertise $89 values for $19.95 simply insult the customers' intelligence. If you advertise dresses at $12.95, formerly $16.95, you are simply saying to women: 'Dear customer, we thought we could sell these garments to you at $16.95, but you were too smart for us. You have decided they are worth no more than $12.95, and that's what we are pricing them.' "

Some Seventh Avenue manufacturers use Ohrbach's as a sensitive barometer of what will sell and what will not. One technique they use is to place two dozen dresses of a new style on sale at the store. If eighteen or more have been bought by the end of the first day, the manufacturers will begin cutting several thousand, confident that a best seller is in the making.[2]

No sales slips are written at the store. Each item bears a single price ticket. If an item is marked down, an entirely new tag is affixed. As Ohrbach's attempts to turn over its merchandise fifteen times a year, more than twice as often as many other similar stores, markdowns come fast if merchandise fails to move.

Style, adroitly advertised and publicized, as well as price has figured in Ohrbach's success. As Ohrbach says: "It is essential that the retail novitiate recognize the utter and absolutely autocratic sway of Dame Fashion and her satellites, style and design, over the world of merchandise." He classifies women shoppers in these four categories:

A. The woman who is highly style conscious and whose purse is able to withstand the onslaughts of high style. Price is no consideration to her. She wants to be among the first to sport the new.

B. The woman who likes style but not to the exclusion of price. Her desire for fashion first may be as keen as that of the other woman. But she must, perforce, keep a weather eye on her purse. She will not buy at the very start of the season. First she must assure herself that the fashion trend is set—she cannot afford to buy a fashion flivver. Second, she must assure herself that the price is not exorbitant.

C. The frugal woman, who is style conscious but who, through habit or necessity, must bide her time. She is quite eager to be up to the fashion. But she must watch her dollars carefully, and therefore she waits until the season is well on before starting to shop. She, also, represents an important group—and an individual pricing problem.

D. Our final type is the woman who buys only when clearances are featured. Women in this group may or may not be fashion conscious—the fact is that few women, these days, do not know the basic style trends. But for economic or other reasons these women buy only when prices are at bedrock.[3]

Women of the last three classes are Ohrbach's regular customers. And in recent years the store has aspired to the "Class A" women with line-for-line copies of creations by French, Italian and Spanish designers. Nathan Ohrbach was made a Chevalier of the Legion of Honor in recognition of his promotion of French imports. Originals by French and Italian designers like Dior, Givenchy, St. Laurent, Chanel, Jacques Heim, Balenciaga, Fabiani, Simonetta, and Capucci have been purchased by Ohrbach's to copy for mass distribution.

Adroit publicity and advertising attempts to keep its customers aware of Ohrbach's fashion achievements. For example, the store's publicity director, Mark Klauser, a former *New York Times* sports writer, once arranged a fashion show for a Ladies' Day crowd of sixty-five thousand attending a Yankee–Red Sox baseball game at Yankee Stadium. Fifteen jeeps carried models wearing sun suits, bathing garb and other summer wear about the field. This stunt helped push Ohrbach's sales above $30,000,000 and its profits over the $1,000,000 mark for the first time shortly after World War II.

Another way that Ohrbach's keeps its name before the public is by furnishing fashions for use on television programs and theatrical productions. Daytime and evening shows with a total of over 150,000,000 viewers a week run the credit line at the end of the show "Fashions by Ohrbach's." Musical and industrial shows in many cities are also costumed by the New York store.

While many stores, at least on Christmas and New Year's Day, advertise themselves as institutions, all of Ohrbach's advertising has been institutional. As specific prices and items are not advertised, there is no need for turning out news of bargains under the pressure of newspaper deadlines. Moreover, the company spends only 1 percent of its total sales for advertising, much lower than the average specialty store.

Five years after Ohrbach's was founded, its advertising was entrusted to Gray Advertising Inc. When William Bernbach and others handling the account there formed their own agency, Doyle Dane Bernbach, Inc., in 1949, Ohrbach's went along with them.

Unusual, gay illustrations, ample white space and short, often humorous copy have characterized Ohrbach's distinctive advertising. Many early advertisements of the store were one-panel cartoons depicting the adventures of a big-eyed, curvaceous young lady called Melisse who always snared her man. This series attracted national attention and the original Melisse, Mildred Oppenheim, the artist who created the character, went into business for herself.

Several paintings from a notable collection of New York scenes commissioned by Ohrbach were used in the store's advertising. This collection of sixty paintings, by ten artists working without restrictions, also was exhibited at the Museum of the City of New York and attracted much favorable criticism in art circles. The artists were Thomas Hart Benton, Aaron Bohrod, Adolf Dehn, George Grosz, Peter Hurd, Fletcher Martin, Paul Sample, Georges Schreiber, Lawrence Beall Smith and Frederic Taubes. Later some abstract illustrations by Erik Nietsche were used in Ohrbach's advertising and proved so abstract that it was suggested that they be repeated upside down.

Humorous drawings by Peter Arno and Paul Rand followed and gave way to equally amusing photographs, sometimes published awry or in fragments. Though copyrighted, one captioned "Don't walk your legs off," and showing a young lady apparently doing so, was copied widely. Another showing bearded men dueling was captioned, "I'd rather die, sir, than give up a woman who shops at Ohrbach's."

In recent years, the whimsical approach in both art and copy—developed by some of the same Doyle Dane Bernbach personnel who have worked on this Ohrbach's account since the agency's inception—has been featured. Perhaps the ad that drew the greatest attention was the 1958 one headlined "I found out about Joan."

This advertisement, which appeared only once, pictured a saucy cat wearing a hat and smoking a cigarette in a holder. The copy consisted entirely of comments by a catty woman explaining how her neighbor Joan dresses well by shopping at Ohrbach's. Thousands of requests for copies of this ad have been made by people from all over the world and granted by the agency.

"We're telling the consumer in all of these ads," says Bernbach, "that no matter what you want, you'll get good quality merchandising at Ohrbach's at a good price. I think that we have built the understanding in the public's mind that you will always get fashion merchandise at a good price at Ohrbach's."[4]

Some idea of the originality and effectiveness of Ohrbach's advertising was revealed by a classroom survey in the Julia Richman High School of New York. With names and addresses deleted, twenty full-page advertisements of big Manhattan and Brooklyn stores from Sunday editions of the *New York Times* and New York *Herald Tribune* were shown to students. Eighty percent of them remembered and identified the Ohrbach's advertisement. Only one other advertisement was recognized by as many as 50 percent. The pages of three stores were identified by 25 percent, eight pages had a smaller score and the remaining seven pages were entirely unrecognized.

Ohrbach's expansion to California came as result of the growth of the fashion industry there. The firm employed the services of a buying office in Los Angeles as early as 1939 and in 1945 opened one of its own.

Three years later, it leased three floors and the mezzanine in a wing of the glittering new Prudential Insurance Company building on fashionable Wilshire Boulevard's "Miracle Mile." Into the 150,000-square feet of floor space went fixtures and decorations, including some mural paintings, costing $2,500,000 and merchandise valued at the same amount.

Lured by newspaper and radio advertising of the same institutional type that had proved successful in New York, thousands were on hand for the initial day's business. Nine minutes after the doors were opened, they had to be closed and, as in the case of the Manhattan opening in 1923, police had to keep order. By afternoon, spot announcements on local radio stations were saying: "Please don't come to Ohrbach's today; come tomorrow or next week." Customers buying bargain nylons, handbags and similar items overwhelmed the store staff, and twenty-five additional cashiers were flown from New York to handle the rush that continued for days.

So well received was the firm in the West that in 1953 it purchased Milliron's, a downtown Los Angeles store dating back to 1905, and spent $1,000,000 modernizing its eleven-story quarters. Using golden scissors, Mrs. Nathan M. Ohrbach cut a ribbon to formally open the refurbished store. A crowd of seventy-five thousand rushed in for opening-day bargains. So crowded was the store at midday that newcomers were admitted only as those inside departed. However, the opening-day aura didn't last long at this branch and, after first shutting down five floors of the building as an economy move, Ohrbach's closed the Milliron store in 1959 because of poor volume results.

Since 1960, Ohrbach's has opened three more stores—in La Mirada, California, Westbury, Long Island, and in the San Fernando Valley outside of Los Angeles. When criticized for this relatively late entry into the booming branch store business, Ohrbach said, "I'd rather be right than first."

Many glamorous shoppers became customers at the Ohrbach's stores in and around Los Angeles. Present at one line-for-line fashion show, for example, were Baroness d'Erlanger, Gene Tierney, Lady Lawford, Princess Pignatelli and many others. Linda Christian told the store how she paid $10 for a coat at Ohrbach's, wore it awhile and then sold it to a thrift shop for $15.

When the Wilshire Boulevard store sold the bankrupt Merry Hull stock of costly children's clothing at a 70 percent markdown, Mrs. Alfred Vanderbilt bought $600 worth of the garments and Lauren Bacall purchased $800 worth.

In 1954, Ohrbach's undertook its boldest move—from the six seventy-five-year-old buildings that had been put together to form the Fourteenth Street store to the heart of New York on West Thirty-fourth Street off Fifth Avenue, just across the street from the Empire State Building. This opportunity came when the venerable James McCreery and Sons store, immortalized in *Life with Father,* closed its doors after becoming unprofitable.

Undaunted by the fact that any store in this location must compete with Macy's and Gimbels to the west and such famous fashion stores as Lord & Taylor, B. Altman & Co. and Arnold Constable nearby on Fifth Avenue, Ohrbach decided to take over the site. A ninety-year lease was arranged and Ohrbach's took possession of the property early in 1954. At a cost of $2,500,000, all eleven floors of the old 501,000-square foot building were rebuilt and remodeled under the direction of designer Raymond Loewy.

Around 100,000 persons crowded into the store on opening day, August 26, 1954, and spent $500,000. "If you live through this, you are ready for Macy's," said the latter in an advertisement welcoming its new neighbor.

The advent of the 1960's brought on a change in the ownership of Ohrbach's, Inc. The company stock had always been closely held by the Ohrbach family, so corporate information has not been made generally available. But enough details have been pieced together for us to come up with this sequence of events:

It had become obvious to Nathan Ohrbach that his son, Jerome Kane Ohrbach—a Cornell University graduate who rose from assistant buyer to president of Ohrbach's—was not interested in taking over completely the reins of the company. Jerome Ohrbach had many other outside interests, was well-known in Wall Street as a large investor in some public companies and was actively connected for many years with the Dreyfus Corporation, which markets the Dreyfus Fund, a mutual fund.

Therefore, in January, 1962, a large undisclosed block of stock in the Ohrbach corporation was sold to the Dutch-American Investing Company, Inc., an affiliate of the Holland-based C. & A. Brenninkmeyer Co. The Brenninkmeyers—who built a European mercantile empire in the years after 1841 with stores in the Netherlands, West Germany, England and Belgium—are even more close-mouthed about their personal affairs than the Ohrbachs.

At that time, Nathan Ohrbach retained the chairmanship of Ohrbach's, Inc., and Jerome Ohrbach continued as president and treasurer. Changes, however, were not long in coming. Jerome Ohrbach resigned in July, 1963 and was succeeded by Elmar Brenninkmeyer. Anthony Brenninkmeyer, his cousin, became a vice president of Ohrbach's. And Nathan Ohrbach gave up the chairman's post in 1965, while retaining his seat on the five-man board of directors, to become a consultant to the company that bears his name. The exact stock ownership now of the Ohrbach and Brenninkmeyer families in the company is unknown.[5]

In 1965, total sales of the entire Ohrbach's organization were estimated at almost $94,000,000. The big New York store had a volume of $33,500,000, while the Newark and Westbury units each sold about $14,250,000 worth of merchandise. In California, sales of the Wilshire store were $15,500,000, of the San Fernando Valley store $10,000,000 and of the La Mirada store $6,000,000.

Morale is high among Ohrbach's four thousand employees. Practically all executives have risen from the ranks. Dining rooms and cafeterias serve good food at low prices. There are sick benefits, life insurance and pension plans. All regular employees receive a week's winter vacation after five years of service in addition to two weeks' vacation in the summer. The company has a revolving loan fund on which employees can draw in financial emergencies.

Ohrbach clerks are given careful instruction in courtesy and grooming but are allowed more latitude in dress than in many other stores. In the summer, for example, salesgirls are permitted "leg makeup properly applied" in lieu of stockings. An Ohrbach girl is supposed to look "crisp and well-put-together." She is instructed: "Don't go in for slouching or slinking, walk naturally—don't rumba."

Employees are invited to make suggestions for the improvement of the store and its operations and a "suggestion committee" distributes cash prizes for those accepted. Employees also are rewarded for the detection of shoplifters.

"A customer owes you nothing," the store tells its employees. "You owe her courtesy by the very fact that she is in your store. It is our aim to make every Ohrbach customer a satisfied one—satisfied not only with any merchandise that she might purchase here but also with the friendly, courteous treatment she receives from each and every employee whom she chances to contact in the store. A customer should never be made to feel that she must buy; she should know that she is perfectly welcome to shop."

Nathan Ohrbach believes that the retail leaders of the future will be college graduates. Thus he has been interested for many years in the New York University Institute of Retail Management, the Fashion Institute of Technology and the High School of Fashion Industries. He also has chairmaned an advisory committee that arranges part-time jobs for retailing students at the College of the City of New York.

Ohrbach believes that, to succeed in retailing, a man or woman must enjoy meeting people, have a feeling for merchandise and enjoy competition. "Retailing," he says, "when stripped of all its details, is found to be the art of pleasing people. Brains, imagination, courage and all the other attributes of youth are demanded by retailing as by no other single industry."

XXII

WEBB'S CITY

"The World's Most Unusual Drugstore"

THE MODERN DRUGSTORE, one of the most amazing of American institutions, is the heir of the itinerant "medicine man" and the ancient apothecary shop. Physicians of Greece and Rome compounded their own prescriptions, but in A.D. 754 an Arab named Abu Coreisch Isa el Szandalani, at the instance of the Caliph of Baghdad, opened in that city probably the world's first apothecary shop. Developments followed in England, Germany and France. Immigrants brought the pharmaceutical traditions of these countries to America.

Elias Durand, a pharmacist with Napoleon's Army, for example, opened a shop in Philadelphia in 1825. It was the first to boast a soda fountain. As early as that date, pharmacists of Philadelphia and Boston were attempting to stabilize retail drug prices. "One evil where there is a difference in price," one of the latter noted, "is that the purchaser either thinks that the one who charged high wronged him as to price, or that the one who charged low wronged him as to quality." It is not surprising that like-minded merchants in the twentieth century, through the National Association of Retail Druggists, advocate state and national fair-trade legislation.

Other drugstore owners believe it more profitable to cut prices. There also are differences of opinion as to what a drugstore should sell. Lascoff's in New York and at least four hundred others carry on in the apothecary tradition, selling only drugs and, in many cases, only drugs prescribed by physicians. A great many more sell many other items as well and may be notable for their customers. One such is Schwab's in Hollywood where film folk gather. Sanborn's of Mexico City is a remarkable institution. Housed in an old palace, it is one of the best eating places in the city and does a big gift and silverware business.

But it is in St. Petersburg, Florida, a pleasant city with so many aged pensioners that the curbs are sloped for wheelchairs, that the world's largest and most extraordinary drugstore is located. By bargains and ballyhoo, it has attained a sales volume of more than $30,000,000 a year and does the largest retail cash business in the South. For years this establishment has advertised itself widely as "Webb's City, The World's Most Unusual Drug Store."

In fact, it might also be called "The World's Most Unusual Meat Store," "The World's Most Unusual Barber Shop," or several other distinctions with equal validity. For the store that sprawls over six city blocks has sixty-seven busy departments, including one selling women's ready-to-wear. There are three restaurants, a beauty shop, a gasoline station and a supermarket. Ten parking lots provide space for 2,000 automobiles. All of this attracts around 45,000 customers a day in a city where the 1960 census counted only 181,298 residents.

But the heart of the operation is the drug department and the drugstore designation permits the place to do business from 9 A.M. to 9 P.M. weekdays and 11 A.M. to 7 P.M. on Sundays. Ten registered pharmacists, aided by twenty-four girl typists and clerks, compound more than nine hundred prescriptions a day in immaculate quarters. The main floor is a super drugstore, and despite the growth of other departments the management asserts that drugs, the huge soda fountain, cosmetics, and related sundries account for a fourth of Webb's huge volume. Everything is sold for cash and only for prescription items is there free delivery service.

The main building is four stories high, with a basement cafeteria.

Across the street is a seven-floor furniture store. Nearby is the Trading Post, essentially a super service station, which also houses sporting goods, paint and hardware stores. Also nearby is the feed and fertilizer store. And some nine miles away, outside the city limits on Gandy Boulevard leading to Tampa, under a five-story electric sign, is Webb's Outpost. This is a little supermarket and a gift, sandwich and souvenir shop which gives tourists information about St. Petersburg and Webb's. Road signs, some of them 750 miles away, also direct motorists to the place.

Responsible for it all is James Earl "Doc" Webb, who has been aptly described as "a peculiar blend of merchant prince and leprechaun"[1] His portrait painted handsomely in oil hangs in the store over the ascending track of the escalator. Of slight stature but immense energy and with a great flair for showmanship, he is a cocky bantam who has found fun and fortune in running a store like a circus. He was born August 31, 1899, in Nashville, Tennessee, of Scotch, Irish and English descent. His formal education ended after the seventh grade but his business education already had begun.

"My father—he was a contractor—had been injured by a truck," Doc once recalled. "Mother and I took over the family. I began making money when I was nine years old. I raised vegetables and sold them. I put on backyards shows, sold lemonade and later peddled both morning and afternoon papers." In his teens he worked around drugstores and had such an affinity for this type of business that "I was manager of a retail drugstore with twelve adults working under me by the time I was twenty," he says.

He was in Knoxville by this time and here earned his informal title of "Doc" by developing a venereal-disease compound which was known through Tennessee and Kentucky as "Webb's 608." Profits from it enabled Webb to buy an expensive Rickenbacker automobile.

"I have always made money and liked making it," Webb says. "By the time I was twenty I had bought a great variety of stocks, but now I own just one kind—Webb's."

After seven years in Tennessee drugstores, where he learned a lot but never bothered to qualify as a registered pharmacist, Webb at twenty-six decided to go into business for himself. Because he liked the climate and there was a real-estate boom there, he chose the west coast of Florida. But, just as he arrived in St. Petersburg with $5,000 and a partner, the boom collapsed and stores began to close.

Undaunted, he opened a tiny cut-rate drugstore with four employees in rented space seventeen by twenty-eight feet. It was in an old building at the south end of the business area adjoining the Negro district, and between the Seaboard and Atlantic Coast Line railroad tracks. The exact spot is now more than occupied by Webb's cigar and magazine department, but a museum replica of the original store is to be found on the fourth floor, labeled "Doc's Original Drug Store." The tracks have since been removed and there is a big Webb's parking lot on the site of the Seaboard station.

The first year's receipts amounted to $38,990.45. With $6,000 in bills unpaid, Webb and his partner then parted and the latter eventually received $18,000 for his interest. Webb says his partner was "too conservative." The next year sales reached $90,000 and Webb started the expansion that eventually took all the space between the tracks. By shrewd purchasing, ruthless price cutting and spectacular promotions, he began to lure crowds to the out-of-the-way location. Sales passed $1,000,000 in 1936 and $2,000,000 in 1939.

One of Webb's most spectacular loss leaders was the three-cent breakfast with which he introduced his basement cafeteria. For this price, you received one egg, two strips of bacon, three slices of toast, grits and ham gravy. After six months, during which the cafeteria became well known, the price was advanced to fourteen cents. During sales this later was cut to nine cents!

Cheeses weighing four thousand pounds have been cut up and sold in a single day. Webb also has sold fifteen tons of bananas and fifty-two thousand pounds of chickens in one day. He sold a freight car of cantaloupes for two cents each, moved a carload of canned peaches in a day and even staged a carload sale of cigars. With sidings on two railroads, he found it easy to handle such shipments. When butter was at seventy-nine cents, Webb's sold some at 19 cents a pound and once marketed $17 automobile tires for $9.95. A cigarette "war" with a rival store ended with Webb's giving away two packs to a customer.

At times, Webb's posts the sale advertisements of rival drugstores with an additional line: "10 per cent off these prices at Webb's." But the height of this sort of thing probably was the sale of two thousand $1 bills at 95 cents each, later the sale of twenty-five hundred more at 89 cents each, and the repurchase a few days later of the "cheap" money at $1.35 per greenback. Mobs jammed the store.

"Any merchant," Webb believes, "should have the right to sell any item in his store at whatever price he decides." His tactics naturally brought him into conflict with the fair-trade laws and at one time he had six law firms employed defending him in various actions. He was successful in having Florida statutes invalidated, the Florida Supreme Court once ruling that inflexible price arrangements "are not in line with our traditional concepts of free competition."

When a "quality stabilization act" was pending in Congress in 1963, he sent a representative to Washington and bought display space in the Washington *Post*[2] to show how he believed the measure would increase the prices of drugs and appliances. "Please kill the quality stabilization act for All America," he asked. It was defeated.

The "Florida Poster Girls," one of Doc Webb's most durable publicity ventures, date from 1939. Each year eight Florida girls are chosen from several hundred on the basis of "beauty, character, talent and charm." Clad in bathing suits and other Florida fashion products, they present fashion shows about the country and otherwise publicize Florida, St. Petersburg and Webb's. Some years, they even invade Hollywood in a Florida-versus-California beauty competition.

Doc Webb's markups have been so low and his promotion expenses so great that at times he had been short of cash when expansion was required. In 1940, he needed $200,000. When local banks couldn't accommodate him and underwriters wanted 10 percent for selling a stock issue, Webb decided to sell $100 preferred shares over the counter. He filed the proper papers, obtained a broker's license and put a big advertisement in the Sunday paper. It concluded, "You have 7 days to buy these securities. . . . Come now! See J. E. Webb." A Monday page said "Today is the Day."

On Tuesday morning, he advertised $73,400 of stock sold and paid for," on Wednesday, $126,600 sold and paid for." On Thursday, a horrified representative of the Securities and Exchange Commission arrived to explain that securities could not be advertised like drugstore bargains. But the advertisement that morning simply said "Thank You." All the stock had been sold.

"At that time," recalls Doc Webb, "I found that we need never fear to be in the hands of the people."

This preferred stock subsequently was retired. Doc Webb owns a majority of the company's common stock and with his officers controls 70 percent of it. The other 30 percent is owned by some five hundred persons, many of them employees or customers. The annual reports reveal a steady increase in volume and unbroken but varying earnings.

Sales increased from $3,693,945 in 1941 to $12,305,000 in 1947, $18,218,837 in 1951 and $44,000,000 in 1954. Earnings ranged from $66,311 on sales of $5,675,000 in 1943 to $333,092 on sales of $16,421,788 for the fiscal year ending August 31, 1950. Sales passed $29,000,000 in 1959. Though it is common for heads of retail enterprises of this volume to earn more, Doc Webb pays himself a salary of only $30,000 a year.

The name, Webb's City, denotes the operation conducted by Webb and his associates. The business is citylike in the sense that more than fifty separate operations are carried on principally under one roof, and that most of the necessities and many of the luxuries of life can be procured in the various "stores." Each store has its own manager who is responsible for purchasing goods and selling them quickly at a modest profit, which Doc Webb says nets between 1 and 2 percent in an average year. The discount for paying cash is sometimes the only profit on an item. Over the store managers are five division heads, and over everybody is Doc Webb as president. Alabama-born Fred B. Scott is executive vice president and general manager. He joined Webb's in 1951 after Air Force service, A & P experience and management of a Dunlap chain department store. Executive vice president, operations is Doc's son, James E. Webb, Jr. He won the Distinguished Flying Cross, Purple Heart and other decorations as a

Ninth Air Force fighter pilot in World War II and ran two businesses of his own before joining his father in 1959.[3] Doc's brother, B. E. Webb, is a senior vice president. Vice presidents also include J. C. Holley, Thomas P. Johnson and Sam Harrington.

"This is not a department store operation at all, though one of the sixty-seven stores is a department store," Doc Webb points out. "Every manager is in charge of his own store and has the responsibility for its operation with help as needed from his division head or from me. Before World War II this was essentially a one-man operation—I had the ideas, planned the remodeling, made the rules and regulations. Now we have more of a team system."

The sixty-seven store managers are almost independent operators, for they hire and fire their own help, act as purchasing agents and are everything that their title implies. Seasonally, the number of employees varies between twelve and fifteen hundred. Turnover is low, morale is high, and many employees are stockholders. A bonus is paid each April, and there is incentive pay in the form of weekly commissions to augment salaries. There are paid vacations, sick leave and an insurance participation plan. Webb is proud of his employees and has announced that one of these days he is going to build a country club and swimming pool for them "and my customers." There are many ten-, fifteen- and twenty-year men in the organization and the attentiveness of clerks gives backing to an observation by an executive that "the employees feel they own the store."

"Most businesses start with one man and I started Webb's," Doc says, "but somewhere along the line you have to have help, and I am lucky to have my staff. You can't build a business staying in an office. The greatest failure in the world came when America's banks closed right and left back in the early thirties. If those bankers had been out in front meeting people and talking to them, the depositors wouldn't have taken out their money. But the bankers were back in their offices and look what happened. . . ."

Doc Webb usually doesn't get to the store and "out in front" until the afternoon, but he has not been idle. The home which he and his attractive wife, Aretta, a businesswoman in her own right, share is equipped with seven telephone lines, three direct to Webb's City, and there are telephone outlets in every room. Doc does most of his business by telephone. When he does arrive at the "office," he probably will breeze in wearing a white suit, one of 150 that he owns, in the jaunty manner of Jimmy Walker or Adolphe Menjou.

After an hour or sometimes less, Webb usually darts restlessly out of the office to do something more exciting. He may grab a microphone and over the public-address system announce a sudden bargain as if he were back selling medicine in the Tennessee mountains.

"Hear this, hear this!" he'll chant. "For the next thirty minutes, the next thirty minutes only, we will sell in the appliance department $25 electric toasters for $9.95 apiece. Hurry, hurry, *hurry!*" From all parts of the area, a mob will converge on the appliance department and in thirty minutes all the toasters may be sold.

If there are circus acrobats performing about the place, as sometimes is the case, Webb may strip to the waist and get into the act. He likes to jump up and down on mattresses. Though now a grandfather, he is a wiry and active athlete. At sixty-eight, he played tennis three times a week. With a partner, he once won the veteran doubles championship of Florida and had no difficulty obtaining a $500,000 insurance policy on his life for the benefit of the store.

Traffic builders for Webb's include a branch post office, second only to the main office in volume, and a free check-cashing service where telephone and all utility bills may be paid. At any time in the day, there will be a line at the check window on the main floor. Checks totaling more than $30,000,000 a year are cashed. This service costs Doc Webb $20,000 or more a year, but it is cheap advertising. Bankers' hours are unheard of at Webb's, and check cashing goes on day and night. Losses from bad checks are infinitesimal—and the few persons who try to impose on the system with bad checks are relentlessly pursued. "We cash more checks than most banks," Doc Webb claims proudly—and he doesn't have to add that a lot of the cash he hands out is spent in the store. While competitors, who encircle him in every direction, have gone largely to credit and premium stamps to increase volume, he has gained without them and Webb's City continues to be a 99 percent cash business.

Doc Webb says he doesn't believe in setting aside any fixed percentage of income for advertising. "There just isn't any yardstick you can apply—you just have to spend what is needed," he declares.

The advertising budget is around $750,000. Everything possible in the way of discounts, "push money" and advertising allowances is obtained from suppliers.

Advertising to Doc Webb means several things. It means first a schedule of full-page and double-page ads in the local newspapers; it means five hundred roadside signs extending as far north as Knoxville, where Doc used to live; it means a cross-country tour for the beauteous Poster Girls in their specially designed bus; it means entertainment of many kinds at Webb's during business hours, either on the main floor, or on a parking lot. There are other things, too, such as radio and TV time, but Doc's major confidence is in black-and-white newspaper advertising with emphasis on the big black letters and figures that announce his bargains.

Many things are conceived by Doc Webb or his staff to keep traffic flowing. A summer special is the manager's sale, in which the various store managers try to outdo each other in the matter of bargains. Entertainers perform five times daily during this period. Sometimes there is a topsy-turvy day, in which the drug department may sell avocados, the cosmetic department may feature gallon cans of motor oil, and the bakery may offer hardware items.

The big stage on the main floor near the fountain has been the scene of many as unusual event. A reptile expert has milked rattlesnakes of their venom for the entertainment of the patrons; aerial acts have been performed; boxing matches have been staged; magicians have done their stuff.

On the No. 1 parking lot, just outside, there have been free elephant rides; clowns have cavorted; people have been shot from cannons; lion acts have been staged. Here, too, Doc Webb has invited his customers to participate in a "Country Fair," which exhibits hobbies, crafts and foods—and the exhibitors were invited to sell their cakes, their bedspreads or whatever, even when they were competing with merchandise in Doc Webb's own stores.

Doc Webb takes an active role in civic affairs, supporting projects he likes and opposing those he thinks unwise. He bought newspaper display space in 1965 to defeat an urban-renewal project that he considered impractical. He has received a "distinguished service to the community" plaque from the Chamber of Commerce, a "citizenship medal" from the Veterans of Foreign Wars and other honors. On the occasion of one, the St. Petersburg *Independent* said: "As if reclaiming and building up an entire area of the city, once low-rated, and advantageously supplying millions of customers, were not enough, Doc Webb has also made his impress on the area in civic directions. It was he who devised the now commonly accepted term 'Sun-coast' to describe the whole Gulf Coast area—in this even antedating the naming of the big Tampa Bay bridge 'Sunshine Skyway'—and he who was the major factor in setting up new and better quarters for St. Petersburg's senior citizens."[4]

Webb says solemnly that two miracles have occurred at Webb's City in recent years "even though we may not be the best of Christians.

"Right after the war when we were expanding faster than we could borrow money, we just about came to the end of our rope. Our newest building program was well along, but we had stretched our finances too far. I said that we had to have $40,000 if we were going to pull out of the hole, and we were actually praying for divine help when we went home from the store one night.

"In the next morning's mail was a check for almost exactly the amount we needed from the U.S. Treasury. We had been trying to get a refund on taxes and we thought that this $40,000 had been returned to us from the Internal Revenue people. Actually, it turned out that the check had been mailed to us by mistake, and we had to pay it back with interest. But we used the money at the time for our building and it was four years before we had to pay it back, and we could afford to do it then. That has always seemed like a miracle to me.

"The other was a different sort of miracle. Webb's ran a highly profitable liquor store for many years—in fact it grew to a place where it had a $2,000,000 gross volume and was providing about half of our gross profits a few years after the war.

"Then I got to thinking that we were having to fire some of our people because they were drinking, and yet we were tempting them to drink with our liquor store. I didn't think that was fair and I could tell our employees didn't think it was right, so I decided to eliminate the liquor store. We did cut it out and here's the miracle—we had a bigger volume of business in Webb's City the next year and our net profits were $75,000 greater than they were when we sold liquor.

"I have always had a feeling that gold shouldn't be the master in any business, and I thought we ought to get out of the liquor business before it got too strong a hold on us. Some of our people didn't agree at the time; they felt that sale of liquor was legal and that there was nothing wrong with our liquor store. But I couldn't hear and read about people getting in trouble because they had been drinking and still feel right about selling it. And we're better off today for being out of that business. A store's principles are just like a person's; they've got to be good or you'll go down. . . ."

Some analysts have tried to figure that Doc Webb's success hinges largely on the fact that St. Petersburg is populated by a bigger-than-average number of oldsters who are looking for an interesting place to spend their pension money. Doc scoffs at this idea, though he is proud that "a lot of people with small incomes are able to live well because they shop at Webb's."

"I just run a fundamentally sound business," Webb declares, "and I could do it just as well in Egypt or Paris if the state would let me operate without interference. The United States is the last country where there is free enterprise, and it's a battle to have it here because of the chain stores and the fair-trade laws.

"But I've whipped 'em on prices and I've whipped 'em on this fair-trade thing. It's nobody's business what I sell an item for after I buy it, and I'm going to keep giving my customers the lowest prices they can find anywhere."

Webb says he would never be interested in adding another "drug-store" in another city. All his efforts have gone into the St. Petersburg operation and his goal is to keep it expanding.

"We definitely plan to be bigger every year than we were the year before," he says. "There has never been a day in forty years that the hammers haven't been ringing somewhere to improve Webb's or make it bigger. I'm sorry about just one thing, and that is that I didn't put our various stores on wheels so they could be rearranged easier. We are always moving around and expanding these units. . . ."

XXIII

THE DISCOUNTERS ARRIVE

Korvette and the Mass Merchandisers

"DO YOU KNOW WHAT DISCOUNTING IS?" the head of a major retail chain once asked.

Then he answered his own question. "It's nothing more than selling inferior merchandise on Sundays."

This facetious comment was untrue when it was expressed and is certainly untrue today. But it symbolizes nevertheless the feeling that many people, both in and out of retailing, have about discount houses, despite their enormous development since World War II.

Discount department stores had total sales of a whopping $13,-300,000,000 in 1965, an estimated $2,500,000,000, or 25 percent, more than the preceding year. This represented 5 percent of total retail sales and brought discounting closer in range to department-store volume of $20,900,000,000.

Their growth, moreover, has been equally spectacular. Sales of discount stores since 1960 have advanced at an annual rate of approximately 40 percent, while total retail volume gained 19 percent and department-store sales increased 15 percent. By mid-1966, a total of 2,684 discount stores were in operation, a 140 percent increase in just six years.

Yet, as big as discounting is now, the origins of many discount stores are humbler than those of most giant retailing establishments. E. J. Korvette, for example, the nation's largest discounter, got its start as a small luggage shop in a second-floor Manhattan walkup. The Two Guys chain began in an eight-hundred-square-foot store next to a New Jersey diner. Other major discounters began in factory buildings, in warehouses and in other offbeat locations.

Department-store executives have called discount stores everything from "a malignant cancer" to "an unsound method of distribution" which "takes it out of the hide of the consumer." Whatever they are called, though, discounters believe that they have succeeded in spurring traditional retailers to do a sharper job of merchandising, advertising and displaying their products to their customers.

As an industry, discounting has few certainties. First, there is no overall agreement as to exactly what a discount house is. The name itself indicates a store that sells merchandise for less. But what merchandise? And less than whom?

A good definition of a discount house is a store that operates at a lower average markup than conventional stores selling the same types of merchandise. Another definition, this one by Perry Meyers, a retailing consultant, calls a discount house "any store which operates on a low expense, low markup basis and which emphasizes competitive pricing as a main attraction to win customers."

But in the discounting field, definitions are rarely all-encompassing. For example, do the above definitions apply to Korvette, the giant of discounting, which has upgraded its merchandising and fixturing to such an extent that it calls its units not discount stores but promotional department stores?

How about such well-known New York stores as Alexander's and Mays? These stores were in business and selling apparel at discount prices long before discounting came into vogue. Nevertheless they term themselves "underselling" stores, rather than discounters.

With this confusion over definitions, it is not surprising to find that there are no precise figures to describe the size of discounting. The Department of Commerce does not compile monthly and yearly sales figures as it does for department stores and other retailing categories—perhaps because of this very confusion—so that even the best estimates of volume are simply that.

Furthermore, food, as well as nonfood, sales of discounters are usually included in estimates of their annual volume. Although food sales currently represent between 15 and 20 percent of total discount industry volume, they have been gaining steadily and add strength to overall sales figures.

Discount houses have frequently been termed revolutionary developments, but they can more precisely be described as evolutionary. For their development has been a gradual one that began long before the modern-day versions were conceived.

Since the early days of the twentieth century, neighborhood and downtown stores have held, either periodically or occasionally, sales when discounts were offered even though the name was not used. "Loss leader" merchandise—where the discounts are so large that the selling price is pushed below the cost to the merchant in order to stimulate traffic in his store—has long been found in department and specialty stores.

For many years, R. H. Macy—the epitome of the traditional department store—used to tell the world that it would "save our customers at least 6 per cent for cash." And then there is the slogan "Nobody but nobody undersells Gimbels."

Another development in the historical evolution of discount stores was the supermarket, beginning with the first one opened by Michael "King" Cullen in Jamaica, New York, in 1930. This method of retailing, particularly the very popular self-service aspects, brought food, and later related items, swiftly and efficiently to the consumer —offering her attractive settings, wide aisles and bargain prices.

With all of its precursors, the discount house as it is now generally known got its start after World War II. There were, to be sure, some discounters operating in the late 1930's, such as the first Masters store. But it wasn't until the opening of the outlet stores in New England, "the cradle of discounting," in abandoned textile mills or old warehouses that discounting really began making rapid strides forward.

The discount-house image at the outset was based on unadorned shelves, plain pipe racks, simple wooden tables, few salespeople ("no service is better than bad service" was the theory), no deliveries and a complete lack of frills. Since they were called "houses" instead of "stores," many people considered these outlets a place to buy only seconds, factory closeouts, irregulars and similar merchandise.

By and large, this has changed significantly. Discounters now sell goods in all general-merchandise categories, have attractive lighting and landscaping in and around their stores and feature extensive, easily-accessible displays. Most of their stores today are one-level, free-standing units in the nation's major metropolitan areas.

Almost from the start, the hard-goods discounters found themselves battling with national-brand manufacturers, who cited fair-trade laws in an attempt to prevent them from price cutting their merchandise. But as these manufacturers saw discounting take on an increasingly larger percentage of their total retail sales, many began to sell to discount stores.

Nowadays discount houses sell brand-name merchandise in profusion at prices generally below the "list," where there is a legitimate one. In fact, the erosion of the list price in many metropolitan centers has been largely due to the constant price pressure of the discounters.[1]

Few manufacturers of television sets, refrigerators and other appliances, including many of the very same companies that initially refused to sell discounters directly, can move their merchandise to the consumer without using discount stores. All of the staple items—toys, hardware, paints, etc.—are carried as a basic part of the inventory of most large and small discount houses.

Discount merchandising has also emerged from a hard-goods emphasis to a more balanced operation that sells both durable and nondurable goods. Some discounters have even grown up specializing in soft goods and have won new customers by offering apparel for men, women and children at apparent discounts. Between 25 and 40 percent of a typical discounter's volume is currently done in soft goods.

The discounters have proceeded still further into the province of department and general-merchandise stores. They have added such extras as service (beauty salons, watch repairing, etc.), automobile tire centers and audio equipment—and earned new customers for their older departments in the process.

What propelled discounting to its present position in the American economy? Perhaps the most important factor was the growth of the suburbs after the end of the Second World War.

As families in even the lower-income brackets moved away from the center of cities and towns, and as the automobile became an essential in many areas for even the simplest shopping tasks, a new type of market was created. The discounters—who moved quickly to those places where new communities developed and who brought new merchandising ideas that had not been tried before—found an audience that welcomed them with open arms.

Moreover, the department-store branches that were built for the suburbs usually didn't include the "basement" or "budget" store that the same companies successfully ran downtown. They thus virtually abdicated the lower-income portions of the suburban market to the onrushing discounters at first.

Discount centers provided many attractions for their customers. Large adjacent parking areas with spaces for thousands of cars, night hours almost every day of the week, and even Sunday openings in some communities were features that brought out larger and larger crowds of shoppers. Because self-selection was the vogue, merchandise was individually packaged for convenient customer handling and inspection.

The bazaarlike atmosphere—with such appurtenances as loudspeaker announcements of "fifteen-minute specials," pretzel and popcorn vendors outside the front doors and nearby carousels and other amusements—made shopping at many discount houses equivalent to a family outing.

As the discounters expanded, many of them utilized the services of concessionaires, or operators of leased departments. Leased departments are nothing new in retailing—some department and specialty stores have long been using them for certain departments like millinery, shoes and fine jewelry—but the concept was carried much further in discount houses.

One reason for the growth in number of lessees was that, with them, discounters were able to reduce the amount of capital investment required to get started, since less inventory had to be purchased by the store owner. Another is that lessees brought a degree of merchandising experience and sophistication in their fields that a large number of store owners originally needed and were willing to pay for. Food lessees, usually big supermarket chains, were taken in as the complete food and nonfood one-stop shopping idea gained momentum among discounters.

The trend toward the use of lessees has considerably abated recently. Leased-department operators who suffered financially when certain stores in which they had concessions went bankrupt have become more cautious, while the discounters—continually gaining more experience and anxious to obtain better control over merchandising and advertising policies—have taken over more departments that had formerly been leased out to others.

In 1962 and 1963 came a "shakeout," with many undercapitalized, poorly merchandised discounters falling by the wayside. Those that have remained, at least the big ones, are currently in a stronger position than they were in the early part of the 1960's,[2] even though discounting failures are by no means a thing of the past.

Three of the most recognizable characteristics that differentiate discount houses from other retailers are:

1. Lower markups. Discounters have from the outset operated at lower gross margins than department stores because their costs of construction, personnel and overall operations have usually been lower. While the differential has narrowed in recent years as discount stores added some of the services they originally disdained—like credit plans, carpeting and expensive fixturing in certain store areas and a greater selection in certain merchandise categories—there generally is still a sizable gap between the two.

Thus the typical department-store markup, figured as a percentage of the selling price, is about 40 percent. On the other hand, average markups of discount stores generally range between 20 and 30 percent.

2. Higher turnover. Inventory turnover, or the number of times

each item of merchandise is sold during the year, is generally acknowledged to be greater among discounters than among department stores. Executives of discounting organizations say that they can turn over their stocks at least six times a year, compared with the typical department-store stock turn of under four.

3. More self-service. Self-service is one of the keynotes of discount houses. With central checkout counters to service many departments and fewer salespeople in the stores, discounters have been able to cut down tremendously on the personnel cost required to man their stores. Consumers have become accustomed to fending for themselves in discount houses and in most cases manage to do it successfully.[3]

No organization has better utilized these techniques of discounting than E. J. Korvette, Inc. From a small second-floor loft opened in October, 1948, the company has gone on to become not only the number one discounter but also one of the country's major merchandising corporations with sales in fiscal 1965 of $720,000,000 and earnings of $10,000,000. It is preparing, moreover, to do battle with two of the best-known giants of retailing—Macy's and Gimbels—with a ten-story store at New York's crossroad, Herald Square, that could push it into first place in the retailing derby in the nation's largest city.

The man who created E. J. Korvette—and also, incidentally, coined the name—is probably the most unorthodox merchant in the United States. His name is Eugene Ferkauf, a shy, wiry, crew-cut native of Brooklyn who, while ignoring the shibboleths of retailing from the outset, nevertheless succeeded in being elected, in 1962, to the Retailing Hall of Fame at the Boston Conference on Distribution.

Gene Ferkauf is continuing to break many of the traditions of the retailing fraternity. He still has no private office, no secretary and no personal files of his own, but shares these facilities with another officer. Although he founded the company and has always been its guiding light and chief executive officer, he had no title until 1955, when his investment bankers—who were brought into Korvette preparatory to a public offering—insisted that he take one. Even then,

Ferkauf picked the nebulous title of chairman of the executive committee to leave himself free for decision making.

In 1965, following a management shakeup, Ferkauf assumed the position of president. Another half-dozen Korvette executives who started with Ferkauf in his first luggage store hold top management posts. But, as in early days, Ferkauf is out of the office more frequently than he is in—constantly walking through his stores and talking to his customers. "I love to go to the marketplace," he says.

Possibly Ferkauf enjoys visiting his Douglaston, Long Island, Korvette City store more than any other. There Korvette has a rectangular 5,600-square-foot art gallery where original works of painting and sculpture are sold to an art-hungry public. Ferkauf likes to spend time in this art gallery, studying the paintings—which range in price from $8 to $35,000—and personally waiting on trade.

The story of Korvette's development is one of merchandising know-how coupled with close attention to an old retailing principle: get the customers in the store with low prices and keep them coming by giving them value for their money. By doing this, Korvette has achieved the distinction of being the most important new merchandiser to emerge in the United States since the end of World War II.

"It doesn't take any special mental processes to become a retailer," Ferkauf believes. Yet how many men could take a thousand-square-foot luggage store, add small appliances and jewelry and from that base build an organization of over forty full-scale general merchandise stores and fifty-nine supermarkets in seven states?

The typical Korvette store contains 275,000 square feet and does an annual volume of $15,000,000 to $20,000,000 in all hard and soft lines. From its base in New York, the company has spread west to Chicago and St. Louis and south to Baltimore and Virginia.

With all this, Ferkauf is a disarmingly uncomplicated man. He claims simply that Korvette has "done more to stretch the buck than anyone in American distribution. I don't know by what percentage we've increased the purchasing power of the American dollar, but I know it's significant."[4]

The Ferkauf success formula can be broken down into these components: Pick good locations. Choose executives for their character and general intelligence. Maintain a close relationship with all employees. Provide customers with the best possible quality and value. Give service only if it is wanted but charge a fair price for it. And convince the public that substantial storewide savings are offered.

Perhaps nowhere is the change that has come over discounting better exemplified than in the Korvette store on Fifth Avenue and Forty-seventh Street in Manhattan. When Korvette first came to the royal row of American retailing in 1962 to occupy the store formerly used by the well-known W. and J. Sloane furniture retailer, skeptics gasped with disbelief. Plain pipe racks on Fifth Avenue?

Ferkauf, however, knew otherwise. He opened a seven-story, crystal-chandeliered store that had carpeting, many higher price lines and fashion apparel ranging up to expensive fur coats and stoles. He built up an elaborate soft-goods operation (that later spread to other Korvette stores), using private-label merchandise and brand-name clothing without the manufacturers' labels when they would not sell to him openly. As a result, the Korvette Fifth Avenue store topped $30,000,000 in sales its first year and has since become a New York tourist attraction.

The year 1965 was a milestone for Korvette because of the major internal changes that the company underwent. Among its activities that year, Korvette:

—Merged with Hill's Supermarkets, Inc., a Long Island supermarket chain doing an annual business of $130,000,000, and brought some of its top executives into the company's senior management ranks. Hilliard J. Coan, who headed Hill's, for example, became Korvette chairman until he resigned in 1966.

—Acquired a Baltimore small-loan and finance company whose credit cards are honored in Korvette's and other stores in that area. Korvette also uses other credit cards, such as the Uni-Card and its own charge card, and now does about 16 percent of its sales on credit.

—Took over its carpeting and furniture lessees, one highly profitable and the other financially beset, and instituted a program of building future stores with these departments as integral units, rather than as adjacent, free-standing buildings.

All of these far-flung activities are a far cry from the beginnings of Korvette. Eugene Ferkauf, born in Brooklyn in 1920, graduated from Tilden High School and went right to work in his father's two small luggage shops near Grand Central Station called Rex Luggage Company. There he learned what retailing was all about and was exposed to his father's principles of merchandising, which included the theory "If you're good to a store, it will be good to you."

After World War II service as a sergeant in the Signal Corps, Ferkauf returned to his father's stores but became quickly discontented. He wanted to test his theory that he could boost sales substantially by chopping the conventional 40 percent markup in half. And so, on a $4,000 investment (partially supplied by his father), Ferkauf rented a second-floor walkup on Manhattan's East Forty-sixth Street and began selling luggage at a discount.

Almost as an afterthought, Ferkauf decided to stock some then hard-to-get electrical appliances and priced them at cost to draw traffic. When he saw that he sold these appliances as fast as he got them in the store, he added small markups—and they still sold.

By ploughing all the profits back into Korvette, Ferkauf found himself running a $2,000,000 business only two years after he started. In 1951, there were three stores, in 1955 there were eight and the expansion program was well under way. Sales totaled $36,000,000 in 1955, $71,000,000 in 1957 and advanced up to $622,000,000 in 1964 in an unparalleled record of retailing growth.

By 1966, Korvette, the biggest volume discounter, was pushing ahead toward the magic $1,000,000,000 sales figure. But the series of top management changes in the previous year, a lack of adequate coordination, financial and merchandising controls and a confused image in its over-all operations affected profitability and created a crisis in the company that Ferkauf felt could only be solved by a merger.

And so a merger was planned with Spartans Industries, Inc., a smaller company that both operates discount stores and manufactures apparel. The Spartans name was chosen for the merged company, with Korvette maintaining its forty-two stores as a division. Ferkauf was named chairman of the executive committee of the enlarged company, but the chairmanship and presidency were given, under the merger plan, to the men who held these posts at Spartans—Charles C. Bassine and Murray Sussman, respectively.

Despite its link-up with Spartans, the name of Korvette will continue to be seen on stores throughout the United States—even in places like Detroit, where Korvette once meant only a type of General Motors sports car. Moreover, the name of Eugene Ferkauf will continue to be remembered because he, more than any other, first put the discount house on the map of American retailing.

Other large discount department-store chains also started their businesses in modest surroundings. For instance, the Two Guys chain, operated by Vornado, Inc., had its genesis in a small hard-goods discount house alongside a diner which was used for an office.

The company was founded with capital of $28,000 in 1947 by two brothers, Herbert and Sidney Hubschman, who opened a twenty-by-forty-foot store in the town of Harrison, New Jersey. The store was located next door to a diner owned by Herbert that was across the street from a tube plant of the Radio Corporation of America, to which the brothers used to run coffee.

They began by selling, on a cash-and-carry basis, cut-price television sets, refrigerators and washing machines for $5 and $10 above their cost, with the customers writing out their own orders. The name they chose for their store was Two Guys from Harrison, which stuck for many years until widespread expansion beyond the confines of New Jersey—and the closing of its last story in Harrison—made it wise to contract the name to the first two words.

The original name, by the way, was based on a competitor's comment about the Hubschmans when he found out that they were underselling him. "Those two bastards from Harrison," he said, and the words—with a slight modification—were taken for the corporate name.

At one time, the company had ten buses in use as mobile showrooms around Woodbridge, New Jersey. Later came a rash of tiny "pup," or, as they are also called, "acorn," stores in New York City and New Jersey.

Today Two Guys is no longer in the pup category. With twenty-six stores containing over 3,600,000 square feet located in five Eastern states, Vornado is now a major factor in discounting. Its sales in 1965 topped $250,000,000 and its earnings were more than $8,000,000. Between 1963 and 1965, volume rose 70 percent and pre-tax profits skyrocketed 230 percent.

The company derived its present corporate name after a 1959 merger between Two Guys from Harrison, Inc., and O. A. Sutton Corporation, an appliance manufacturer. The Hubschmans held the two top executive posts until Sidney left the company in 1963 after some policy friction and Herbert died in 1964.

Since then the management of Two Guys has been under the direction of Frederick Zissu, a Wall Street lawyer who joined the company in 1949 and now serves as Vornado's chairman, and Murray J. Siegel, president and chief executive officer.

Mr. Siegel operated the leased soft-goods departments at the Two Guys stores for seven years but was bought out in 1961 because, he says, "It got to a point where as a concessionaire I was too damn big."[5] In 1965, leased-department sales accounted for less than 5 percent of Vornado's total value, compared with 50 percent as recently as 1958.

Vornado has emerged unshaken from abortive merger negotiations with Arnold Constable, the New York specialty store, and Arlan's Department Stores, another discount chain. It is continuing its own expansion program—becoming an anchor store in a New London, Connecticut, enclosed-mall shopping center, for example—and expects to move both north and south from its present base in the Middle Atlantic states.

Another discounting success tale can be told about Interstate Department Stores, Inc. Here is an instance where a company did a complete about-face from an outright reliance on conventional merchandising to an emphasis on discount retailing—and in so doing became one of the major factors in the field.

Sol Cantor, the president of Interstate and long a dynamic spokesman for discounting, was running an ordinary forty-six-unit department-store chain in smaller cities whose roots went back to 1928. In 1957, he visualized the advantages of discount merchandising and tried out an experimental unit in Copley, Pennsylvania.

It worked, so the next year he opened his first discount store and found it to be much more profitable than his other stores. In 1959, therefore, he bought the two-store White Front chain in Los Angeles, the following year he took over the ten-store Topps chain in the East and he was on his way.

"We are rebels in the retail field," says Mr. Cantor, "and we must continue to think of ourselves that way."

By thinking of himself as a rebel, Mr. Cantor has created a retailing empire that now consists of sixty discount stores—under the White Front name on the West Coast and the Topps name in the East and Middle West. His conventional stores are now down to thirty-two but his total sales in 1965 totaled $433,000,000, of which more than 80 percent came from discounting.

Much of this growth, says Mr. Cantor, "is due to the fact that we are attracting customers from the middle and upper income brackets. Bare pipe racks are out; we are going more and more to chandeliers, carpets on the floor and chrome display devices."

The list of discounters who are attracting wider groups of customers can be extended almost indefinitely. Stores run by King's Department Stores, Inc., the Zayre Corporation, National Bellas Hess and other big companies in the field have become important elements in the overall retailing pattern throughout the country by merchandising for all elements in their communities.

There has been, moreover, a step-up of entries into discounting by other types of merchandisers. As these companies, which have already won their spurs in retailing, gain more experience in discounting and realize its benefits, their interest in and enthusiasm for discount stores can be expected to grow.

In this category, for example, are the department-store chains that have developed discount-store divisions. Included here are L. S. Ayers & Co., with its Ayr-Way stores; Allied Stores Corporation, with its Almart stores; and the Dayton Company, with its Target stores.

Many variety-store chains also have discount divisions. From a single store in March, 1962, S. S. Kresge Company has pushed its K-Mart division into the number two spot among all discounters in terms of annual volume and the number one spot in terms of units.

Other variety-store companies in discounting incude the F. W. Woolworth Company, with its Worth Mart stores; J. J. Newberry Company, with its Britt stores; and Neisner Brothers, Inc., with its Big-N stores.

Finally, many of the supermarket chains are involved in discounting to a large extent. Besides operating as lessees in discount stores run by others, food chains have started discount divisions of their own. Grand Union Company has its Grand-Way stores, Food Fair Stores owns J. M. Fields, Inc., the Kroger Company has the Thriftown stores and Jewel Tea Company runs the Turnstyle stores.

As other retailers move into discounting and as the discounters develop into major merchandising organizations, some of the clear-cut differences between department stores and discount houses are disappearing. Discounters are offering additional amenities to make shopping more pleasant, while department stores have met low-margin merchandisers on their own ground by offering discounts in certain categories themselves.

Despite this blending—or perhaps because of it—the discount store shows every indication of continuing as a potent force on the retailing scene. The big Korvette, Two Guys, White Front and similar stores in the suburbs are betting on an uninterrupted growth in the affluence, purchasing power and standard of living of middle-class Americans. Few retailers, it would seem, are betting against them.

NOTES

I. PEDDLERS TO PALACES

1. H. Gordon Selfridge, *The Romance of Commerce* (London, John Lane the Bodley Head, Ltd., 1918), pp. 121–38. Also H. Pasdermadjian, *The Department Store* (London, Newman Books, 1954).
2. National Retail Merchants Association, *Financial and Operating Results of Department and Specialty Stores,* for year ended January 31, 1965. Reported in the *New York Times,* March 5, 1965.
3. Tom Mahoney, "Shopping Centers—the Big Success Story," *The Rotarian,* January, 1964, pp. 34–37, 57.
4. Caroline Bird, "Macy's of Moscow," *Coronet,* March, 1959. Also J. E. Evans, "Russian Retailing," *Wall Street Journal,* November 19, 1956, p. 1, 21; Audrey R. Topping, "On Sale at GUM, Moscow's Super Shop, *New York Times Magazine,* July 28, 1963, pp. 13, 46–48.
5. Phineas T. Barnum, *Struggles & Triumphs* (Buffalo, 1883).
6. Leonard Sloane, "G. Fox: Bit of Hartford History," *New York Times,* December 23, 1965, p. 27, 33.
7. Betty Morgan, "Pivirotto Has a Sure Grip on Helm at Joseph Horne," *Women's Wear Daily,* September 28, 1965.
8. Leonard Sloane, "Iowa's Younkers: Friendly Store," *New York Times,* April 11, 1966, p. 55, 59.
9. Leonard Sloane, "Brigham Young's Store Moves with Times," *New York Times,* April 8, 1966, pp. 37, 42.
10. Joseph H. Appel, *The Business Biography of John Wanamaker* (New York, The Macmillan Co., 1930), p. 52.
11. Lawrence B. Romaine, "Benjamin Franklin the Father of the Mail Order Catalog," *The American Book Collector,* December, 1960, pp. 25–28. Also, earlier, *Direct Advertising.*

12. Jerome S. Kriska, "The Abercrombie & Fitch Pitch," *Women's Wear Daily,* April 21, 1966, pp. 1, 10–11. Also James V. O'Gara, "The Shop That Sells Dreams," *Coronet,* September, 1957, pp. 104–108.
13. Samuel Feinberg, *What Makes Shopping Centers Tick* (New York, Fairchild Publications, Inc., 1960), pp. 41–43.
14. Emerson Chapin, "Japanese Shops Go Underground," *New York Times,* May 24, 1964, VIII, pp. 1, 16.

II. THE HUDSON'S BAY COMPANY

1. These are definite distinctions of the venerable company, according to A. R. Huband, secretary of its Canadian Committee. The oft-applied phrase "oldest trading company in the world" must be weighed with the fact that Stora Kopparbergs Bergslags AB, Sweden's oldest industry and the oldest stock firm in the world, was chartered in 1347. Its activities today include mining, iron and steel, pulp and paper, and it might be described as a trading company. The Muscovy Company, established in 1554, exists but is nonoperating. The Shell–St. Gobain Company of France claims to have made glass since 1668.
2. *A Brief History of the Hudson's Bay Company* (a fifty-page booklet published by the company) includes a bibliography of more than eighty volumes on its history. See also Ray Gardner, "The Story of the Hudson's Bay Company," *Maclean's,* August 15 and September 1, 1949, condensed as "Beads to Billions," *Reader's Digest,* March, 1950, pp. 84–87. Most scholarly of all is E. E. Rich's *Hudson's Bay Company 1670–1870* (Toronto, McClelland and Stewart Ltd., 1960), 3 vols.

III. BROOKS BROTHERS

1. Maurice C. Carroll, "A Stylish Robbery at Brooks Bros.," New York *Herald Tribune,* January 22, 1964.
2. Leonard Sloane, "John Wood Marks 20th Year at Helm of Brooks Brothers," *New York Times,* April 16, 1966.

IV. TIFFANY'S

1. "Hoving Raced by Plane to New Hampshire for Needed Tiffany Stock," *Wall Street Journal,* August 22, 1955. Hoving was born December 2, 1897, in Stockholm, Sweden, graduated from Brown University and had been an executive of R. H. Macy & Co., Montgomery Ward, Lord & Taylor and Bonwit Teller.
2. *New York Times,* October 21, 1955.
3. At Marble House, a Vanderbilt home at Newport for the benefit of The Preservation Society of Newport County. *Life* photographers

covered it and the magazine ran three pages of pictures on August 12, 1957.

4. Causing a Nashville, Tennessee, newspaper to carry the headline: "General Shoe Buys Tiffany's." Actually General Shoe increased its holdings of Hoving Company stock to 65 percent.
5. *New York Times,* New York *Herald Tribune,* New York *Journal-American,* September 10, 1965.
6. Charles Lewis Tiffany wrote an account of the American jewelry trade in Chauncey M. Depew's *One Hundred Years of American Commerce* (New York, D. O. Haynes, 1895), pp. 589–594.
7. Robert Koch, *Louis C. Tiffany, Rebel in Glass* (New York, Crown, 1964). Interest has revived in this glass.

V. THE SINGER COMPANY

1. Annual reports. Also, Edmund K. Faltermayer, "It's a Spryer Singer," *Fortune,* December, 1963, and "Singer," *Forbes,* October 15, 1964.
2. Tom Mahoney, "The Machine That Sews Everywhere," *Reader's Digest,* January, 1951. Also, John Kobler, "Mr. Singer's Money Machine," *Saturday Evening Post,* July 7, 14, 21 and 28, 1951.
3. Bourne reported the sewing machine industry in Chauncey M. Depew's *One Hundred Years of American Commerce* (New York, D. O. Haynes, 1895), pp. 525–539.

VI. FILENE'S

1. Eben Jordan was a Maine-born ribbon clerk who became a partner of Benjamin L. Marsh. On his father's death in 1895, Eben Jordan, Jr., became head of the store. Edward J. Mitton, then vice president; his son, George W., who became president in 1916; and his son, Edward R., who became president in 1937 and was still chairman in 1966, contributed importantly to the growth of the enterprise. *Women's Wear Daily,* February 21, 1966, estimated the volume of Jordan Marsh and its New England branches at more than $160,000,000 and, January 5, 1966, placed sales of its Miami, Florida, branches at more than $40,000,000.
2. Paul M. Mazur and Myron S. Silbert, *Principles of Organization Applied to Modern Retailing* (New York, Harper & Brothers, 1927).
3. Tom Mahoney, "Fabulous Filene's," *Future,* July, 1947, and *Reader's Digest,* August, 1947.
4. Mary La Dame, *The Filene Store* (New York, Russell Sage Foundation, 1930), pp. 273–74. Book presents a detailed account of employee relations.
5. Filene's basement has been described many times, including "Filene's Automatic Bargain Basement," *Retail Management,* March, 1945.

6. A. Lincoln Filene, *A Merchant's Horizon* (Boston, Houghton Mifflin, 1924), p. 11, and Edward A. Filene, *The Way Out* (New York, Doubleday, Page and Co., 1924), pp. 178–79, gave their statements on need for a business to plan for future, the latter saying: "A businessman is a failure, although he makes millions of dollars, if he creates a business so dependent upon his personal administration that it disintegrates after his death." Edward A. Filene also wrote *More Profits from Merchandising* (A. W. Shaw, 1925), *The Model Stock Plan* (New York, McGraw-Hill, 1930), a book still used; *Successful Living in This Machine Age* (New York, Simon & Schuster, 1931); *Next Steps Forward in Retailing* (New York, Harper & Brothers, 1937). Lincoln Filene wrote *Unfair Trade Practices—How to Remove Them* (New York, Harper & Brothers, 1934) and, with Ralph E. Flanders, Morris Leeds and Henry Dennison, *Toward Full Employment* (New York, Whittlesey House, 1938).
7. Gerald W. Johnson, *Liberal's Progress* (New York, Coward-McCann, Inc., 1948), pp. 21–35.
8. *Women's Wear Daily,* February 21, 1966, placed Filene's downtown volume for the previous year in the $85,000,000 to $90,000,000 category with nearly $60,000,000 more from nine branches as a result of greater emphasis on "serious fashion."

VII. F. & R. LAZARUS & COMPANY

1. Investment Company Institute, February 4, 1966, release.
2. Tom Mahoney, "When FDR Juggled Thanksgiving," *American Legion Magazine,* October, 1964. President Roosevelt also wanted to change Thanksgiving from Thursday to Monday but abandoned that part when Protestant church leaders objected. Instead of warning the Ohioans as planned, he announced advancing of the date on August 14, 1939, at Campobello, Nova Scotia, in the course of a vacation fishing trip.
3. *Fortune,* February, 1947.
4. *Business Week,* May 14, 1955.
5. *Women's Wear Daily,* January 5, 1966.
6. *New York Times,* December 31, 1963, "The Man at A & S." New York *Post* February 18, 1965.
7. *New York Times* and *Women's Wear Daily,* January 12, 1966, had lengthy biographical articles recounting his achievements.

VIII. MARSHALL FIELD & COMPANY

1. Leonard Sloane, "On State Street It's Still Marshall Field," *New York Times,* December 21, 1965, pp. 55, 63.
2. Lloyd Wendt and Herman Kogan, *Give the Lady What She Wants* (Chicago, Rand, McNally & Company, 1952). Literature on Field's

also includes John Tebbell, *The Marshall Fields* (New York, E. P. Dutton, 1947); Emily Kimbrough, *Through Charley's Door* (New York, Harper & Brothers, 1950); Robert W. Twyman, *History of Marshall Field & Co.* (Philadelphia, University of Pennsylvania Press, 1954). This book quotes Field archives and has a bibliography listing 50 books and more than 150 shorter works with references to the store.

3. Peg Zwecker, "Chicago's All-Out Welcome for Philip," Chicago *Daily News,* March 18, 1966, p. 22.
4. *Women's Wear Daily,* April 11, 1960.
5. Tebbell, *op. cit.,* pp. 136–37.
6. "Marshall Field, the Store," *Fortune,* December, 1945.

IX. BRENTANO'S

1. While Kroch's & Brentano's has been advertised as "the world's largest bookstore," this distinction seems to belong to Foyle's of London, which has nine acres of floor space and more than four million volumes. See George Kent, "The World's Biggest Bookseller," *Saturday Review,* October 7, 1950, pp. 14–16.
2. Bennett Cerf, "The Story of Brentano's," *Saturday Review,* March 4–11, 1950.
3. Stanton Griffis, *Lying in State* (New York, Doubleday & Company, 1952), pp. 62–72.

X. MACY'S

1. Margaret Case Harriman, *And the Price Is Right* (Cleveland and New York, World Publishing, 1958).
2. Ralph M. Hower, *History of Macy's of New York 1858–1919* (Cambridge, Harvard University Press, 1946).
3. Curtiss S. Johnson, *The Indomitable R. H. Macy* (New York, Vantage Press, 1964).
4. Curtiss S. Johnson, *America's First Lady Boss* (Norwalk, Conn., Silvermine Publishers, 1965).
5. Leonard Sloane, "A Fourth Generation Retailer," *New York Times,* June 23, 1963. Also, *Time* cover article, January 8, 1965.
6. Wheelock H. Bingham and David L. Yunich, "Retail Reorganization," *Harvard Business Review,* July–August, 1965.
7. Leonard Sloane, "The Merchant's View," *New York Times,* November 17, 1963.

XI. THE FOOD GIANTS

1. "The True Look of the Supermarket Industry 1965," *Super Market Merchandising,* April, 1966.

2. J. C. Furnas, "Mr. George and Mr. John," *Saturday Evening Post,* December 31, 1938.
3. Progressive Grocer, *Consumer Dynamics in the Super Market* (New York, privately printed, 1966).

XII. RICH'S

1. Tom Mahoney, "The Store That Married a City," *Saturday Evening Post,* December 3, 1949, pp. 34, 176–80. Also Professor Henry Givens Baker, *Rich's of Atlanta* (University of Georgia, School of Business Administration, 1953).
2. Among the many honors received by Neely was the 1952 Gantt Medal of the American Management Association. In 1962, he received an honorary Doctor of Laws Degree from Mercer University, and the Georgia Institute of Technology named its Nuclear Research Center for him.
3. Dick Rich received an honorary Doctor of Laws Degree from Emery University in 1965. He has served as trustee of Young Harris College and been active in more than forty civic, religious and charitable organizations. He was Georgia's "Citizen of the Year" and received the Rotary Club's Armin Maier Cup for outstanding community service in 1953, the National Retail Merchants' Association Gold Medal in 1963. He served as chairman of the Atlanta Arts Alliance, Inc., formed to raise funds for the Atlanta Memorial Cultural Center, a complex housing an art gallery and performing-arts facilities. It honors the memory of 122 members of the Atlanta Art Association killed June 3, 1962, in a plane crash at Paris, France.

XIII. F. W. WOOLWORTH CO.

1. Carl Rieser, "What's Come Over Old Woolworth?," *Fortune,* January, 1960, pp. 92–98, 212–18. *Don Wharton,* "See What's Happened to the 5 & 10!" *Reader's Digest,* February, 1962, pp. 241–44. "The Old Five-and-Ten Spreads New Wings," *Business Week,* November 14, 1964, pp. 58–67.
2. John K. Winkler, *Five and Ten, The Fabulous Life of F. W. Woolworth* (New York, Bantam, 1957), pp. 7–9. Winkler had access to company records.
3. *Woolworth's First 75 Years* (published by the company, 1954), pp. 22–26.
4. She married Prince Alexis Mdivani, Count Kurt von Hawgwitz-Reventlow, Cary Grant, Prince Igor Troubetzkoy, Porfirio Rubirosa, Gottfried von Cramm and Prince Doan Vinh Na Champacak.
5. Winkler, *op. cit.,* p. 233.

XIV. THE J. L. HUDSON COMPANY

1. Oscar Webber, "J. L. Hudson, The Man and the Store," reprint of a November 8, 1954, address to the Newcomen Society of North America. Besides much little-known family history, this includes the only public statement for many years of the store's sales figures. Also, Tom Mahoney, "Hudson's of Detroit," *Coronet,* October, 1955, pp. 67–69.
2. Leonard Sloane, "In Detroit—Hudson's," *New York Times,* December 10, 1965, pp. 73, 80.
3. William T. Noble, "Joseph L. Hudson, Jr., Detroit's Merchant Prince," *Detroit News Pictorial Magazine,* September 12, 1965, pp. 7–16.
4. "History of the Men's Wear Industry 1890–1950," *Men's Wear,* February 10, 1950, pp. 206–249.
5. "The hardest hit city was Detroit," writes Caroline Bird in *The Invisible Scar* (New York, David McKay, 1966). "The unemployed auto workers could not pay their rent; landlords could not pay taxes; banks could not realize on mortgages; the city could not pay on its municipal bonds, and so could not borrow money to keep relief going." Pp. 103–104.
6. "Artists Paint Michigan," *Life,* August 23, 1948.
7. "Men Make Their Own Dignity," Detroit *Free Press,* March 10, 1961.

XV. SEARS, ROEBUCK AND CO.

1. Investment Company Institute release of February 4, 1966. Sears stock worth $109,798,000 was then held by 34 mutual funds. A survey of 16 funds more than a decade earlier found 10 holding 320,100 Sears shares at the end of 1954, according to Arthur A. Werfel, *Women's Wear Daily,* June 28, 1955.
2. Used as a headline by *Changing Times,* October, 1950, in summarizing *Catalogues and Counters, A History of Sears, Roebuck and Company,* by Boris Emmet and John E. Jeuck (Chicago, University of Chicago Press, 1950), a 788-page volume that gives the history of the enterprise in great detail.
3. The Detroit *News,* October 15, 1965, p. 7-C. Two Sears employees, Daniel Kleczkowski, twenty-four, and Mark Rebrovich, eighteen, trailed the bandits, hailed a police car and were given principal credit for recovery of $9,780 and the arrests.
4. James C. Worthy, Sears personnel department, in *Harvard Business Review,* January, 1950. Also Harvey E. Runner, New York *Herald Tribune,* January 18, 1950.
5. A 1932 Calvin Coolidge letter, catalogued in 1954 by Paul Hoag, Gilmanton, Massachusetts, autograph dealer, advised a contractor that "Sears are sending" some building supplies by freight and instructed

him to haul them to his Vermont farmstead, which he was then modernizing.

6. Kenneth McKenna, "Forgotten Men of Business," New York *Herald Tribune,* March 9, 1961.
7. In its "50 years ago" department, *Printer's Ink,* August 27, 1948, reproduced an advertisement headed "An Infamous Lie" offering $100 reward for detection of the man who started the story that "Mr. Ward is a mulatto Negro."
8. Made from 1908 to 1911 by the Lincoln Motor Car Works, Chicago. It had five forward speeds and was popular on Texas farms. One preserved by Frank Stokes, Covina, California, was pictured in *Horseless Carriage Gazette,* January–February, 1954, p. 14.
9. In his retirement, Lessing Rosenwald has assembled one of the world's greatest collections of prints at Alverthorpe, his estate at Jenkintown, Pennsylvania. He has enriched the National Gallery of Art and the Library of Congress with gifts of rare books and prints.
10. John Reddy, "The General Who Built the World's Largest Store," *Reader's Digest,* January, 1964, pp. 181–85.
11. An earlier effort to sell life insurance through a Hercules subsidiary from 1934 to 1938 was less successful and it was sold.
12. John McDonald, "Sears Makes It Look Easy," *Fortune,* May, 1964, pp. 120–27. Includes a listing of ten critical decisions that have led to company's success.
13. The fall 1965 catalog, described as the largest ever issued by Sears, had 1,812 pages, 634 of them in color, and weighed six pounds. The 1966 spring-summer catalog had 1,604 pages and weighed half a pound less.
14. Julian Lewis Watkins, *One Hundred Greatest Advertisements in History* (New York, Dover Publications, 1959), p. 199. "No book on great copy would be complete without this most famous of all salesmen in print," said Watkins. "More than a thousand pages of the strongest selling copy ever written—any page, any item, any year."
15. The Dallas *Morning News* obituary of April 21, 1954, described Scott as one "who cared more for people's welfare and culture than for a personal fortune."
16. *Amerika Illustrated,* Issue No. 41, 1959.
17. *Wall Street Journal* and other newspapers of September 22, 1959.

XVI. LANE BRYANT

1. Details of Mrs. Bryant's early life were obtained from her by Tom Mahoney in a series of interviews for a magazine article, "$49,000,000 Business in Round Figures," *The Independent Woman,* October, 1950, and condensed as "Maternity Mart—The Story of Lane Bryant," *Reader's Digest,* November, 1950.

2. Recipients of the individual award have included Mrs. Mary Pulvino Cariola, Rochester, N.Y.; Mrs. Dorothy Y. Goble, San José, Calif.; Mrs. Maria Isabel de Atiles Moreau, San Juan, Puerto Rico; Mrs. Lester G. Auberlin, Detroit; Dr. Jessie Royer Greaves, Paoli, Pa.; Danny Kaye, Beverly Hills, Calif.; Rev. W. L. Buffington, Augusta, Ga. Among others, group awards have gone to the Henry Street Settlement, New York; League of Women Voters, Des Moines, Ia.; Parents and Friends of Mentally Retarded Children, Bridgeport, Conn. International awards have gone to Oscar J. Arrelano, Manila, Philippines; Joao Napoleao de Andrade, Rio de Janeiro, Brazil; James Jacob Macobane, Basutoland, Africa; Mlle. Denise Legrix, Paris, France.

XVII. J. C. PENNEY COMPANY

1. James C. Penney, *Fifty Years with the Golden Rule* (New York, Harper & Brothers, 1950).
2. Godfrey M. Lebhar, *Chain Stores in America 1859–1950* (New York, Chain Store Publishing Corporation, 1952).
3. Alfred Law, "From Overalls to Fashion Wear," *Wall Street Journal,* October 22, 1964.

XVIII. BULLOCK'S AND I. MAGNIN

1. William H. Kilner, *Letts 1862–1923* (Los Angeles, privately printed, 1927).
2. "A Store for the Motorized Carriage Trade," *Architectural Forum,* May, 1948.
3. Leonard Sloane, "Retailers in Hot Proxy Fight," *New York Times,* July 5, 1964.

XIX. NEIMAN-MARCUS

1. "From Skies to Store," *Life,* August 30, 1954, pp. 14–15.
2. Frank X. Tolbert, *Neiman–Marcus, Texas* (New York, Henry Holt, 1953) and many others. The store has a lengthy bibliography of all published about it.
3. *A Taste of Texas* (New York, Random House, 1949).
4. George Sessions Perry, *American Cities* (New York, McGraw-Hill, 1947).
5. Charlotte Curtis, "Neiman-Marcus and the Last of the Big-Time Spenders," *New York Times,* September 16, 1965.

XX. L. L. BEAN, INC.

1. Genealogical records of many generations of Beans are listed in L. L. Bean, *My Story, The Autobiography of a Down-East Merchant* (Freeport, Maine, 1960), pp. 34–35, 78–79. Some are pictured.
2. This and most of the other details of this chapter are from a 1954 interview by Tom Mahoney with L. L. Bean at Freeport, supplemented by correspondence, especially a lengthy letter from him dated October 12, 1965, the day before his ninety-third birthday.
3. Important national notice began for the business with the October 13, 1941, issue of *Life* which, pp. 122–27, published a four-page picture feature, "Maine's Bean Outfits Sportsmen Everywhere." The December, 1941, issue of *Reader's Digest,* pp. 112–15, condensed Webb Waldron's "Bean, the Happy Hunter," from the *Kiwanis Magazine* of the same month. The *Saturday Evening Post* published Arthur Bartlett's "The Discovery of L. L. Bean," December 14, 1946, pp. 30–31, 92–99.
4. Except for ten shares each given three employees, all stock was held in the family at incorporation in 1934. Carl Bean and the late John T. Gormen, a son-in-law, were named vice presidents in the first election of officers November 16, 1934. Mr. Gorman died in 1959.
5. The workings of L. L. Bean has been the subject of a case study by the Harvard University Graduate School of Business Administration, also of articles in *Business Week* (September 6, 1952, pp. 46–49) and *Sales Management* (September, 1955).
6. *Playboy,* May, 1963, pp. 119–120.
7. Dated June 2 and October 29, 1954, respectively. Published *My Story,* p. 103.

XXI. OHRBACH'S, INC.

1. Selma Robinson, "Even the Rich Love Bargains," *McCall's,* June, 1964.
2. Herbert Brean, "High Style Cash-and-Carry," *Life,* January 26, 1953.
3. Nathan M. Ohrbach, *Getting Ahead in Retailing* (McGraw-Hill Book Company, New York, 1935).
4. Leonard Sloane, "Ohrbach's Offbeat Approach," *New York Times,* January 26, 1964.
5. Leonard Sloane, "Ohrbach's Names a New President," *New York Times,* July 6, 1963.

XXII. WEBB'S CITY

1. Hyman Goldberg, "Million-Dollar Medicine Man," *Cosmopolitan,* February, 1953, pp. 104–111. Other accounts of the rise of "Doc"

Webb include: Paul Gardner and Allan Gould, "Pink Pills and Pin-Ups." *Collier's,* November 22, 1947, pp. 97–98; *Fortune,* January, 1948, pp. 92–95, 124–128, condensed by *Reader's Digest,* pp. 109–112, as "The World's Most Unusual Drugstore." Tom Mahoney, "The Drug Store That Became a City," *Pageant,* April, 1955, pp. 110–14.

2. Washington *Post,* August 8, p. D20, and August 20, 1963, p. A14.
3. Career of James E. Webb, Jr., was recounted in detail by Dick Bothwell in "Look Out! Here Comes Another 'Doc' Webb," St. Petersburg *Times,* January 26, 1964.
4. St. Petersburg *Independent,* January 21, 1960.

XXIII. THE DISCOUNTERS ARRIVE

1. Walter Henry Nelson, *The Great Discount Delusion* (New York, David McKay Company, 1965).
2. E. B. Weiss, *A Reappraisal of New Rental Trends* (New York, Doyle Dane Bernbach, Inc., 1964).
3. Leonard Sloane, "Discount Stores Broaden Inroads," *New York Times,* July 19, 1964.
4. "Everybody Loves a Bargain," *Time,* July 6, 1962.
5. Leonard Sloane, "Two Guys Stores Are Expanding," *New York Times,* October 9, 1964.

INDEX

A & P, 12, 172–83
Abercrombie & Fitch Co., 14
Abraham & Straus, 91, 93, 108–9, 113, 160
Abramson, N. H., 34
Accounting system, 182
Acme Markets, 185
Adler, Max, 233
Advertising, 59, 104, 130, 154–55, 156, 194, 230–31, 238, 239, 314
Advertising: newspapers and magazines, 10–11, 45, 47, 53, 89, 124, 130, 170, 205, 218, 239, 278, 291, 295–96, 317–20; other media, 15, 44, 89, 130, 164, 173, 205, 218, 278
Africa, 67, 72, 199
Air conditioning, 82
Albert Malsin Scholarships, 256
Aldens Inc., 14
Alexander, Sir Douglas, 73, 75
Alexander's, 337
Alldredge, Melvin W., 181
Allen, Frederick Lewis, 45
Allied Stores Corporation, 9, 15, 16, 78, 348
Allstate, 223, 234–35
Allstate Life Insurance Company, 235
Almart stores, 348
Alstores Realty Corporation, 16
Alterations, 316
Altman, Benjamin, 109
Altman (B.) & Co., 109
A.M.C. Wholesale Corporation, 90–91
American Coffee Corporation, 176
American Motors Inc., 213
American Retail Federation, 101
Amory, Viscount, 19, 35
Anderson, Clifford O., 204
Anderson, Eddie, 126
Anderson, Ross F., 111
Angstadt, Earle K., 14
Ann Page Division, 176
Arkwright, Preston S., 197
Arlan's Department Stores, 347
Arnett, Mahlon, 282, 284
Arnold, Dorothy, 146
Arnold Constable, 7, 347
Art department, 217–18
Art of Tying the Cravat (Balzac), 45
Asher, Louis, 230–31
Associated Dry Goods Co., 7
Associated Merchandising Corp., 32, 90, 93, 108, 188, 189, 194, 207, 280
Astor, John Jacob, 7, 25
Auerbach, Beatrice Fox, 8
Automatic Bargain Basement, 86, 88
Automobiles, 11, 15, 223, 231, 234–35, 273
Avon Cosmetics, 5
Ayers (L. S.) & Co., 13, 90, 348
Ayres, William E., 181

Backhaus, C. Walton, 204
Baker, Crowdus, 222
Baldridge, Letitia, 52, 238
Ballantyne, R. M., 24
Bamberger (L.) & Co., 164, 168, 169
Bardshar, Sybil, 142
Bargain Basement, Automatic, 86, 88
Barker, J. M., 236
Barnum, Phineas T., 6, 58
Barron, C. W., 232
Barrows, Arthur, 233

Basement budget operations, 32, 47, 82, 86–89, 95, 103, 117, 124, 150, 207, 216, 340
Bassine, Charles C., 346
Batten, William M., 261, 268–69, 270, 272
Baylis, George, 291
Bean, Carl, 303
Bean, Guy, 301
Bean, Leon, 303
Bean, Leon Leonwood, 299–309
Bean, Tom, 303
Bean (L. L.), Inc., 299–309
Beaver, The, 24
Beaver House, 29
Bendel (Henri), 14
Bent, George P., 74–75
Bergdorf, Herman, 14
Bergdorf Goodman, 14
Bergengren, Roy Frederick, 85–86
Bergquist, Walter L. L., 113
Berman, Milton, 110
Bernbach, William, 318, 319
Best & Co., 13
Best's Apparel, 17
Best sellers, 136, 139–40, 141, 142, 148
Bigelow, H. M., 277
Big-N stores, 349
Billing, 79, 271, 315, 316
Bixler's, 53
Black, Starr & Frost, 54
Blanton, C. E., 210
Bloomingdale, Samuel, 108
Bloomingdale's, 108–9, 110, 113
Blum, John A., 164
Bode, H. W., 199–200
Bohack (H. C.) & Co., Inc., 185
Bolton, James, 71, 122
Bond's, 13
Bon Marché, 13–14, 15–16
Bon Marche, Inc., 311
Bon Marché (France), 2
Bonwit Teller, 14
Book Chat, 139
Book clubs, 144–45, 236
Book stores and departments, 33, 78, 106, 117, 130, 133–40, 142
"Boston Store," 78
Bourne, Commodore Frederick G., 72–73
Bramley, Norman W., 291
Branagan, B. A., 184
Branch, Judson B., 235
Branch operations, 46, 53, 79, 82–83, 107, 110, 111, 131, 133, 140, 142, 145–46, 165, 168, 195, 212, 216–17, 231, 235, 292–93, 340
Brandeis, Louis D., 84
Brazil, 147
Breakfast at Tiffany's, 52–53
Brenninkmeyer, Anthony, 322
Brenninkmeyer, Elmar, 322
Brentano, Arthur, 135–39, 141
Brentano, Arthur, Jr., 138, 140, 141, 143–45
Brentano, August, Sr., 134–35, 136
Brentano, Lowell, 138, 140
Brentano, Simon, 136, 138
Brentano's, Inc., 133–48
British Woolworth Company, 199, 203, 204
Britt stores, 349
Broadway-Hale Stores, Inc., 275
Brockey, Harold, 193
Brombacher (A. F.) & Co., 6
Brooker, Robert Elton "Tom," 12
Brooks, Daniel H., 41
Brooks, Frederick, 43, 44
Brooks, Henry, 41
Brooks, Henry Sands, 40–41
Brooks, Winthrop Holley, 45–46
Brooks Brothers, 36–50
Brown, E. M. H., 34
Browning, King & Company, 7
Bruce, Eleanore, 164
Bruder, Charles F., 76
Bryant (Malsin), Lena (Lane), 244
Bryant (Malsin), Raphael, 245, 255
Budget Stores (Hudson), 207
Buildings and real estate, 29, 30, 79, 81–82, 104, 105, 106–7, 108, 110, 117, 119–20, 129–32, 134–35, 161–62 181–82, 187–88, 202, 203, 207, 215–16, 260, 267, 271–72, 325–26
Bullock, John Gillespie, 274–81
Bullock's, Inc., 91, 113, 273-74, 277–83
Bullock's-Magnin, 282–85
Bulova Watch Company, 51
Bunker, Charles C., 131
Burbridge, Richard, 3
Burcham, Lester A., 204
Burchill, Herbert, 76–77
Burdine's, 112
Burger, Ralph W., 180–81
Burnham, Daniel H., 79, 82
Butler, Charles E., 136
Butler Bros., 15–16
Button, James W., 223
Byars (J. B.) Company, 265
Byrne, Cornelius J., 131

Caldwell, Clarence B., 242
Callahan, T. M., 262–63
Canada, 19–35, 177, 237
Candy, Walter W., Jr., 274, 282, 284, 285
Cantor, Sol, 347–48
Capwell (H. C.) Company, 91
Carney, Thomas J., 233

Carpenter, Horace, Jr., 216
Carson, Pirie and Company, 122
Carson Pirie Scott & Co., 9
Cartier, Inc., 8
Case, C. P., 201, 203
Cash-and-carry, 170, 175, 202, 263, 314, 331
Cash boys, 122
Caswell-Massey, 6
Catalogs (*see also* Mail order), 12, 56, 77, 117, 222–26, 235, 239–41, 243, 250, 255, 270–71, 293–94, 300, 304, 307, 308
Censorship, 147–48
Cerf, Bennett, 138
Chain Store Age, 17
Chain stores (*see also* specific chain), 12–13, 101, 171, 172, 177–78, 238, 265–66
Chandler & Co., 78
Chaplin, Fredrick L., 204
Charga-Plate, 79
Charge accounts, 98, 153, 163, 175, 288
Charles, King, 23
Charlton, Earl, 202
Chester, Philip Alfred, 20, 30
China department, 117, 160
Christian, J. Gordon, Jr., 181
Christmas, 89, 149, 151, 164, 217, 241, 318
City of Paris, 8, 142
City Stores Company, 98
Civil War, 10, 42–43, 71, 159, 211
Clark, Carlos B., 214–15
Clark, Edward, 66, 69–71
Clothing sizes, 250–55
Coan, Hilliard, Jr., 344
Cokesbury, 133
Cole, Henry, 175
Coleman, W. A., 133
Collins, Kenneth, 164
Collyer, Barbara, 164
Colombo, Frank, 209
Comité des Foires, 297
Community activities, 92, 103–4, 160, 189–90, 195, 205, 209, 213–15, 270, 307–8, 331, 333; disaster aid, 10, 128, 256–57; grants and awards, 60, 83, 94–95, 98–99, 196, 217–18, 238–39
Comparison buying, 153, 163, 315
Complaints, handling, 33, 120, 152, 179
Confidential, 294
Constable (Arnold), 347
Consumer Award for Personal Fashion Discrimination, 296
Consumer Distribution Corporation, 94
Continental Clothing House, 82
Continental Oil Co., 20–21
Controllers' Congress of the National Merchants Association, 214
Cook, Charles, 61
Cooper, Sir Patrick Ashley, 20, 30–31, 34
Cooperatives, 94
Corley, Frederick D., 129
Cornwell, Alfred L., 203
Cory, Thomas K., 91, 93
Coulter, J. D., 210
Country Club Plaza, 15
Cox, Muriel, 99
Credit, 109, 156, 163, 205, 259, 270, 344
Credit cards, 344
Credit unions, 85–86
Crosby, Enoch, 5
Cross (Mark), 8
Crowell Collier Publishing Company, 133
Cullen, Michael, 170–71, 338
Cummins, Ray, 112
Cunningham Drug Stores, 12
Cushman, Austin T., 221, 243
Custin, Mildred, 14
Customers: consideration for, 37–40, 44, 118, 119, 178–79, 188–89, 218–20, 238–39, 279–80, 285, 292, 294–95, 299–300, 305–6, 315, 316; famous, 14, 36–37, 39, 42, 44, 45, 46, 48, 52, 56–57, 59, 60, 74, 88–89, 116, 126–27, 134, 135, 138, 146–47, 286–87, 290, 304, 305, 321; letters, 152; publications for, 45, 53, 76, 139, 257, 270; services, 14–15, 21, 33, 98, 161, 195–96, 208, 280, 339; shopping service, 38–39, 117, 127–28, 152, 196, 219
Custom tailoring, 42, 47
Cycle billing, 79

Dahl, Francis, 84
Dale, Charles M., 204
Dale, Richard I., 204
Daniels, Alfred H., 112
Daniels & Fisher Stores Co., 9
David, Donald, 99
Davidson, David W., 131
Davidson, Harry E., 204
Davidson, J. Edward, 110
Davies, Alfred I., 243
Davis, Jacob E., 185
Davis, Lester F., 204
Davison-Paxon, 165, 191
Dawley, Melvin, 7
Dayton Company, 14, 90, 348
Decentralization, 165, 177, 274
Deliveries, 8, 104, 110, 117, 121–22, 151–52, 158, 161, 219, 314
Department stores (*see also* specific store), 9–10, 157–58; cooperative, 94

Deposit accounts, 163
Depression, the, 11–12, 14–15, 29–30, 64, 86, 101, 109, 128, 131, 140, 185, 214, 265, 292
Deyo, Charles W., 203
Di Scipio, Alfred, 77
Discount operations, 15, 98, 180, 205, 216, 255, 329, 336-49
Display and decoration, 96–97, 102–3, 117, 170, 190, 216–17
Diversification, 76, 272
Dodd, Alvin E., 90, 236
Doering, Otto C., 229, 233
Douglas, Paul H., 257
Downsbrough, George A., 77
Doyle Dane Bernbach Inc., 318, 319
Drug stores and departments, 12–13, 185, 324–34, 199, 208
Duff-Gordon, Lady, 235
Dutch-American Investing Company, Inc., 322

Eastland, 108, 215, 216
Eaton, Timothy, 27
Eberhard, Roy, 113
Echo, The, 85
Edward A. Filene Good Will Fund, Inc., 94
Ehrgott, John D., 181
Eisenhower, Gen. and Mrs. Dwight D., 287
Elizabeth II, Queen, 23
Ellis, J. L., 58, 59
Employees, 11–12, 31–32, 48, 62–63, 81, 123–24, 146, 182, 188, 197, 218–20, 238, 241; arbitration, 84–85; credit unions, 85–86; education, 31, 256; profit sharing, 241–42, 256, 260, 304; stockholders, 222, 330; training and recruiting, 11, 33–34, 79, 81, 83–84, 130, 137–38, 166, 167, 182, 197, 205, 208, 220, 221–22, 242–43, 263, 267–68, 269, 294, 322–23; wages and hours, 33, 85, 123, 192, 196–97, 203, 212, 330; welfare provisions, 31, 130, 177, 197, 215, 241–42, 269, 294, 322–23, 330; women, 8, 111, 119, 158
Emporium, 90, 91
Encyclopaedia Britannica, 235–36
"Equal-store" concept, 168
Escalator, 98
Escobosa, Hector, 125, 283
Europe, 12–13, 17, 67, 70, 72, 77, 199

Fair of Chicago, The, 13
Fair trade, 153, 163–64, 238, 315, 334, 339
Famous Barr Co., 8, 13
Farwell, Field and Company, 118
Fashion, 37, 38, 114–15, 152–53, 167–68, 235, 238, 244–58, 260, 270, 317–18; advisory boards, 79; shows, 2, 14, 97, 114, 196, 292, 318
Federated Department Stores, Inc., 93, 95, 98, 99, 100–15, 283–84
Fedway, 113
Fentress, Calvin, 235
Ferkauf, Eugene, 342–46
"Feuds," 164
Field, Marshall, 118–26, 176
Field, Marshall, II, 126
Field, Palmer and Leiter, 118
Field, Stanley, 125, 126
Field (Marshall) & Company, 116–32, 150
Fieldcrest Mills, 130–31
Fields (J. M.), Inc., 349
Figgins, Weston P., 112
Filene, Edward Albert, 80–86, 91–94, 98–99
Filene, Lincoln, 80–84, 90, 91, 93, 95, 98
Filene, William, 79–81
Filene Cooperative Association, 84–85
Filene-Finlay simultaneous translator, 92–93
Filene's, 78–79
First National Stores, 185
Fish, Mrs. Stuyvesant, 65
Fisher, E. D., 210
Fitzgerald, F. Scott, 45
Fitz-Gibbon, Bernice, 164
Fitzhugh, Gilbert W., 77
Flags, 216–17
Fogerson, Harry B., 204
Foley Brothers, 109–10
Food Fair Stores, 185, 349
Food stores and departments, 32, 170–86, 223, 235, 349
Forbes and Wallace Inc., 13
Forman (B.), 17
Forman (B.) Company, 90
Fortas, Abe, 114
"Fortnights," Neiman-Marcus, 296–97
Fox, Gerson, 8
France, 2–3, 64, 142–44, 147–48
Frank, Glenn, 99
Franklin, Benjamin, 12
Franklin Simon, 14
Franzheim, Franz, 110
Fraser, Sir Hugh, 3
Frazer, Arthur, 124
Frederick, Donald E., 131
Frederick & Nelson, 131-32
French, William T., 91
French, Amos Tuck, 141
Frenchman, The (Halsman), 147–48
Friden Inc., 76

Friedman, Lillian, 142
Frost, Edward J., 92, 93, 95
Frost, Owen C., 110–11
Fuller Brush Company, 5
Funck, Pierre, 126
Fuoss, Robert M., 114
Fur trade, 19–26, 30, 31, 34, 239

Galeries Lafayette, 2–3
Gallico, Paul, 293
Galt & Bro., 53–54
Gamble, Bert, 14
Gamble Skogmo Inc., 14
Gandhi, Mahatma, 67
Gantt, Henry Laurence, 192
Garden State Plaza Corporation, 166
Garfinckel (Julius) & Co., 37, 49–50
Gazette, 70
General Merchandise, 271
Genesco, Inc., 14, 49, 53
George VI, King, 23
Gertz, 15
Getchell, Margaret, 158–59
Gilbert, Cass, 202
Gilbert, Lewis, 198
Gilbreth, Frank B., 83
Gilchrist Co., 78
Gilman, George F., 173–74
Gilmore, Electra W. W. B., 290
Gimbel, Adam, 7
Gimbel, Bernard F., 7–8, 194
Gimbel, Bruce Alvah, 8
Gimbel Brothers Inc., 7–8, 164, 338
Gittler, Sydney, 315
Gluckman, Harold, 216
Goldberg, Jack, 96
Golden Rule stores, 259–64
Goldman, Harry, 230
Goldsmith, Jack L., 113
Goldsmith's (Memphis), 112–13
Goldwaters, Inc., 9
Gomme, Lawrence, 137–38
Goodman, Edwin, 14
Goodspeed's, 78
Gordon, Ben, 193
Gorman, Jack, 303
Goulding, Dr. Frank, 68
Graham, John, 16
Grand Union Company, 8, 349
Grand-Way stores, 349
Grant (W. T.), 12
Gray Advertising Inc., 318
Great American Tea Company, 173–74
Great Atlantic & Pacific Tea Company, Inc., 12, 172–83
Great Britain, 3, 64, 70, 199
Green (H. L.), 12
Griffin, W. E., 303
Griffis, Stanton, 140–42, 144–45, 147
Griffs, Nixon, 133, 145
Groseilliers, Médart Chouart, Sieur des, 22–23
Gruen, Victor, 16, 17, 216
Gruenther, Gen. M., 114
Guarantees, 10–11, 59, 161, 225, 240–41, 305
GUM, 2
Gunmere, Francis B., 96
Gunther Jaeckel, Inc., 7

Hager, Christopher, 7
Hager & Bro., Inc., 7
Hahner, Marcella, 130
Hale (J. M.) & Brothers, 262, 265
Hall, Joseph B., 185
Halle Bros. Co., 14
Hall (Robert), 13
Halliburton's, 111
Harbaugh, Rose Oller, 130
Harms, J. W., 210
Harrigan, Edward F., 204
Harrington, Sam, 330
Harris, Sherwin, 183
Harris, W. Robert, 204
Harrods, Ltd., 3, 91
Hartford, George Huntington, 12, 173–74, 176
Hartford, George Ludlum, 174, 176, 177, 179, 181, 182
Hartford, Huntington, 176
Hartford, John Augustine, 174–79, 181
Hart (L.) & Son Co., Inc., 13
Hart Schaffner & Marx, 82
Harvest House Cafeterias, 199
Harvey, Fred, 15, 125
Haverhill Cheap Store, 154–55
Hayes, Shailer, 303
Hearn, George Arnold, 7
Hearn's, 7
Hecht Co., 13
Helicoid, 17–18
Herpolsheimer Co., 13
Hess, Max, 14–15
Hess Brothers, 14–15
Hettrick, Ann Mary, 150
Heydt, George F., 63
Higbee Co., 9
Hill's Supermarkets, Inc., 344
Himmelstein, Anna, 245
Hochschild, Kohn & Co., 13
Hodgkinson, Harold Daniel, 95–96, 98, 99
Hoffman, Claire Giannini, 238
Holley, J. C., 330
Holmes (D. H.), 8
Holt, William A., 277, 279
Hooper, Horace Everett, 235–36
Hopkins, Ernest Martin, 96, 99

Horne (Joseph) Company, 8, 90
Houser, Theodore V., 234, 236, 243
House-to-house selling, 5, 267
Hoving, Walter, 7, 51–53, 64
Hoving Corporation, 51, 53
Howard, William H., 164
Howe, Elias Jr., 68–70
Hoyt, Newton H., Jr., 76
Hubschman, Herbert, 346–47
Hubschman, Sidney, 346–47
Hudson, J. Gilbert, 210
Hudson, Joseph L., 209
Hudson, Joseph L., Jr., 209–10
Hudson, Joseph Lothian, 206, 209, 210–14
Hudson, Joseph Lothian (grandnephew), 207
Hudson, William H., 209
Hudson (J. L.) Company, 16, 90, 117, 150, 206–20
Hudson Motor Car Company, 212–13
Hudson's Bay Co., 19–35, 91
Hudson's Bay Oil and Gas Co. Ltd., 20–21, 35
Hughes, Albert W., 268
Hughes & Hatcher, 13
Hunting-Fishing and Camping (Bean), 305–6
Hutchins, Horace, 142, 145
Hutton, Barbara, 202
Hutzler Brothers Company, 91

Ice shipment, 25
India, 67
Installment selling, 66–68, 70–71, 225
Insurance, 223, 234
International Council of Shopping Centers, 16
Interstate Department Stores, Inc., 347–48
Inventory control, 153, 182, 188, 208, 223, 238, 269
Irving Trust Co., 140

Jaffe, Lillian, 238
James II, King, 24
Japan, 3, 17, 67, 72, 75, 76, 199
Jarman, W. Maxey, 14
Jarman's (W. Maxey) General Shoe Company, 53
Jay, Byron, 181
Jeffrey, Robert M., 291
Jenkins, Read, 209–10
Jewelry, 13, 51–65, 78, 225
Jewelry Industry Council, 54
Jewel Tea Company, 349
Johnson, Guy, 262–63
Johnson, Howard W., 114
Johnson, Lyndon B., 14, 150, 222
Johnson, Mrs. Lyndon B., 286
Johnson, Thomas P., 330
Johnson-Stevens Company, 265
Johnston, Thomas W., 169
Jones, George, 73–74
Jones, John Paul, 114
Jones (F. S.) and Company, 265
Jordan, Ambrose, 69
Jordan, Eben, 8–9, 78
Jordan, Ray H., 269
Jordan Marsh Company, 8–9, 16, 78
Joske Brothers Co., 13
June, Frank T., 74–75
June Manufacturing Company, 74–75

K-Mart, 348
Kane, Joseph, 10
Kane, William J., 181
Kaufman and Baer Company, 7
Kaufmann's, 13
Kavanaugh, Mrs. Kathryn, 132
Keeshan, William P., 283, 284
Kellstadt, Charles H., 243
Kennedy, Joseph P., 130
Kenny Shoe, 204
Kent, Sol, 196
Keswick, William Johnston, 20, 34–35
Khrushchev, Mrs. Nikita, 243
Kilgour, D. E., 20
Kindall, Alvah, 96
Kindersley, Sir Robert, 29
King Kullen, 171
King's Department Stores, Inc., 348
Kinney Shoe Corporation, 199
Kirby, Allan P., 204
Kirby, Fred, 201, 202
Kircher, Donald P., 66, 73, 75–76
Kirkbride, Frank C., 204
Kirkwood, Robert Campbell, 198, 204
Kirstein, Louis E., 89, 90, 91–93, 95, 108
Kittle, Charles M., 233
Klauser, Mark, 318
Klein, Jerome, 257
Klein, Sam, 312, 313
Klein (S.) on the Square, 312
Knight, Richard L., 114
Knox, Seymour, 201
Knox, Seymour H., 204
Korvette (E. J.), Inc., 337, 342–46, 349
Krensky, Harold, 99
Kresge (S. S.) Company, 12, 348
Kress (S. H.), 12
Kroch, Adolph, 141
Kroch's & Brentano's, 133, 141
Kroger, Bernard H. "Barney," 184–85
Kroger Company, 184–85, 349
Krogh, Egil E., 125
Krul, Joe, 219–20
Kunz, Dr. George Frederick, 61–62

Laboratories, 153, 231, 271
Labouisse, Henry R., 77
Lachman, Lawrence, 113
La Forge, Abiel T., 158–59
La Forge, Margaret Getchell, 158–59
Lambert Brothers, 13
Landsman, Herbert S., 114
Lane Bryant, 244–58
Lane Bryant Annual Awards, 257
La Salle & Koch Company, 165
Lascoff's, 325
Lasser, J. K., 142
Latin America, 237
Laverty, Roger M., 183
Lazarus, Charles Y., 108
Lazarus, Fred (son of Simon), 104, 105
Lazarus, Fred, Jr., 100–2, 105–7, 109–10, 114, 115
Lazarus, Fred, III, 107
Lazarus, Jeffrey, 105–6, 107
Lazarus, Maurice, 99, 114, 115
Lazarus, Ralph, 100, 109, 114, 115, 284
Lazarus, Ralph (son of Simon), 104–5
Lazarus, Robert, 105–6, 107–8
Lazarus, Robert, Jr., 108
Lazarus, Simon, 104
Lazarus, Simon (grandson of Simon), 105
Lazarus (F. & R.) & Co., 90, 93, 100–15
Leahy, David T., 206–7
Leased departments, 340–41
Lebor, John, 111, 114
Lee, William, 96
Leftwich, James T., 203–4
Lehman Brothers, 99
Leiter, Levi, 118, 122–23
Leonard, Marvin, 14
Leonard, Obadiah, 14
Leonard's, 14
Lerner Stores Corporation, 13
Leslie, Warren, 295
Letts, Arthur, 275, 276–77, 278
Levine, Max, 110
Lewis, Thomas, 131
Liberman, Isaac, 7
Liggett (L. K.), 12
Lightner, Milton C., 73, 75
Lincoln, Robert Todd, 125
Lincoln and Therese Filene Foundation, 98
Lind, Jenny, 58
Liners, bookstore branches on, 145–46
Linz Brothers, 13
Liquor, 22, 210, 223, 333–34
Literary Guild, 145
Liverman, Harry, 248, 249, 255
Lloyd, Francis Guerin, 43–44
Lloyd, Mary, 291
Lloyd Center, 16–17
Loeb, Albert, 231–32
Loewy, Raymond, 108, 110
Lord, Samuel, 7
Lord & Taylor, 7
Loss leaders, 170, 327, 338
Louis Comfort Tiffany Foundation, 60
Lowell, Ralph, 99
Luckey, Platt and Company, 13
Lunde, Marvin Co., 239
Lundy, James M., 169
Lusk, William T., 52, 60
Lynn, John W., 204

Mabley, Christopher R., 211
Mabley & Carew, 211
Macy, Rowland Hussey, 154–59, 163, 169
Macy (R. H.), 10, 111, 113, 117, 128, 130, 149–69, 207, 321, 338
Magnin, E. John, 283
Magnin, Grover, 283
Magnin, Mary Ann, 282–83
Magnin (I.) and Co., 113, 125, 273–74, 282–83
Magowan, Robert A., 184
Maher, Pat, 111
Maidman, Irving, 51
Mail order (*see also* Catalogs), 12, 39, 146–47, 158, 184, 222–23, 225–30, 236–38, 250, 255, 300, 306-7
Maine Hunting Shoe, 302–3
Malsin, Albert, 247–52, 253
Malsin, Lane (Lena) Bryant, 244
Malsin, Raphael Bryant, 247, 255–56
Mandel Bros., Inc., 9
Manufacturing, 40, 47, 66–75, 116, 122, 129, 130–31, 166, 172, 174, 231, 249–50, 302–3
Mapes, Eugene, 43, 44–45
Marcus, Edward, 291
Marcus, Herbert, 288–90
Marcus, Herbert, Jr., 291
Marcus, Lawrence, 291
Marcus, Stanley, 286–87, 288, 290–92, 294–98
Margolies, Joseph, 141
Marks, Edwin M., 113
Markups, 54, 143, 170, 171, 307, 311, 314–15, 316, 328, 337, 341, 345
Marlborough, Duke of, 24
Marshall, Joseph, 118, 120
Marshall Field & Company, 116–32, 150
Martin, Frank F., 32
Masters, 338
Materials handling, 102
Maternity clothes, 244–50, 253
Maxim's, 3
Maxwell, Rolland A., 169
May, Morton D., 13

May Department Stores Co., 8, 13
Mays, 337
Mazur, Paul, 99, 108, 111
McBain, Hughston M., 110, 129–31
McCarthy, Joseph, 147
McCauley, Zula, 295
McConnell, Fowler B., 233–34
McCracken (J. N.) Company, 265
McCrory (J. J.), 12
McCurdy, 17
McCurdy, William F., 239
McKenzie, George Ross, 72
McKesson & Robbins, 7
McKinlay, John, 128–29
McKinsey, James O., 128–29
McLeod, William, 95
McLoughlin, Dr. John, 26
Mecklin, Clive, 136
Meier, Jack L., 9
Meier, Julius L., 9
Meier & Frank, 9, 16
Men's clothing, 36–50, 212
Merchandise lines, 3–4, 9–10, 21–22, 32–33, 47–48, 52, 76, 104, 146, 151, 152, 157, 161, 173, 180, 205, 207–8, 223, 267, 326–7, 339
Merchandise Mart, 128, 130, 176
Merrill, Charles A., 184
Merz, Charles, 99
Metcalf, Gordon M., 243
Meyers, Perry, 337
Midtown Plaza (Rochester), 17
Miller, Byron D., 203
Miller, William, 114
Miller & Rhoads, 13
Mills (William) & Son Inc., 7
Milwaukee Boston Store, 78, 111
Mitchell, James P., 150
Mitsukoshi, 3
Molloy, Ernest L., 149, 167–68
Montgomery Ward, 12, 222, 224, 233, 234–35, 266
Moore, Charles M., 64
Moore, Gene, 52
Moore, John Chandler, 61
Moore, Louis de Bebian, 52
Moore, Robert L., 89
Moore, W. H., 202
Moore and Evans Company, 225
Moore and Smith, 200–1
Moore's (John C.) Silverware Company, 59–60
Morgan, J. P., 61
Morgan (Henry) & Co., 20, 34
Muir & Mirrieless, 2
Munro, Alan B., 204
Murphy (G. C.), 12
Murray, James Richard, 20, 33
Myer, Charles A., 243
Nakat Packing Corporation, 176
Nascopie, 28–29
National Bellas Hess, 348
National Retail Dry Goods Association, 214–15
National Retail Merchants Association, 101, 113
Neely, Frank H., 191–93
Neely, Rae Schlesinger, 191–92, 194
Neidlinger, George, 72
Neiman, A. L., 288, 290
Neiman, Carrie Marcus, 288–90
Neiman-Marcus, 87, 286–98
Neiman-Marcus Awards, 296
Neisner Brothers, Inc., 349
Nelson, Donald M., 231, 233
Nelson, Nels, 131
Newberry (J. J.) Company, 12, 16–17, 349
Newman-Benton Stores, 255
Nichols, J. C., 15
Night openings, 15
Nonfood items, 180
Nordiska, 296
Northern Stores, 21, 34
Northgate, 15–16
Northland, 16, 108, 215–16
North West Co., 25
Nugent-Johnson wedding, 222, 286
Nusbaum, Aaron E., 227–28
Nyquist, O. Philip, 181
Nystrom, Dr. Paul H., 90

Oak Hill Clothing Bazaar, 10
Obata, Guy, 293
O'Connor Moffatt & Co., 165
Odd-cent pricing, 160, 162, 275, 312–13
Odell, Carl, 235
Ogilvie & Mather, Inc., 239
Ohio State Council of Retail Merchants, 101
Ohrbach, Jerome Kane, 322
Ohrbach, Nathan M., 310–14, 315, 316, 317, 322, 323
Ohrbach's, Inc., 310–23
Oliver, Lucien E., 243
On-approval policy, 119
O'Neil (M.), 13
On Going Away, 45
Open-book selling, 38–39
Oppenheim, Mildred, 318
Order handling, 229–30, 255, 304, 307
Organization, 83, 102, 109–10, 157, 168, 177, 269, 329–30
Orosi-Back, 2
Orr (John) and Garlick's, 91
Orton, Stewart, 110
Osterweis, Steven L., 91
Otis, Emma Penniman, 200

Pacific Fur Co., 25
Packaged produce and meat, 179
Palley, George T., 254
Palmer, James L., 129–31
Palmer, Potter, 118–19
Panama Railroad Co., 91
Parsons, Frank, 83
Parsons, Hubert Templeton, 203
Patent pool, 69
Patman, Wright, 265
Patterns, 76
Paynter, J. W., 210
Peacock, C. D., 54
Peck, Carson C., 201, 202
Peck, Fremont C., 204
Peddlers, 5–6, 9, 13, 155
Penney, James Cash, 259–60
Penney, Reverend, 261–62
Penney (J. C.) Building, 271–72
Penney (J. C.) Company, 22, 259–72
Perkins, Harry D., 131
Perkins, John, 96
Perlin, A. B., Jr., 210
Perot Malting Co., 6
Personal shopping service, 117, 127–28, 152, 219
Petzold, Herman G., 214
Petzold, William T., 214
Pierce, James E., 204
Pierce (S. S.) Co., 7
Pirie, John T., 9
Pivirotto, Richard R., 8
Plaid Stamps, 180
Platt, Henry B., 60
Pneumatic cash tubes, 98
Pollock, E. J., 236
Popular Dry Goods Co., 14
Premiums, 105, 173, 229
Price, William T., 181
Pricing, 3, 7, 21, 43, 56, 59, 104, 118, 119, 153, 156, 160, 162–64, 189, 238, 263–64, 275, 307, 312–13, 327, 329, 334
Printemps, 106
Pritzlaff, Charles, 126–27
Private labels, 163, 172, 270
Promotion and publicity (*see also* Advertising), 52–53, 96–97, 102, 104, 130, 150, 179, 190, 208, 291, 293, 298, 317–18, 327, 331, 332
Public-address system, 82
Public relations (*see also* Community activities; Customers), 130, 164, 177–79, 188, 228–29, 238–39, 260–61
Purchasing, 86-87, 90-91, 102, 120, 168, 193–94, 223–24, 231, 238, 269, 270, 274, 315
Purdy, C. Milburn, 204
Quaker Maid Company, 176
Quality control, 82, 153, 223, 231, 304
Queen Mary club, 87

Raasch, John E., 11
Radisson, Pierre Esprit, 22–23
Randolph, W. F., 210
Rapaczak, Alfonse, 216
Raymond's, 78
Ready-to-wear, 40, 81, 211, 315
Reed, Austin, 87
Reed, William P., 78
Reed's (Jacob) Sons, 7
Regan, R. B., 210
Related selling, 208
Rental services, 19
Restaurants, 34, 117, 125, 158, 199–200, 327
Retail Clerks International Association, AFL-CIO, 11–12
Retailing, evolution of, 1–17
Retailing Hall of Fame, 98–99, 176, 234, 342
Retail Research Association, 90, 91, 108
Retail Store Employees, Independent Union of, 85
Returns and refunds, 33, 117, 119, 120, 189
Revolving credit, 109
Rheder, Henry, 280
Rheder's, 275
Rich, Morris, 188–89
Rich, Richard H., 193, 194, 195
Rich, Walter Henry, 190–195, 197
Rich Foundation, 196
Richmond, Kenneth C., 113
Rich's, Inc., 187–97
Rike, David L., 112
Rike-Kumler Company, 90
Rike's, 112–13
Roberts, John S., 204
Rockefeller, John D., 5
Roebuck, Alvah Curtis, 225–27
Roebuck (A. C.), Inc., 225–26
Rogers Peet Co., 13
Roosevelt, President, 101, 243
Rosenwald, Julius, 224, 227–33, 239, 241–42
Rosenwald, Lessing, 233
Rothschild, Simon Frank, 108
Rothschild, Walter N., 113
Rothschild, Walter N., Jr., 113
Ruml, Beardsley, 150
Rupert, Prince, 23, 24
Russia, 2, 15, 26, 73
Russian American Fur Company, 26
Ryan, Bruce, 141

Safeway Stores, Inc., 183–84
Saint, Thomas, 68
Saks Company, 7
Saks Fifth Avenue, 7, 87
Sale, Charles Vincent, 29
Salzberger, Henry X., 112
Sammons, Wheeler, 99
Sams, Earl Corder, 263, 264–65, 266, 268
Sanborn's, 325
Sanger Brothers, 111
Sanger-Harris, 111–12
Saturday closings, 44
Saunders, Walter E., 204
Schieffelin & Co., 6
Schlesinger, Theodore, 9
Schlumberger, Jean, 52
Schoff, James S., 110, 113
Schwab (Friedrich) & Co., 77
Schwab's, 325
Schwartz, A., 14
Schwartz, Leonard, 133, 145
Scotese, Peter G., 111
Scotland, 71–72
Scott, Elmer L., 231, 241
Scott, Fred B., 329
Scott, Temple, 138
Scruggs-Vandervoort-Barney, Inc., 8
Sears, Richard Warren, 224–31, 241
Sears, Roebuck and Co., 12, 111, 112, 191, 221–43, 266
Sears Motor Buggy, 231
Sears Readers Club, 236
Sears (R. W.) Watch Company, 224–25
Security forces, 151
Seegal, Herbert C., 169
Seegal, Samuel, 96
Seelig (Sam) Company, 183
Selfridge, Harry Gordon, 124–25
Self-service, 32, 170–72, 179, 186, 205, 315–16, 342
Selkirk, Lord, 25
Service charges, 98
Sewing Machine Combination, 69–70
Sexual Behavior in the Human Male (Kinsey), 148
Shahtoosh, 298
Shapiro, Richard G., 99
Shaver, Dorothy, 7
Shaw, George Bernard, 139, 140
Shedd, John G., 124, 126, 128, 129
Sheen, Ronald E., 20, 33, 34
Shepard, Mrs. George, 41–42
Sheridan, George V., 101
Sherman Act, 163
Shield, Lansing P., 183
Shillito's, 100, 103–4, 107, 109
Shipping (*see also* Delivery), 151–52, 219, 227, 229–30, 301
Shoe operation, 117
Shoppers' World, 16
Shopping centers, 15–18, 195, 199, 215–16, 223, 267
Shreve, Crump & Low, 53, 78
Sibley, Lindsay & Curr Co., 78, 125
Siegel, Henry, 162
Siegel, Murray J., 347
Siegel Cooper New York, 162
Silbert, Myron S., 111, 114
Simmons, W. E., 209–10
Simon, Franklin, 14
Simon & Schuster, 148
Simpson, James, 27, 125, 128, 131
Simpson, John R., 91, 93
Simpson, Sir George, 25–26
Simpson-Sears Limited, 223, 237
Singer, Isaac Merritt, 66, 68
Singer Building, 202
Singer Company, 43, 66–67, 122
Sivage, Gerald A., 116, 131
Sizes, women's clothing, 250–55
Size selling, 106
Skaggs, Marion Barton, 183
Skagmo, Phil, 14
Skinner, J. Fletcher, 230–31
Slattery (E. T.) Co., 78
Slee, Ackley, 96
Sloane (W. & J.), 8
Slogans, 162, 164, 194, 310, 314
Smiley, Donald B., 149
Smith, Hubert P., 204
Smith, William M., 13
Snaith, William, 108
Soda fountain, 324
Solomon, Sidney, 113
Sostrin, Morey, 9
South America, 17–18, 71, 237
Spartans Industries, Inc., 345–46
Specialty stores (*see also* specific store), 9, 79, 81
Sperry & Hutchinson, 180
Sporting goods, mail-order, 299–309
Stahl, John, 39
Stair, George W., 146
Stanford, Eric M., 284
Stanley Home Products, 5
St. Clair, William H., 131
Stearns (R. H.) Co., 78
Stern Bros., 13
Stewart, Alexander Turney, 10
Stewart, A. T., 128
Stewart & Co., 7, 10
Sticht, J. Paul, 114
Stix, Baer & Fuller, 14
Stoner, Owen, 99
Strathcona (Donald A. Smith) Baron, 27–28
Straus, Edward, 166
Straus, Herbert, 165–66

Straus, Isidor, 160, 165
Straus, Jack I., 149, 163–64, 166–67
Straus, Jesse, 165–66
Straus, John, 166
Straus, Kenneth, 166
Straus, Lazarus, 159–60
Straus, Nathan, 160, 165, 166
Straus, Percy, 165–66
Straus (L.) & Sons, 159–60
Strauss, David H., 190
Strawbridge, G. Stockton, 13
Strawbridge & Clothier, 13, 91
Streamer, Volney, 138
Street, William S., 131
Stritzinger, Chris, 291
Stromenger, John E., 204
Struthers, George H., 223
Stutz, Geraldine, 14
Subsidiaries, 166, 176, 179, 215–16
Suburbs, 165, 183, 199, 210, 215–16, 340
Suggestion system, 84
Sumner, Keith L., 204
Supermarkets, 170–86, 349
Sussman, Murray, 346
Sutherland, Chief Executive, 34
Sutherland, Hugh W., 20, 33
Sutton (O. A.) Corporation, 347
Switchboards, 207

Talmadge, Eugene, 222
Target stores, 348
Taste of Texas, A (McDuff and Trahey), 293
Taylor, Frederick W., 192
Taylor, George Washington, 7
Taylor (John) Dry Goods Store, 111
Taylor (William) Son & Company, 90
Teeter, Mrs. Lulu S., 106
Telephone exchange, private, 195
Thalhimer Brothers, Inc., 8
Thanksgiving, 101–2, 164, 208, 217
Thefts, 63, 123
Thimonnier, Barthélemy, 68
Third National Bank, 213
Thomas, Winky, 141
Thorne, George R., 12
Thorp (J. H.) & Co., Inc., 6
Thriftown stores, 349
Thurso Paper and Pulp Company, 77
Tiffany, Charles Lewis, 57–60, 61
Tiffany, Louis Comfort, 60, 126
Tiffany & Company, 51–65, 293
Tiffany Favrile, 60
Tips to Trappers, 239
Titche-Goettinger Co., 14
Topps, 348
Town & Country, 255
Trademarks, 41, 45, 65, 74–75, 163, 169
"Trade Palace," 13
Trading stamps, 180
Traub, Marvin A., 113
"Travelers," Brooks, 39–40
Treasure Island stores, 271
Truex, Van Day, 52
Truman Merry-Go-Round (Allen and Shannon), 147
Tudor, W. Wallace, 242
Turnover, 341–42
Turnstyle stores, 349
Twentieth Century Fund Inc., 94–95, 99
Two Guys, 337, 346–47, 349

Unions, 11–12, 144
Unitization, 274, 281

Valentine, Robert G., 83
Valentine, Robert Macy, 159
Valentine's Manual, 42–43
Variety chain, 12–13, 198–205
Vaughan, Donald G., 45
Venezuela, 17–18
Verdier, Felix, 8
Victor Talking Machine Company, 163
Vicuña, 298
Vigilant, 28
Ville de Paris, La, 2
Vogel, Edward J., 181
Vornado, Inc., 346
Vose, Elliott E., 77

WABE-FM, 196
Walgreen (Charles R.), 13
Wall, Ashbel T., 46, 48
Wallstrom, H. K., 210
Waltham Watch Co., 87
Wanamaker, John, 10–11, 128, 150, 176
Wanamaker, Rodman, 11
Wanamaker's, 10–12
Ward, Montgomery, 12, 125, 228
Ward, Virginia, 142
Ware, Dexter H., 210
Warehousing and storage, 102, 106–7
Warren Company, 225
Wasmuth, Thomas C., 112
Watkin, Sir Edward, 26
Watson, Edward, 113
Watson, Thomas J., Jr., 53, 92
Weaver, Phyllis, 127
Webb, B. E., 330
Webb, Frederick, 39
Webb, James E., Jr., 329–30
Webb, James Earl "Doc," 326–35
Webb, James R., 204
Webber, James B., 209, 214
Webber, Joseph L., 209, 214
Webber, Oscar, 209, 214
Webber, Richard H., 209, 214